C000240505

Employment Law

An advisers' handbook

Thomas Kibling is a practising barrister and has previously worked in citizens advice bureaux and law centres.
Tamara Lewis is a solicitor who works in the employment unit of the Central London Law Centre.

Both authors have written and lectured extensively on employment law.

The Legal Action Group is a national, independent charity which campaigns for equal access to justice for all members of society. Legal Action Group:

- provides support to the practice of lawyers and advisers
- inspires developments in that practice
- campaigns for improvements in the law and the administration of justice
- stimulates debate on how services should be delivered.

Employment Law

An advisers' handbook

FOURTH EDITION

Thomas Kibling, BARRISTER
and
Tamara Lewis, SOLICITOR

Legal Action Group
2000

Fourth edition published in Great Britain 2000
by Legal Action Group
242 Pentonville Road, London N1 9UN

First edition 1991
Second edition 1994
Third edition 1996

British Library Cataloguing in Publication Data
A CIP catalogue record for this book is available from the British Library.

ISBN 0 905099 93 1

Phototypeset by RefineCatch Limited, Bungay, Suffolk
Printed by Bell & Bain Ltd, Glasgow

Preface

We are constantly asked to recommend a book which covers the wide range of employment problems in a clear and practical form. There is no obvious book to recommend. We have written this book to fill that gap. In particular, we have aimed to provide lay advisers, trade union officials and lawyers with a handbook which is a real support in identifying the relevant law and issues of evidence and which can be used as a self-contained guide while running unfair dismissal and discrimination cases. The book therefore devotes as much space to evidence, precedents and checklists as to setting out the law. Due to this practical emphasis, further research may be necessary on the law itself in new, developing or complex areas, eg, TUPE and EU law.

Employment law is a large subject and inevitably there will be some omissions. We have, however, attempted to cover the major areas of contract issues, unfair dismissal and unlawful discrimination. Certain areas of employment law are dealt with more thoroughly than others. This is not accidental. We have attempted to give more space to those subjects which cause most frequent problems for advisers of workers. Because of the complexity of the subject and the dangers of over-simplification, the law on race, sex and disability discrimination has been treated in particular detail.

As a result of changes of government and the increasing influence of Europe, employment law has rapidly expanded and many new areas have been introduced. As far as possible, we have tried at least to signal most of these new areas. This had led to some new chapters and re-arrangement of information from previous editions. For a clear overview of the contents and lay-out of the book, it is best to look at the contents list on pages vii–xi. Note that although we use the word 'worker' throughout this book, it is used in its non-legal meaning. Within employment law, different rights are available to workers of varying employment status and terms such as 'employee' and 'worker' have precise legal definitions.

The law as is known is stated as at 1 February 2000. Where possible, reference has been made to more recent law at proof stage.

Tamara Lewis
Thomas Kibling

Acknowledgements

The development of Central London Law Centre's employment unit has been greatly assisted by a small group of volunteers, who have shown remarkable commitment over the past eleven years. We are particularly indebted to Nicholas O'Brien, Martin Westgate and Ann Cutting who have provided such long-standing support, and also to Catherine Scrivens. We would also like to thank Robin Allen for his continuing support for our work. Finally, a big thank you to Philip Tsamados, both for his contribution towards this edition and for his invaluable work alongside Tamara as a full-time member of the law centre's employment unit since May 1991.

In relation to this fourth edition, thank you also to Martin Westgate for his suggestions in relation to the race and sex discrimination section. Any mistakes, of course, remain our own. We would also like to thank all at LAG for their encouragement and support.

Contents

APPENDICES 365

Table of cases

Table of statutes

Table of statutory instruments

Table of European legislation

Table of Codes of Practice

Abbreviations

ACAS	Advisory, Conciliation and Arbitration Scheme
CA	Court of Appeal
COET	Central Office of Employment Tribunals
CRE	Commission for Race Equality
DDA	Disability Discrimination Act 1995
DPA	Data Protection Act 1998
EAT	Employment Appeal Tribunal
EAT Rules	Employment Appeal Tribunal Rules 1993 SI No 2854
ECJ	European Court of Justice
EDT	Effective date of termination
EOC	Equal Opportunities Commission
EPCA	Employment Protection (Consolidation) Act 1978
EPD	Equal Pay Directive (75/117/EEC)
EqPA	Equal Pay Act 1970
ERA 1996	Employment Rights Act 1996
ERA 1999	Employment Relations Act 1999
ET	employment tribunal
ETA	Employment Tribunals Act 1996
ETD	Equal Treatment Directive (76/207/EEC)
ET Regs	Employment Tribunals (Constitution and Rules of Procedure) Regulations 1993 SI No 2687
GOQ	genuine occupational qualification
HRA	Human Rights Act 1998
JES	job evaluation scheme
MSC	Manpower Services Commission
NMWA	National Minimum Wage Act 1998
PIDA	Public Interest Disclosure Act 1998
RRA	Race Relations Act 1976
SDA	Sex Discrimination Act (1975, unless otherwise stated)
SOSR	some other substantial reason
SSP	statutory sick pay
SSP Regs	Statutory Sick Pay (General) Regulations 1982 SI No 894

TULR(C)A	Trade Union and Labour Relations (Consolidation) Act 1992
TUPE Regs	Transfer of Undertakings (Protection of Employment) Regulations 1981 SI No 1794
TURERA	Trade Union Reform and Employment Rights Act 1993
WA	Wages Act 1986

Introduction

CHAPTER 1

Terms and conditions of employment

The contract of employment

1.1   Every worker has a contract of employment, which consists of a number of terms, some of which are express terms, some implied and some statutory. Express terms are those agreed between the employer and worker whether in writing or orally. Implied terms are not expressly agreed but are implied into the contract of employment by the courts. Some implied terms are universal (ie, they apply to all contracts of employment) and others are implied as a natural consequence of a specific contract of employment, either because the term is so obvious that the employer and worker would have agreed to the term if asked to consider it, or because the contract could not work without the term being incorporated. Statutory terms form part of the contract and exist as a consequence of Acts of parliament. Employment protection rights (such as the right not to be unfairly dismissed or unlawfully discriminated against) are examples of such terms.

Express terms

1.2   An express term is one which has been the subject of discussion and acceptance by the employer and worker. These terms are usually put in writing but this is not necessary. The main express terms are usually found in the letter of appointment or in the written contract of employment. Sometimes they are found in other documents such as the staff handbook, the rule book or collective agreement. The contract of employment often expressly incorporates the provisions of the staff handbook as part of the employment contract. The main express terms are usually:

- the rate of pay, and how often the worker will be paid;
- the hours of work;
- any terms and conditions relating to holidays and holiday pay;
- sick pay;
- notice pay; and
- the disciplinary rules and grievance procedure.

As these are the main terms and conditions of employment, the employer is obliged to supply most workers with written details of these terms.[1-2]

1–2 Employment Rights Act (ERA) 1996 s1(1).

Implied terms

1.3   In the absence of express terms, employment contracts need terms to be implied into them in order to make them workable, meaningful and complete. Implied terms of fact are used to fill a gap in the express terms on the basis that the term would have been agreed between the employer and worker had they discussed it.[3] Furthermore, the courts have appreciated that as employment contracts involve personal contact between the parties, it is necessary to have terms implied into them so that they can operate smoothly, such as the implied term of mutual trust and confidence. The courts will imply a term only if it is absolutely necessary to do so, or if it is clear that the employer and worker would have agreed to the term if it had been discussed. The courts will not intervene and imply a term just because one of the parties has entered into an unreasonable contract.[4]

1.4   Custom and practice may give rise to an implied term if the custom and practice is reasonable, notorious and certain. Reasonable means that the term is fair, notorious requires the term to be well known, and certainty requires the term to be sufficiently precise so that the term is possible to state,[5] for example, the employer closes the factory for a trade holiday and gives all staff paid holidays for that week.[6] A term can also be implied by looking at what has happened between the particular worker and the employer in practice, for example, if the employer has given five weeks' holiday every year to the worker without exception this may create a right by custom and practice.

Mutual trust and confidence

1.5   This is the most widely applied and influential of all the implied terms. The employer must not, without reasonable and proper cause, conduct him/herself in a manner likely to destroy or seriously damage the relationship of trust and confidence with the worker.[7] This term also applies to the worker as well. The following are examples of breaches of this implied term:

– physical or verbal abuse;[8]

---

3 *Lister v Romford Ice and Cold Storage Co Ltd* [1957] AC 555.
4 *Aparau v Iceland Frozen Foods plc* [1996] IRLR 119, EAT.
5 *Sugar v Ridehalgh and Sons Ltd* [1931] 1 Ch 310.
6 *Quinn v Calder Industrial Materials Ltd* [1996] IRLR 547.
7 *Woods v WM Car Services (Peterborough)* [1982] ICR 693, CA.
8 *Western Excavating (ECC) v Sharp* [1978] ICR 221, CA.

- sexual harassment[9] and the failure to support someone who has been the victim of harassment at work;[10]
- moving a senior worker to an inadequate office or location;
- imposing a disciplinary penalty when unwarranted or where the disciplinary procedure is not followed.[11]

Not to act arbitrarily, capriciously or inequitably

1.6   An employer treating a worker arbitrarily, capriciously or inequitably without good reason will be in breach of this term. Failing to give a worker a pay increase without good cause when other workers are given an increase has been held to be a breach of this term.[12]

Good faith and fidelity

1.7   This term lasts during employment but not after its termination. Any action by a worker which seriously harms the employer's business will be in breach of this term.[13] Likewise, the employer who discloses to a third party information about a worker without good reason or consent will be in breach of this term. Examples are:

- carrying on business in competition with the employer;[14]
- the use of the employer's list of customers including their business requirements.[15]

Workers cannot use confidential information for their own personal benefit during their employment.

Not to disclose trade secrets

1.8   The worker cannot disclose, either during employment or after it has ended, the employer's trade secrets. Most workers will not have access to information which would amount to a trade secret. The true nature of a trade secret is something which the outside world does not or could not ascertain, such as a process, a chemical formula, eg, the ingredients of Coca Cola, and not just confidential

---

9   Ibid.
10   *Wigan BC v Davies* [1979] ICR 411, EAT.
11   *Post Office v Strange* [1980] IRLR 515, EAT.
12   *FC Gardiner Ltd v Beresford* [1978] IRLR 63, EAT.
13   *Boston Deep Sea Fishing and Ice Co v Ansell* (1888) 39 Ch D 339, CA.
14   *Hivac Ltd v Park Royal Scientific Instruments* [1946] 1 All ER 350; [1946] Ch 169, CA.
15   *Faccenda Chicken Ltd v Fowler* [1986] IRLR 69, CA.

information which the employer does not want the worker to use after s/he leaves.[16]

To obey reasonable and lawful orders

1.9   The worker is obliged to obey reasonable and lawful orders. Lawful means both a requirement of parliament as well as an order given within the ambit of the employment contract. If the worker is asked to perform a function outside the employment contract which is unreasonable, this order can be refused. (However, refusal to obey a reasonable order outside the contract could still lead to a fair dismissal.)

Care of employer's equipment

1.10   The worker owes the employer a duty to look after the employer's equipment and machinery. The failure to exercise due care, leading to loss to the employer could constitute a disciplinary matter. This will arise if the worker has injured a third party, as the claim will usually be against the employer.[17]

To employ a competent workforce

1.11   The employer owes a duty to employ a competent and safe work-force,[18–19] safe plant and equipment, to have a safety system at work and to pay attention to workers' complaints in relation to safety matters.[20]

To provide a safe working environment

1.12   The employer owes a duty to provide a safe working environment.

To deal promptly with grievances

1.13   The employer is under a duty to afford workers an opportunity to obtain reasonably and promptly redress of any grievance that they may have.[21–22]

---

16   Ibid.
17   The worker may have to indemnify the employer.
18–19   *Hudson v Ridge Manufacturing Co* [1957] 2 All ER 229, QBD.
20   *British Aircraft Corporation v Austin* [1978] IRLR 332, EAT.
21–22   *W A Gould (Pearmak) Ltd v McConnell* [1995] IRLR 515, EAT.

1.14   All these implied terms are normally treated as fundamental terms of the employment contract, so the employer's breach will usually entitle the worker to claim that s/he has been constructively dismissed, if s/he does not delay in making the claim. An employer can usually dismiss a worker without notice if s/he has breached a term which would be applicable such as the term of trust and confidence.

Statutory terms

1.15   Due to the unequal bargaining power between workers and employers, successive governments have found it necessary to incorporate into the employment contract certain terms protecting workers during, and on termination of, employment. The most important statutory terms give the worker the right to receive notice, redundancy pay, to return to work after maternity leave, not to be unfairly dismissed and not to be discriminated against on grounds of race, sex or disability. Furthermore, the Working Time Regulations 1998[23] incorporate into the employment contract certain rights such as a limit on the number of hours to be worked each week and annual holidays.[24]

1.16   Apart from the provisions on unlawful discrimination and maternity rights, a worker qualifies for these rights after a given period of continuous employment. Once the worker has qualified for these rights, they become part of the employment contract and it is not possible for the worker and employer to agree a contract which excludes those rights except in respect of redundancy payments with certain fixed-term contracts.

Varying the terms of employment

1.17   Any term of the employment contract can be varied by consent of the parties. Each time a worker receives a pay increase there is a variation to the employment contract by consent. If the employer tries to vary any term of the employment contract but does not get the worker's consent, that variation is not recognised as lawful.[25] The courts will treat the worker as having consented to the variation if s/he does not

---

23   SI No 1833.
24   *Barber v RIB Mining (UK) Ltd* [1999] IRLR 308.
25   *Rigby v Ferodo Ltd* [1988] ICR 29, HL.

object to the change within a reasonable period of time. This is often referred to as a variation by affirmation. It is therefore important that the worker objects to any proposed variation as soon as possible. It is not necessary for the worker to keep repeating his/her objection; once is sufficient if it is clear and unequivocal. But an objection cannot hold the position open forever.

1.18   Where an employer insists on varying terms without the worker's consent, the worker's refusal to agree will rarely be the end of the matter. The employer may impose the changes anyway, such that the worker's normal options are to resist, resign or, if relevant, sue for any unlawful deduction or breach of contract. Alternatively, a worker may claim that s/he has in reality been dismissed and is now working on an alternative contract.[26]

1.19   Many of the options may lead to the worker's dismissal. Whether or not a worker will succeed in an unfair dismissal case depends on eligibility to claim and the normal principles of fairness (see below). It does not automatically follow that dismissal for opposing a change of contract will be unfair, or even if it is, the worker may not get much by way of compensation.

1.20   Employers have been known to terminate the employment contract and offer a new contract which contains the variation as a means of getting round the worker's lack of consent to the variation. This approach is only lawful if the full contractual period of notice is given to terminate the employment contract and it is clear that the original contract is being terminated. It is not sufficient to notify the worker that after a period of time the contract will be treated as having been varied. The worker will probably be able to claim unfair dismissal in respect of the first contract and continue to work under the second contract.[27]

The right to written particulars of employment

1.21   Most workers are entitled to receive, within two months of the start of their employment,[28] a written statement of particulars of their employment. These particulars must include:

---

26 *Hogg v Dover College* [1990] ICR 39, EAT; *Alcan Extrusions v Yates and Others* (1996) 565 *IDS Brief* 13. There are other options too, eg, discrimination.
27 *Rigby v Ferodo Ltd* [1988] ICR 29, HL.
28 ERA 1996 s1(2).

- the names of the employer and employee;
- the date on which employment began, including any period of continuous employment with a previous employer;
- rates of pay or methods of calculating pay and frequency of payment;
- hours of work, including normal working hours;
- terms relating to holidays, including public holidays and holiday pay;
- rules relating to sickness or injury and sick pay;
- pension arrangements;
- the employee's job title or a brief description of the work for which s/he is employed;
- place of work, including details of any mobility clause, and the employer's address;
- the length of notice required by each party;
- if employment is not intended to be permanent, the period for which it is expected to continue, or if a fixed-term contract, its expiry date;
- any collective agreements which directly affect the terms and conditions of employment;
- certain details[29] if the worker is required to work outside the UK for a period of more than one month;
- the disciplinary procedure;[30] and
- the name of a person to whom the worker can apply if s/he is dissatisfied with any disciplinary decision or seeking redress of any grievance relating to his/her employment.

Where there is a change in any of the terms, the employer is required to notify the worker in writing within one month of the change.[31]

1.22   At least the first nine items listed above must be contained in a single document (the principal statement). The others may be contained in separate statements such as the staff handbook. Where an employer has supplied a written contract containing all the required particulars, this will probably comply with the law. Where there are no particulars on a point, this should be stated.

1.23   The statement of terms is not itself the contract. It is strong but

29   ERA 1996 s1(4)(k).
30   Where the employer and any associated employer employed fewer than 20 people at the time employment commenced, s/he need not provide the disciplinary procedure: ERA 1996 s3(1).
31   ERA 1996 s4.

not conclusive evidence of what the contractual terms are.[32] If no proper statement is supplied within two months, the worker can apply to an employment tribunal (ET) at any time up to three months from termination of employment for the ET to determine what particulars ought to have been given in the statement.[33] In practice workers tend not to apply to the ET unless there is a dispute over their entitlement to, eg, holidays. It is useful to remember that it is automatically unfair to dismiss a worker, regardless of length of service, because s/he has demanded a s1 statement (as it is known); see para 6.69 below.

1.24   A worker can make an ET claim for a determination of particulars even if s/he left within the first two months of employment, as long as s/he has worked at least one month. The duty on the ET is to determine what has been agreed by the employer and the worker (including a term which is required to be implied), but not to remake a contract or decide what should have been agreed. It is the contractual relationship alone which is relevant. It is for the ET to make findings of the terms and conditions of the contract as initially made and then consider whether there have been subsequent variations. Where there has been no express nor apparent agreement, it may be possible for the ET to infer a term from the surrounding circumstances or from custom and practice.

1.25   A claim to the ET can be made by a worker when employed and within three months after dismissal.[34]

Wrongful dismissal

1.26   Unlike unfair dismissal, which is a statutory right, wrongful dismissal is a contractual right. It arises when an employer terminates the employment contract contrary to the terms of the contract (eg, failure to give proper notice, or breach of another contractual term such as failure to follow the contractual disciplinary procedure).

1.27   The general rule is that either party can end the contract by giving the appropriate notice and without cause or reason. Where a worker has committed an act of gross misconduct, the employer may end the contract without giving notice. What amounts to gross misconduct

---

32 *Robertson and Jackson v British Gas Corporation* [1983] IRLR 302; [1983] ICR 351, CA.
33 ERA 1996 s11.
34 Ibid.

depends on the facts of each case but it is an act which completely undermines the employment contract. Some employment contracts define what amounts to gross misconduct; some acts such as theft and physical assault are obvious acts of gross misconduct and do not need stating. Although gross misconduct entitles the employer to dismiss without giving notice, whether the dismissal is fair is a separate question under the unfair dismissal provisions of the Employment Rights Act 1996 (ERA).

1.28   A wrongfully dismissed worker can recover damages for breach of contract. Where the breach of contract is the failure to give proper notice, compensation will usually be the loss of earnings (pay and other benefits, eg, use of a company car) for the notice period, subject to mitigation. The worker is expected to take all reasonable steps to reduce the claim by seeking alternative employment and claiming social security benefits. Any money received in the notice period from these sources will be set off against the claim. It is not possible to recover compensation for mental distress or injury to feelings caused by the breach of contract,[35] although it might be possible to get stigma damages, but this will only arise in very limited circumstances.[36]

1.29   Where failure to give contractual notice means the worker falls short of the necessary service for a statutory right (eg, falls short of one year's service to claim unfair dismissal, or is not in employment when a new Act comes into force), the value of the worker's claim may be more than net pay for the notice period. It could include compensation for the lost opportunity of bringing an unfair dismissal claim which would be assessed by reference to the amount of compensation which the ET might award, reflecting the chance that the claim might not succeed.[37]

1.30   Where the breach of contract is failure to follow a contractual disciplinary procedure prior to dismissal, the amount of compensation is hard to predict. In some cases, it may be wages for the length of time it would have taken to go through the compulsory disciplinary procedures.[38] It is also possible to argue that if the following of the disciplinary procedure might have resulted in the worker not being dismissed (the main purpose of a disciplinary procedure is to cure problems rather than legitimate dismissals), then compensation

35   *Addiss v Gramophone* [1909] AC 488.
36   *Bank of Credit and Commerce International SA v Ali* [1999] IRLR 508, HL.
37   *Raspin v United News Shop Ltd* [1999] IRLR 9, EAT.
38   *Gunton v Richmond LBC* [1980] IRLR 321, CA.

should be assessed on a more generous basis, namely compensation to reflect the lost chance of continued employment (the loss of wages subject to a percentage reduction to reflect this lost chance).[39]

1.31   Claims for breach of contract based on failure to follow disciplinary procedures are hard to prove and should be approached with caution. Most disciplinary procedures are not contractual but offer guidance rather than impose mandatory obligations, and failure to hold a disciplinary hearing or give a warning prior to dismissal will not necessarily be a breach of contract.

1.32   A worker who has been wrongfully dismissed can claim in the ET, county court or High Court, subject to the value of the claim. The rules are complex and should be checked.[39A] As a rough guide, most claims may be started in the High Court if worth more than £15,000 (£50,000 if there is also a personal injuries claim). Claims worth more than £15,000 may be county court or High Court, depending on specified factors. There is also a small claims track in the county court. Alternatively, certain contract claims arising or outstanding on the termination of a worker's employment may be brought in an ET, currently for up to £25,000.[39B]

Statutory minimum notice

1.33   ERA 1996 s86 sets out minimum notice periods though the contract may require more. An employer must give at least:

- one week's notice to a worker who has been continuously employed for one month or more but less than two years;
- one week's notice for each whole year of continuous employment of two years or more, but less than 12 years. For example, a worker employed for 5 years 11 months, would be entitled to at least five weeks' notice of dismissal.
- 12 weeks' notice for continuous service of 12 years or more. For example, a worker employed for 16 years, would be entitled to at least 12 weeks' notice.

A worker employed for one month or more need give only one week's notice when resigning. In some situations, neither contractual nor statutory notice needs to be given,[40] eg, a dismissal for gross

---

39   *Raspin v United News Shops Ltd* [1999] IRLR 9, EAT.
39A See the Practice Direction supplementary to the Civil Procedure Rules Part 7.
39B Employment Tribunals Act 1996 s3.
40   ERA 1996 s86(6).

misconduct or a resignation due to the employer's fundamental breach.

1.34   A worker can claim for wrongful dismissal including the failure to give statutory minimum notice in the ET within three months of the effective date of termination.

References

1.35   There is usually no obligation on an employer to provide a worker with a reference on termination of the employment contract. The exception is where a reference is required by a regulatory body such as the Financial Service Authority (FSA) to ensure that financial services are only handled by authorised and competent persons.

1.36   If an employer does provide a reference to a third party, that employer owes a duty of care to whom the reference is provided. Furthermore, a corresponding duty is owed to the worker who is the subject matter of the reference. It is necessary for the reference to be true, accurate and fair. Also the reference must not give an unfair or misleading impression overall, even if the discrete components are factually correct.[41]

1.37   In *Spring v Guardian Assurance plc*,[42] the House of Lords recognised that a worker could sue an employer if a negligent reference is given as either a breach of an implied term of the contract or in negligence. The duty imposed on the employer is to ensure that the reference is fair, just and reasonable and that the author of the reference should take all reasonable care to ensure that there is no misstatement.

1.38   A number of employers provide references and then attach a disclaimer for liability for that reference. It might be open to the court to set aside the disclaimer under the provisions of the Unfair Contract Terms Act 1977 if the disclaimer is deemed unreasonable.[42A]

1.39   In practical terms, it can be hard for a worker to do anything if s/he suspects a bad reference has been given. Often s/he cannot obtain a copy of the reference, even from the proposed new employer. Although the reference could be obtained once a case had been started, this is not helpful if s/he does not know whether there are

---

41   *Bartholomew v Hackney LBC* [1999] IRLR 246.
42   [1994] IRLR 460
42A   *Brigden v American Express Bank Ltd* [2000] IRLR 94, HC.

has good grounds to go ahead at all. The legal rights described above would usually only be enforceable in the county court or High Court, which is rarely a practical option without legal aid. Sometimes the best thing to do is to send a solicitor's letter to the former employer warning him/her of the consequences of unjustified references. This may prevent the employer doing it again.

1.40   An employer may victimise a worker by giving an adverse reference or no reference because the worker alleged discrimination during his/her employment or brought a case after leaving.[43] At the moment, victimisation or discrimination taking place after the worker's employment has ended is not covered by the Race Relations Act 1976 (although this has been doubted[44]) or probably the Disability Discrimination Act 1995. However, victimising a woman after she has left due to an allegation of sex discrimination made by her while still in employment amounts to unlawful sex discrimination.[45] The advantage of this is that it is a claim which can be brought in an ET and the questionnaire procedure can be used to obtain a copy of the reference before starting any case.

1.41   Because of the above difficulties, it is usually important to obtain an agreed reference as part of any settlement negotiated on an unfair dismissal or discrimination case.[46]

The Data Protection Act 1998

Introduction

1.42   The Data Protection Act 1998 (DPA) replaced the Data Protection Act 1984. The DPA will substantially come into force on 1 March 2000. The new provisions are still based on the 'data protection principles' (data to be processed fairly and lawfully, be adequate, relevant and not excessive, be accurate, not kept any longer than is necessary, processed in accordance with workers' rights, and must not be transferred to another country which does not provide similar protection in respect of the keeping of data). The purpose of the DPA is to regulate when and how information concerning workers may be

---

43   See para 9.82 for definition of victimisation under the Sex Discrimination Act 1975, Race Relations Act 1976, Disability Discrimination Act 1995.
44   *Coote v Granada Hospitality Ltd (No 2)* [1999] IRLR 452.
45   *Coote v Granada Hospitality Ltd (No 2)* [1999] IRLR 452.
46   See para 16.85.

obtained, held and disclosed. 'Data' is specifically defined and includes computerised records (both mainframe, laptop, and hand-held computers), health records (including in-house occupational health records), as well as manual records.

1.43   As part of the regulatory provisions, the DPA imposes registration procedures and provides enforcement powers. Data subjects (workers who have records kept on them) are entitled to have formal access to information on them to know to what use the information is being put. In addition, a worker can prevent the processing of personal data concerning him/her if the data is likely to cause unwarranted damage or distress.

Entitlement to secure data

1.44   Section 7 of the DPA entitles a worker to be informed as to:
   – a description of the data being kept on the worker;
   – a description of the potential recipients of this data;
   – the reason why this data is being kept.

1.45   Section 8 of the DPA entitles a worker to:
   – a clear and understandable copy of the data, including details as to from where the data came;
   – if the personal data is processed by automatic means (such as the assessment of the worker's reliability from a time clock system) which significantly affects, or might affect, the worker, then to be informed 'of the logic involved in that decision-making'.

1.46   The employer (the data controller) is only obliged to provide the information requested on the payment of a prescribed fee. In the majority of cases the maximum fee that the employer (the data controller) will be able to charge is £10.[47] The employer (the data controller) will have to respond to a request 'promptly' and in any event within 40 days beginning with the day the request was received and the fee paid.

Exceptions

1.47   The employer (the data controller) is not required to provide the requested information if the consequence of providing the informa-

---

47   Data Protection (Subject Access) (Fees and Miscellaneous Provisions) Regulations 2000 SI No 191 – to come into force on 1 March 2000.

tion would cause the identification of another person such as the author of an appraisal, reference (see below), or a report; unless the other person has consented to the disclosure of their name, or it is reasonable in all the circumstances to comply with the request notwithstanding the lack of consent. In determining whether it is 'reasonable in all the circumstances' regard must be had to the duty of confidentiality, the efforts made to secure consent, and any express refusal by the individual of disclosure of the information.

1.48 DPA s7(9) excludes the disclosure of references provided for education, training or future employment. In addition, excluded data includes the process of the appointment of civil servants, management forecasts or planning used for the conduct of the employer's business and negotiations where the personal data consists of records of the intentions of the employer (the data controller) in those negotiations and which would be likely to prejudice those negotiations.

Enforcement

1.49 A worker is entitled to bring a claim for compensation for any damage suffered due to the employer (the data controller) breaching any of the provisions contained in the DPA and can further apply for an order to rectify, block, erase, or destroy data which is inaccurate. Compensation will be awarded if there is financial loss. A claim is brought in the county or High Court.[48]

1.50 The former Data Protection Registrar is to become the Data Protection Commissioner who will have extended powers. The Data Protection Commissioner can investigate complaints, go to court for access to information and to secure compensation. Importantly, the new powers in the DPA impose an obligation on the Data Protection Commissioner to publish a Code of Practice and to serve information notices requiring employers (the data controller) to provide certain information. Failure to comply with any information notice will be an offence. An employer (the data controller) can apply to the Data Protection Tribunal against any information notice.

1.51 Employers must be registered if they are to hold information on their workers. It is an offence not to be registered and to hold information, and knowingly or recklessly failing to comply with the terms of the register is punishable with a fine.

48 DPA ss10(4) and 14.

Contracts of employment: Key points

- All workers have a contract of employment. Most employment contracts are verbal. They carry the same status as written contracts, the only difference being that they are harder to prove.
- The statutory statement of the main terms and conditions of employment is not the contract of employment but will often be strong evidence of what is the contract.
- The terms of the employment contract are either express terms (discussed and agreed by the employer and worker) or implied terms (not discussed but forming part of the contract).
- To determine what constitutes the contract of employment, start with the first communications: the job advertisement, the interview, the letter of appointment, the initial written documents, etc. Having established the original contractual agreement, then look for any variations which were applicable at the material time.
- Some of the most important terms of the employment contract are put in by Acts of parliament and are referred to as statutory terms. The majority of these terms are implied into the employment contract to protect workers against unfair treatment. The most important are the rights against unfair dismissal, unlawful discrimination, and victimisation for union membership.
- Contractual terms are varied from time to time during the course of employment. When dealing with a contractual dispute it is important to ascertain the nature of the contract at the time of the dispute.

General guide to useful evidence

- All documents, including the letter of appointment, the s1 statutory statement of the main terms and conditions of employment, the staff handbook, and any other written procedures.
- The custom and practice at the workplace.
- The terms and conditions that similar workers enjoy.

CHAPTER 2

Trade unions

Dismissal or detriment for trade union activities

2.1   Trade unions members are afforded protection from dismissal, unfair selection for redundancy and action short of dismissal. It is automatically unfair to dismiss a worker if the sole or principal reason for dismissal is that the worker:

- was or proposed to become a member of a trade union,[1]
- had taken part, or proposed to take part, in the activities of a trade union,[2]
- was not a member of any trade union, or has refused or proposed to refuse to become or remain a member.[3]

It is automatically unfair to select an employee for redundancy on one of the above grounds.

2.2   It is unlawful for an employer to take action short of dismissal against a worker for the purpose of:

- preventing or deterring the worker from being or seeking to become a member of a trade union,[4]
- preventing or deterring the worker from taking part in the activities of a trade union,[5]
- compelling the worker to be or become a member of a trade union.[6]

A worker can complain of dismissal by reason of union membership not only where the dismissal was due simply to having joined the union, but also where the introduction of union representation into the employment relationship was what led the employer to dismiss.[7]

2.3   Trade union activities includes not only official and expressly authorised union activities but also other union activities with some nexus to the workplace which takes place at the 'appropriate time'.[8] This includes recruitment and organisation,[9] acting or being involved

---

1   TULR(C)A 1992 s152(1)(a).
2   Ibid s152(1)(b).
3   Ibid s152(1)(c).
4   Ibid s146(1)(a).
5   Ibid s146(1)(b).
6   Ibid s146(1)(c).
7   *Speciality Care Plc v Pachela* [1996] IRLR 248.
8   *Dixon and Shaw v West Ella Developments Ltd* [1978] IRLR 151.
9   *Lyon Scherk v St James Press* [1976] IRLR 218.

in grievances and complaints,[10] meetings and voting,[11] and industrial action.[12]

2.4   Appropriate time is defined as a time which is either outside a worker's working hours or is within hours at a time which, in accordance with arrangements agreed with, or consent given by, the employer, it is permissible for the worker to take part in union activities.[13] Working hours are those hours which the worker is required to be at work.

Industrial action

2.4A   There are special rules regarding whether a worker dismissed while taking industrial action can claim unfair dismissal (see paras 6.64– 6.67 below).

Time off for trade union duties and activities

Officials

2.5   Regard must be had to provisions of the ACAS Code of Practice, *Time Off for Trade Union Duties and Activities 1998* which aims to aid and improve the effectiveness of relationships between employers and trade unions. Any Code of Practice may be taken into account by ETs when considering a claim which concerns the subject matter of the Code.

2.6   An employer must permit an independent trade union official to take time off during working hours for the purposes of carrying on trade union activities.[14] The trade union duties defined are; negotiations with the employer, matters related to or connected with collective bargaining and matters in relation to which the trade union is recognised. Paragraph 12 of the ACAS Code lists duties which are likely to be treated as trade union duties.

.7   The employer must permit a worker who is an official of an independent recognised trade union to take time during working hours for the purpose of undergoing training in respect of matters

---

10 *Brennan and Ging v Ellward (Lancs) Ltd* [1976] IRLR 378.
11 *British Airways Engine Overhaul Ltd v Francis* [1981] IRLR 9.
12 *Crowther v British Railways Board* EAT 762/95.
13 TULR(C)A 1992 ss152(2), 146(2).
14 Ibid s178(2).

concerning industrial relations.[15] This training must be approved by the TUC or by the official's own trade union.[16] Paragraph 18 of the ACAS Code provides further guidance as to the type of training covered. This right is likely to be extended to workers' representatives.[17]

2.8   The amount of time off must be reasonable in all the circumstances. Paragraph 4 of the ACAS Code provides further guidance as to what is reasonable and regard must be had to the size of the organisation, the production process, the need to maintain a public service, and safety considerations. The test is objective and requires the balancing of the competing interests of both parties.[18]

2.9   Where time off is given during working hours the worker is entitled to be paid and the employer cannot allow time off if the worker agrees it will not be paid.[19]

2.10   Note also that the Employment Relations Act 1999 (ERA) entitles a worker, where there is a reasonable request, to be accompanied by a work colleague or trade union official at disciplinary and grievance hearings.[20]

Members

2.11   The employer must allow a worker who is a member of a recognised independent trade union to take time off during working hours for the purpose of taking part in any activities of the union and any activities in relation to which the worker is acting as a representative of the union.[21]

Remedies

2.12   A worker can complain to an ET about the failure to permit time off or a failure to pay for time off permitted for trade union activities.[22] The claim must be presented within three months of the refusal or

15   Ibid s168.
16   Ibid s168(2).
17   Consultation paper on *Employees' information and consultation rights on transfers of undertakings and collective redundancies.*
18   *Chloride Silent Power Ltd v Cash* EAT 95/86.
19   *Beecham Group Ltd v Beal* [1983] IRLR 317.
20   ERA 1999 ss10–15, particularly s10(7). See also paras 6.13A–6.13C below.
21   TULR(C)A 1992 s170.
22   Ibid ss168(4), 170(4) and 169(5).

failure to pay.[23] Where there has been a failure to give time off the ET can award compensation which it considers just and equitable.[24]

Recognition

2.13 It is not within the ambit of this book to talk about recognition and collective bargaining generally. However it is noteworthy that the new ERA 1999 provides for a trade union recognition procedure, which will be triggered by a formal written request by an independent trade union or a group of two or more independent trade unions which wish to be recognised in an undertaking employing more than 20 workers, specifying the group of workers on behalf of whom it is or they are seeking to recognise.

Check off

2.14 The employer is not entitled to make deductions from a worker's pay for trade union dues unless the worker has authorised the deduction in writing and the worker has not withdrawn the authorisation.[25] If the employer has made unauthorised deductions, a worker can present a claim to the ET.[26]

The statutory duty to consult in respect of collective redundancy dismissals

2.15 The Trade Union and Labour Relations (Consolidation) Act 1992 (TULR(C)A 1992) s188 contains rules regarding consultation with trade union or employee representatives where redundancies of 20 or more employees are proposed. TULR(C)A 1992 and ERA 1996 were amended by the Collective Redundancies and Transfer of Undertakings (Protection of Employment) (Amendment) Regulations

---

23 Ibid s171.
24 Ibid s172(2).
25 Deregulation (Deduction from Pay of Union Subscriptions) Order 1998 SI No 1529.
26 TULR(C)A 1992 s68(A).

1999[28] to meet the requirements of the EC Directive.[29] This includes dismissals for any reason not related to the individuals concerned, eg, reorganisation or restructuring dismissals as opposed to dismissals for redundancy in the normal sense (as in paras 7.51–7.60 below).

2.16   Consultation must take place with the appropriate representatives of any employees who may be affected by the proposed dismissals or by measures taken in connection with those dismissals.[30] If not, the employers must consult correctly elected employee representatives.[31] Consultation should be undertaken by the employers with a view to reaching agreement with the representatives and should include ways of avoiding or reducing the numbers of dismissals.[32]

2.17   The information which must be disclosed in writing is the reason for the redundancy proposals, the numbers and descriptions of the workers whom it is proposed to dismiss as redundant, the total number of workers employed at the establishment in question, the proposed method of selection, the manner in which the dismissals are to be carried out and the proposed method of calculating the redundancy payments.[33]

2.18   With redundancy dismissals the consultations must take place in good time. Where it is proposed to make 100 or more workers redundant, then the consultation must be at least 90 days before the first of the dismissals is to occur; at least 30 days before, where at least 20 but less than 100 workers are proposed to be made redundant.[34]

2.19   For meaningful consultation to take place, it is strongly arguable that it should start as soon as the employers seriously think redundancies are possible, and should not wait until a provisional decision has been made as to how many, who they are and how the dismissals will take place.

Collective consultation on business transfers

2.20   The interpretation of the EC Business Transfers Directive[35] is found in the Transfer of Undertakings (Protection of Employment) Regula-

---

28 SI No1925, in force 28 July 1999.
29 98/59/EC, consolidating and replacing Directives 75/129 and 92/56.
30 TULR(C)A s188(1B)(a).
31 Ibid s188(1B)(b); s188A(1).
32 Ibid s188(2).
33 Ibid s188(4).
34 Ibid s188(1A).
35 77/187/EEC.

tions 1981,[36] the provisions of which were added to by the Trade Union and Labour Relations (Consolidation) Act 1992 (TULR(C)A 1992).

2.21   As a consequence of an ECJ ruling[37] there is now the obligation to consult with not only recognised trade unions but also workers representatives to give effect to the Acquired Rights Directive article 10. This ruling resulted in the implementation of the Collective Redundancies and Transfer of Undertakings (Protection of Employment) (Amendment) Regulations 1995 now amended by the 1999 Regulations.[38]

2.22   Employers must consult with either the trade union or, if there is none, with correctly elected employee representatives.[39] Consultation must be with the representatives of any employees of the transferor or transferee, whether or not employed in the undertaking to be transferred, who may be affected by the transfer or measures taken in connection with it.[40]

2.23   The nature of the information required to be provided is set out in regulation 10(2) of the 1995 Regulations, including confirmation of the transfer, when it will take place and the reason for it, plus the legal, economic and social implications of the transfer for the affected workers. Thus, information must be delivered or posted to the trade union or the employees' representative in sufficient time before a relevant transfer to enable consultation to take place (see regulation 10 (2)).

Remedies for failure to consult on redundancies or transfers

2.24   If the employer fails to inform or consult, the remedy is to complain to an ET. If the appropriate representative is the trade union then the complaint is made by the trade union and, if the workers' representative, then by the workers' representative.[41] The remedy is in two stages. The first stage is a declaration that the employer has failed to consult and an ET may award compensation to each affected

36   SI No 1794.
37   *EC Commission v United Kingdom* [1994] IRLR 412.
38   SI No 1925.
39   TUPE Regs reg 10(2A).
40   Ibid reg 10(1).
41   TULR(C)A s189(2); TUPE Regs reg 11(1).

employee.[42] The second stage applies if the employer fails to pay, in which case the individual employee must apply to an ET.[43]

2.25   Where an ET declares that there has been inadequate consultation on collective redundancies, it can make a protective award, ordering the employer to pay remuneration to individual employees for the protected period. This period starts when the first dismissal takes effect (or the date of the ET award if earlier), and lasts for as long as the ET thinks just and equitable having regard to the seriousness of the employer's default. It cannot exceed 90 days' pay.[44] The award is intended to compensate the worker for the lack of consultation and it is not necessarily relevant that the worker has lost earnings as a result (eg, s/he may have got a new job immediately). On the other hand, it is not intended to punish the employer as such and therefore a purely technical breach of the rules may lead to no award. A general starting point would be the number of days that the actual consultation fell short of the period of required consultation, with an adjustment made according to the seriousness of the employer's failure.

2.26   Where there is a failure to comply with the TUPE Regulations on information and consultation, an ET can order the employers to pay appropriate compensation to individual employees up to a maximum of 13 weeks' pay for each employee. Again the ET must take account of the seriousness of the employer's failure.[45]

---

42   TULR(C)A s189(2); TUPE Regs reg 11(4).
43   TULR(C)A s192; TUPE Regs reg 11(5).
44   TULR(C)A s189(4).
45   TUPE Regs reg 11(11).

International obligations

European law

3.1   The law of the European Union has become increasingly influential in the employment field, most obviously in the fields of sex discrimination, transfers of undertakings and health and safety. The following is only a brief and simplified outline of the basic principles as to how individuals in member states including the UK may rely on legislation and case-law from the EU.[1]

3.2   The advantage of EU legislation is that its ambit is often wider than the UK legislation. Wherever possible, UK legislation should be interpreted consistently with any relevant EU directive.[2] Where there is an irreconcilable conflict between UK and EU law, the latter can be applied to individual cases in the ET only in the limited circumstances described below.

3.3   Where a question arises as to the interpretation or applicability of EU law, any UK court or tribunal can ask the European Court of Justice (ECJ) to give a preliminary ruling. UK courts can choose to interpret EU law themselves, but where there is no further route of appeal, ie, the House of Lords, the ECJ must be referred to.

The Treaty of Rome and its Articles

3.4   The EEC[3] was established by the Treaty of Rome and it is this Treaty which provides the original basis for the establishment of employment rights. On 1 May 1999, the Treaty of Amsterdam came into force, renumbering the articles of the Treaty of Rome and making other amendments.

3.5   On the whole, the Treaties impose obligations on member states which are enforceable only by other member states. However, some key articles are 'directly applicable' and have 'direct effect'. This means they can be used in claims brought by individual citizens of the member states, even though they may not have been implemented by the relevant member state. If necessary, such articles override conflicting national law.

---

1 See also the relevant chapters.
2 *Pickstone v Freemans* [1988] IRLR 357; [1988] ICR 697, HL; *Litster v Forth Dry Dock and Engineering Co* [1989] IRLR 161; [1989] ICR 341, HL; *Finnegan v Clowney Youth Training Programme* [1990] IRLR 299, HL; *Marleasing SA v La Commercial Internacional de Alimentacion SA* [1992] 1 CMLR 305, ECJ; *Webb v EMO Air Cargo (UK) Ltd* [1993] IRLR 27, HL.
3 Subsequently renamed the EU.

3.6   Under the Treaty of Rome, the articles with direct effect were article 119 requiring men and women to receive equal pay for equal work, and article 48 prohibiting discrimination in work on grounds of nationality against nationals of other member states.

3.7   On 1 May 1999, the Treaty of Amsterdam came into force, amending the Treaty of Rome in a number of ways and renumbering the articles. Most importantly for employment law, article 119 was renumbered as article 141 and expanded to include a reference in the Treaty to equal treatment for the first time. It is unlikely that this addition will have direct effect. Article 48 was renumbered article 39. There is also a new article 13 which will enable the EU to issue directives and take other action to combat discrimination based on sex, racial or ethnic origin, religion or belief, disability, age or sexual orientation. On 25 November 1999 the European Commission proposed two draft anti-discrimination directives under article 13: the first would outlaw discrimination in employment on grounds of race, ethnic origin, religion, disability, age and sexual orientation. The second would prohibit race discrimination in employment and other areas.[4]

Directives

3.8   The European Parliament together with the Council and the Commission can make regulations, issue directives and make recommendations.[5] An increasing number of directives are being issued. Examples of important directives issued over the years are:

- 76/207/EEC on the implementation or the principle of equal treatment for men and women as regards access to employment, vocational training and promotion, and working conditions. This is known as the Equal Treatment Directive;[6]
- 77/187/EEC safeguarding employees' rights on transfers of undertakings, businesses or parts of businesses. This is known as the Acquired Rights Directive;[7]

---

4 Draft directives and accompanying documentation are available on the website of the Directorate for Employment and Social affairs, www.europa.eu.int/comm/dg05/key_en.htm.
5 Treaty of Rome, article 189.
6 See para 9.9.
7 See para 6.92.

– 93/104/EEC concerning certain aspects of the organisation of working time. This is known as the Working Time Directive.[8]

A member state must implement the contents of a directive into its own national law by a given date. If it fails to do so, an individual may be able to claim rights under the directive, but only if the directive has 'direct effect'.[9] For this, the directive, and the relevant provision, must be clear, precise and allow no exceptions.[10]

3.9   Provided that the directive has direct effect, a worker employed by the state or an 'emanation' of it, can claim against his or her employer the rights given by the directive. This is to prevent the state, in any of its guises, taking advantage of its own failure to comply with EU law. Unfortunately a worker who is not employed by an 'emanation of the state' cannot claim under the directive against his or her employer. However, if s/he suffers loss as a direct result of the UK government's failure to implement the directive, s/he may be able to sue the government for compensation.[11]

3.10   On the whole, the UK has now implemented most EU Directives by national legislation. However, there are still a few areas where greater rights appear to exist under a directive[12] and in such cases, it is unsatisfactory that private sector workers may have lesser rights than their public sector colleagues.

What is an emanation of the state?

3.11   A useful definition of 'emanation of the state' is in *Foster v British Gas*,[13] where the ECJ said that the Equal Treatment Directive could be used by individuals employed by any body made responsible by the state for providing a public service under the control of the state and which has special powers for that purpose. An 'emanation of the

---

8   See para 4.46.
9   And if the conditions in the next paragraph apply.
10 *Van Duyn v Home Office* [1975] 3 All ER 190, ECJ.
11 *Francovich v Italian Republic* [1992] IRLR 84, ECJ; *(1) Brasserie du Pecheur SA v Federal Republic of Germany (2) R v Secretary of State for Transport ex p Factortame Ltd* [1996] IRLR 267, ECJ; *R v HM Treasury ex p British Telecommunications plc* [1996] IRLR 300, ECJ; *Secretary of State for Employment v Mann and Others* [1996] IRLR 4, EAT; *Dillenkofer and Others v Federal Republic of Germany* [1997] IRLR 60, ECJ; *Potter and Others v Secretary of State for Employment* [1996] 576 *IDS Brief* 3, CA.
12 For example, the current definition of 'indirect discrimination'.
13 [1991] IRLR 268, HL.

state' includes local government, health authorities,[14] the police,[15] the Post Office and nationalised industries.[16] In some circumstances, privatised industries may remain an 'emanation of the state'. A useful case is *Griffin v South West Water Services Ltd*.[17] In stating that a privatised water company was an emanation of the state, the court emphasised that it is the service, not the body, which needs to be under state control. The *Foster* case gives indicators as to when an employer may be considered an emanation of the state, but these will not always apply, for example, it is not necessary to be under the control of central government.[18] The governing body of a voluntary aided school can be considered an emanation of the state for these purposes.[19]

Human Rights Act 1998

3.12   As part of the government's manifesto commitment, the Human Rights Act (HRA) 1998 has been passed in order to incorporate the European Convention on Human Rights[20] into domestic law. It comes into force on 2 October 2000. Until incorporation the only redress under the Convention was to claim against the UK in the European Court of Human Rights in Strasbourg. The Convention was ratified by the Labour Government in 1951 and came into force in 1953. The first interstate application brought under the Convention was against the UK concerning the colonial rule in Cyprus. The Greek Government petitioned the European Commission and complained that 'The exceptional measures adopted by the British administration authorities in Cyprus have meant the denial of nearly all human rights and fundamental freedoms in the island'. This petition was successful much to the horror of the UK: 'We never conceived of the Convention being used against us like this'.[21] Individual petitions

---

14 *Marshall v Southampton and South-West Hampshire AHA* [1986] IRLR 140; [1986] ICR 335.

15 *Johnston v Chief Constable of the Royal Ulster Constabulary* [1986] IRLR 263; [1987] ICR 83, ECJ.

16 *Foster* (n13 above). But see also *Doughty v Rolls-Royce plc* [1992] IRLR 126, CA.

17 [1995] IRLR 15, HC.

18 *NUT v Governing Body of St Mary's Church of England (Aided) Junior School* [1997] IRLR 242, CA.

19 *NUT* ibid.

20 European Convention of Human Rights and Fundamental Freedoms 1950.

21 Telegram from the Minister of State, Lord Perth, to the Governor of Cyprus.

have been permitted since 1966. Since 1966 there have been over 6,000 applications against the UK. In 1998 alone 300 applications were made.

3.13 The purpose of the HRA 1998 is to require the courts to interpret domestic legislation so far as is possible to give effect to the rights imposed by the articles of the Convention. Where it is not possible to do so, the domestic legislation remains unaltered thereby preserving parliamentary sovereignty. Another shortfall in the effectiveness of the HRA 1998 is the failure to introduce a Commission for Human Rights (like the CRE or EOC) to ensure its implementation and effective operation and the failure to incorporate article 13 of the Convention, which guarantees an effective remedy if the Convention is violated.

The Articles of the Convention

3.14 Section 1 of the HRA 1998 incorporates articles 2–12 and 14 of the Convention. The HRA 1998 does not include article 13. The failure to incorporate article 13 is likely to be challenged on the basis that the HRA 1998 is in breach of the Convention!

3.15 The important articles which will have an impact in the employment field include article 4 (right not to be held in slavery and to be protected against forced or compulsory labour), article 5 (right to liberty and security of the person), article 6 (right to a fair and public hearing within a reasonable period of time), article 8 (the right to respect for private life), article 9 (freedom of religion), article 10 (the right to freedom of expression) and article 11 (the right to peaceful assembly and the freedom of association with others). Importantly, article 14 declares:

> the enjoyment of the rights and freedoms set forth in this Convention shall be enjoyed without discrimination on any ground such as sex, race, colour, language, religion, political or other opinion, national or social origin, association with a minority, property, birth or other status.

Although article 14 is not a free-standing right, the other articles must be read in conformity with article 14.

3.16 Many of the rights and fundamental freedoms under the Convention are not unqualified. For example, articles 8–11 may be subject to restrictions on a number of grounds 'in accordance with the law' which are deemed 'necessary in a democratic society'. The scope of article 11 can be restricted by reference to national and public safety. In the *GCHQ* case[22] it was permissible to prevent those engaged in the administration of the state from belonging to a trade union.

Link with other international human rights

3.17 In addition to article 14, the European Court of Human Rights when considering a claim will frequently have regard to other relevant international human rights provisions. For example, in *Chahal v United Kingdom*[23] the court had regard to both the UN Torture Convention and the International Covenant on Civil and Political Rights in considering the scope of 'inhuman and degrading treatment' in article 3.

3.18 The ECHR has said that the discharge of lesbians and gay men from the armed forces and investigations into their homosexuality were breaches of the right of privacy under article 8 of the European Convention of Human Rights. Article 13 was also violated in that there was no effective remedy in the UK.[24]

Who can claim under the HRA 1998?

3.19 Under the HRA 1998, it is unlawful for public authorities to behave in a manner contrary to the Convention.[25] The practical implications for employment law are very uncertain.[26] It seems that workers employed by obvious public authorities such as government departments and local authorities should be able to enforce directly the Convention rights (although the mechanism is not entirely clear). Workers employed by bodies 'some of whose functions only are of a public nature', eg, GP practices which have both NHS and private patients, may not generally be able to claim. This is because only the public functions of such mixed bodies will be covered and the employment relationship may be seen as a private function. Workers employed in the private sector alone will be unable to make direct

---

22 *Council of Civil Service Unions v Minister for the Civil Service* [1985] AC 374; [1985] IRLR 28, HL.
23 (1997) 23 EHRR 622.
24 *Smith and Grady v UK* [1999] IRLR 734; 88 EOR 49, ECHR.
25 HRA 1998 s6.
26 For useful early analysis, see the two articles in (December 1998) *Industrial Law Journal* Vol 27 No 4 p 275–308.

claims. However, as 'public authorities' are defined to include courts and tribunals,[27] any worker may be able to challenge procedures restricting his or her access to bringing or processing a claim, eg, regarding the deposit payments following a pre-hearing assessment or the statutory defences and exclusions in discrimination cases. ETs must also interpret domestic law consistently with the Convention as far as possible.

3.20   Claims may be brought only by individuals who are, or are likely to be a victim of a breach of the Convention.[28] Article 34 of the Convention provides 'The Court may receive applications from any person, non-governmental organisation or group of individuals claiming to be the victim of a violation of the right set forth in the convention'.

3.21   A court can award damages against a public authority which will be assessed in accordance with article 41 of the Convention.[29]

27   HRA 1998 s6(3)(a).
28   Ibid s7(7).
29   Ibid s8(4).

Part I

Wages

CHAPTER 4

Pay and the protection of wages

For complete chapter contents, see overleaf

Introduction

4.1 The payment of wages, and the intervals at which payments are made, is a matter of agreement between the employer and worker. It is a fundamental term of the employment contract to pay wages and the failure to do so (unlike a genuine miscalculation)[1] will entitle the worker to claim constructive dismissal[2] and to recover the wages owing either in the employment tribunal (ET) or civil courts (county court or High Court) for breach of contract or as an unlawful deduction from wages under the Employment Rights Act (ERA) 1996.[3]

4.2 The employer is under a statutory duty to give workers a written statement which includes the scale, or the method of calculating wages,[4] and the intervals at which wages will be paid, whether weekly or monthly or by some other period.[5] The employer is obliged to account in writing to the worker for all deductions made from wages at or before each pay day, whether it is for tax, national insurance or for any other reason.[6] This duty is usually discharged by issuing itemised pay statements.

4.3 The employer's obligation in most work situations is to pay the wages contractually agreed. There is usually no obligation to supply work.[7] The worker's obligation is to be willing and able to perform his/her contractual duties. The failure to do so entitles the employer to deduct a sum equal to the proportion of the time when the worker was not willing to work.[8]

Payment in cash and deductions from pay: the legal framework

The legislation

4.4 Since 1831 there has been statutory protection for certain workers in respect of their entitlement to be paid 'a current coin of the

---

1 *Cantor Fitzgerald International v Callaghan* [1999] IRLR 234.
2 *Gillies v Richard Daniels Co* [1979] IRLR 457 and see para 6.41.
3 ERA 1996 Part II (Protection of Wages). This is only enforceable in the ET.
4 ERA 1996 s1(4)(a).
5 ERA 1996 s1(4)(b). See para 1.21.
6 ERA 1996 s8.
7 *William Hill Organisation Ltd v Tucker* [1998] IRLR 313; *Collier v Sunday Referee Publishing Co* [1940] 4 All ER 234; [1940] 2 KB 647.
8 *Miles v Wakefield MDC* [1987] IRLR 193, HL.

realm',⁹ ie, cash for their services. This legislation was introduced to combat the growing practice in the early 19th century of employers paying workers by way of tokens or goods instead of wages. These tokens were valid only in the employer's shop. Employers were not only motivated by profit; they also had religious and paternalistic reasons for doing this. Many of these 'tommy' shops were operated by religious philanthropists who refused to sell alcohol or goods likely to corrupt morals.

4.5   In addition to the right to be paid in cash, the subsequent Truck Acts protected workers in respect of deductions from wages and fines imposed by their employers.¹⁰ The Wages Act (WA) 1986 repealed the Truck Acts 1831 to 1940 and the Payment of Wages Act 1960.¹¹ The WA 1986 abolished a worker's right to be paid in cash, and removed the protection against deductions from wages. Since 1 January 1987 employers have been entitled in certain circumstances (see para 4.15 below) to make deductions from wages as long as they comply with the notification provisions. The WA 1986 has been repealed and re-enacted in ERA 1996 Part II.

4.6   ERA 1996 Part II allows employers, if they satisfy the necessary requirements, to make deductions from the pay of workers. There is no control in respect of the extent of the deduction unless the worker is employed in retailing, unlike under the Truck Acts. The provisions are therefore regulatory rather than protective. ERA 1996 s13 deals with the employer's right to make deductions from a worker's wages. ERA 1996 s18 limits the size of the deduction that can be made from the wages of retail workers for cash shortages and stock deficiencies.¹² However, even the limited protection afforded to retail workers is removed on their final pay day.¹³

Who is covered?

4.7   ERA 1996 Part II covers most categories of workers and extends the definition of worker beyond the restrictive definition of 'employee' in the unfair dismissal provisions.¹⁴ The definition of 'worker' covers those who have entered into, or work under, a contract of employ-

---

9   Truck Act 1831 s1.
10   Truck Amendment Act 1887 and Truck Act 1896.
11   WA 1986 s11.
12   ERA 1996 ss17 and 18.
13   ERA 1996 s22.
14   ERA 1996 s230.

ment and any other contract whereby the individual undertakes to do or perform personally any work or services for another party to the contract whose status is not, by virtue of the contract, that of a client or customer of any profession or business undertaking carried on by the individual.[15] This has included agency workers on the books of an employment agency.[16]

4.8   Those working in retail employment are given additional protection in respect of the amount of the deductions that can be made in any given week during their employment on account of cash or stock deficiencies,[17] being no more than 10 per cent of the gross wage due on any given pay day, and to continue to recover up to 10 per cent in the following weeks until the full sum is recovered. In the final week of employment any amount which remains outstanding can be recovered by the employer.[18] Deductions other than for cash or stock shortages are not subject to this 10 per cent ceiling.

4.9   This protection was introduced because of the widespread practice of employers in retailing of deducting cash and stock deficiencies from wages. The worst employers were garage owners, who would hold workers responsible for unpaid fuel bills which were often in excess of the wages owing, resulting in the worker owing money to the employer for the privilege of working![19]

4.10   Retail employment means employment which involves the carrying out by the worker of retail transactions directly with members of the public and the collection by the worker of amounts payable in connection with retail transactions such as the sale and supply of goods and services.[20] This definition covers workers in shops, banks, building societies, petrol stations, restaurants (waiters and cashiers), homeworkers, those working on the 'lump' in the building trade, and workers involved in the delivery and sale of produce such as those who do milk rounds.

4.11   ERA 1996 Part II excludes workers who carry on a business or profession where the other party is a client.[21] This would exclude professionals such as solicitors, doctors, and dentists and also sole traders and taxi drivers. ERA 1996 Part II also covers Crown

---

15 Ibid.
16 *Allied Medicare Ltd v Westwood* (1996) 568 IRLB 18, EAT.
17 ERA 1996 s18.
18 Ibid s22.
19 *Bristow v City Petroleum* [1987] IRLR 340, HL.
20 ERA 1996 s17.
21 Ibid s230(3).

employment (civil servants),[22] but not those employed in the armed forces.[23]

Payment of wages

4.12   A worker who started employment after 1 January 1987 may be paid by credit transfer or by cheque. A worker employed prior to this date who has a contractual right to be paid in cash continues to enjoy this right. However, if an employer refuses to continue to pay the worker in cash, there is very little that the worker can do. A claim for unfair constructive dismissal is unlikely to succeed if the employer argues that the change in paying wages was introduced for sound administrative and/or safety reasons; the reason for any subsequent dismissal would be some other substantial reason justifying the dismissal.

Unauthorised deductions from wages

Definition of 'wages'

4.13   For the purpose of ERA 1996 Part II, 'wages' are given a wide definition, covering 'any sums payable to the worker by his employer in connection with his employment, including any fee, bonus, commission, holiday pay or other emolument referrable to his employment',[24] including guarantee payments, statutory sick pay and maternity pay.[25] The courts have held that wages do not include notice pay (unless the worker is working out his/her notice or is treated as doing so).[26] Discretionary and ex gratia payments are wages if there is a reasonable expectation that the worker will receive the payment.[27] The failure by a restaurant to pay the full 15 per cent fixed service charge to the staff was held to be recoverable as a deduction from wages.[28] The definition has also included commission that becomes payable after the termination of the worker's contract, provided that it is in connection with the employment.[29]

4.14   Certain payments are expressly excluded from the definition of

---

22   Ibid s191.
23   Ibid s192.
24   Ibid s27.
25   Ibid.
26   *Delaney v Staples (t/a Montfort Recruitment)* [1992] IRLR 191, HL.
27   *Kent Management Services Ltd v Butterfield* [1992] IRLR 394, EAT.
28   *Saavedra v Aceground Ltd* [1995] IRLR 198.
29   *Robertson v Blackmore Franks Investment Management Ltd* [1998] IRLR 376.

wages including loans and advances on wages, expenses including a car mileage allowance,[30] pensions, allowances or gratuities in connection with the worker's retirement, redundancy payments, and benefits in kind.

When deductions can be made

4.15 ERA 1996 Part II prevents the employer from making any deduction from the wages of workers unless it is:

a) authorised by statute.[31] This enables the employer to deduct from wages the PAYE tax and national insurance payments as required by law or following an order of a court (maintenance payments, fines, etc);

b) authorised by a 'relevant provision in the contract'.[32] There is no requirement that the term of the contract should be in writing and the term in question can be an implied rather than express term. However, it is necessary for the employer to notify the worker in writing of the existence of the term, and to explain its effect;[33] or

c) previously agreed in writing by the worker that the deduction may be made.[34]

If the worker gives prior consent in writing to the deduction being made, it will be an authorised deduction. This consent cannot be retrospective. Where the written consent is to make deductions in respect of stock shortages, it must have been given before the shortage arose.[35] Similarly, the employer cannot receive any payment from the worker unless the payment satisfies one of the three conditions above. This prevents the employer recovering payments by demand rather than deduction.

4.16 Even if the above three conditions are absent, the employer is entitled to deduct money:

a) in respect of any overpayment of wages and/or expenses;[36]

b) for a statutory purpose to a public authority (eg, taxes owing to the Inland Revenue);

---

30 *Southwark (LBC) v O'Brien* [1996] IRLR 420.
31 ERA 1996 s13.
32 Ibid.
33 Ibid.
34 *Pename Ltd v Paterson* [1989] IRLR 195, EAT.
35 *Discount Tobacco and Confectionery Ltd v Williamson* (1993) 475 IRLB 5, EAT.
36 ERA 1996 s14 and *Sunderland Polytechnic v Evans* [1993] ICR 392.

c) as a consequence of a strike or industrial action;

d) for any contractual obligation to pay to a third party (eg, union dues);

e) in satisfaction of a court or tribunal order requiring the worker to pay the employer;[37] or

f) if the deficiency in payment is attributable to an error of computation. However a conscious decision not to make the payment as the employer believes that there is a contractual right not to make the payment does not amount to an error of computation.[38]

What amounts to a deduction?

4.17   Where the total amount of any wages that are paid by an employer to a worker is less than the total amount of the wages that are properly payable to the worker on that occasion, the amount of the deficiency will be treated as a deduction made by the employer from the worker's wages,[39] even where there is a 100 per cent deduction.[40] Any unauthorised deduction from any of the different types of 'wages' or a non-payment of them,[41] such as the failure to pay statutory sick pay, maternity pay or accrued holiday pay,[42] is recoverable in the ET.

Remedies and time limits

4.18   The worker can make a claim to the ET asking for a declaration that the employer has made unauthorised deductions and an order that the employer repay the sums deducted.[43] This claim must be made within three months of the date of the deduction or, if the worker has made a payment to the employer, of the date when the payment was made.[44] If the employer made a series of deductions, the time limit runs from the last deduction.[45] The time limit runs from the latest date on which payment could be made under the contract rather than the actual date of payment.[46] The ET can extend the time limit if it was not reasonably practicable for the claim to have been made within the

37   ERA 1996 s14.
38   *Yemm v British Steel* [1994] IRLR 117.
39   ERA 1996 s13(3).
40   *Delaney v Staples* [1991] IRLR 112, CA.
41   *Kournavos v JR Masterton and Sons* [1990] IRLR 119, EAT.
42   *Greg May (CF and C) v Dring* [1990] IRLR 19, EAT.
43   ERA 1996 s23.
44   Ibid s23(2).
45   Ibid s23(3).
46   *Group 4 Nightspeed Ltd v Gilbert* [1997] IRLR 398.

three-month period.[47] The extension provision adopts the same form of words as is used for the unfair dismissal provision and it can be assumed therefore that the worker will experience the same problems with ERA 1996 Part II claims as with unfair dismissal claims[48] if the time limit is missed.

4.19 Wages owed may be claimed either under ERA 1996 Part II as a deduction, or as a breach of contract, in the county court or High Court or, if the contract has been terminated, in the ET. There may be advantages in claiming under Part II even though it seems a more artificial concept, eg, as counterclaims may be made against contract claims but not against Part II claims. Also, the employer may have a genuine entitlement to the money, but not to acquire it by helping him/herself out of the pay packet. If that happens and the worker wins his/her Part II claim, the employer loses the right to claim in respect of the same sum in the county court or High Court.[48A]

ET claim for breach of contract

.20 Since 12 July 1994 once a worker's employment has ended s/he can bring a claim in the ET for breach of contract, eg, for holiday pay, wages owing or notice.[49] It is not possible to bring proceedings in the ET for compensation arising out of personal injuries sustained at work, or claims concerning living accommodation or clauses in restraint of trade.

21 Many claims, eg, for wages owing (though not notice) could alternatively be brought under ERA 1996 Part II as an unlawful deduction. Since the employer can counterclaim if an action is commenced for breach of contract in the ET, an ERA 1996 Part II claim will be preferable where there is a choice. An employer cannot start proceedings for a breach of contract. There is a three-month time limit from the end of employment for bringing a claim unless it is not reasonably practicable to do so within that period. Any counterclaim must be made within six weeks of receipt of the claim. There is a maximum ceiling of £25,000 for a claim in the ET.

---

47   ERA 1996 s23(4).
48   See para 16.16.
48A *Potter v Hunt Contracts Ltd* [1992] IRLR 108, EAT.
49   Implemented by Employment Protection (Consolidation) Act 1978 (EPCA) s131(8) and the Employment Tribunals (Extension of Jurisdiction) (England and Wales) Order 1994 SI No 1623.

The difference between ET and county or High Court claims

4.22 A contract claim in the county or High Court differs procedurally from one in an ET in that:

a) there is no entitlement to legal aid if the claim is presented in the ET, but legal aid, subject to means and merits, is available for a claim in the county or High Court provided it is above the small claims limit;

b) the time limit in the county or High Court is six years whereas in the ET it must be brought within three months of termination, though in some circumstances the cause of action may have arisen in the previous six years;[50]

c) legal costs will only be awarded against a worker in the ET if the worker has acted frivolously, vexatiously, abusively, disruptively or otherwise unreasonably in bringing proceedings,[51] but in the county or High Court costs will normally be awarded to the party who wins (unless it is a small claims case);

d) interest is payable on an ET award six weeks after the decision. In the county or High Court interest is assessed as from the date on which the sum is due;

e) if a worker has a claim in excess of £25,000 and issues in the ET that worker cannot receive the excess in the county court or High Court as it would be an abuse of process to do so.

National minimum wage and wages councils: the legal framework

The legislation

4.23 Since 1909[52] workers in the 'sweated trades' have had the statutory right to be paid a minimum rate of pay. The trade boards were created in industries where there was no collective bargaining machinery. In 1945 the trade boards were replaced by wages councils.[53] Each wages

---

50 Employment Tribunals Extension of Jurisdiction (England and Wales) Order 1994 SI No 1623 reg 7.
51 ET Regs Sch 1 r12.
52 Trade Boards Act 1909.
53 Wages Councils Act 1945.

council was not only directed to set a minimum rate of pay for its industry but also to lay down minimum holiday entitlements. Once the minimum entitlements were decided, the Secretary of State for Employment would ratify them and thereby give the provisions statutory force.

4.24   The Wages Act 1986 (WA) Part II substantially altered the scope of the wages councils and those workers entitled to protection. In order to reduce the scope of the wages councils, and those covered by their provisions, it was necessary for the Conservative government to de-ratify from the International Labour Organisation (ILO) convention 26 (which requires all member states to have a minimum wage fixing machinery) prior to enacting the WA 1986 Part II. It was the first time that one of the 94 member states had denounced any of the ILO conventions which seek to provide minimum protection for workers worldwide.

4.25   Wages councils were empowered to set minimum rates of pay and overtime rates after 39 or 40 hours in any given week. They could also limit the amount taken into account for provision of living accommodation. They no longer had the power to make provisions for holidays or holiday pay.

4.26   The Agricultural Wages Act 1948 provides for similar powers to be vested in agricultural wages boards which cover farm workers, and those employed in the agricultural industry. These boards and their powers under the 1948 Act remained unaltered by the WA 1986.

4.27   From 30 August 1993 wages councils were abolished[54] as part of the then government's commitment to deregulation in the employment field. It was argued that the limited and piecemeal protection afforded by wages councils suppressed job opportunities for workers joining the labour market for the first time. This was a fallacious and unsustainable argument.

4.28   The National Minimum Wage Act 1998 introduced for the first time a national minimum wage although in the past there had been minimum pay for certain vulnerable groups of workers.[55] The National Minimum Wage Regulations 1999 came into force on 1 April 1999 and introduced for workers over 22 an hourly rate of £3.60 an hour[56] unless the worker has commenced work under an accredited training programme where the hourly rate is £3.20 an

---

54 TURERA 1993 s35.
55 WA 1986.
56 National Minimum Wage Regulations 1999 SI No 584 reg 11.

hour.[57] The rate for 18 to 21-year-olds is £3.00 an hour.[58] Under the National Minimum Wage Act, a 'worker' means anyone working under a contract of employment or any other contract to perform personally any work or services, except to a professional client or business customer. It includes agency workers and homeworkers.[58A] Excluded from an entitlement to a minimum wage are workers under the age of 18,[59] those employed on a contract of apprenticeship,[60] undergraduates on sandwich courses,[61] au pairs and nannies and companions who are treated as a member of their employer's family,[62] and members of the employer's family who live at home.[63] If a worker is not paid the national minimum wage s/he will be entitled to recover the shortfall[64] as an unlawful deduction from pay or on termination of employment as a breach of contract claim before the employment tribunal or in the county court.

4.29   From 1 November 1998 a worker has been protected from suffering a detriment as a consequence of enforcing a right under the national minimum wage provisions on his/her behalf or on behalf of another worker.[65] If an employee is dismissed, it will be treated as automatically unfair regardless of the worker's age or length of service.[66]

4.30   As well as individuals taking cases, the enforcement of the national minimum wage is done presently by officers of the Inland Revenue and Contributions Agency. These officers can serve an enforcement notice in respect of the shortfall of wages and can serve a penalty notice which requires the employer to pay a financial penalty to the secretary of state equal to twice the hourly amount of the national minimum wage in respect of each worker to whom the failure to comply relates for each day of non-compliance with the enforcement notice.[67] This penalty is recoverable as a civil debt by the officer.

---

57   Ibid reg 13(2).
58   Ibid reg 13(1).
58A National Minimum Wage Act 1998 ss54(3), 34–35.
59   National Minimum Wage Regulations 1999 reg 12(1).
60   Ibid reg 12(2)–(4).
61   Ibid reg 12(8), (9).
62   Ibid reg 2(2)(a) and para 37.
63   Ibid reg 2(2)(b), (3), (4) and para 38.
64   National Minimum Wage Act 1998 s17.
65   Ibid ss23 and 24.
66   Ibid s25.
67   Ibid s21.

4.31   It is also a criminal offence not to pay the national minimum wage or not to keep or preserve the prescribed records punishable by a fine up to £2,000.[68]

Holiday pay

4.32   Prior to the Working Time Regulations (WTR) 1998, workers did not have a right to paid holidays unless the employer agreed to paid holidays and it then became a contractual right. This situation has been changed by the WTR (see para 4.46 below). The WTR provide that all workers will be entitled to annual leave. Every worker who has been continuously employed for 13 weeks is entitled to at least four weeks' holiday as from 23 November 1999.[69] This must be taken in the leave year in which it is due and this entitlement cannot be substituted by payment in lieu of the holiday except on the termination of employment.[70] A worker can take leave by giving the correct notice specifying the proposed leave days.[71] The notice must be given twice as many days in advance of the first day proposed for leave as the number of days proposed in total.[72] If the employers object to leave being taken on those dates, they must give counter-notice as many days in advance of the earliest date as the total number of days in the worker's notice.[73] For example, a worker wanting to take two days' leave, must give at least four days' notice. If the employers wish to refuse that leave, they must give at least two days' counter-notice. Note that workers and employers may have agreed a different notification procedure by a relevant agreement under the rules.[74]

4.33   Where a worker is paid for bank holidays, it appears that these bank holidays will be offset against the annual holiday, unless the contract gives additional rights. The worker's leave year for the purpose of the WTR begins on the date (if any) specified in the employment contract or, if there is no leave year identified, it starts when

---

68   Ibid s31.
69   Working Time Regulations 1998 SI No 1833 reg 13.
70   Ibid reg 13(9)(b).
71   Ibid reg 15.
72   Ibid reg 15(3).
73   Ibid reg 15(4)(b).
74   Ibid reg 2(1), 15(5).

the worker's employment began (or for workers employed before 1 October 1998, the year starts 1 October).[75] The WTR provides for a minimum entitlement. There is nothing to prevent an employer agreeing to give additional holidays beyond the legal minimum entitlement. It is an obligation on the employer to supply the worker, within two months, with a statement giving details of any terms and conditions relating to holidays, public holidays and holiday pay, including any entitlement to accrued holiday pay on termination of employment.[76]

4.34   On the termination of employment, workers are entitled to receive a payment for any holidays outstanding, calculated proportionally to the leave year.[77] If the contractual holiday entitlement is greater than the WTR minimum, pay in lieu of the additional holiday will only be payable on termination if there is an express right to do so under the contract or a clear term implied by custom and practice. Some contracts exclude accrued holiday pay if the dismissal is for gross misconduct. This is permissible regarding any additional contractual rights, but probably not under the WTR.

4.35   If the employer refuses to pay holiday pay, a claim can be made in the ET for an unauthorised deduction from pay[78] or for breach of contract in the ET (if the worker's employment has ended) or the county or High Court.

Sick pay

Statutory sick pay

4.36   Since 6 April 1983[79] every employer has been obliged to pay statutory sick pay for the first 28 weeks of absence on account of sickness in any period of three years. Usually after 28 weeks the worker will claim incapacity benefit, paid direct by the state.

4.37   The employer makes the payment on behalf of the government and is entitled to claim a contribution which is deducted from the payment of national insurance contributions. It is an administrative

---

75   Ibid reg 13(3)(b).
76   ERA 1996 s1(4)(d)(i).
77   Working Time Regulations 1998 reg 14.
78   ERA 1996 Part II.
79   Social Security and Housing Benefits Act 1982 Part I.

process which results in many workers not getting sick pay when off work due to illness. Those workers who do not qualify for statutory sick pay claim, if entitled, from the DSS.[80] Payment is made after three waiting days' 'qualifying period' for each occasion that the worker is incapable of working due to some specific disease or bodily or mental disablement.[81] Workers do not have to qualify again if two periods of sickness fall within eight weeks.[82]

4.38 Statutory sick pay is a flat-rate payment. Details of the statutory sick pay rates, the entitlement provisions and the remedies available for non-payment can be found in the Child Poverty Action Group's *Welfare Benefits Handbook* (annual). It is worth noting that unpaid statutory sick pay is recoverable under ERA 1996 Part II.

4.39 In order to be eligible for statutory sick pay a worker must be an employee employed under a contract of service (see para 6.14), aged under 65 and have earnings of at least the lower earning limit.

Contractual sick pay

4.40 The statutory sick pay provisions are a minimum entitlement when away from work on account of sickness. About 80 per cent of workers are covered by a contractual sick pay scheme which generally makes up the difference between the statutory sick pay figure and normal wages for a fixed period of time in any given year. Such a scheme will be provided by an express term of the contract. It is possible to imply a term that the worker is entitled to normal pay if it is the custom or practice at the workplace to continue to pay workers off sick their normal pay. However, there is no longer a presumption that workers are entitled to the normal rate of pay when off sick.[83]

41 It is a requirement for the employer to provide workers with a written statement of any terms and conditions relating to entitlement when incapable of work due to sickness or injury, including any provisions for sick pay.[84]

---

80 Statutory Sick Pay (General) Regulations 1982 SI No 894 (SSP Regs).
81 SSP Regs reg 2.
82 Social Security and Housing Benefits Act 1982 s2.
83 *Mears v Safecar Security* [1982] IRLR 183, CA.
84 ERA 1996 s1(4)(d)(ii).

Itemised pay statements

4.42   Employers are obliged to provide workers with an itemised pay statement at or before each pay day.[85] There is no requirement on the worker to request an itemised pay statement. It is an absolute right.[86] Itemised pay statements must include the gross pay, details of all deductions from the gross pay, and the net pay. If the net pay is paid in different ways, the amount and method of payment of each part of the net pay must also be itemised.[87] If the employer supplies the worker with a written statement of a fixed deduction to be made each pay day (such as the repayment of a season ticket loan), the employer must detail the nature of this deduction only once every 12 months.[88]

4.43   If the employer fails to give a worker an itemised pay statement, or deductions are made which were not notified, the worker can apply to the ET for a declaration to this effect, and ask the ET to exercise its discretion to make a compensatory award. The declaration is mandatory, the compensation award is discretionary. The maximum amount of compensation that can be awarded is calculated by taking the date of application to the ET and determining the amount of the deductions (difference between the gross and net pay) on each of the pay days in the previous 13 weeks.[89]

4.44   As ignorance of the law is no defence, employers should be made to pay a compensatory award somewhere near the maximum figure. If the reason why the employer has failed to provide itemised pay statements is due to fraud or dishonest conduct, it is likely that the ET will be more willing to make a high award. The compensation is intended to act as a penalty on the employer for non-compliance and it does not matter whether the employer has accounted for the sums deducted to the Inland Revenue and therefore ends up paying twice.[90] The Employment Appeal Tribunal (EAT), in a decision in 1979, decided that a small award was not appealable as the provisions had come into effect only recently and the employer was a busy professional person in sole practice.[91] Twenty years later, the EAT has

---

85   Ibid s8.
86   *Coales v John Woods and Co (Solicitors)* [1986] IRLR 129, EAT.
87   ERA 1996 s8.
88   ERA 1996 s9.
89   Ibid s12(4).
90   *Cambiero v Aldo Zilli & Sheenwalk Ltd t/a Signor Silli's Bar* EAT/273/96; May 1998 *Legal Action* 21.
91   *Scott v Creager* [1979] ICR 403; [1979] IRLR 162, EAT.

taken a stronger position[92] and it is unusual for employers to get away with such leniency. It is important to stress to the ET that the failure to supply these statements is often indicative of some unlawful practice by the employer; usually the failure to make the appropriate tax and national insurance returns. It can also cause the worker practical inconvenience.

4.45   Workers who do not get itemised pay statements should check with the Inland Revenue and the Department of Social Security to discover whether the employer has been committing a fraud by not paying the requisite tax or national insurance, and if so, national insurance contributions for the missing payments should be secured by way of credited contributions.[93]

Working Time Regulations 1998

4.46   The Working Time Regulations (WTR) 1998 came into force on 1 October 1998 in order to implement two EC Directives on the organisation of working time[94] and young workers.[95] Workers are given a wide definition and includes those who undertake other forms of work in addition to workers under a contract of employment. Those covered include temporary workers, and agency workers but not those who are self-employed.[96]

4.47   There are a number of jobs and professionals excluded for the time being from the protection afforded by the WTR. Those working in the transportation sector (air, rail, road, sea, inland waterway), fishing, doctors in training[97] and occasionally the police force and other emergency services. Employment as a domestic servant in a private household is excluded from much of the protection, although the holiday entitlement remains.[97A]

4.47A   Almost all the protections in the WTR except for annual leave do not apply where the worker works on 'unmeasured working time'.[97B] If only part of the worker's time is unmeasured, the regulations do

92 *Cambiero* ibid.
93 See CPAG's *Welfare Benefits Handbook* (annual).
94 No 93/104/EC.
95 No 94/33/EC.
96 Working Time Regulations 1998 reg 2(1).
97 Ibid reg 18.
97A Ibid reg 19.
97B Ibid reg20(1).

not apply to that part.[97C] It is unclear exactly what this means. The exception is intended to apply where due to the specific nature of the work done, the duration of the worker's working time is not measured or predetermined, or it can be determined by the worker him or herself. The regulations give examples as managing executives or other persons with autonomous decision-making powers; family workers; or workers officiating in religious ceremonies. The DTI Guidance suggested that an indicator may be if the worker has discretion over whether to work or not on a given day without needing to consult the employer. Some employers are attempting to interpret this exception widely but advisers should resist this. High-powered, self-regulating managing directors should probably be covered, but not junior workers who are forced by higher management to work limitless unpaid overtime.

4.48   Regulation 4(1) imposes a contractual obligation on the employer not to require a worker to work more than an average of 48 hours per week.[97D] The employer also has a separate duty subject to criminal sanctions to take all reasonable steps to ensure no more than 48 hours per week are worked.[97E] The 48 hours is usually averaged over 17 weeks although for some workers it will be 26 weeks.[97F] A collective or workforce agreement cannot modify or exclude the 48-hour ceiling, but in certain circumstances it can extend the period over which hours are averaged.[98] Night workers should not average more than eight hours in each 24-hour period, again averaged over 17 weeks. A collective or workforce agreement can modify or exclude this entitlement.[99]

Rest periods

4.49   Each worker is entitled to a minimum daily rest period of 11 consecutive hours unless working on a shift pattern.[100] (Shift workers are entitled to the same protection as other workers regarding the number of hours of work.) Young workers are entitled to 12 consecutive hours daily rest.[101] Daily rest periods do not apply where there

---

97C Ibid reg 20(2).
97D *Barber v RJB Mining (UK) Ltd* [1999] IRLR 309, HC.
97E Working Time Regulations 1998 reg 4(2).
97F Ibid reg 4.
 98 Ibid reg 23(b).
 99 Ibid reg 23(a).
100 Ibid reg 10(1).
101 Ibid reg 10(2).

have been unusual and unforeseeable circumstances or exceptional events which are temporary and require immediate performance.

4.50   In addition to the daily rest periods the worker is entitled to a weekly rest period of at least 24 consecutive hours in any given week which may be averaged out over a fortnight.[102] Young workers are entitled to a weekly rest period of 48 consecutive hours although this can be reduced to 36 hours if justified by technical or organisational reasons.[103] Many of the rules regarding night work and daily and weekly rest breaks do not apply in special areas where continuity of service or production may be necessary, eg, work in hospitals, prisons, security, media, gas, water and electricity, refuse collection, post, tourism.[103A]

4.51   Every worker is entitled to a minimum 20-minute rest break during the working day if more than six hours is worked.[104] Young workers are entitled to 45 minutes if more than four and a half hours are worked. Again there is an exception to this entitlement if there are unusual and unforeseen circumstances or exceptional events. There is no requirement for the rest periods to be paid although there may be a contractual entitlement to be paid.

Annual leave

4.52   See above at para 4.32.

Contracting out of the 48-hour week

4.53   The employer can agree with the worker to enter into a written agreement to exclude the 48-hour entitlement and this agreement can be for a specific period or indefinitely although the worker is entitled to bring the agreement to an end without the employer's consent.[105] If the worker is dismissed or suffers a detriment for refusing to enter into an opt out agreement or for bringing one to an end, s/he can bring a claim to the ET.[106] It is not possible to contract out of the other provisions of the WTR. Some employers are cutting contractual

102   Ibid reg 11.
103   Ibid reg 11(3).
103A Ibid reg 21.
104   Ibid reg 12.
105   Ibid reg 18.
106   ERA 1996 ss45A and 101A.

hours to 48, with a consequential pay-cut, even where the worker wants to continue with the longer hours. The cut in hours is probably lawful as a matter of contract if it is done in order to comply with the regulations, but whether the pay-cut is lawful may depend on whether pay is explicitly linked to hours worked.

Enforcement

4.54   The statutory enforcement of the working hours is carried out by the health and safety enforcement authority and the local authority, depending on the industry, and the breach of the obligations can result in criminal proceedings punishable by a fine.

4.55   The failure to give rest periods and breaks and paid holidays can be enforced by the worker in the ET and the ET can award compensation according to what is just and equitable having regard to employer's default and any attributable loss for the worker.[107] It is unlawful to dismiss or subject a worker to a detriment because of insisting on their rights under the WTR (see para 6.78).

4.56   A worker has the right not to be subjected to any detriment because s/he has refused or proposes to refuse to comply with a requirement imposed in contravention of the WTR. It is also automatic unfair dismissal to dismiss an employee for that reason.[108] This could apply to a worker's insistence on taking breaks or refusing to work more than 48 hours. It may be particularly important in the latter case, as it seems a worker cannot claim compensation in an ET, but can only go to the county court or High Court for a declaration as to breach of contract and, most unlikely, an injunction.[109] This is not a practical remedy and it may be simpler for a worker, having made sure s/he is protected, to inform the employer politely and in writing that in accordance with the WTR s/he is not willing to work more than 48 hours. Obviously a worker needs to tread carefully and be sure of his or her rights (especially as the law is still untested) before upsetting an employer in this way.

4.57   The regulations make it an offence for an employer not to comply with any of the relevant requirements including the keeping of adequate records.[110]

---

107   Working Time Regulations 1998 reg 30.
108   See ERA 1996 ss45A and 101A for this and related reasons.
109   See *Barber v RJB Mining (UK) Ltd* [1999] IRLR 309, HC.
110   Ibid reg 9. But see Working Time Regulations 1999 SI No 3372 reg 4(2) which modifies the need for record-keeping for opted-out workers.

Wages: Key points

- Employers are obliged to pay wages to workers who are willing and able to work even if the workers are not required to do so. The only exception is where the contract has an express term allowing the employer to lay off workers when there is no work and without pay. Such a term is unusual and can only be relied on for a short period of time.
- Employers are not allowed to make deductions from wages unless there is a statutory requirement to make deductions (tax and national insurance), where it is a term of the employment contract, or where the worker has agreed in writing to the deduction.
- Any deduction made without authority can be recovered by claiming in the ET under ERA 1996 Part II.
- The majority of workers are entitled to the national minimum wage and the failure to pay the minimum wage will entitle the worker to recover the shortfall and the employer will be committing a criminal offence and can be fined.
- Workers are entitled to paid holidays and to limits on the hours worked and to breaks under the Working Time Directive.
- Workers are entitled to receive itemised pay statements at or before each pay day.
- Men and women are entitled to equal pay for equal work. The Equal Pay Act 1970 and EU law apply. Part-timers are generally entitled to pro rata pay and non-cash benefits. (See Chapter 3.)

General guide to useful evidence

- The pay slips, P45, P60 and other tax records.
- Details of what other, similar workers enjoy.
- Information from the Health and Safety Executive on the Working Time Regulations.

Equal pay

For complete chapter contents, see overleaf

The legal framework

The legislation

5.1   The Equal Pay Act (EqPA)1970 and, in particular, the concept of equal value introduced by the Equal Pay (Amendment) Regulations 1983 SI No 1794, are difficult to understand and apply. EU law has been particularly influential in this area, especially the Treaty of Rome article 119, now numbered 141. This book outlines the key issues so that potential cases may be identified. 'Like work' claims can be relatively straightforward to run in the ET, but complex and lengthy procedures are involved for 'equal value' claims and we only touch on the necessary evidence and procedural issues. An adviser considering running an equal value claim for the first time should talk to someone who has done it before.

5.2   The EqPA 1970 and the Sex Discrimination Act (SDA) 1975 cover separate ground. Although the EqPA 1970 most often applies to pay, in fact it covers discrimination between men and women in relation to any contractual term, eg, a holiday entitlement or right to have a company car. If unsure which statute applies, both should be cited in the application to the ET. Indeed, due to the difficulty in some situations of knowing which is the appropriate legislation, it is safer always to claim under article 141, the Equal Pay Directive (EPD) and the Equal Treatment Directive (ETD) as well as the EqPA 1970 and SDA 1975.[1] Note that sex discrimination in pay or contract terms on grounds of gender reassignment is covered by the SDA 1975.

3   The Equal Opportunities Commission has issued a code of practice on equal pay, which is admissible in evidence in any ET case under the EqPA 1970 or SDA 1975. Where relevant, it must be taken into account by the ET.

Who is covered?

4   The EqPA 1970 is wider than the unfair provisions of the ERA 1996. It protects workers employed under a contract of service or apprenticeship and the self-employed having contracted to execute work personally.[2] Both men and women can claim under the EqPA 1970.

---

1   The way to do this is to write in the ET1 that the claim is made 'under article 141 and/or the EPD and ETD and/or the EqPA 1970 and/or the SDA 1975'.
2   EqPA 1970 s1(6).

Using EU law

5.5   All UK workers can claim under article 141 in the ET in relation to discrimination in pay. Article 141 requires that 'men and women should receive equal pay for equal work' and is expanded by the Equal Pay Directive (75/117/EEC) which can also be relied on in national courts against any employer.[3] In many circumstances EU law is superfluous because it duplicates rights which exist under UK law. However, in respect of pensions and some other limited matters, EU law may be needed because of exclusions and omissions from the UK legislation.

What does article 141 mean by 'pay'?

5.6   Unlike the EqPA 1970, article 141 does not apply to all terms and conditions, but only to pay. Article 141 defines pay as 'the ordinary basic or minimum wage or salary and any other consideration, whether in cash or in kind, which the worker receives, directly or indirectly, in respect of his employment from his employer'. This wide definition was confirmed by the ECJ in *Garland v British Rail Engineering*,[4] which added that the consideration may be 'immediate or future, provided that the worker receives it, albeit indirectly, in respect of his employment from his employer'.

5.7   Both contractual[5] and statutory redundancy pay[6] fall within article 141, although payment by the redundancy fund when the employer defaults is not covered.[7] Some payments made by employers under a statutory obligation, eg, statutory sick pay,[8] may also be within article 141. Most significantly, article 141 covers contributions towards and benefits paid under contractual pension schemes,[9] whether supplementary to,[10] or contracted-out from,[11] the state pension scheme.

---

3   *Pickstone and Others v Freemans* [1988] IRLR 357, HL.
4   [1982] IRLR 111; [1988] ICR 420, ECJ.
5   *Hammersmith and Queen Charlotte's Special Health Authority v Cato* [1987] IRLR 483; [1988] ICR 132, EAT.
6   *Barber v GRE Assurance Group* [1990] IRLR 240, ECJ.
7   *Secretary of State for Employment v Levy* [1989] IRLR 469, EAT.
8   *Rinner-Kühn v FWW Spezial-Gebaüdereinigung GmbH* [1989] IRLR 493, ECJ.
9   See paras 11.73 to 11.81 on retirement.
10   *Bilka-Kaufhaus GmbH v Weber von Hartz* [1986] IRLR 317, ECJ.
11   *Barber* (n6 above).

Compensation for unfair dismissal constitutes pay within article 141.[12]

The comparable man

Requirement for a comparator

5.8 Under the EqPA 1970 (unlike the SDA 1975) a woman must find an actual man with whom she can compare herself. She cannot simply ask the ET to infer that her terms and conditions are less favourable than those of a man would have been.

The same employment

5.9 The male comparator must be employed by the same or an associated employer. Under the EqPA 1970 an employer is an associated employer where one company owns another or where two companies come under the control of a third person.[13] However, the test under article 141 is simply whether the comparator is employed in the same establishment or service, and comparison should not be confined to associated employers.[14] Relevant factors are whether each employer is directly or indirectly controlled by the same third party, the extent and nature of control, and whether they form part of the same establishment or service.[15] The comparator must be employed at the same establishment or at another establishment in Great Britain where common terms and conditions of employment[16] apply generally or to workers of the relevant classes.

5.10 Workers employed by a direct services organisation established to submit an in-house tender in compliance with the requirements of the Local Government Act 1988 may compare themselves with other employees of the same council provided common terms and conditions

12 *R v Secretary of State for Employment ex p Seymour-Smith and Perez* [1999] IRLR 253 ECJ.
13 EqPA 1970 s1(6).
14 *Scullard v Knowles and Southern Regional Council for Education and Training* [1996] IRLR 344; (1996) 67 EOR 44, EAT
15 Ibid.
16 Cf, *Leverton v Clwyd CC* [1989] IRLR 28, HL, on the meaning of 'common terms and conditions'. For more detail of the application of this test, see *British Coal Corporation v Smith* [1996] IRLR 404, HL.

apply.[17] Where article 141 applies,[18] but not under the EqPA 1970, a woman may compare herself with a predecessor, who left before she started.[19] She may also be able to compare herself with a successor.[20]

Comparable jobs

The nature of the comparison

5.11   A woman may compare herself with a man in the same employment if:

a) she is doing like work, ie, work which is the same or of a broadly similar nature, and where any differences in the work they actually do are relatively unimportant;[21] or

b) she is doing work rated equivalent to his in a study which evaluates their work in terms of the demand made on each worker under various headings, eg, effort, skill and decision[22] (such a study is usually known as a job evaluation scheme); or

c) she is doing work of equal value in terms of the demand made on each worker, eg, under such headings as effort, skill and decision.[23]

Where the jobs seem fairly similar, it is safer to claim at the same time both 'like work' and, in the alternative, 'work of equal value'.[24] Then if the ET decides that some of the differences between the jobs are significant, it can immediately turn to the equal value claim and appoint an independent expert to assess the jobs.[25]

5.12   The following points should be noted.

–   A woman can choose which man she wants to compare herself with and may choose more than one. If several women are bringing claims, each could choose two or three comparators (more

---

17   *Ratcliffe and Others v North Yorkshire CC* EAT 501/92, (1993) 496 *IDS Brief* 2.

18   See para 5.6 and also para 9.8.

19   *Macarthy's v Smith (No 2)* [1980] IRLR 209, CA; *Albion Shipping Agency v Arnold* [1981] IRLR 520; [1982] ICR 22, EAT.

20   *Diocese of Hallam Trustee v Connaughton* 1128/95 (1996) 569 *IDS Brief* 4, EAT.

21   EqPA 1970 s1(2)(a) and (4).

22   EqPA 1970 s1(2)(b) and (5).

23   EqPA 1970 s1(2)(c), added by the 1983 Regulations (see para 5.1).

24   This is where no job evaluation scheme (JES) applies.

25   See para 5.21. An independent expert need not be appointed.

may irritate the ET). Choosing more than one man as comparator reduces the risk of losing because the particular man chosen is in some way not typical, eg, he has been favoured because he is infirm or red-circled for a non-discriminatory reason.

- Even if there is a man in the same employment doing like work or work rated as equivalent under a job evaluation scheme (and getting the same pay), a woman may still compare herself with a different (higher paid) man who is doing work of equal value.[26] (This prevents equal pay claims being defeated by the presence of one or two low-paid men in predominantly female areas of work.)
- Where there has been a job evaluation scheme, a woman may only compare herself with a man rated (and paid) higher than herself, (a) if her job is sufficiently similar to claim like work, or (b) if she is relying on an equal value claim, where there are reasonable grounds for supposing that the job evaluation scheme was based on a system which discriminates on grounds of sex.[27]
- Under article 141 a woman in an equal value claim may compare herself with a man whose work turns out to be of less value than hers,[28] although she can claim only pay equal to his. ETs now commonly accept this under the EqPA 1970 as well.

Like work

13   In deciding whether a woman is doing 'like work' to her comparator, the ET should consider the matter in two stages.[29]

1) Is the work done by the woman and her comparator the same or of a broadly similar nature? At this stage, the ET should make a general consideration of the type of work and the skill and knowledge required to do it. So, eg, women cleaners who clean offices and toilets should easily pass the test when compared with male cleaners who clean offices and urinals.

2) Are any differences between the work done by the woman and her comparator of practical importance in relation to the terms and conditions of employment? In other words, if the jobs were both done by members of the same sex, would you expect the differ-

26   *Pickstone and Others v Freemans* [1988] IRLR 357, HL.
27   EqPA 1970 s2A(2).
28   *Murphy and Others v Bord Telecom Eireann* (1988) 19 EOR 46; [1988] IRLR 267, ECJ, where a woman's work was in fact found to be of higher value than her male comparator's, even though she was paid less.
29   *Capper Pass Ltd v Lawton* [1976] IRLR 366, EAT.

ences in their tasks to warrant a difference in pay? Trivial differences or differences which in the real world are unlikely to be reflected by a pay difference should be disregarded.

The ET must look at the tasks actually carried out by the woman and her comparator, rather than to a (perhaps artificially inflated or understated) job description.[30]

5.14   In any 'like work' claim, detailed evidence of the work of both the woman and her comparator needs to be presented to the ET. Often it can take an entire day at the ET to draw out all the elements of each job. If there are several women bringing a joint case, it is usually a good idea for each of them to give evidence as to the nature of the job. This reduces the risk of key elements being omitted.

Job evaluation schemes

5.15   A study measuring the relative value of jobs, either solely of the woman and her comparator, or of some or all workers in the same employment, is commonly known as a job evaluation scheme (JES). There are many methods of evaluation, but the principal distinction is between analytic and non-analytic schemes. An analytic JES is one which evaluates jobs according to a breakdown of demands and characteristics. Factors such as responsibility, working conditions, physical and mental requirements are weighted and measured. A non-analytic JES compares jobs on a 'whole-job' basis, eg, by ranking and paired comparisons. There are dangers that a JES may itself be directly or indirectly discriminatory, eg, because it over-values traditional male skills and attributes, such as physical strength.

5.16   Where there is an existing JES which is both analytic[31] and non-discriminatory,[32] it can serve two functions:

1) a woman may claim equal pay and other terms and conditions equal to those of a man whose work has been rated as equivalent under such a JES;[33]

2) where a woman's work has been rated of less value than a man's under such a JES, she will fail in a claim under EqPA 1970 s1(2)(c) that her work is of equal value to his.[34]

---

30 *Shields v E Coombes (Holdings) Ltd* [1978] IRLR 263, CA.
31 *Bromley and Others v H and J Quick* [1988] IRLR 249, CA.
32 As defined by EqPA 1970 s2A(3).
33 EqPA 1970 s1(2)(b) and see above.
34 EqPA 1970 s2A(1) and (2).

Sometimes an employer may commission a JES after an equal value claim has been started in an attempt to block the claim. In order to have any effect, the JES must be completed at the latest by the final hearing, and it is in the ET's discretion whether it is willing to stay proceedings if the JES is not ready.[35] A 'completed' JES means one which has been accepted by the employers and workers as a valid study, even though it may not yet have been implemented.[36]

5.17 Where the employer uses a JES which bands job points in advance (eg, 210–239 points will be put at grade 5; 240–279 points at grade 6), a woman obtaining 210 points can demand to be paid equally with a man obtaining anything up to 239 points.[37]

Equal value claims

5.18 Equal value claims tend to become extremely long and drawn out, with a number of interlocutory hearings as well as up to three full hearings, each of which may last one or more weeks in the ET. Although some trade union officials in some parts of the country have succeeded in completing equal value cases within a year, on the whole the complexity of the statutory provisions means that cases take two or more years to complete. Expert evidence and legal representation is almost certain to be used by one or both parties and cases tend to be extremely time-consuming and expensive. For these reasons, equal value cases are usually brought by more than one worker (and sometimes by hundreds or thousands) or with an agreement with the employer that all similarly circumstanced female workers will get the benefit (including back pay) of any favourable decision in a test case.

5.19 It is difficult to generalise, but the procedural steps in an equal value claim are often as follows (once the originating application and notice of appearance have been lodged and documents exchanged).

a) There is a preliminary hearing at which the ET decides whether to order an independent expert's report.

b) There is a second hearing where the ET decides whether the work is of equal value.

c) There is a third hearing where the employer puts forward any

---

35 *Avon CC v Foxall and Others* [1989] IRLR 435; [1989] ICR 407, EAT.
36 *Arnold v Beecham Group Ltd* [1982] IRLR 307; [1982] ICR 744, EAT.
37 *Springboard Sunderland Trust v Robson* [1992] IRLR 261, EAT.

material factor defence. Sometimes this issue is dealt with at the second hearing.

The preliminary hearing

5.20   Prior to the introduction of new regulations in 1996,[38] an ET could dismiss hopeless cases at the preliminary hearing, for example because the woman's job was obviously less demanding than the man's in terms of skill, effort, decision, etc, or because it had been given a lower value than a man's on an analytical non-discriminatory Job Evaluation Scheme. However the EAT has now said that even if the ET does not order an independent expert's report because the case seems hopeless, it should still permit the parties to get their own experts' reports and argue the substantive merits of the case at a second hearing.[39] The ET may still consider the proceedings to be frivolous or vexatious and threaten costs, but it can only do so if the parties are notified in advance that this will be the subject of the hearing.

The independent expert and the second phase

5.21   At the preliminary hearing the ET may refer the case to an independent expert to prepare a report. An ET may choose, after consulting the parties, to make its own assessment whether the work is of equal value without referring the matter to an independent expert.[40] Often the parties will each instruct their own expert. Avoiding an independent expert can reduce delays in the procedure.

5.22   Where an ET still decides to refer the matter to an independent expert, certain procedures must be followed. These are set out in detail in regulations.[41] The ET gives the expert a date for completion of the report and sets intervals for progress reports.[42] The ET's brief to the expert is sent to the parties. If delays are caused by the conduct of

---

38 Sex Discrimination and Equal Pay (Miscellaneous Amendment) Regulations 1996 SI No 438.

39 *Wood & Others v William Ball Ltd* [1999] 646 IDS Brief 9, EAT.

40 EqPA 1970 s2A(1), as amended by the Sex Discrimination and Equal Pay (Miscellaneous Amendments) Regulations 1996 SI No 438. See also the Industrial Tribunals (Constitution and Rules of Procedure) (Amendment) Regulations 1996 SI No 1757.

41 Employment Tribunals (Constitution and Rules of Procedure) Regulations 1993 SI No 2687 (ET Regs) Sch 2 as amended by Employment Tribunals (Constitution and Rules of Procedure) (Amendment) Regulations 1996 SI No 1757.

42 ET Regs Sch 2 r8A(4) and (8) as amended by SI 1996 No 1757.

the parties, then the expert must say so and the ET can strike out the ET1 or ET3 or order costs.[43]

5.23   The expert collects written submissions and materials; interviews the woman, her comparator, supervisors and anyone else relevant; and then writes a final report, which should conclude whether or not the jobs are of equal value. The final report is circulated to the parties, who then decide whether to agree its contents. Sometimes a case settles at this stage. Otherwise a second full hearing occurs. The ET may receive the independent expert's report as evidence at this hearing and either party may call additional evidence (but not as to the factual basis of the independent expert's report). Since the expert's reasoning and conclusion can really only be challenged by other experts, one or both parties usually calls their own expert evidence at the hearing. The ET may choose whether to follow the conclusion of the independent expert. After the ET's decision, the case may end or be settled or go on to a final hearing regarding the employer's defence.

5.24   The following points should be noted.

1) Although either party may obtain its own expert report, the ET cannot order the woman to co-operate with the employer's expert[44] nor the employer to allow the woman's expert onto the premises to see what is actually done (this is usually considered very important). These matters need negotiation between the parties and reciprocal access should be agreed.

2) Once the ET has received it in evidence, the independent expert's report is conclusive on issues of fact. If it contains factual errors which could damage the woman's case (eg, it omits part of her job or includes in the comparator's job description things he does not do), evidence must be called to prove the errors at the start of the second hearing and before the independent expert's report is admitted as evidence by the ET.

3) The independent expert's opinion has no special status,[45] but an ET may well find it very convincing simply because it is independent. However, the ET should form its conclusion on all the evidence and make its own decision as to whether the work is of equal value.

4) If the independent expert's report is very flawed or, for some

---

43   ET Regs Sch 2 r8A(10) to (10E) as amended by SI 1996 No 1757.
44   *Lloyds Bank v Fox and Others* [1989] IRLR 103, EAT.
45   *Tennant Textile Colours v Todd* [1988] IRLR 3; (1988) 23 EOR 39, NI CA.

reason, it becomes clear that the independent expert is not fit to appear as such, the ET may refuse to allow the report in evidence. Unfortunately, the result may be the instruction of a further independent report with significant additional delay. Alternatively, the ET may exercise its power to decide the matter without reference to an independent expert.

The defence hearing

5.25 At the third hearing (or sometimes at the second hearing) the employer may argue that even if the work is of equal value, the pay variation is genuinely due to a material factor other than sex. This defence applies to all equal pay claims and is set out below.

Defences

5.26 Even where there is like work, work rated as equivalent or work of equal value, the employer has a defence under EqPA 1970 s1(3) if s/he proves on a balance of probabilities that the variation between the woman's and the man's pay (or other terms) is due to a genuine material factor other than sex. In claims based on like work or work rated as equivalent under a JES, such a factor must be a material difference between the woman's case and the man's. When the scope of the EqPA 1970 was broadened to introduce equal value claims, employers were given a wider defence, ie, in addition to such a material difference, it can also be any other material factor.

The material difference defence

5.27 Originally this defence was limited to personal factors differentiating the woman and her comparator. For example, a man could legitimately receive higher pay because of his longer service or better skills or productivity or because of red-circling. However, the House of Lords decision in *Rainey v Greater Glasgow Health Board*[46] widened the interpretation of the defence to include circumstances other than the personal qualifications or merits of the workers concerned. There is now little practical difference between the defence that can be used on like work and JES cases and that for equal value cases.

---

46 [1987] IRLR 26; [1987] ICR 129, HL.

The material factor defence

5.28   The nature of this defence has been greatly influenced by decisions of
the ECJ, although its interpretation by ETs and the Employment
Appeal Tribunal has been inconsistent. The ECJ in *Bilka-Kaufhaus
GmbH v Weber von Hartz*[47] said the employer's defence must relate to
a legitimate economic need of the enterprise. In *Rainey*, the House of
Lords said the defence could include administrative needs.

5.29   The material factor must not be based, wholly or partly, upon
gender differences (see below). In the past, the case-law was unclear
on whether it is enough for the employer to provide a neutral explanation, or whether the pay differential needs to be objectively justified.
Although the House of Lords in *Rainey* said that a pay difference
needs justification under EqPA 1970 s1(3) in the same way that
indirect sex discrimination must be justified under the SDA 1975,[48] it
was only considering a situation of unintentional indirect discrimination. More recently, in another case[49] the House of Lords has said
that there is a valid defence if a pay difference is merely explained by
genuine factors which are not tainted by sex discrimination. The
employer only needs to go further and justify the differential if sex
discrimination is involved.

5.30   It is uncertain whether the ECJ would agree with this. In the
major cases before the ECJ, it has always required objective justification, but these cases happen to have involved indirect discrimination.
Indeed, even where the indirectly discriminatory factor cannot be
identified, where jobs are segregated and the female group is paid on
average less than the male, the ECJ has said that the employer must
show that the pay difference is based on objectively justified factors.[50]
For further examples, see para 5.41 below on indirectly discriminatory pay practices.

What is a genuine material factor?

5.31   The word 'genuine' simply means the factor must be the true reason
for the pay difference and not a sham or pretence.[51] A 'material' factor

---

47   [1986] IRLR 317, ECJ.
48   See para 9.77.
49   *Strathclyde Regional Council v Wallace* [1998] IRLR 146; 78 EOR 51, HL.
50   See *Enderby v Frenchay Health Authority and Secretary of State for Health* [1993]
     IRLR 591; (1993) 52 EOR 40, ECJ. See also *British Road Services Ltd v Loughran*
     [1997] IRLR 92, NI CA.
51   *Strathclyde Regional Council v Wallace* (n49, above).

is one which is 'significant and relevant'.[52] This means 'significant' in the sense that it is the cause of the pay difference. It does not in itself mean that the factor must be 'objectively justifiable'.

5.32   The employer's defence may be based on several factors. Where an employer can only partially justify a pay differential, an ET may accept the justification to that extent.[53]

5.33   As well as personal differences between the workers concerned, the following are examples of genuine material factors, although whether the defence is made out will depend on the specific circumstances in each case:

– market forces and other economic considerations;
– administrative efficiency;
– geographical differences, eg, London weighting;
– unsocial hours, rotating shift and night working;
– experience and qualifications.

Some equal value cases have confused matters relevant to evaluating the relative worth of each job such as skill, responsibility, effort, with material factors which would justify a pay difference. The EAT in *Davies v McCartneys*[54] suggested that the employer could use as a defence the very matters which were relevant in determining whether a job was of equal value. This approach has been criticised and is open to doubt: once two jobs have been evaluated as equal in terms of these separate demands, an employer ought not to be able to justify a pay difference by saying that s/he personally values one job more highly.

5.34   There is a dispute over whether it can be a defence that the pay difference was based on a mistake or misunderstanding.[55] It is in any event advisable to investigate fully the facts relied on by the employer as a basis for the defence. For example, in one case, an employer's assertion that library van drivers (mostly male) needed to be paid at a higher rate so as to encourage them to remain in the job was disproved by an analysis of the job turnover figures.[56]

52   *Rainey v Greater Glasgow Health Board* (n46, above).
53   *Enderby* (n50, above).
54   [1989] IRLR 439, EAT. This may be only obiter given the actual findings in the case.
55   *Mcpherson v Rathgael Centre for Children and Young People* [1991] IRLR 206, NI CA, though *Yorkshire Blood Transfusion Service v Plaskitt* [1994] ICR 74, EAT probably represents the better view.
56   *Lucas Salter and Stedman v West Sussex County Council* (unreported) Southampton ET 1323–30/90.

Not a sex-based explanation

5.35 The employer must prove there is no direct or indirect sex discrimination within the material factor defence that s/he puts forward.[57] Sometimes this is quite easy, eg, if the worker compares herself with a man who is obviously more skilled and where there are also more skilled women on the higher pay. Generally speaking, if an employer can show there is no gender disproportionality between those in the higher and those in the lower pay groups, an ET is likely to accept that s/he has proved the factor is not discriminatory. Alternatively, the employer may prove that any such disproportionality arises by chance or is irrelevant to the levels of pay.

5.36 The woman may take it upon herself to prove direct sex discrimination, eg, by relying on something she was told or has found out about the true reason for her lower pay; for example, she has heard that the employer believes women will work for less pay than men. Alternatively, the factor put forward by the employer may itself contain an element or history of direct sex discrimination, which is readily apparent or becomes clear on examination, eg, in one case[58] a material factor defence of red-circling was rejected because it was based upon previous direct sex discrimination, excluding women from male pay and jobs in the 1960s.

5.37 A market forces defence can be discriminatory where there is job segregation, since female-dominated jobs tend to be paid less precisely because they are traditionally carried out mainly by women. For example in *Ratcliffe v North Yorkshire County Council*[59] a council's DSO reduced the pay of catering assistants (who were almost exclusively female) in order to compete successfully on a compulsory competitive tendering exercise. Three women brought an equal value case comparing themselves with male council workers, such as road sweepers and refuse collectors, whose work had been rated equivalent under a job evaluation scheme. The House of Lords rejected the Council's argument that the DSO had to be able to compete on the open market. This defence was based on sex because the Council's competitors could pay less on the open market precisely because such work was done mainly by women.

5.38 Although there is some ambiguity in the case-law, it seems that a

---

57 *Byrne v Financial Times* [1991] IRLR 417, CA.
58 *Snoxell v Vauxhall Motors Ltd* [1977] IRLR 123; [1977] ICR 700, EAT.
59 [1995] IRLR 439; (1995) 63 EOR 49, HL.

factor which amounts to direct discrimination can never be justified.[60] Alternatively, the pay difference is due to indirect discrimination, eg, part-time workers being paid less than full-time workers[61] or paying more for previous experience in a male-dominated industry. Sometimes the true (and indirectly discriminatory) reason is hidden or not obvious, eg, a woman is really being paid less because she cannot work unsocial hours, whereas the employer contends that the pay differential is because she is less competent at her job. Indirect discrimination in pay must be objectively justified. In order to do that, the employer must show:[62]

a) there is a real need on the part of the undertaking;
b) the measures chosen by the employer are appropriate for achieving the objective in question; and
c) are necessary to that end.

The Burden of Proof Directive,[63] to be implemented by 22 July 2001, broadly confirms the existing case-law.

5.39   It is important that the pay system is clear and easy to understand; this has become known as transparency.[64] A transparent system is one where workers understand not only their rates of pay but the components of their individual pay packets. The ECJ has said that where an employer operates a pay system which is wholly lacking in transparency but appears to operate to the substantial disadvantage of one sex, the onus will be on the employer to explain and justify objectively the differential, even if the individual worker cannot identify why she has been paid less.

Summary

5.40   In summary, the key principles relating to the defence are as follows:

– the onus is on the employer to prove any defence;

---

60 See definition under the SDA 1975, paras 9.38–9.50 below. See also *E Coombes (Holdings) Ltd v Shields* [1978] IRLR 263; [1978] ICR 159, CA, although beware the obiter comments made in *Strathclyde Regional Council v Wallace* (n49 above).
61 *Jenkins v Kingsgate (Clothing Productions) Ltd (No 2)* [1981] IRLR 388; [1981] ICR 715, EAT.
62 The test was set out by the ECJ in *Bilka-Kaufhaus GmbH v Weber von Hartz* [1986] IRLR 317 and adopted by the House of Lords in *Rainey v Greater Glasgow Health Board* [1987] IRLR 26.
63 See para 9.55.
64 Code of Practice on Equal Pay, paras 19–20.

- the material factor must not be discriminatory, either directly or indirectly;
- the material factor must be significant and relevant, but unless any discrimination is involved, a neutral explanation will suffice;
- if the factor involves direct discrimination, it (probably) cannot be justified;
- if the factor involves indirect discrimination, the employer must objectively justify it;
- where pay is governed by merit, flexibility, training or seniority, the comments of the ECJ in the *Danfoss* case[65] should be borne in mind (see below);
- for service-related pay, see comments of the ECJ in *Nimz v Freie und Hansestadt Hamburg*[66] (see below).
- where the pay system is wholly lacking in transparency, the onus will be on the employer to justify a pay differential which appears substantially to disadvantage one sex.

Indirectly discriminatory pay practices

5.41   Equal Pay Directive article 1 requires 'the elimination of all discrimination on grounds of sex with regard to all aspects and conditions of remuneration'. Hence EU law (and domestic law) has developed to prohibit indirect discrimination in pay. Most discrimination in pay systems takes the form of indirect or hidden discrimination.[67] The concept is similar to that of indirect discrimination under the Race Relations Act (RRA) 1976 or SDA 1975 s1(1)(b),[68] although without the restrictive wording. In particular, it is not necessary to identify a requirement or condition, and any discriminatory pay practice is covered. For example, the ECJ has suggested that an incremental pay structure using subjective criteria such as 'quality of work' may be discriminatory.[69] The Burden of Proof Directive[70] defines indirect discrimination broadly in accordance with the case-law.

---

65 *Handels-og Kontorfunktionaerernes Forbund i Danmark v Dansk Arbejdsgiverforening (acting for Danfoss)* [1989] IRLR 532, ECJ.
66 [1991] IRLR 222.
67 Equal Pay Code, para 24.
68 See paras 9.51–9.54.
69 *Danfoss* (n65, above).
70 See paras 5.38 and 9.55.

5.42   The Equal Pay Code of Practice provides useful guidance on how to identify discriminatory elements in pay systems. Access to bonuses, for example, tends to be available more in jobs done by men.[71] It may be clear that women generally are paid less well than men, but it may not be possible to identify the requirement or practice causing this.[72] In *Enderby*[73] the ECJ said that where the pay of a predominantly female group is significantly lower than the pay of a predominantly male group doing work of equal value, the employer is required to show objective reasons for the differential.[74] The higher the proportion of women in the lesser paid group, the more likely it is that justification is required. However, it is not necessary for the underpaid group to be almost exclusively women.[75]

5.43   It is a common defence that the different pay rates were arrived at by independent and distinct collective bargaining processes. This is not sufficient where the outcome is a disparity between the mainly female group and the mainly male group, even if no direct or indirect discrimination can be identified within each process.[76] Otherwise an employer could easily circumvent the principle of equal pay by using separate bargaining processes.[77]

5.44   The ECJ's most explicit guidance on what may be considered justifiable or not in indirect discrimination is in *Danfoss* (above). In that case, the employers awarded pay increments on the basis of a number of criteria, ie, flexibility, quality of work, vocational training and seniority. It was not apparent to the workers precisely how the level of each person's pay had been arrived at, but the net effect was that women were on the whole paid less than the men. The ECJ said that where a pay system is characterised by a total lack of transparency, that is, where it is impossible to tell precisely how each worker's pay level was reached, and where there is a statistical imbalance between

---

71   Equal Pay Code, para 29a. See also (1999) 84 EOR 4 on local government bonuses.
72   See above, para 5.39 on 'transparency'.
73   See n50.
74   Though see *Specialarbejderforbundet i Danmark v Dansk Industri acting for Royal Copenhagen A/S* (see n77 below), which seems to qualify *Enderby*, at least in the context of piece-working.
75   *Strathclyde Regional Council* (n49, above).
76   *Enderby* (n50, above) and *Strathclyde Regional Council*, ibid.
77   See also *Nimz v Freie und Hansestadt Hamburg* [1991] IRLR 222, ECJ; *Kowalska v Freie und Hansestadt Hamburg* [1990] IRLR 447, ECJ. See further the possibly contradictory position of the ECJ in *Specialarbejderforbundet i Danmark v Dansk Industri, acting for Royal Copenhagen A/S* [1995] IRLR 648; 64 EOR 42, ECJ.

the pay of male and female workers, the onus is on the employer to justify the difference.

5.45   The ECJ then examined each of the criteria. It recognised that proportionally fewer women were likely to score highly on criteria such as flexibility, vocational training and seniority. Therefore, where statistics indicated that women were generally paid less than men on the basis of flexibility or vocational training criteria, the employer must justify the use of each criterion by showing it was 'of importance for the performance of the specific duties entrusted to the worker concerned'.

.46   The ECJ took a radical position in respect of merit payments. It said that if women were, on the whole, paid less on the basis of 'quality of work', this could not be justified because 'it is inconceivable that the work carried out by female workers would be generally of a lower quality'. In other words, the employer must be directly discriminating.

47   In *Danfoss*, the ECJ said the employer need not justify the use of the seniority criterion because that was obviously justifiable. However, in the subsequent case of *Nimz v Freie und Hansestadt Hamburg*,[78] the ECJ changed its mind. It said that service-related pay also needs justifying where it has an adverse impact on women in the workforce. In providing an objective justification, an employer must in particular show a relationship between the nature of the duties performed and the experience acquired with time.[79] So, for example, service-related pay increments may be justified for the first few years of employment where a worker is rapidly learning and improving in a job, but unjustified thereafter.

Part-time workers

48   Many ECJ cases concern lower pay and benefits for part-time workers.[80] There is a general recognition that a far higher proportion of women than men are in part-time work and the issue has been whether employers can justify the differential. In the key case of *Bilka-Kaufhaus GmbH v Weber von Hartz*,[81] a German department

78 [1991] IRLR 222.
79 There is no reason why this argument cannot also be used in challenging the effect of service-related pay on black workers under the RRA 1976.
80 See section on part-time working, para 11.11 below.
81 [1986] IRLR 317. See also *Jenkins v Kingsgate (Clothing Productions) (No 2)* [1981] IRLR 388, EAT.

store (in line with West German state legislation) excluded part-time workers from its occupational pension scheme. The ECJ said that where a pay practice, applied generally, operated to disadvantage more women than men, it would infringe article 141 unless it were objectively justifiable.[82]

5.49   Working full-time is not a justification in itself for receiving greater hourly pay. Nor would the ECJ in *Rinner-Kühn*[83] accept as justification an argument that part-timers were less integrated into the business than full-timers. However, it may be justification if an employer can show that for economic or administrative reasons it needs to discourage part-time working.

5.50   In another case, the ECJ has said that a civil service rule whereby job-sharers progress up an incremental pay-scale only in accordance with time actually worked and therefore at half the speed of full-timers with equal competence, cannot be justified merely on the grounds of saving costs.[84] In contrast to the ECJ's approach, the Court of Appeal has allowed a rather weak justification where a voluntary severance scheme was calculated on the basis of hours worked and therefore earnings at the termination date, not giving credit for greater average hours and earnings in previous years.[85] This can adversely affect women changing from full-time to part-time work after maternity leave. Unfortunately it seems that restricting overtime supplements to cases where the normal full-time working hours are exceeded is not unlawful.[86]

5.51   Statutory entitlement to certain payments such as redundancy pay, sick pay and unfair dismissal compensation is often subject to requirements, eg, length or hours of service, which may have indirectly discriminatory effect. There have been several major cases challenging such requirements.[87]

5.52   In addition to the above, to comply with the EU Directive on part-time work[88] the government will be making regulations to ensure that

82   See para 5.38 for more detail on this definition.
83   [1989] IRLR 493, ECJ.
84   *Hill & Stapleton v Revenue Commissioners and Department of Finance* [1998] IRLR 466, ECJ.
85   *Barry v Midlands Bank PLC* [1998] IRLR 138, CA, but it is arguable that the CA has not correctly applied the *Bilka-Kaufhaus* test.
86   *Stadt Lengerich v Helmig* [1995] IRLR 216; 60 EOR 45, ECJ.
87   *Rinner-Kühn* [1989] IRLR 493, ECJ; *R v Secretary of State for Employment ex p EOC* [1994] IRLR 176; (1994) 54 EOR 30, HL; *R v Secretary of State for Employment ex p Seymour-Smith and Perez* [1999] IRLR 253, ECJ.
88   97/81/EC; Employment Relations Act 1999 ss19–21.

part-time workers are treated no less favourably than full-timers in specified circumstances.

The equality clause

.53 When a claim succeeds, the way the EqPA 1970 operates is to insert an equality clause into the contract of the woman. Each contractual term that is less favourable than the equivalent term in the contract of the comparable man is modified to make it equal. Once the woman's contract is modified, it remains so even if her male comparator leaves or is promoted or demoted.

54 It is irrelevant that, looking at the contracts as a whole, the woman may be said to be equally treated. For example, where a woman receives less basic pay, but better holiday and sick pay, she is nevertheless entitled to have her basic pay increased to the male level.[89] Similarly under article 141, the ECJ has said that the principle of equal pay entails equality in each component of remuneration and does not look at whether the total benefits are the same.[90]

Time limits for claiming and remedies

Remedies

5 If a woman succeeds in her claim, any less favourable term in her contract is modified so that, for example, she is no longer paid less than the male comparator. She may also be awarded pay arrears, or compensation in relation to any non-pay term. Under article 141, a part-timer suffering indirect discrimination may have her contract modified so that she receives proportionally the same benefits as full-timers.[91]

6 Under the EqPA[92] an ET could not award compensation for any period more than two years before the ET application was lodged. Following an ECJ ruling that this limitation may not be compatible

---

89 *Hayward v Cammell Laird Shipbuilders* [1988] IRLR 257, HL.
90 *Barber v GRE Assurance Group* [1990] IRLR 240, ECJ.
91 *Kowalska v Freie und Hansestadt Hamburg* [1990] IRLR 447, ECJ.
92 EqPA 1970 s2(5).

with EU law, the EAT has extended the limit for backdated pay awards to six years at least.[93]

5.57　ETs have power to award interest on pay arrears[94] and are prepared to do so. This partly counters the effect of the delays in the ET procedure, so advisers should always seek interest on any claim or settlement.

Time limits

5.58　The time-limit for lodging equal pay claims is governed by EqPA 1970 s2(4), which is not well drafted. Until further clarification is forthcoming from the ECJ[95] the time-limit should be taken as six months from leaving a job.

93　*Levez v TH Jennings (Harlow Pools) Ltd (No 2)*; *Hicking v Basford Group Ltd* [1999] IRLR 764, EAT, plus see Highlights at p761.

94　Employment Tribunal (Interest on Awards in Discrimination Cases) Regulations 1996 SI No 2803.

95　As asked by HL in *Preston and others v Wolverhampton Healthcare NHS Trust and Others* [1998] IRLR 197; [1998] ICR 227, HL.

Part II

Unfair dismissal and redundancy

Statutory protection

For complete chapter contents, see overleaf

The legal framework

The legislation

6.1   The statutory right not to be unfairly dismissed was first introduced by the Industrial Relations Act 1971. The Trade Union and Labour Relations Act 1974[1] repealed the Industrial Relations Act and introduced provisions strengthening the unfair dismissal provisions.

6.2   New employment rights were introduced by the Employment Protection Act 1975, which created the Advisory, Conciliation and Arbitration Service (ACAS), whose conciliation officers are allocated to every unfair dismissal and discrimination case, with a view to bringing about a settlement.[2] The Employment Protection Act also introduced the right to maternity pay and guarantee payments, it recognised the role of trade unions in redundancy dismissals and it strengthened a worker's right to receive a written statement of the main terms and conditions of employment.

6.3   The Employment Protection (Consolidation) Act (EPCA) 1978 consolidated and re-enacted the major legislation on workers' rights relating to their employment contracts and termination of employment. EPCA 1978 consolidated the Redundancy Payments Act 1965, the Contracts of Employment Act 1972 and substantial parts of the Trade Union and Labour Relations Act 1974 and the Employment Protection Act 1975.

6.4   The Employment Rights Act (ERA) 1996, with the Employment Tribunals Act (ETA) 1996, repealed and replaced the EPCA 1978, forming a consolidated code. The ERA 1996 incorporates the employment protection provisions together with those of the Wages Act 1986, the Sunday Trading Act 1994 and the Betting, Gaming and Lotteries Act 1963. The ETA 1996 consolidates the provisions of EPCA 1978 and the Trade Union and Labour Relations (Consolidation) Act 1992 so far as they concern the powers of the employment tribunals and the Employment Appeal Tribunal.

6.5   The Employment Relations Act 1999 broadly reflects the proposals in the White Paper, *Fairness at Work*. The upper limit on awards for unfair dismissal has been increased from £12,000 to £50,000, the additional award increased to an amount not less than 26 weeks and not more than 52 weeks, and certain statutory awards

---

1   Trade Union and Labour Relations Act 1974 s1.
2   Employment Protection Act 1975 s2(1).

will be increased in September each year referable to the retail price index. The Act also introduces other rights such as the right of workers to be permitted to be accompanied by a fellow worker or trade union official at a disciplinary and grievance procedure, who will be entitled to address the hearing; an entitlement to reasonable unpaid leave to deal with domestic incidents and the extension by regulation to statutory maternity leave.

6.6   The Trade Union and Labour Relations (Consolidation) Act (TULR(C)A) 1992 dealt in the main with the consolidation of the trade union laws. The Employment Act 1980 reinforced the importance of the Codes of Practice produced by ACAS and the secretary of state.[3] At the same time, the Employment Act 1980 reduced the effectiveness of unfair dismissal protection by removing the burden of proof from the employer to become a neutral burden.[4]

6.7   The Trade Union Reform and Employment Rights Act (TURERA) 1993 made further reforms to trade union laws and abolished the right to minimum rates of pay and, in particular, continued the legislative reform of trade unions. It extended the law on trade union elections, ballots and financial affairs, trade union membership, unjustifiable disciplinary action and industrial action. Further provisions were introduced in respect of action short of dismissal on trade union grounds, the provisions on check-off arrangements, and the citizen's right to challenge unlawful industrial action.

6.8   TURERA 1993 also made some major changes to the rights of individuals now to be found in the ERA 1996. These included the right not to be unfairly dismissed for asserting certain statutory rights, and adequate compensation for employees who are not re-employed pursuant to a re-employment order made by an ET.

6.9   TURERA 1993 also made a number of changes to ET powers and procedures. The main purpose has been to reduce the delays in the hearing of ET claims which could have been resolved by increasing the resources made available to ETs rather than tinkering with the rules of procedure. The changes remove the right to have a full tribunal determine claims relating to unlawful deductions from wages, insolvency claims, breach of contract claims, and (with the consent of the parties) other claims. It is also possible for parties to settle claims without the involvement of ACAS if advised by an independent qualified lawyer or a relevant independent adviser (officers, officials,

3 Employment Act 1980 s3(8)(a) and (b).
4 Ibid s6.

employees or members of an independent union who have been certified by the union as being competent[5] and advice centre workers who have been certified as being competent and who have not been paid for the advice[6]) who are insured against negligent advice.[7] The increased responsibility on ETs to hear breach of contract claims has increased the burden on limited resources. Claims are increasing across the board. In 1998/99, 74,006 applications were made to the ET, of which 68% were resolved by the ET.[8]

Codes of practice

6.10   In deciding whether a dismissal is fair or unfair, the ET is primarily concerned with the fairness of procedures followed by the employer prior to dismissal. This is why the secretary of state or ACAS are empowered to produce codes of practice. These codes provide employers with practical guidance on how to draw up and effectively operate disciplinary rules and procedures. The importance of the Codes of Practice has recently been reinforced by the courts.[9]

6.11   The ACAS Code on disciplinary practice and procedures[10] gives guidance on conduct dismissals, although the procedures set out are equally applicable to other types of dismissal. Its essential feature of the disciplinary process is for an employer to give fair and appropriate warnings to a worker and to give the worker an opportunity to respond to any allegations being made before decisions are made.[11]

6.12   There are a number of other Codes including the disclosure of information to trade unions, time off for union duties and activities, the elimination of racial, sex and disability discrimination,[12] and equal pay.[13]

6.13   The ET and other courts are under a statutory obligation to consider the relevant provisions of the Codes[14] in reaching their decision.

---

5   TULR(C)A 1992 s5.
6   TULR(C)A 1992 s5.
7   ERA 1996 s203.
8   *Labour Market Trends* (published September 1999).
9   *Lock v Cardiff Railway Co Ltd* [1998] IRLR 358.
10 Employment Protection Code of Practice (Disciplinary Practice and Procedures) 1977 para 1. Note that ACAS are to issue a new Code on Disciplinary and Grievance Procedures.
11 Ibid para 10.
12 See paras 9.2 and 13.2.
13 See para 5.3.
14 TULR(C)A 1992 s207, HSWA 1974 s17, SDA 1975 s56A, RRA 1976 s47, DDA 1995 s53.

Significant breach of the provisions of the code by an employer should generally result in a finding of unfair dismissal or unlawful conduct.[15]

The right to be accompanied to disciplinary and grievance hearings

6.13A Where a worker is invited or required to attend a disciplinary or grievance hearing and reasonably requests to be accompanied at the hearing, the employers must allow the worker to choose a trade union representative or another of the employers' workers to accompany him or her.[15A] This companion may address the hearing and confer with the worker during the hearing, but may not answer questions on behalf of the worker.[15B]

6.13B The employers must allow a worker to take time off during working hours to accompany another of the employers' workers.[15C] If the chosen person cannot attend the proposed time for the hearing, the employers must postpone the hearing to any reasonable time suggested by the worker within five working days of the original date.

6.13C ACAS have issued a draft Code of Practice on disciplinary and grievance procedures which contains guidance on this new statutory right. A worker can complain to an ET if this right is denied. The ET can award compensation up to two weeks' pay.[15D] A worker must not be subjected to any detriment because s/he has tried to exercise this right or has accompanied another worker. It would also be automatically unfair dismissal to dismiss an employee for this reason.[15E]

Eligible categories

Employees and the self-employed

6.14 In order to claim unfair dismissal, a worker must be employed (ie, work under a contract of service). A worker who is self-employed (ie, working under a contract for services) is not entitled to bring a claim.

---

15 *Polkey v AE Dayton Services* [1987] IRLR 503; [1988] ICR 142, HL; *West Midlands Co-operative Society v Tipton* [1985] IRLR 116; [1986] ICR 192, HL.

15A ERA 1999 s10. This is not yet in force, but is likely to be brought in shortly.

15B Ibid s10(2). Nevertheless employers may choose to give this additional right under their existing disciplinary procedure.

15C Ibid s10(6).

15D Ibid s11.

15E Ibid s12.

The distinction between these two types of workers can be extremely blurred and difficult to distinguish.[16]

6.15   Unfortunately, there is no clear guidance given by the courts to distinguish between those who are employed and those who are self-employed. An 'employee' is simply defined as someone who has entered into, or works under, a contract of employment.[17] A 'contract of employment' means 'a contract of service or apprenticeship, whether express or implied, and (if it is express), whether it is oral or in writing'.[18]

6.16   There is no single test which determines whether a worker is employed or self-employed although there have been a large number of cases trying to establish the approach to be adopted to determine this issue. The approach the courts usually apply is referred to as the multiple test which requires all aspects of the relationship to be considered and then to ask whether it could be said that the worker was carrying on a business on his/her own account.[19] The multiple test requires the consideration of a number of factors.

6.17   The first factor is whether there is a mutual obligation to supply and perform work. This is the most important single factor. If no such obligation exists, the ET will conclude that the worker is not an employee.[20] In *O'Kelly v Trusthouse Forte plc*,[21] butlers who worked in a hotel as 'regular casuals' were not employees, even though they were provided with work on a regular basis, since the hotel was not in fact under an obligation to provide such work. On the other hand, in *Nethermere (St Neots) Ltd v Gardiner and Taverna*[22] a group of homeworkers were deemed employees because, over a period of time, their employer had provided work, which the workers were obliged to accept and perform. This became in effect an implied term of the contract. More recently casual workers were held not to be workers.[23]

6.18   The second main factor is the purpose and intention of the parties. The ET will look at the purpose of the contract and what the parties intended when they formed it. It is the nature of the

---

16   *Stevenson Jordan and Harrison v MacDonald and Evans* [1952] 1 TLR 101, CA.
17   ERA 1996 s230.
18   Ibid.
19   *O'Kelly v TrustHouse Forte* [1983] IRLR 369, CA.
20   *Carmichael v National Power plc* [2000] IRLR 43, HL.
21   [1983] IRLR 369; [1983] ICR 728, CA.
22   [1984] IRLR 240; [1984] ICR 612, CA.
23   *Carmichael v National Power plc* [2000] IRLR 43, HL.

agreement and the actual performance of the contract which counts, not simply the label attached to the relationship by the parties. Just because a worker is told by an employer that s/he is self-employed does not mean that is the true legal position. Nor is it conclusive that a worker is paying tax on a self-employed basis, although that will be one of the relevant factors.[24]

6.19 The degree of control exercised by the employer is the third factor. Historically this factor alone was the conclusive test. Now it is simply one of the criteria to be considered. If the worker controls when, where and how s/he performs the work, this degree of autonomy would suggest that s/he is self-employed. However, if the employer has the power to tell the worker when, where and how to perform, it would indicate that the worker is an employee.[25]

6.20 Finally, the method and mode of payment to the worker may be a relevant factor. If pay is referable to a period of time rather than productivity, this suggests that the worker is an employee.

6.21 'Contract workers', 'temp workers' or 'casual workers' may or may not meet the definition of a 'employee'. Agency workers are unlikely to be treated as employees of the organisation to which they are assigned although they may be employed by the agency which assigns them.[26] If these workers are 'employees' and meet the other eligibility requirements (see below), they can claim unfair dismissal. However, the absence of mutuality of obligation will prevent the worker from being treated as an employee for the purpose of bringing a claim.

Upper age limit

6.22 A worker cannot claim unfair dismissal if s/he has reached the 'normal retirement age' at his/her place of work or, if there is no normal retirement age, if s/he has reached 65.[27] The 'normal retirement age' is usually the contractual retirement age unless it can be shown that most or all other employees retire at a different age.[28] However, the

---

24 *Massey v Crown Life Insurance Co* [1978] ICR 590; [1978] IRLR 31, CA.
25 *Ready Mixed Concrete (South East) v Minister of Pensions and National Insurance* [1968] 2 QB 497.
26 *McMeechan v Secretary of State* [1997] IRLR 353, CA.
27 ERA 1996 ss109(1) and 156.
28 *Waite v GCHQ* [1983] ICR 653; [1983] IRLR 341, HL. Note that the legal view as to what is the normal retirement age in a particular situation can be complex.

'normal retirement age' cannot be reduced below the contractual retiring age unless the contract has been lawfully varied.[29]

Working abroad and ship workers

6.23 It used to be the case that a worker who, under his or her contract of employment ordinarily worked outside Great Britain, could not claim unfair dismissal.[30] It was often unclear on the facts whether this exclusion applied. The ERA 1999 abolished this exclusion.[31] Whether or not a dismissed worker can now claim unfair dismissal will depend on the wider principles of conflict of laws. This is rather a complex question, which is beyond the scope of this book. However an employee working in Great Britain at the time of dismissal may well be able to claim.

6.24   Special rules apply to employment on a ship.[32]

Categories excluded from claiming unfair dismissal

6.25 Workers in Crown employment (eg, working for government departments) can generally claim unfair dismissal though there are some partial exceptions, eg, where a national security certificate has been issued and, currently, for members of the armed services.[33] Members of the police service are also excluded[34] as are share fishermen and women.[35] Advisers should check the exact wording of the legislation and up-to-date amendments where any of these exclusions may apply. Special rules also apply to employees of foreign and Commonwealth missions.[36]

Contracting out

6.26 Failure to renew a fixed-term contract amounts to a dismissal in law. Workers employed on a fixed-term contract can therefore claim

---

29 *Bratko v Beloit Walmsley* [1995] IRLR 629. See para 11.78 on age discrimination and retirement ages.
30 ERA 1996 s196.
31 ERA 1999 s32(3).
32 ERA 1996 ss199(7) inserted by ERA 1999 s32(4).
33 See ERA 1996 ss191–193, Sch 2 para 16; ERA 1999 s41 and Sch 8 once implemented.
34 ERA 1996 s200.
35 Ibid s199.
36 This can be complex. See the State Immunity Act 1978.

unfair dismissal provided they meet the other eligibility requirements. Waiver clauses which meet specific requirements used to
be able to exclude a worker's ability to claim unfair dismissal, but
these are no longer effective for dismissals after 25 October 1999
where the contract and waiver were not entered before 25 October
1999[37] (although they are still effective to exclude claims for statutory
redundancy).

Illegal contracts of employment

6.27 An illegal contract of employment is not enforceable in the courts
and a worker will be unable to claim unfair dismissal.[38] An employment contract will be illegal in the following circumstances.

- Where, to the worker's knowledge, the contract of employment
  involves a fraud on the Inland Revenue, eg, the employer is not
  paying the appropriate tax on the worker's wages. A common
  indication of a fraud is when wages are wholly or partly in cash.
  The essential question is whether the worker actually knew that
  the employer was not paying the appropriate tax, not whether s/he
  ought to have known. If the worker did not know, the contract is
  not illegal.[39]
- Where the performance of the employment contract is prohibited by statute, the prohibited period will not count towards
  the required length of continuous employment for an unfair
  dismissal claim. A worker must be continuously employed for
  one year after the end of the prohibited period in order to
  qualify.
- Where the performance of the contract is prohibited by common
  law. A contract for an immoral purpose, eg, procuring prostitutes,
  or for a criminal purpose, eg, gun-running, will not be recognised
  by the ET. It is necessary for the main purpose of the employment
  to be the immoral or criminal purpose rather than it being an
  incidental part of the employment contract.[40] The conduct and
  relative moral culpability of the parties may be taken into account
  when deciding whether a contract is illegal.[41]

---

37 ERA 1999 s18(6).
38 *Tomlinson v Dick Evans U Drive* [1978] ICR 639; [1978] IRLR 77, EAT.
39 *Newland v Simons and Willer (Hairdressers) Ltd* [1981] IRLR 359; [1981] ICR 521,
    EAT.
40 *Coral Leisure Group Ltd v Barrett* [1981] IRLR 204; [1981] ICR 503, EAT.
41 *Newcastle Catering Ltd v Ahmed and Elkamah* [1991] IRLR 473, CA.

Qualifying service

Length of continuous employment

6.28   To claim unfair dismissal, a worker must have been continuously employed for one year at the effective date of termination (EDT).[42] There is no longer a requirement to work a specific number of hours in a week to qualify for the right not to be unfairly dismissed. There is no minimum service requirement, eg, where dismissal is related to pregnancy or maternity,[43] related to trade union membership or activities,[44] related to the worker being an elected representative for collective redundancy or transfer consultation purposes,[45] related to a worker asserting his or her statutory rights[46] or a health and safety dismissal.[47]

Weeks which count towards continuous service

6.29   Continuous employment is measured by 'qualifying' weeks. It is broken by a week that does not qualify with the result that the worker will have to start again in accruing the one year continuous service.[48] If during all or part of a week a worker is away on account of holiday or sickness or other recognised absence, that week will nevertheless count.[49] Equally, if a worker resigns or is dismissed in one week and re-engaged in the subsequent week, each week counts and continuity is not broken.

Continuity if the worker leaves work and returns

6.30   The period of continuous employment must be of unbroken service except in limited circumstances. Where a worker is absent from work but the contract continues, there is no problem and continuity is preserved. In some circumstances, even though the contract is terminated because the worker leaves, when s/he subsequently returns to the job continuity is preserved and the weeks of absence will count

42   Unfair Dismissal and Statement of Reasons for Dismissal (Variation of Qualifying Period) Order 1999 SI No 1436.
43   ERA 1996 s99.
44   TULR(C)A 1992 s152.
45   ERA 1996 s103.
46   Ibid s104 and *Mennell v Newell & Wright* [1997] IRLR 519.
47   ERA 1996 s100.
48   ERA 1996 Part XIV Chapter 1.
49   ERA 1996 s212.

towards his/her continuity of employment. Continuity is preserved where the worker is absent from work in any of the following circumstances:

- wholly or partly because of pregnancy or confinement. This is subject to a maximum of 26 weeks except where the absence and return is in accordance with statutory maternity leave;
- on account of a temporary cessation of work – when the employer lays off workers through lack of work;
- because of sickness or injury, subject to a maximum of 26 weeks;
- in such circumstances that, by arrangement or custom, s/he is regarded as continuing in employment for all or any purposes.[50] This can be helpful when, eg, an employer agrees that a worker may leave to visit family overseas and return subsequently to the same employment;
- is reinstated or re-engaged through ACAS conciliation following dismissal,[51] a reinstatement or re-engagement order made by the ET,[52] or a compromise agreement to withdraw a claim.[53]

The presumption of continuity

31   The period of continuous employment begins on the day someone starts work[54] and is presumed to continue[55] until the EDT.[56] The presumption of continuity is very important for workers, since it means that it is for the employer to prove there has been a break which is not recognised by the law as preserving continuity.[57]

Identifying the EDT

32   The EDT is identified in the same way as for time limit purposes[58] except that, for purposes of calculating length of continuous service, it is artificially extended when the employer fails to give notice. In those circumstances, the EDT is when the minimum statutory notice period, not the contractual notice period,[59] would have expired.

---

50   Ibid.
51   Ibid s219.
52   Ibid s111.
53   Ibid s203.
54   Ibid s211(1)(a).
55   Ibid s210(5).
56   Ibid s97.
57   Ibid s210(5).
58   See para 16.15 below.
59   *Fox Maintenance v Jackson* [1977] IRLR 306; [1978] ICR 110, EAT.

Change of ownership of the business

6.33   Continuity of employment is preserved where there is a change in the
        ownership of the business.[60] For the effect of the Transfer of Under-
        takings Regulations, see paras 6.91 onwards.

'Contract workers, casuals and temps'

6.34   With the deregulation of the labour market, workers are employed on
        an increasingly insecure basis under a number of labels which have
        no legal meaning. Whether or not contract and casual workers can
        claim unfair dismissal depends on whether they meet the eligibility
        requirements set out in this chapter. In particular:

        – Are they an employee? This is a question of fact having regard, in
          particular, to the issue of mutual obligation.
        – Do they have the requisite length of service? Remember that a
          series of fixed-term contracts without a break will be added
          together.
        – Have they been dismissed? Failure to renew a fixed-term contract
          is a dismissal in law.

        It is no longer possible to exclude the right to claim unfair dismissal
        on expiry of fixed term contracts by written waiver clauses.[61] Whether
        or not the failure to renew a fixed-term contract is in practice fair or
        unfair, will be subject to the usual reasonableness test (see below).
        However, it cannot necessarily be assumed that just because the con-
        tract was for a fixed-term period, non-renewal is fair.

What is a dismissal?

6.35   To bring a claim for unfair dismissal, the worker must have been
        dismissed in a way recognised by the ERA 1996.[62] There are various
        types of dismissal:

        – termination by the employer;
        – expiry of a fixed-term contract;

---

60 Transfer of Undertakings (Protection of Employment) Regulations 1981 SI No
    1794 reg 5.
61 ERA 1999 s18(6). See para 6.26.
62 ERA 1996 s95.

- forced resignation;
- resignation amounting to constructive dismissal.

Termination by the employer

6.36 Usually the employer terminates the employment with or without notice.[63] Therefore, there is no doubt that this has taken place, but employers seeking to avoid an unfair dismissal claim often deny that the worker was dismissed. If there is a dispute over whether a dismissal has occurred, it is for the worker to show on the balance of probabilities that s/he has been dismissed. If the ET cannot decide this issue on the available evidence, the worker's claim will fail.[64]

6.37 Sometimes an employer's words are ambiguous. The ET will look at the purpose and effect of those words in the light of all the surrounding circumstances and, in particular, the conduct of the parties and what happened before and after the disputed dismissal.[65] The ET must then decide how a 'reasonable' worker would have interpreted the employer's words.[66] If the employer's words clearly indicated a dismissal, they will be taken literally and the ET will not usually consider the parties' intentions.[67] The only exception is where the dismissal (or resignation) took place in 'the heat of the moment', for example, as a result of an argument between the employer and worker.[68] If the employer retracts the dismissal soon afterwards, the ET may consider that s/he was entitled to do so. The period of time in which a party may retract depends on the circumstances but usually it should be shortly afterwards.[69]

6.38 A similar principle applies where a worker resigns in the heat of the moment and instantly retracts the resignation. If the employer refuses to accept the retraction, the ET may consider the worker to have been dismissed. Similarly, where the worker is immature or of below average intelligence and resigns while under emotional stress, the ET will not necessarily treat those words as constituting a resignation, if the worker never intended it.[70]

---

63 ERA 1996 s95(1)(a).
64 *Morris v London Iron and Steel Co* [1987] ICR 855; [1987] IRLR 182, CA.
65 *Tanner v D T Kean Ltd* [1978] IRLR 110.
66 *J & J Stern v Simpson* [1983] IRLR 52, EAT.
67 *Sothern v Franks Charlesly and Co* [1981] IRLR 278, CA.
68 *Martin v Yeoman Aggregates Ltd* [1983] IRLR 49.
69 *Sovereign House Security Services v Savage* [1989] IRLR 115, CA.
70 *Barclay v City of Glasgow DC* [1983] IRLR 313.

Expiry of a fixed-term contract

6.39   Non-renewal of a fixed-term contract on its expiry is treated as a dismissal.[71] A fixed-term contract is a contract for a specific term and at its commencement the termination date is ascertainable.[72]

Forced resignation

6.40   If the worker resigns as a result of the employer saying that s/he must resign or otherwise be dismissed, this counts as a dismissal.[73] The difficult issue for the ET to decide is whether the resignation was forced.[74] A worker should be wary of resigning in these circumstances, because it may be difficult to prove that s/he was threatened in this way.

Constructive dismissal

6.41   If the worker resigns in response to a fundamental breach of the employment contract by the employer, this is a 'constructive dismissal'.[75] Constructive dismissal is usually difficult to prove and a worker should be very careful about resigning if s/he wants to be able to claim unfair dismissal.

6.42   Whether there has been a fundamental breach of contract is determined by reference to the contractual terms.[76] The reasonableness of the parties' behaviour is not relevant in establishing whether there was a constructive dismissal, although it will be relevant when considering whether the constructive dismissal was unfair. So, for example, if the employer gives the worker an instruction which is unreasonable but which is allowed by the contract, there is no breach of contract and therefore no constructive dismissal.[77]

Fundamental breach of contract

6.43   Not every breach of contract is a 'fundamental breach'[78] which entitles a worker to claim constructive dismissal. Before resigning, a worker

---

71   ERA 1996 s95(1)(b).
72   *BBC v Dixon* [1979] IRLR 114; [1979] ICR 281, CA.
73   *Martin v MBS Fastenings (Glynwed) Distribution Ltd* [1983] IRLR 198.
74   *BBC v Dixon* (n72 above).
75   ERA 1996 s95(1)(c).
76   *Western Excavating (ECC) Ltd v Sharp* [1978] IRLR 27.
77   *Western Excavating (ECC) v Sharp* [1978] IRLR 27; [1978] ICR 221, CA.
78   A 'fundamental breach' may also be called a 'repudiatory breach'.

needs to consider which term of the contract an employer has broken. A contract may comprise many terms both written and oral, and these terms may be express or implied terms. A large number of constructive dismissal claims are based on the employer breaking one of the following implied terms:

- not to subject the worker to capricious or arbitrary treatment;
- trust and confidence;
- to take reasonable care for the health and safety of the worker.

It is difficult to be sure when a breach is sufficiently serious to be a 'fundamental breach' and there are no hard-and-fast rules as this determination is for the ET to decide. The working relationship will be relevant and, what in one job situation may amount to a fundamental breach, in another will not. The ET will ask itself whether the employer's conduct, objectively considered, is calculated or likely to breach the implied term of trust and confidence.[79] The following are examples of what might amount to a fundamental breach: a significant reduction in pay[80] (rather than a genuine miscalculation[81]), a change in the worker's status or job content,[82] changes of work hours[83] or place of work, provided the change was not contemplated by the parties when the employment contract started.[84] The change must not be one which is permitted by the contract.

.44   Sometimes a single breach of contract is enough if it is sufficiently serious. Alternatively the worker can rely on a series of breaches, where each breach in isolation might not constitute a significant and fundamental breach, but taken together they do. This is known as the 'last straw' doctrine.[85]

An anticipatory breach

.45   When an employer breaks a term of a contract with immediate effect, this constitutes an actual breach. When the employer merely indicates in advance a clear intention to commit a fundamental breach, this is called an 'anticipatory breach'. A worker who resigns as a

---

79 *Malik v BCCI* [1997] IRLR 462.
80 *Industrial Rubber Products v Gillon* [1977] IRLR 389, EAT.
81 *Cantor Fitzgerald International v Callaghan* [1999] IRLR 234.
82 *Ford v Milthorn Toleman* [1980] IRLR 30, CA.
83 *Derby CC v Marshall* [1979] IRLR 261; [1979] ICR 731, EAT.
84 *Courtaulds Northern Spinning v Sibson* [1988] IRLR 305; [1988] ICR 451, CA.
85 *Lewis v Motorworld Garages Ltd* [1985] IRLR 465.

result of an anticipatory breach may claim constructive dismissal.[86] However, a worker should be careful not to resign prematurely where the employer has not finally decided to commit the fundamental breach. The employer may still be willing to negotiate. For example, an invitation to use the grievance procedure in response to a proposed step will indicate that the employer has made no final decision. Equally, an employer's statement that, 'I expect you to co-operate in the manner asked of you', is only a forceful request, falling short of an actual breach of contract.

When to resign[87]

6.46   Once the worker is sure that the employer has committed an actual or anticipatory breach, s/he must resign fairly promptly, since any delay may be taken by the ET as acceptance of the employer's conduct. A worker is often reluctant to resign before s/he has found another job and this can cause problems. If the conduct of the employer is the effective but not the sole cause for the resignation this is sufficient. Therefore if a worker resigns as a consequence of securing another job but the seeking of alternative employment was driven by the fundamental breach the worker is entitled to claim constructive dismissal.[88]

6.47   How long a worker can afford to delay depends on the facts of each case. Delay is very risky where the employer's breach has immediate impact on the worker, eg, a pay cut, and particularly where the worker has to behave differently to comply with the breach, eg, new duties or location. It may be legitimate to object in writing and request a short trial period before resigning.[89] There is less urgency where the breach has no immediate impact, eg, a change in retirement age or sick pay entitlement, provided a written protest is made immediately.

6.48   When the worker does resign, s/he should make it clear that it is in response to the employer's fundamental breach and not for any other reason. A worker is not precluded from bringing a claim for constructive dismissal because no mention is made at the time of

---

86   *Harrison v Norwest Group Administration Ltd* [1985] IRLR 240.
87   For fuller treatment of ways to handle an employer's unilateral variation of the contract see T Lewis and M Westgate, 'Unilateral change of contractual terms by employers' July 1989 *Legal Action* 13.
88   *Jones v F Sirl & Son (Furnishers) Ltd* [1997] IRLR 493.
89   See, eg, *Bevan v CTC Coaches* (1989) 373 IRLIB 10, EAT.

resignation that it is a constructive dismissal, but it may be hard to prove.[90]

Deemed dismissal

6.49 Until recently a woman who was not permitted to return from statutory maternity leave was deemed to have been dismissed. This concept no longer applies.[91]

Situations where there is no dismissal

6.50 Where an unforeseen event occurs which makes future performance of the employment contract impossible or radically different, eg, terminal sickness or imprisonment, the contract is frustrated and the worker cannot claim s/he has been unfairly dismissed. This is, however, very rare. Employers sometimes try to claim frustration inappropriately, eg, in cases of ordinary long-term sickness. Given the change in emphasis towards the treatment of lengthy sickness arising from the DDA 1995, frustration in these circumstances should apply less readily.

6.51 Termination by mutual agreement means the worker cannot claim unfair dismissal or other rights dependent on a dismissal having taken place. It is not always obvious whether a mutual termination has taken place. Voluntary redundancy depends on the facts; it may be a dismissal, although likely to be fair.[92] Similarly, early retirement, unless involuntary, is usually a mutually agreed termination. Workers need to be careful. A dismissal accompanied by a settlement package, however small, may appear later to an ET to indicate a mutually agreed termination.

6.52 An employer cannot deprive a worker of the right to claim unfair dismissal by agreeing in advance that the contract will automatically terminate on the happening of a certain event, eg, the worker's late return from holiday. This would effectively circumvent the ET's jurisdiction and is invalid.[93]

---

90 *Weathersfield Ltd v Sargent* [1998] IRLB 609.
91 See paras 7.94 onwards.
92 *Burton, Allton and Johnson v Peck* [1975] IRLR 87, QBD; *Birch and Humber v University of Liverpool* [1985] IRLR 165, CA.
93 ERA 1996 s203 and *Igbo v Johnson Matthey Chemicals* [1986] ICR 505; [1986] IRLR 215, CA.

What is an unfair dismissal?

The two stages

6.53   ERA 1996 s98 sets out how an ET should decide whether a dismissal is unfair. There are two basic stages.

1) The employer must show what was the reason, or if more than one, the principal reason for the dismissal.[94] The reason must be one of the five potentially fair reasons set out in ERA 1996 s98(2).
2) The ET then must decide in accordance with ERA 1996 s98(4) whether it was fair to dismiss the worker for that reason.

The reason for the dismissal

6.54   The potentially fair reasons are the following:

– a reason relating to the worker's capability or qualification for performing work of the kind s/he was employed to do;[95]
– a reason relating to the conduct of the worker;[96]
– the worker is redundant;[97]
– the worker could not continue to work in the position s/he held without contravention of a duty or restriction imposed by or under an enactment;[98]
– for some other substantial reason of a kind such as to justify the dismissal of a worker holding the position which the worker held.[99]

If the employer cannot show the reason for dismissal, the dismissal will be automatically unfair. If there are several reasons, the employer must establish the principal reason. The dismissal will be unfair if the reason shown is insignificant, trivial or unworthy.[100]

6.55   The reason for dismissal will be the set of facts known to the employer at the time of dismissal or a genuine belief held on reasonable grounds by the employer which led to the dismissal.[101] An employer may give one reason for dismissal at the time or immediately afterwards and advance another once ET proceedings have

94 ERA 1996 s98(1).
95 Ibid s98(2)(a).
96 Ibid s98(2)(b).
97 Ibid s98(2)(c).
98 Ibid s98(2)(d).
99 Ibid s98(1)(b).
100 *Gilham and Others v Kent CC (No 2)* [1985] ICR 233; [1985] IRLR 18, CA.
101 *Abernethy v Mott, Hay and Anderson* [1974] ICR 323; [1974] IRLR 213, CA.

started. It is the reason for the dismissal at the time of the dismissal which is relevant. The ET will be reluctant to accept a change of reason if raised at the hearing for the first time, particularly if it will cause prejudice to the worker and the worker will not have had the fullest opportunity to answer the allegations made.[102]

Was it fair to dismiss for that reason?

6.56   ERA 1996 s98(4) sets out the statutory test of fairness:

> the determination of the question whether the dismissal is fair or unfair (having regard to the reason shown by the employer)—
>
> (a) depends on whether in the circumstances (including the size and administrative resources of the employer's undertaking) the employer acted reasonably or unreasonably in treating it as a sufficient reason for dismissing the employee, and
>
> (b) that question shall be determined in accordance with equity and the substantial merits of the case.

The ET must take into account a number of considerations in deciding the fairness of a dismissal under s98(4). The relevant factors vary according to the reason for the dismissal.[103] However, there are also broad considerations which apply to all s98(4) dismissals.

Employer's size and administrative resources

6.57   In deciding whether a dismissal is fair, an ET must have in mind the size and administrative resources of the employer. This is particularly relevant when considering the actions taken by an employer prior to dismissal. The larger the employer, the greater the obligation to operate proper disciplinary, grievance and consultative procedures.

Equity and the substantial merits of the case

6.58   Equity requires that an employer treats workers consistently; an arbitrary or capricious dismissal will be inequitable. If, on a different occasion, the employer failed to dismiss another worker for a similar offence, the dismissal may well be inequitable and therefore unfair. The employer must offer an explanation for the difference in treatment.[104]

---

102 *Hotson v Wisbech Conservative Club* [1984] ICR 859; [1984] IRLR 422, EAT.

103 See below, sections dealing with each reason and relevant issues.

104 *Post Office v Fennell* [1981] IRLR 221, CA; *Harrow LBC v Cunningham* [1996] IRLR 256.

Procedural unfairness

6.59   The House of Lords in *Polkey v AE Dayton Services*[105] stressed the importance of procedures and the obligation on an employer to carry them out fairly in relation to each of the four potentially fair reasons for dismissal. Failure to consult and adopt fair procedures will now in itself render a dismissal unfair except in exceptional circumstances. The employer will be able to justify failure to consult, etc, only if s/he could reasonably conclude at the time of dismissal and in the light of what s/he knew at that time, that consultation would be 'utterly useless or futile'. An example would be where a worker was caught in the act of stealing. An employer is not required to show a deliberate and conscious decision that consultation would be useless or futile. It is only necessary for the employer to show that the employer, acting reasonably, could have failed to consult in the particular circumstances.[106]

6.60   *Polkey* is probably the most important decision since the introduction of the right not to be unfairly dismissed. Unfortunately the consequences for compensation have not been good. An ET can find a dismissal unfair on *Polkey* principles, but award only nominal compensation because it believes the dismissal would have occurred in any event had a proper procedure been adopted. However, if the dismissal is substantially unfair rather than merely procedurally unfair, the ET must make an award referable to the loss the worker has suffered as a consequence of his/her dismissal.[107] It is, therefore, important to show that the dismissal was substantially unfair rather than merely procedurally unfair.[108] If the employer wants to maintain that the amount of compensation should be reduced, it is for him/her to prove that dismissal was inevitable even if the proper procedure had been adopted.[109]

The band of reasonable responses

6.61   The real question is not whether the ET would itself have chosen to dismiss the worker in the circumstances, but whether the decision to

---

105   [1987] IRLR 503.
106   *Dufy v Yeoman and Partners* [1994] IRLR 642.
107   *Leonard v Strathclyde Buses Ltd* [1998] IRLR 693.
108   Also see para 14.25 below on compensation.
109   *Heron v Citylink (Nottingham)* [1993] IRLR 372.

dismiss fell within the band of reasonable responses. The ET may think that the dismissal was harsh, but nevertheless within 'the band of reasonable responses' open to the employer. Within such a band, one employer might reasonably retain the worker whereas another employer might reasonably dismiss him/her. If so, then it is not unfair dismissal, even if the ET would not have dismissed.[110] This test has been challenged as being wrong in law.[111] If the decision is upheld on appeal, it will be as important as the *Polkey* decision. In *Haddon* the approach is whether the ET believed that it was unfair with no artificial consideration of the band of reasonable responses of an employer.

6.62   This is a very important concept which results in many claims of unfair dismissal being rejected. It is to be noted that s98(4) gives no scope or support for this approach. It is a judicial creation which benefits only the employer and removes any meaningful role for the ET members, who are appointed for their industrial experience and common sense.

Automatically fair or unfair dismissals

6.63   Certain dismissals are not subject to the reasonableness test and are treated as automatically fair or unfair. This category is being expanded all the time. In many cases, it is also unlawful to subject a worker to a detriment short of dismissal. Note that as only employees can claim unfair dismissal, where workers in the wider sense are dismissed, their claim would usually be for an unlawful detriment (although the exact wording of ERA 1996 should be checked).

Dismissal during industrial action

.64   The law is due to change shortly (see below), but until then, the position is as follows. A worker dismissed while taking unofficial industrial action cannot claim unfair dismissal.[112] The only exception is if s/he is dismissed for specific reasons related to maternity, health and safety or whistle-blowing. Broadly speaking, industrial action is unofficial unless some or all of its participants are members of

110 *British Leyland (UK) v Swift* [1981] IRLR 91, CA.
111 *Haddon v Van den Bergh Foods Ltd* [1999] IRLR 672, EAT.
112 TULR(C)A 1992 s237(1) and (1A).

a trade union which has authorised or endorsed the action.[113] There are complicated rules on this.

6.65   Where a worker is dismissed while taking part in 'official' industrial action or while the employer is conducting a lock-out, the position is less straight-forward.[114] An ET will have no jurisdiction to hear the worker's unfair dismissal claim if all those taking part in the action or affected by the lock-out were also dismissed and none were re-engaged within three months. This is designed to protect workers against selective or targeted dismissals. Again there is an exception for maternity, health and safety and whistle-blowing dismissals.

6.66   The new law will make it automatically unfair dismissal to dismiss a worker during the first eight weeks of industrial action (or subsequently, if the employer has not taken reasonable procedural steps to resolve the dispute) because s/he took protected industrial action.[115] It also covers later dismissals, where the worker had stopped taking industrial action within the eight weeks. Basically it is official action which is protected. No minimum service or upper age limit applies. It would seem that outside the eight-week protected period or if the action is unofficial, the current law continues to apply.

Automatically unfair dismissals and detriments short of dismissal

Pregnancy, maternity and dependant leave dismissals

6.67   It is automatically unfair to dismiss a woman or select her for redundancy due to pregnancy or maternity, and no minimum qualifying service is required.[116] A woman who is dismissed while pregnant but for non-related reasons can claim ordinary unfair dismissal but only if she has the usual qualifying service. It is automatically unfair to dismiss a woman or select her for redundancy, and it is unlawful to subject her to a detriment short of dismissal, for a reason connected with any of the following:[117]

---

113   Ibid s237(2).
114   See ibid s238.
115   Ibid s238A to be inserted when ERA 1999 Sch 5 s16 is implemented.
116   ERA 1996 s99(1)–(3).
117   ERA 1996 s99 (dismissal), s105(1) (redundancy), s47C (detriment), and see Maternity and Parental Leave, etc Regulations 1999 SI No 3312.

a) due to the employee's pregnancy or, where dismissal ends the ordinary or additional maternity leave period, because s/he has given birth;[118]

b) because she took or sought to take the benefits of ordinary maternity leave;[119]

c) because she took or sought to take additional maternity leave, parental leave or time-off for care of dependants under ERA 1996 s57A;[120]

d) because she refused to sign a workforce agreement (related to parental leave) or because she is a workforce representative or candidate;[121]

e) due to a requirement or recommendation for a health and safety suspension (see below);[122]

f) if she is made redundant during the ordinary or additional maternity leave period and not offered any *existing* suitable alternative vacancy.[123]

There are exceptions for small employers (below five employees) in relation to AML and for offers by associated employers.[124]

5.68   If a woman is dismissed while pregnant or at the end of her maternity leave, she is entitled to written reasons for her dismissal, whether or not she asks for them, and regardless of her length of service.[124A]

5.68A   It is also unlawful to subject a worker to a detriment and automatically unfair to dismiss him or her because s/he took or tried to take parental leave or time-off for the care of dependants (see below).[124B] Once the part-time workers regulations are passed (see paras 11.11–11.14 below), it is likely that those rights will similarly be protected.

Dismissal for asserting a statutory right

5.69   It is automatically unfair to dismiss a worker or select him/her for redundancy for alleging that the employer has infringed a statutory

---

118 Maternity and Parental Leave, etc Regulations 1999 reg 20(3)(a)(b), (4).
119 Ibid reg 20(3)(d).
120 Ibid reg 20(3)(e).
121 Ibid reg 20(3)(f)(g).
122 Ibid reg 20(3)(c).
123 Ibid reg 20(1)(b).
124 See ibid reg 20(6) and (7) for details.
124A ERA 1996 s92(4).
124B Maternity and Parental Leave, etc Regulations 1999 reg 20(3)(e).

right or for bringing proceedings to enforce such a right.[125] The statutory rights covered are: minimum notice; any right conferred by the ERA 1996, the ERA 1999, and the TULR(C)A 1992 which can be enforced in an ET, eg, rights to ante-natal care, itemised pay slips, statements of terms and conditions; the right not to have unlawful deductions from wages; right to time off for trade union activities; the right not to suffer action short of dismissal which prevents, deters, penalises or compels union membership; and the right not to have unauthorised deductions for union contributions or a union political fund.

6.70   As long as the worker's allegation is made in good faith, it does not matter whether s/he is correct in thinking s/he has the right or that it has been infringed. It is also unnecessary for the worker to specify the right, as long as s/he has made it reasonably clear to the employer what the right was. Workers qualify for this protection regardless of their length of service and age above normal retirement date.[126]

6.71   This concept is similar to the law prohibiting victimisation for taking up issues of race or sex discrimination and there are likely to be similar difficulties of proving the link between a dismissal and the assertion of a statutory right. It is therefore wise to make any request, eg, for payslips or clarification of terms and conditions, in writing.

Health and safety

6.72   It is automatically unfair to dismiss or select for redundancy a worker who, in circumstances of danger which s/he reasonably believes to be serious and imminent:

- takes appropriate steps for self-protection or to protect others and does not act negligently in doing so; or
- refuses to work in the place of work, when s/he cannot reasonably be expected to avert the danger.[127]

There have been few cases on the meaning and scope of this protection. However, successful ET cases have included dismissals for refusal to drive defective vehicles and a dismissal of a young female employee who refused to take rubbish alone at night to a deserted

---

125   Ibid s104.
126   ERA 1996 ss104 and 105(7).
127   ERA 1996 s100.

dump.[128] The EAT has confirmed that steps taken to protect members of the public are also covered, eg, a chef who was dismissed for refusing to cook food which he considered unfit for human consumption.[129] Circumstances of danger can include danger of violence from other workers.[130]

.73 Where there is no health and safety representative at the workplace or it is impracticable for the worker to raise the particular issue through the representative, it is also automatically unfair to dismiss a worker who brings to the employer's attention by reasonable means conditions of work which s/he reasonably believes are harmful or potentially harmful to health and safety. The reasonableness of the worker's actions will be judged by reference to all the circumstances, including the worker's knowledge and the facilities and advice available to him/her at the time. It is also unlawful to subject the worker to any detriment short of dismissal on these grounds.[131]

74 Workers with a specific health and safety duty under statute or by agreement with the employer have a similar right not to be dismissed or subjected to detrimental treatment because they carry out or propose to carry out their health and safety duties. There is no minimum service requirement and no upper age limit to claim unfair dismissal for these reasons.[131A] As with trade union dismissals, a health and safety representative who has been dismissed may be entitled to interim relief and enhanced compensation.[132]

5 Note that the Public Interest Disclosure Act 1998[133] can also be invoked in some circumstances where health and safety of work colleagues or the public may be endangered.

Dismissal of workers' representatives and trade union membership

6 It is automatically unfair to dismiss a worker or select him/her for redundancy for membership or proposed membership of an independent trade union or for refusing to join. It is also automatically

---

128 See (1996) 544 *IDS Brief* 4 for a round-up and *Kerr v Nathan's Wastesavers* at p 27.
129 *Masiak v City Restaurants (UK) Ltd* [1999] IRLR 780, EAT.
130 *Harvest Press Ltd v McCaffrey* [1999] IRLR 778, EAT.
131 ERA 1996 s44.
131A Ibid ss108(3), 109(2).
132 Ibid s44.
133 See para 6.81.

unfair to dismiss a worker for taking part or proposing to take part in the activities of an independent trade union at an appropriate time.[134] Subjecting the worker to a detriment short of dismissal is also unlawful. An appropriate time is outside working hours or, with the employer's consent, within working hours. An independent trade union is one which is not under the control or domination of the employer. Note that a worker can claim unfair dismissal for these reasons regardless of his/her length of service or upper age.[135] This protection is extended to workers' representatives.[136]

Not declaring spent convictions

6.77   The Rehabilitation of Offenders Act 1974 gives certain workers the right not to disclose previous convictions which are 'spent' as a result of the passage of a specified length of time. The length of time depends on the nature of the conviction and the rehabilitation period ranges from six months to ten years. It is automatically unfair to dismiss a worker for failing to disclose a 'spent' conviction.[137] There is still the need to satisfy the qualifying requirements as with ordinary unfair dismissal claims. It is to be noted that exception orders can be made to exclude the protection of the 1974 Act.[138]

Minimum wage, working time and tax credits dismissals

6.78   It is automatic unfair dismissal to dismiss a worker or select him/her for redundancy for any of the following reasons, regardless of length of service or upper age:[138A]

a) in connection with rights under the Working Time Regulations;[138B]
b) because of qualifying for a minimum wage rate or seeking to enforce the minimum wage etc.;[138C]
c) because the worker took action to secure the benefit of a tax credit and certain related reasons.[138D]

---

134   TULR(C)A s153 and ERA 1996 ss47 and 103.
135   ERA 1996 ss108(3) and 109(2).
136   Ibid ss47 and 103.
137   Rehabilitation of Offenders Act 1974 s4(3)(b).
138   Rehabilitation of Offenders Act 1974 s4(3)(b); *Wood v Coverage Care Ltd* [1996] IRLR 264.
138A   ERA 1996 s108(3), s109(2).
138B   Ibid s101A.
138C   Ibid s104A. See para 4.23 above on the National Minimum Wage.
138D   Ibid s104B.

Sunday Trading Act 1994

5.79 A shop worker[139] or a betting worker is treated as protected (if s/he is not required to work only on a Sunday and has not provided an opting-out certificate)[140] and so can refuse to work on a Sunday. A written notice called an 'opting-out notice' can be given to the employer objecting to working on a Sunday. At any time an opting-in notice can be served by the worker signifying a willingness to work on a Sunday. A protected shop worker or protected betting worker will be treated as automatically unfairly dismissed if the reason, or where there is more than one reason the principal reason, for dismissal is the refusal to do shop work or betting work on a Sunday.[141] No minimum service is required, nor is it necessary to be below normal retirement age.[142] S/he also has the right not to be subjected to a detriment.[143]

Trustees of occupational pension schemes

5.80 The dismissal of a worker is treated as automatically unfair if the reason relates to any function discharged as a trustee of an occupational pension scheme.[144] No minimum service qualification or upper age limit applies.[145] Detrimental action short of dismissal is also unlawful.[146]

Protection for whistleblowers

5.81 Public inquiries have found that in many of the major disasters of the last decade, workers were aware of the danger but afraid to speak out. Partially as a response to this, the Public Interest Disclosure Act 1998 (PIDA 1998) introduced a new Part IVA into the ERA 1996[147] to provide public interest whistleblowers with protection against victimisation. The provisions are complex and should be read closely before taking any action. The Current Law Statutes annotated notes to the PIDA 1998 provide an excellent commentary incorporating the parliamentary background to the Act.[148]

139 Ibid s232.
140 Ibid s36.
141 Ibid s101.
142 Ibid ss108(3) and 109(2).
143 Ibid s46.
144 Ibid s102.
145 Ibid ss108(3) and 109(2).
146 Ibid s46.
147 In force 2 July 1999.
148 Sweet & Maxwell. Also available from Public Concern at Work 020 7404 6609. See also introductory feature at (1999) 621 IRLB 2.

6.82   The protection covers workers[149] (not just employees), contractors, agency workers, homeworkers, NHS professionals (even if self-employed) and trainees.[150] It is automatic unfair dismissal to dismiss an employee because s/he has made a 'protected disclosure' of information.[151] No minimum service or upper age limit applies. A worker also has a right not to be subjected to a detriment for that reason,[152] eg, disciplinary action or lack of promotion. A threat could also amount to a detriment.

6.83   The worker is only protected if s/he discloses certain categories of information ('a qualifying disclosure') and makes the disclosure to the correct person and in the correct way.[153] A 'qualifying disclosure' means any disclosure of information which the worker reasonably believes tends to show one or more of the following:[154]

- that a criminal offence has been, is being or is likely to be committed;
- that a person has failed, is failing or is likely to fail to comply with a legal obligation;
- that a miscarriage of justice has occurred, is occurring or is likely to occur;
- that the health and safety of any individual has been, is being or is likely to be endangered, eg, risks to hospital patients, train passengers or consumers as well as to work colleagues;
- that the environment has been, is being or is likely to be damaged;
- that information tending to show any of the above has been, is being or is likely to be concealed.

It does not matter that the information is confidential, but the worker must not commit an offence by making the disclosure, eg, by breaching the Official Secrets Act 1989. The worker is protected even if the particular malpractice is not occurring, as long as s/he reasonably believed that it was.

6.84   ERA 1996 ss43C–43H sets out to whom protected disclosures may be made and in what circumstances. It is important to read these

---

149   As defined by ERA 1996 s230(3) and s43K.
150   See ERA 1996 ss43K, 191, 193, 196 and 200, and Current Law Statutes commentary for who is covered and exceptions.
151   ERA 1996 s103A.
152   Ibid s47B.
153   Ibid s43A.
154   Ibid s43B.

carefully, but in general, internal disclosures[155] are more readily protected. For example, a worker who makes disclosure to someone with managerial responsibility only needs an honest and reasonable belief about the malpractice. The same applies to disclosure made to someone authorised by an employer under a procedure,[156] eg, an internal whistleblowing procedure, which allows the matter to be raised with a trade union or health and safety representative, an external auditor or retired director or its lawyers. There is no requirement to have such an internal procedure, but employers may find that it encourages internal disclosure first. During parliamentary debate, the government and the sponsors of the bill consistently expressed the view that trade unions would have a valuable role both in framing such procedures and in being authorised to receive disclosures. There is a Health Service Circular giving guidance to NHS trusts on appropriate policies and procedures on whistleblowing.

Disclosures can also be made in certain circumstances to a person prescribed by the secretary of state,[157] eg, in the Public Interest Disclosure (Prescribed Persons) Order 1999.[158] The prescribed regulators include (as appropriate) the Charity Commissioners, the Inland Revenue Commissioners, the Data Protection Registrar, the Director General of Electricity Supply or Gas Supply or Water Services, the Director of the Serious Fraud Office, the Health and Safety Executive, the Environment Agency, the Rail Regulator, the Civil Aviation Authority, and local authorities responsible for health and safety or consumer protection. Disclosure can be made to these regulators even if the matter has not been raised internally first, provided that the worker makes the disclosure in good faith and reasonably believes that the relevant failure falls within a matter for which that regulator is prescribed and that the information disclosed and any allegation made is substantially true.

Disclosures can be made in the course of obtaining legal advice[159] even if not in good faith. However, if the lawyer is authorised to pass on the disclosure, eg, by communicating with the employer, then the worker's good faith is necessary in the usual way. Disclosures to trade union lawyers would also be covered, but it is less certain if the

---

155 Ibid ss43C, 43E.
156 Ibid s43C(2).
157 Ibid s43F.
158 SI No 1549. Obtainable from the Stationery Office.
159 ERA 1996 s43D.

disclosure is to a trade union official, but for the purpose of getting legal advice. Trade unions may be best advised to set up specific advice lines to cover this situation. Disclosure to a trade union official for other purposes must otherwise fit one of the other categories of protected disclosure, eg, as part of an authorised internal procedure (see above).

6.87   Wider disclosures, eg, to the media, MPs or police, are protected only in more limited circumstances, including that it is reasonable in all the circumstances to make the disclosure and it is not made for personal gain.[160] Except where the disclosure relates to a failure of an exceptionally serious nature,[161] the worker must already have made disclosure to his/her employer or reasonably fear a detriment if s/he raises it with his/her employer or a prescribed regulator, or if there is no prescribed regulator, s/he must reasonably fear a cover-up by the employer.[162] Any term in an agreement or contract of employment which tries to gag a worker by imposing confidentiality will be void, provided the disclosure is otherwise within the ERA 1996.

6.88   Remedies are similar to those for ordinary unfair dismissal except that there is no ceiling on the compensatory award.[163–164] Interim relief may also be claimed if the ET application is lodged within seven days from the effective date of termination.[165]

Dismissal because of the transfer of an undertaking

6.89   It is automatically unfair to dismiss a worker due to the transfer of an undertaking unless the dismissal is for an economic, technical or organisational reason entailing changes in the workforce of either the transferor (the selling employer) or the transferee (the buying employer).[166] If so, the ET will decide the fairness of the dismissal in the usual way.

6.90   It is the employer who must prove that the dismissal was for an economic, technical or organisational reason. The ET should interpret this defence narrowly and dismissing workers in order to satisfy

---

160   Ibid s43G.
161   Ibid s43H.
162   Ibid s43G.
163–164   Public Interest Disclosure (Compensation) Regulations 1999 SI No 1548 reg 3(a). Available from the Stationery Office.
165   ERA 1996 ss128, 129.
166   TUPE Regs reg 8(1) and (2).

the buyer's requirements and obtain a good price is not an 'economic' reason which is acceptable. See paras 6.106 to 6.108 and below.

The Transfer of Undertakings Regulations

91 The Transfer of Undertakings (Protection of Employment) Regulations 1981[167] (the TUPE Regs) protect workers' rights on transfer of the business in which they are employed. Where there is a transfer to which the TUPE Regs apply, the new employer effectively stands in the shoes of the old employer, and workers maintain continuous service for the purpose of all statutory rights. The TUPE Regs also transfer the existing contractual terms and conditions, as well as any outstanding liabilities and rights.[168] The TUPE Regs apply to the whole of the UK.

92 The TUPE Regs were brought in to implement the European Business Transfers Directive.[169] This means they should be interpreted as far as possible in line with decisions of the ECJ under the Directive.[170] The law is constantly developing through decisions of the ECJ and UK courts. Developments need to be monitored. A new Transfer Directive has now been adopted and a new set of transfer regulations should be introduced in the UK by 17 July 2001.

What is the method of transfer?

3 Much of the case-law has concerned when the TUPE Regs apply and what form of transfer, as well as what kind of undertaking, is covered. Until the decision of the ECJ in *Süzen v Zehnacker Gebaudereinigung GmbH Krankenhausservice*,[171] it had seemed that most situations were covered. However, the *Süzen* decision has changed the emphasis, particularly in respect of labour-intensive undertakings, where a key factor will be how many employees have been transferred (see below). The following are broad guidelines taken from the case-law as

---

167 SI No 1794.
168 TUPE Regs reg 5.
169 No 77/187.
170 Where there is a conflict between the TUPE Regs and the Directive, similar rules apply as when UK legislation has not fully implemented EU law on sex discrimination. See chapter 3.
171 [1997] IRLR 255, ECJ.

to when TUPE will apply, but the particular facts of every case will be important.

6.94   A transfer may occur in many different ways,[172] although the most common means is by a straightforward sale of a business, eg, a restaurant chain under a brand name is sold by one company to another with little visible change. It may also take place by some other form of disposition such as granting a lease, franchise, contract or gift, even if ownership of physical property has not been transferred. Note that a share take-over is not a transfer, since ownership remains in the same legal person, ie, the company.

6.95   A transfer may take place as a result of a series of transactions[173] provided the business retains its identity, for example:

- a factory is transferred back from a lessee to the owner, who then sells it on to another company;[174]
- a NHS trust cleaning contract transfers between two successive contractors (the first contractor hands back the cleaning services at the end of its contract, which are immediately transferred on to the second contractor) if the undertaking is labour intensive;
- a local authority grant is removed from one voluntary sector organisation and given to another to provide the same services.[175]

Has an 'undertaking' been transferred?

6.96   The undertaking transferred must be a stable economic entity, but it need not own any tangible assets. For example, it could be a labour-only contract such as the provision of cleaning services, in-house catering or management of a shopping centre.[176] On the other hand, an 'entity' cannot be reduced to an activity alone (see para 6.101). Either the whole undertaking or a severable part of it must be transferred, eg, the transfer of one shop in a chain or contracting out a cleaning or catering service. Non-commercial ventures are covered,[177] eg, non-profit enterprises, voluntary organisations, free advice

---

172   TUPE Regs reg 3(2).
173   TUPE Regs reg 3(4)(a).
174   *P Bork International A/S v Foreningenaf Arbedjsledere i Danmark* [1989] IRLR 41, ECJ.
175   *Dr Sophie Redmond Stichting v Bartol and Others* [1992] IRLR 366, ECJ.
176   But see *Süzen* (n171 above) on necessary elements of labour-intensive transfers.
177   As from 30 August 1993, and arguably before that; *Dr Sophie Redmond Stichting v Bartol* (n175 above).

centres, charities, NHS trusts[178] and local education services.[179] It can include transfers between subsidiary companies within a corporate group.[180]

6.97   The undertaking must be transferred in a recognisable form from one employer to another. The overall test is whether the business in question retains its identity, this being indicated in particular by the continuation or resumption of its operation by the new employer.[181] An entity is 'an organised grouping of persons and assets facilitating the exercise of an economic activity which pursues a specific object- ive'.[182] The greater the similarity between the business run before and after the transfer, the more likely it is to satisfy this test. So, for example, a chocolate factory which is sold to be converted into a nightclub, would be a mere sale of assets and not of an undertaking. However, the business need not be identical before and afterwards in the way that it is run.

6.98   Case-law has suggested certain guidelines in deciding whether a business has retained enough of its identity on transfer to be covered by the TUPE Regs, although no single factor needs to be present in every case and an overall assessment must be made. In weighting factors, the type of undertaking must also be taken into account.[183] ETs must take a purposive approach, ie, remember that the purpose of the TUPE Regs and the Directive is to protect workers. Relevant factors will be:

– the type of business or undertaking concerned, eg, the under- taking may consist only of the right to provide services; the size of the undertaking is irrelevant;
– whether the business's tangible assets, such as buildings and equipment, are transferred. It is not essential that ownership (as opposed to use) of assets is transferred.[184] If the business solely comprises services, transfer of assets will be particularly unimportant;
– the value of the intangible assets, eg, goodwill, at the time of transfer and whether they are transferred. However, it is not

---

178 *Porter and Nanayakkara v Queen's Medical Centre (Nottingham University Hos- pital)* [1993] IRLR 486, HC.
179 *Kenny and Others v South Manchester College* [1993] IRLR 265, HC.
180 *Allen and Others v Amalgamated Construction Co Ltd* [2000] IRLR 119, ECJ.
181 *Spijkers v Gebroeders Benedik Abbatoir CV* [1986] CMLR 296, ECJ.
182 *Süzen* (n171, above).
183 *Allen and Others v Amalgamated Construction Co Ltd* [2000] IRLR 119, ECJ.
184 *Allen* (n183 above).

essential for there to be a transfer of tangible or intangible assets, what matters most is the transfer of responsibility for the operation of the undertaking;

- whether or not the majority of employees are taken over by the new employer;[185]
- whether customers are transferred and the degree of similarity between the activities carried on before and after the transfer;
- the period, if any, during which those activities are suspended.

It does not matter if the new employer intends to integrate the transferred undertaking into its own business, provided that immediately after transfer the entity carries on the same activities as before and so retains its identity.[186] To say otherwise would make the TUPE Regs largely ineffective as every business is likely to wish to integrate any new business it has acquired.

6.99   Applying these guidelines will not always be easy. For example, in one case[187] there was a transfer of an undertaking to provide medical services, even though the method of provision would change. The object of the undertaking remained the same, even though the method of achieving that object changed as medical science developed. By contrast, there was no transfer where an NHS trust hospital shop selling newspapers, magazines, confectionery and flowers was changed on transfer to a major chain convenience store with a much wider range of goods, longer opening hours and a more commercial outlook. The ET considered that the identity of the original shop had been replaced by an entirely new and different concept.[188] These examples are simply illustrative. It is essential to give detailed examination to all the facts.

Contracting out

6.100   It is now established[189] that the TUPE Regs can cover the contracting-out of services, often as a result of a compulsory competitive tendering

---

185   See comments below at para 6.101 regarding *Süzen* and contracting out.
186   *Farmer v Danzas (UK) Ltd* (1995) 518 IRLB 14, EAT.
187   *Porter and Nanayakkara v Queen's Medical Centre (Nottingham University Hospital)* [1993] IRLR 486, HC.
188   *(1) Matthieson (2) Cheyne v United News Shops Ltd*, EAT 554/94.
189   *Rask and Christensen v ISS Kantineservice A/S* [1993] IRLR 133, ECJ; *Dines and Others v (1) Initial Health Care Services Ltd (2) Pall Mall Services Group Ltd* [1994] IRLR 336; [1995] ICR 11, CA.

exercise in the public sector. Following the principles set out above, it is necessary to show that an economic entity has been transferred and continues in an identifiable form. This entails a comparison of the operation before and after transfer by reference to the above guidelines, although in contracting-out situations it is recognised that the contract is often purely for services and no tangible assets are transferred.

6.101   The ECJ in *Süzen* said that an 'entity' cannot be reduced to the activity it is carrying out. An entity's identity also emerges from other factors, eg, workforce, management structure, operating methods and resources. Therefore, in a labour intensive sector, where there is no transfer of significant tangible or intangible assets, there may be no transfer unless the new employer takes over a major part of the employees (in terms of numbers and skills).[190] However, the Court of Appeal has said the importance of *Süzen* has been overstated. It is still necessary to consider all the facts characterising the transaction in question. The failure to appoint any of the former employees does not point conclusively against a transfer. It is also relevant to consider why the employees were not taken on, eg, in a deliberate attempt to avoid the TUPE Regs.[191]

6.102   The undertaking must be a stable economic entity and not one where the contracted service is itself of limited duration, whoever is running it. For example, in one case the transfer of part of a building contract for the construction of a canteen was not covered by the TUPE Regs.[192] It is different where complete works projects are transferred.[192A]

6.103   Examples where the TUPE Regs have applied include:

–   the contracting-out of cleaning services by a bank which had previously employed one cleaner to do the work;[193]
–   the transfer of hospital cleaning services from one contractor at the end of its contract to another;[194]

190 *Süzen* (n171, above). Allen (n183 above).
191 *ECM (Vehicle Delivery Service) v Cox* [1999] IRLR 559, CA.
192 *Ledernes Hovedorganisation, acting on behalf of Ole Rygaard v Dansk Arbejdsgiver-forening, acting on behalf of Stro Molle Akustik A/S* [1996] IRLR 51, ECJ. This principle should not be applied too widely: *BSG Property Services v Tuck* [1996] IRLR 134, EAT.
192A Allen (n183 above).
193 *Schmidt v Spar-und Leihkasse der fruheren Amter Bordesholm, Kiel und Kronshagen* [1994] IRLR 302, ECJ.
194 *Dines and Others v (1) Initial Health Care Services Ltd (2) Pall Mall Services Group Ltd* (n189 above).

- a college's termination of a catering contract in order to provide its own catering service;[195]
- the contracting-out to a college of prison education previously provided by the local education authority;[196]
- the transfer of a subsidy or grant by a public body, eg, a local authority, from one advice agency to another with similar aims.[197]

The National Health Service and Community Care Act 1990 governs transfers from local health authorities to NHS trusts.[198] The Education Reform Act 1988 covers transfers to grant-maintained or opted-out schools.

Which workers are protected?

6.104   The TUPE Regs protect workers who are employed with the transferor immediately before,[199] ie, at the moment of,[200] the transfer. Workers dismissed in advance of the transfer but for a connected reason are deemed to be employed immediately before the transfer.[201]

6.105   Where part of an undertaking is transferred, the TUPE Regs protect only those workers 'assigned' to that part.[202] A worker may be assigned to the transferred part even though s/he carried out duties for other parts of the original employer's business.[203] An ET must look at all the facts, such as time spent in each part, value given, and allocation of costs and contractual terms.

Dismissal due to the transfer

6.106   It is automatically unfair to dismiss a worker for a reason connected with the transfer, unless the reason is for an economic, technical

---

195   *Campion-Hall v (1) Wain (2) Gardner Merchant Ltd* (1996) 561 *IDS Brief* 5, EAT.

196   *Kenny and Anor v South Manchester College* [1993] ICR 934; [1993] IRLR 265, HC.

197   *Dr Sophie Redmond Stichting v Bartol and Others* (n175 above).

198   See also *Gale v Northern General Hospital NHS Trust* [1994] IRLR 292, CA.

199   TUPE Regs reg 5(3).

200   *Secretary of State for Employment v Spence and Others* [1986] ICR 651; [1986] IRLR 248, CA.

201   *Litster v Forth Dry Dock and Engineering Co Ltd* [1989] ICR 341; [1989] IRLR 161, HL.

202   *Botzen and Others v Rotterdamsche Droogdok Maatschappij BV* [1986] 2 CMLR 50, ECJ.

203   *Duncan Webb Offset (Maidstone) Ltd v Cooper and Others* [1995] IRLR 633, EAT; *Buchanan-Smith v Schleicher and Co International Ltd* (1996) 561 *IDS Brief* 9, EAT.

or organisational (ETO) reason entailing changes in the workforce.[204] Case-law is divided as to whether an ETO reason can exist once the reason is proved to be connected with the transfer.[204A] If there is an ETO situation the ordinary principles to determine unfair dismissal claims will apply as the reason for dismissal is treated as a dismissal for some other substantial reason. To claim ordinary or automatic unfair dismissal, the worker must be an employee with one year's service[205] and have been dismissed in law. This includes constructive dismissal and failure to renew a fixed-term contract.[206]

6.107   It is a question of fact whether a dismissal is connected with a transfer. There is a rebuttable presumption that dismissals at the time of a transfer are connected with it, but a dismissal may also be connected with it if it takes place in advance or some time afterwards. There is no fixed time period afterwards within which a dismissal will be deemed 'connected'.

6.108   To avoid an automatically unfair dismissal, any 'economic' reason must relate to the conduct of the business itself and not just to secure an enhanced sale price.[207] A contracting-out situation can be ambiguous and will depend on the facts of the case. For example, where it is a condition of the contract that a new contractor reduces the contract price by reducing staff, what is the reason for the dismissals of the redundant staff ? Is it simply a cost saving relating to the conduct of the business which would have happened whether or not there was a transfer, or is it just a way to reduce the cost of the contract to prospective bidders?[208] The main restriction on the ETO exception is the qualification that it must entail changes in the workforce. This means the employer cannot simply change a worker's contractual terms, eg, to harmonise with the existing workforce, but there must

204 TUPE Regs reg 8(1) and (2).
204A *Kerry Foods Ltd v Creber and Others* [2000] IRLR 10, EAT; *Whitehouse v Chas A Blatchford & Sons Ltd* [1999] IRLR 492, CA; *Warner v Adnet Ltd* [1998] IRLR 394, CA.
205 Collective Redundancies and Transfer of Undertakings (Protection of Employment) (Amendment) Regulations 1995 SI No 2587. See also *MRS Environmental Services Ltd v Marsh and Another* (1996) 571 *IDS Brief* 2.
206 See para 6.34 for the rights of workers on temporary contracts.
207 *Wheeler v (1) Patel (2) J Golding Group of Companies* [1987] IRLR 211; [1987] ICR 631, EAT; *Gateway Hotels Ltd v Stewart and Others* [1988] IRLR 287, EAT. Although see *Whitehouse and Kerry* (n204A above).
208 See *Whitehouse v Chas A Blatchford & Sons Ltd* [1999] IRLR 493, CA, which is a strange interpretation of a factual situation–see IRLR commentary at p450. See also several confusing cases relating to the interrelationship between regulations 8(1) and (2) including *Kerry* (n204A above).

be a change in the overall numbers of the workforce or a change in job functions.[209]

The effect of a transfer

6.109 Where the TUPE Regs apply, the new employer stands in the shoes of the old employer for most purposes. The contractual terms and conditions are transferred[210] as are all the transferor's rights, powers, duties and liabilities under or in connection with the contract.[211] This would include wages owed, liability for discrimination by the former employer[212] and possibly tortious liability, eg, for negligence leading to personal injury.[213] It seems it also covers liability for a protective award due to a transferor's failure to consult on collective redundancies.[213A] It probably also transfers acquired continuous service for statutory employment rights.[214]

6.110 Occupational pension schemes are excluded from the TUPE Regs in so far as they cover old age, invalidity or survivors' benefits.[215] This includes benefits of early retirement under the NHS pension scheme.[216] Although accrued pension rights should be preserved,[217] there is probably no entitlement to continued membership or contributions.[218] The precise legal position regarding transfer of pensions is still being tested and case-law should be watched.

6.111 If the TUPE Regs apply to a particular worker, s/he must claim for any transferred rights or unfair dismissal against the transferee, even if s/he never started work for the new employer and was dismissed in advance of the transfer but for a connected reason.[219] However, if dismissal by the transferor was for an ETO reason, the worker

209 *Berriman v Delabole Slate Ltd* [1984] IRLR 394, CA.
210 TUPE Regs reg 5(1).
211 Ibid reg 5(2).
212 *DJM International Ltd v Nicholas* [1996] IRLR 76, EAT.
213 *Secretary of State for Employment v Spence and Others* (n200 above); *Bernadone v Pall Mall Services Group* [1999] IRLR 617, HL.
213A See paras 2.20–2.25. *Kerry Foods Ltd v Creber and Others* (n204A above).
214 Although this is usually preserved in any event by ERA 1996 s218(2).
215 TUPE Regs reg 7(2). See also art 3 of the Directive.
216 *Frankling v PBS Public Sector Ltd* [1999] IRLR 212.
217 Art 3(3) of the Directive.
218 *Walden Engineering Co Ltd v Warrener* [1993] IRLR 420, EAT; *Adams and Others v Lancashire CC and BET Catering Services Ltd* [1997] IRLR 436, CA.
219 *Stirling District Council v Allan and Others* [1995] IRLR 301, Court of Session.

may have to sue the transferor.[219A] If in doubt whether the TUPE Regs apply or as to the transferor's reason for dismissal, it may be safest to claim in the alternative against the old employer and the apparent transferee.

Changing the terms and conditions

6.112 The TUPE Regs preserve the contractual terms and conditions and prohibit changes due to the transfer alone. It seems that an employer's attempt to impose new terms and conditions, even if s/he has secured the workers' agreement (expressly or by affirmation) will be ineffective if the change is due to the transfer. So, for example, a worker retained by the new employer ostensibly on changed terms and conditions could subsequently insist on the previous terms still applying.[219B] However, if the worker is dismissed by the transferor and offered new terms and conditions by the transferee, which s/he accepts, the new terms and conditions will apply. His or her only remedy will be any claim regarding the dismissal (see paras 6.106–6.108).[220]

6.113 Workers still need to be careful. This protection exists only if the reason for the change of terms is the transfer. This is very likely if the change occurs at the time of the transfer, but a subsequent change may be harder to resist. A worker may be better off, legally and practically, to remain with a new employer and assert the old terms and conditions, rather than resign or refuse to transfer[221] and claim constructive dismissal. Although under the TUPE Regs, a worker may resign and claim constructive dismissal where a substantial change is made to his/her working conditions to his/her detriment,[222] the normal fairness test will apply unless automatic unfairness can be proved. For this it must be shown that the constructive dismissal was connected with the transfer, but that it was not for an ETO reason which entailed changes in the workforce.[223]

219A *Kerry Foods Ltd v Creber and Others* (n204A above).
219B *Foreningen A F Arbejdsledere i Danmark v Daddy's Dance Hall A/S* [1988] IRLR 315, ECJ; *Credit Suisse First Boston (Europe) Ltd v Lister* [1998] IRLR 700, CA.
220 *Wilson and Others v St Helens BC; British Fuels Ltd v Baxendale & Meade* [1998] IRLR 706, HL; *Ministry of Defence v Clutterbuck and Others* (2000) 632 IRLB 9, EAT.
221 *Merckx and Anor v Ford Motors* [1996] IRLR 467, ECJ.
222 TUPE Regs reg 5(5). This wording is different to the usual constructive dismissal test at para 6.41, but probably means the same.
223 See above on dismissal connected with the transfer.

Transfer of undertakings regulations: Key points

– Many situations are now covered by the TUPE Regs and a purposive approach should be adopted.
– The mechanism of the transfer does not matter, provided there
  is a change of legal person responsible for running the undertaking, who acts as employer.
– The key test is whether an identifiable and stable economic
  entity has been transferred. This entails a comparison of the
  undertaking immediately before and after the transfer.
– The TUPE Regs can cover contracting-out of services; the services reverting in-house; and the transfer of the service between
  two successive contractors.
– For labour-intensive undertakings, a key factor will be whether
  the majority of employees are transferred.
– Protected workers are those who are employed immediately
  before the transfer or who are dismissed in advance but in
  connection with the transfer, unless their dismissal was for an
  ETO reason entailing changes in the workforce.
– Where part of an undertaking is transferred, a worker must
  have been assigned to that part, even if s/he has carried out
  some duties for non-transferred parts.
– It is automatically unfair to dismiss (or constructively dismiss)
  a worker in connection with the transfer except for an ETO
  reason entailing changes in the workforce, in which case the
  ordinary test of fairness will apply. The normal eligibility rules
  for claiming unfair dismissal apply.
– Where a worker is covered, rights, liabilities and contractual
  terms transfer, eg, wages owed, liability for previous discriminatory acts and continuous service, but probably excluding continuing membership of occupational pension schemes.
– For consultation on transfers, see para 2.20.

General guide to useful evidence

– Evidence comparing the nature of the undertaking before and
  after the transfer by reference to factors such as location, staff,
  customers, product and service.
– Legal and other documents relating to the transfer and any
  related transfers of assets and staff.

Reasons for dismissal

For complete chapter contents, see overleaf

Capability or qualification dismissals

7.1   An employer may claim that a dismissal related to the capability or qualifications of the worker for performing work of the kind s/he was employed to do.[1] The statutory definition of 'capability' is 'capability assessed by reference to skill, aptitude, health or any other physical or mental quality'.[2] 'Qualification' means 'any degree, diploma or other academic, technical or professional qualification relevant to the position which the employee held'.[3]

Skill dismissals

7.2   A skill dismissal is one that is due to the worker's inability to perform the job to the standard expected by the employer. It includes situations where that standard is higher than the norm in the industry.[4]

The reasonableness test: ERA 1996 s98(4)

7.3   It is important to note that the employer need not prove in the ET that the worker actually was incompetent. The employer need show only that s/he genuinely and reasonably believed that the worker was incompetent. The test is as follows.

- Did the employer honestly believe that the worker was incompetent or unsuitable for the job?
- If so, was such belief held on reasonable grounds?
- In forming such a belief, did the employer carry out a proper and adequate investigation? In most cases, this would include giving the worker an opportunity to answer the criticisms.[5]

Other factors are relevant to the fairness of the dismissal. An ET usually expects the employer to have taken steps to remedy the worker's shortcoming before dismissing, eg, by offering support and/or supervision, or retraining, setting targets and monitoring progress. The extent of assistance that should have been offered depends on the employer's administrative resources and size of enterprise.

7.4   It is rarely fair to dismiss a worker on the basis of one act of

1 ERA 1996 s98(2)(a).
2 Ibid s98(3)(a).
3 Ibid s98(3)(b).
4 *Brown v Hall Advertising* [1978] IRLR 246, EAT.
5 *McPhie and McDermott v Wimpey Waste Management* [1981] IRLR 316, EAT.

incompetence. The exception is where the consequences are so serious that to continue to employ the worker would be too risky and dangerous, eg, when a mistake is made by an airline pilot or a coach driver.[6] In this type of situation, dismissal without retraining or being given the chance to improve would usually be fair.

.5   The ET may also take into account whether the employer had any alternative vacancy which could have been offered to the worker prior to dismissal. An employer will not be expected to create a vacancy or new job for the worker. The failure to offer alternative employment is not an overriding factor in capability dismissals but it is a relevant consideration, particularly where a large employer had appropriate vacancies which were not offered to the worker.

Aptitude and mental quality dismissals

.6   An 'aptitude' dismissal may be because a worker is inflexible at work or is difficult or disruptive or not prepared to adapt.[7] 'Mental quality' would include a worker's lack of drive or having a personality which has a detrimental effect on colleagues' work or on customers.[8] If a worker has not satisfied the necessary standards required by the employer due to carelessness, negligence or idleness, this is more appropriately dealt with as misconduct rather than incapability.[9]

The reasonableness test: ERA 1996 s98(4)

7   The employer must show that the worker's inflexibility or other mental quality was detrimental to the business. Prior to dismissal, the employer should have given sufficient and adequate warnings detailing the alleged shortcomings and the worker ought to have been provided with a reasonable opportunity to improve. As usual, the employer's size and administrative resources will be relevant in judging the adequacy of the procedures followed.

Sickness, injury and other health dismissals

An employer who dismisses a worker for ill-health or sickness

6 *Alidair Ltd v Taylor* [1978] IRLR 82; [1978] ICR 455, CA.
7 *Abernethy v Mott, Hay and Anderson* [1974] ICR 323; [1974] IRLR 213, CA.
8 *Bristow v ILEA* (1979) EAT 602/79.
9 *Sutton and Gates Ltd v Boxall* [1978] IRLR 486.

absences may be dismissing on grounds of capability or conduct.[10] It will be a dismissal for conduct if the employer believes that the worker is not ill but is using sickness as an excuse not to work. Since different considerations will be relevant to the fairness of dismissing for conduct, it needs to be established what was the principal reason for dismissal. This section deals with capability. Note that in some circumstances, a worker may gain protection from the Disability Discrimination Act 1995 (see below).

7.9   There are two distinct forms of absence from work as a result of ill-health:

1) several intermittent absences, not necessarily for the same reason; and
2) a prolonged continuous absence due to a single medical condition.

The proper steps for an employer to take, prior to dismissing a worker, depend on whether the ill-health was intermittent or continuous. In respect of both situations, it is necessary for the employer to have regard to the whole history of employment and take into account a range of factors such as the nature of the illness, the length of absences, the likelihood of the illness recurring, the need of the employer to have the worker's work done, and the impact on others of the worker's absence.[11]

Intermittent absences

7.10   Before dismissing, the employer must have made it clear to the worker what level of attendance was expected. If the employer is dissatisfied with the worker's attendance record, s/he should conduct a fair review of the record and give the worker an opportunity to explain the reason for the various absences.[12] Any warning after the review should make it clear that the worker may be dismissed if there is no improvement. If there is no satisfactory improvement following a warning, dismissal will usually be fair.[13]

7.11   An employer also ought to take into account the following factors:

– the length of absences and periods of good health;
– the likelihood of future absences;

10 See para 7.34 below.
11 *Lyncock v Cereal Packaging* [1988] IRLR 510.
12 *Rolls-Royce v Walpole* [1980] IRLR 343, EAT.
13 *International Sports Co v Thompson* [1980] IRLR 340, EAT.

- the nature of the worker's job and the effect of absences;
- the consistent application of the employer's absenteeism policy;[14]
- any dismissal ought to be handled in a sympathetic, understanding and compassionate manner.[15]

A single period of prolonged absence

.12 The basic question is whether in all the circumstances the employer could be expected to wait any longer and, if so, how much longer.[16] Each case depends on its own facts and an employer cannot hold rigidly to a predetermined period of sickness after which any worker may be dismissed.

.13 An ET would expect the employer to have found out the true medical position and to have consulted with the worker before making a decision. A medical report on the implications and likely length of illness should generally be obtained from the worker's GP or a company doctor or independent consultant. The employer should be willing to consider a report from the worker's own GP or specialist as well as from a company doctor. Whereas the latter may be more familiar with working conditions, the former may be better placed to judge the worker's health.

.14 The employer must get the worker's consent to obtaining a medical report. If a worker refuses to see a company doctor or allow any medical report, s/he increases the risk of being fairly dismissed. The worker is entitled to see the report before it is sent to the employer and to make amendments with the doctor's consent. If the doctor does not consent, the worker has the right to attach a personal statement to the report.[17]

.5 Once the employer has the report, a meeting should be arranged to discuss its contents with the worker. There will be very few circumstances where an employer can justify a failure to discuss the situation with the worker and it would have to be an utterly pointless exercise.[18] In general, the employer must take such steps as are sensible in the circumstances to discuss the matter and become informed of the true medical position.[19] Consultation will often throw new light

---

14 Inconsistency may also indicate discrimination.
15 *Lyncock v Cereal Packaging* [1988] IRLR 510; ICR 670, EAT.
16 *Spencer v Paragon Wallpapers* [1976] IRLR 373, EAT.
17 Access to Medical Reports Act 1988.
18 *Polkey v AE Dayton Services* [1987] IRLR 503; [1988] ICR 142, HL.
19 *East Lindsey DC v Daubney* [1977] IRLR 181; ICR 566, EAT.

on the problem, bringing up facts and circumstances of which the employer was unaware.[20]

7.16   The employer's decision ought to be based on the following factors:

- the nature and likely duration of the illness;
- the need for the worker to do the job for which s/he was employed and the difficulty of covering his/her absence. The more skilful and specialist the worker, the more vulnerable s/he is to being fairly dismissed after a relatively short absence;
- the possibility of varying the worker's contractual duties. An employer will not be expected to create an alternative position that did not already exist nor to go to great lengths to accommodate the worker.[21] However, a large employer may be expected to offer any available vacancy which would suit the worker.

There is rarely any useful purpose served by issuing a warning to a worker who is long-term sick. The issue relates to the worker's capability, not conduct, and the consequence of a warning may be counter-productive.[22]

7.17   Sometimes the nature of the illness or injury is such that a worker may never be able to perform his/her contractual duties again or any performance would be radically different from what s/he and the employer envisaged at the outset. If this happens, the contract of employment may be 'frustrated' and just come to an end (see para 6.50 above). Since the employer will not have actually dismissed the worker, the worker cannot claim unfair dismissal.[23] The courts are extremely reluctant to say that an employment contract has ended in this way because of the dire consequences for the worker.

7.18   A worker suffering from long-term ill-health may succeed in a claim under the DDA 1995, where s/he would have failed in an unfair dismissal claim. The DDA 1995 places greater obligations on the employer, eg, to modify the worker's duties or actively find alternative employment.

---

20   Ibid.
21   *Garricks (Caterers) v Nolan* [1980] IRLR 259, EAT.
22   *Spencer v Paragon Wallpapers* [1976] IRLR 373, EAT.
23   See paras 6.35–6.50 above on types of dismissal under the ERA 1996.

Dismissals due to other physical quality

7.19 An 'other physical quality' would include an injury or loss of faculty which affected the worker's ability to perform the job.[24] Although outside the scope of this book, note that an injury sustained at work may give rise to a personal injury claim against the employer, including compensation for loss of earnings. Workers may also gain protection from the DDA.[25]

The reasonableness test: ERA 1996 s98(4)

7.20 The employer will usually be able to justify dismissal if the injury is such that it is impossible or dangerous for the worker to perform his/ her job. Before dismissal, the employer should consult the worker concerning the injury and its consequences for future employment. It may be possible for the worker to retrain or use aids to overcome the loss of faculty. An employer should offer any suitable alternative vacancy.

Qualification dismissals

7.21 A qualification dismissal is one where a worker loses a qualification or fails to obtain a qualification which was a condition of his/her employment. A common example is disqualification from driving when having a licence is a necessary requirement of the job. This requirement need not be expressly stated in the contract where the job clearly entails driving duties.[26] An employer may also require a qualification during the worker's employment which the worker does not possess and is unable or unlikely to acquire. An employer's insistence on certain qualifications may be indirect discrimination contrary to the RRA 1976 or SDA 1975.[27]

The reasonableness test: ERA 1996 s98(4)

7.22 Where a worker loses a qualification which s/he is required to have under his/her contract or which is necessary for the job, it may be fair to dismiss. The employer would not usually be expected to create an alternative job, but s/he should make an effort appropriate to the size

---

24 See chapter 13 below on disability.
25 See chapter 13.
26 *Tayside RC v McIntosh* [1982] IRLR 272, EAT.
27 See paras 9.51 onwards.

and administrative resources of the enterprise and the availability of vacancies.

7.23   An employer may require new qualifications because of the introduction of new technology or a different mode of operation. It may be fair to dismiss a worker who fails to acquire the new qualification if the employer can justify the need for it. The employer must also act reasonably in the introduction of the requirement, eg, by offering retraining. Failure to give a worker a fair and proper opportunity to satisfy the new requirement will make the dismissal unfair.[28]

Capability or qualification dismissals: Key points

- Capability dismissals cover sickness and injury dismissals as well as dismissals relating to the ability to do a job.
- Qualification dismissals relate to relevant qualifications to do the job which may be academic, technical or professional.
- Sickness and injury dismissals fall into two categories, the long-term sickness case and intermittent absence from work. The employer has to satisfy different requirements depending on the category.
- It is a requirement with long-term sickness/injury dismissals for the employer to obtain a medical report (to find out the nature and likely duration of the illness/injury) and to discuss this report with the worker before dismissing. See also the adjustments suggested under the DDA 1995.
- With sickness and injury dismissals, the employer will be able to dismiss fairly only if s/he can demonstrate that it is necessary in the best interest of the business.
- Only in exceptional cases will a dismissal for a first act of incompetence be fair. The exceptions concern workers who are responsible for the safety of members of the public such as airline pilots or bus drivers.

General guide to useful evidence

- With sickness dismissals, a copy of all the medical reports. If the employer did not rely on a medical report, get a report from the worker's GP for use at the ET hearing.

28 *Evans v Bury Football Club* (1981) EAT 185/81.

- Get details of the sickness record of other workers. This might be evidenced by the SSP records. If other workers have had more time off, then it is likely to be important and would show inequitable treatment (or even unlawful discrimination).
- If the dismissal is due to incompetence, get information on the consequences of the incompetence and also try to discover whether any other workers have committed similar acts and whether they were dismissed.

Conduct dismissals

7.24 Unlike with capability and qualification dismissals, there is no statutory definition of conduct dismissals. Perhaps surprisingly, parliament and the courts have made no serious attempt to define exhaustively what forms of misconduct may justify dismissal. Nevertheless, there are a number of activities which are recognised as potential misconduct and are usually listed in the disciplinary procedure if there is a written contract of employment:

- theft or other dishonesty;
- violence and fighting;
- unauthorised absenteeism[29] or lateness;
- disobedience;
- being under the influence of alcohol or drugs;[30]
- threatening or abusive language;
- behaviour undermining the implied term of fidelity and good faith.

Some acts of misconduct amount to 'gross misconduct'. The main relevance of this concept is that an employer dismissing for gross misconduct need not give notice under the contract.[31] Unfair dismissal is a separate issue. It may be fair or unfair to dismiss a worker for gross misconduct. However, as gross misconduct involves more serious forms of misconduct, it is more likely to be fair to dismiss for a single act than for a single act of less serious misconduct. It has to be recognised that conduct outside working hours might give rise to a

29 This may be a capability issue; see para 7.8 above on health.
30 Ibid.
31 See wrongful dismissal, summary dismissal and gross misconduct, para 1.27 above.

breach of the employment contract; for example, a cashier shoplifting on his/her day off is going to be in breach of the implied term of trust and confidence.[32]

Theft and other dishonesty

7.25   It is imperative to understand the difference between the criminal law and unfair dismissal law. Many workers feel that the ET is the arena for them to clear their name. Unfortunately the real issue is not whether the worker actually committed the offence but whether, in the circumstances, it was reasonable for the employer to dismiss. An ET may well find that a worker was fairly dismissed for suspected theft, even though by the time of the ET hearing s/he has been acquitted. What counts is whether the employer, at the time of dismissal and having carried out reasonable investigations, genuinely and reasonably believed that the worker committed the theft.[33] Equally, it does not automatically justify a dismissal that a worker has been charged with a criminal offence.

7.26   A worker may be dismissed for an act of dishonesty, whether at work or outside work[34] and against the employer, a fellow worker or the public. Dishonesty dismissals often relate to offences peculiar to the working environment such as borrowing money without authorisation, fraudulent expense claims,[35] unauthorised use of the employer's property[36] and clocking offences.[37]

The reasonableness test: ERA 1996 s98(4)

7.27   In order to dismiss for dishonesty fairly, the employer must:

- genuinely believe that the worker was dishonest;
- hold that belief on reasonable grounds; and
- have carried out proper and adequate investigations.[38]

If the employer is unable to ascertain which of a group of workers

---

32   *Thomson v Alloa Motor Co Ltd* [1983] IRLR 403.
33   *British Home Stores v Burchell* [1978] IRLR 379; [1980] ICR 303, EAT. See also below on the reasonableness test.
34   *Singh v London Country Bus Services* [1976] IRLR 176, EAT.
35   *John Lewis and Co v Smith* (1981) EAT 289/81.
36   *Bartholemew v Post Office Telecommunications* (1981) EAT 53/81.
37   *Engineering Services v Harrison* (1977) EAT 735/77.
38   *British Home Stores v Burchell* (n33 above); *Weddel and Co v Tepper* [1980] ICR 286; [1980] IRLR 96, CA.

was guilty of the dishonesty, the employer may fairly dismiss all of them solely on reasonable suspicion, provided that:

- after proper investigation, the employer tries and is unable to identify which worker is guilty;
- the employer genuinely believes, on reasonable grounds, that one or more of the group is guilty; and
- any member of the group was capable of having carried out the dishonest act.[39]

It will be inequitable and unfair to dismiss only some members of the group to which the employer has narrowed things down.

7.28   It is very important that the employer follows a fair procedure and investigates properly. The degree of appropriate investigation depends on a number of factors including the complexity of the case,[40] the nature of the offence, the size and administrative resources of the employer[41] and whether the worker confessed to the misconduct[42] or was caught red-handed.[43]

7.29   The employer's disciplinary procedure should be followed in conducting the investigation, or in the absence of a procedure, what the ET deems a fair procedure in order to ensure justice. Regard will be had to the ACAS code of practice in the absence of a procedure. The disciplinary procedure should state what acts of misconduct are considered by the employer to be gross misconduct, the various stages of the procedure itself, the right to be represented and the right of appeal against any decision reached.[44] Furthermore, it is a requirement of the rules of natural justice that a worker knows the allegations made against him/her, that s/he has an opportunity to answer those allegations fully and that the conduct of the investigation and internal hearings is in good faith.[45] A failure to follow a contractual disciplinary procedure will often, but not necessarily, result in a finding of unfair dismissal.[46]

39 *Monie v Coral Racing* [1980] IRLR 464; [1981] ICR 109, CA; *Whitbread and Co v Thomas* [1988] IRLR 43; ICR 135, EAT.
40 *British Home Stores v Burchell* (n33 above).
41 ERA 1996 s98(4).
42 *Parker v Clifford Dunn* [1979] ICR 463; [1979] IRLR 56, EAT.
43 *Scottish Special Housing Association v Linnen* [1979] IRLR 265, EAT.
44 Employment Protection Code of Practice (Disciplinary Practice and Procedures) 1977.
45 *Khanum v Mid-Glamorgan Area Health Authority* [1978] IRLR 215; [1979] ICR 40, EAT.
46 *Stoker v Lancashire CC* [1992] IRLR 75; *Westminster CC v Cabaj* [1996] IRLR 399, CA.

7.30   Since dishonesty is gross misconduct, dismissal for a single act is usually justified and warnings are not usually appropriate. It is important to emphasise long service and, if relevant, the extent of the dishonesty, on the worker's behalf. The ET cannot simply consider whether the investigation was fair. It must also consider whether it was reasonable to dismiss in all the circumstances.[46A] It may not be fair to dismiss a worker for dishonesty taking place outside work, particularly if it does not bear on the work situation. Similarly, in relation to any other criminal acts or convictions occurring off work premises, whether a dismissal is fair will depend on a number of factors, such as adverse publicity, implications for the work-place, relevance to the job and whether the conduct outside work could be said to breach the implied term of trust and confidence (see above).[47]

Violence or fighting dismissals

7.31   Violence or fighting usually constitutes gross misconduct even if the employer's disciplinary procedure does not explicitly describe it as such.[48] Nevertheless, this does not mean that a dismissal for violence is automatically fair. An employer must carry out an investigation and take into account all relevant matters,[49] eg, the nature and circumstances of the violence, whether it was in public view, the proximity to machinery or dangerous objects,[50] the status of the workers, the length of service[51] and the nature of any provocation.

7.32   The employer should speak to the parties involved and any witnesses. If the employer cannot ascertain who was responsible for the violence, the employer may dismiss all concerned if it was serious.[52] It will not usually help a worker who participated in fighting to say that another worker initiated it.

7.33   An employer should be consistent. Departing from a previous course of action without warning, eg, dismissing a worker for an offence for which previous workers have not been dismissed, will usually make the dismissal unfair.[53]

46A *Wilson v Ethicon Ltd* [2000] IRLR 4, EAT.
  47 See also para 11.90 below on offences affecting gay men which have no heterosexual equivalent.
  48 *CA Parsons and Co v McLoughlin* [1978] IRLR 65, EAT.
  49 *Taylor v Parsons Peebles* [1981] IRLR 119, EAT.
  50 *Greenwood v HJ Heinz and Co* (1977) EAT 199/77.
  51 *LB Ealing v Goodwin* (1979) EAT 121/79.
  52 *Monie v Coral Racing* [1980] IRLR 464, CA.
  53 *Post Office v Fennell* [1981] IRLR 221, CA.

Dismissals for unauthorised absences or lateness

7.34   Dismissals for absenteeism may relate to capability and ill-health.[54] Conduct absenteeism is where a worker is absent without authority and it is usually a form of bad time-keeping. A common form of unauthorised absenteeism is where a worker returns late from a holiday.

General absenteeism

7.35   An employer is rarely entitled to dismiss for a single occasion of lateness or absenteeism. The usual situation is when a worker is frequently late or absent from work. Some large employers set out in the contract of employment an 'expected level of attendance' below which a worker will be dismissed. However, it is not necessarily fair to dismiss a worker who falls below this level. The employer should fairly review the worker's attendance record and the reasons for the absences. Appropriate warnings should be given after the worker has had the opportunity to explain. If there is no improvement, the worker's subsequent dismissal is likely to be fair.[55]

7.36   As well as fairness in procedures, the ET will take into account:

- the worker's age, length of service and performance;
- the likelihood of an improvement in attendance;
- the effect of absences on the business;[56]
- the known circumstances of the absence, eg, a temporary domestic problem.[57]

Even if the reason given for the absences is sickness, the employer does not necessarily have to obtain a medical report, particularly if there is no link between the various absences.

Late return from holiday

7.37   Where an employer has warned the worker in advance that failure to return from holiday on the due date will be treated as gross misconduct, it will be easier to justify a dismissal. Unless the worker can put forward compelling reasons why s/he should not be dismissed,

54 See para 7.8 above.
55 *International Sports Co v Thompson* [1980] IRLR 340, EAT.
56 See ACAS Advisory Handbook *Discipline at Work* (1987) on the importance of these considerations.
57 *Post Office v Stones* (1980) EAT 390/80.

dismissal will be fair.[58] Usually the employer should wait until the worker comes back to work or invite an explanation by post. However, if there is a significant delay and no obligation under the contract of employment to consult prior to dismissal, the employer may be able to dismiss the worker before his/her return to work, although the ET would expect some efforts by the employer to get an explanation.[59]

7.38 Sometimes an employer informs the worker that if s/he returns late from holiday, s/he will be taken to have dismissed him/herself. Legally this is not recognised as a resignation or mutual termination. The worker cannot be deprived of the right to claim unfair dismissal in this way.[60]

Disobedience

7.39 This type of dismissal usually arises when a worker refuses to obey an order or instruction of the employer. The instruction may or may not be one with which the worker is required to comply under the contract of employment.

The reasonableness test: ERA 1996 s98(4)

7.40 The two key considerations are: (a) the nature of the employer's instruction, and (b) the worker's reason for refusal to comply.

7.41 A worker is entitled to refuse any unlawful,[61] unreasonable or dangerous instruction. Although the starting point is whether the worker is obliged to comply with the instruction under the employment contract, this does not necessarily determine whether a refusal is reasonable.[62] It may be unfair to dismiss a worker who refuses to obey a contractual instruction or fair to dismiss a worker who refuses to obey a non-contractual order. A worker who fails to co-operate with an employer's request to do non-contractual overtime,[63] to adapt to new technology[64] or otherwise go along with a reorganisation[65] will often be found to have acted unreasonably and to be fairly dismissed.

7.42 Where a worker is required to comply with a contractual term

58 *Rampart Engineering v Henderson* (1981) EAT 235/81.
59 *London Transport Executive v Clarke* [1981] ICR 355; [1981] IRLR 166, CA.
60 See para 6.35 above on what constitutes dismissal under the ERA 1996.
61 *Morrish v Henlys (Folkestone)* [1973] 2 All ER 137; [1973] ICR 482, NIRC.
62 *Redbridge LBC v Fishman* [1978] IRLR 69; [1978] ICR 569, EAT.
63 *Horrigan v Lewisham LBC* [1978] ICR 15, EAT.
64 *Cresswell v Board of Inland Revenue* [1984] 2 All ER 713; [1984] IRLR 190, Ch D.
65 *Ellis v Brighton Co-operative Society* [1976] IRLR 419, EAT.

which has not previously been operated and which will cause inconvenience or hardship, the employer must give reasonable advance notice. If no notice is given, a worker may be entitled to refuse to comply with the instruction in the short term[66] on this ground alone.

7.43 The ET must consider also the worker's reason for refusing to obey the instruction and it should weigh up the competing interests and take into consideration the nature of the contractual relationship between the employer and worker generally. There may be good reason for the worker's refusal, eg, a pregnant woman refusing to work close to a VDU screen, a risk to the worker's safety in handling money or a risk of civil liability.[67]

Dependency on drugs or alcohol or possession of drugs

.44 Taking or possessing drugs at work, and sometimes out of work, tends to be treated as gross misconduct. Drinking at work may be treated as misconduct depending on the circumstances and what the contract says. Dependency on drugs or alcohol is now more likely to be treated by an enlightened employer as a medical condition[68] and will not be referred to as an act of misconduct in the disciplinary procedure. The advantage of treating this as a health issue is that the requirements relating to capability dismissals apply. These are more conducive to helping the worker, as medical reports will be obtained and appropriate treatment will be encouraged.

Dependency on alcohol or drugs

.45 The employer must have a genuine and reasonable belief, based on proper and adequate investigation, that the worker is dependent. The worker should be given the chance to answer the allegations and to obtain a medical or specialist report if s/he wishes, particularly if the employer treats it as a sickness issue.

.46 In deciding whether to dismiss, the following factors will be relevant:

– whether the contract of employment or disciplinary procedure treats alcohol/drug dependency as a matter of conduct or capability;

---

66 *McAndrew v Prestwick Circuits* [1988] IRLR 514, EAT.
67 *UCATT v Brain* [1981] ICR 542.
68 See above on capability/health dismissals and *Strathclyde RC v Syme* (1979) EAT 233/79.

- whether the worker is responsible for the safety of others, eg, a coach driver or operator of dangerous machinery. If so, the worker should not be permitted to continue on the job. The employer may dismiss or transfer the worker to safer duties;
- whether the person works in an environment which is potentially dangerous to others or him/herself, eg, an electrician. Similar considerations apply; and
- whether there is a risk of adverse publicity or harm to customer relations (which would be a dismissal for 'some other substantial reason').

Taking or possessing drugs in or out of work

7.47   Most employers are naïve about the different types of drugs and their effect, so summary dismissal is common for using or possessing drugs, particularly when at work. Unfortunately this naivety extends to many ETs, who take a hard line on any drug-related dismissal. In one case, a worker was arrested for possession of cannabis off the premises during a lunch break. His summary dismissal without investigation or consultation after five years' service was considered fair.[69]

7.48   It will usually be fair to dismiss a worker for using or possessing drugs when there is a risk of adverse publicity, harm to customer relations or other harm to the employer's business interests.[70] However, if the possession or use of drugs is outside the work environment, not a matter of public knowledge and could not harm the business, the worker may be able to show that dismissal is unfair.[71]

Drinking at work

7.49   This may not be a matter of alcohol dependency at all and it will not necessarily be misconduct to drink at work. This will depend on whether the contract or disciplinary procedure expressly lists drinking as misconduct or, if not, whether the worker and employer clearly contemplated that it would be misconduct. This depends on the nature of the job, factors such as proximity to dangerous equipment and custom and practice.

---

69 *Mathewson v RB Wilson Dental Laboratory* [1988] IRLR 512, EAT.
70 This would be a dismissal for 'some other substantial reason'.
71 *Norfolk CC v Bernard* [1979] IRLR 220, EAT.

Conduct dismissals: Key points

- Only with acts of gross misconduct will an employer be able to dismiss for a first offence. Usually acts of gross misconduct will be set out in the disciplinary procedure.
- Whether the dismissal is fair or unfair will depend primarily on the procedure adopted by the employer rather than the nature of the offence itself. Employers will be expected to follow their disciplinary procedure. If there is no disciplinary procedure, the ET will take into consideration what type of procedure a reasonable employer would have followed.
- In deciding the issue of fairness, the ET will expect the employer to have had reasonable grounds for suspecting the worker of misconduct, to have carried out reasonable investigations and subsequently come to a reasonable conclusion.
- The ET's function is not to determine whether the worker was guilty of the offence. The ET has to determine whether the employer acted reasonably in dismissing the worker. If the worker was not guilty, then it is unlikely to be a fair dismissal although this is not always the case.

General guide to useful evidence

- It is important to get a copy of the disciplinary procedure and to see whether the employer followed it.
- Get evidence whether the disciplinary hearing was fair and properly conducted. Had the decision already been made to dismiss?
- Find out whether any other workers have committed similar acts of misconduct and not been dismissed.

Redundancy dismissals

The right to a redundancy payment was introduced by the Redundancy Payments Act 1965. Not until the general unfair dismissal provisions came into force in 1972[72] was a worker able to challenge the

---

72 Under the Industrial Relations Act 1971.

fairness of a redundancy dismissal. Two issues arise with a redundancy dismissal. First, the worker's entitlement to a redundancy payment which may be a contractual entitlement over and above the statutory minimum payment and, second, whether the worker has a claim for unfair dismissal. In addition, there are several potentially automatically unfair redundancy dismissal situations, which are dealt with above (see paras 6.68 onwards).

The definition of 'redundancy'

7.51   In broad terms, there are three main redundancy situations:
1) closure of the business as a whole;
2) closure of the particular workplace where the worker was employed; and
3) reduction in the size of the workforce.

The statutory definitions are a little more complex.

Closure of the business

7.52   . . . an employee who is dismissed shall be taken to be dismissed by reason of redundancy if the dismissal is wholly or mainly attributable to—
(a) the fact that his employer has ceased or intends to cease—
    (i)   to carry on the business for the purposes of which the employee was employed . . .[73]

The closure may be permanent or temporary,[74] eg, closure of a restaurant for refurbishment. The employer's decision to close cannot be challenged unless it is a sham.[75]

Closure of the workplace

7.53   A dismissal is deemed to be for redundancy if it is attributable wholly or mainly to the fact that the employer 'has ceased or intends to cease . . . to carry on that business in the place where the employee was so employed'.[76] This situation can arise when a large employer closes down one retail outlet or one branch of a restaurant chain. The facts

---

73 ERA 1996 s139(1).
74 Ibid s139(6).
75 *H Goodwin v Fitzmaurice* [1977] IRLR 393, EAT.
76 ERA 1996 s139(1)(a).

must be checked against these definitions; there is no redundancy situation unless the wording is satisfied.[77]

.54–7.56 For some time there was a difference of approach by the courts as to whether a worker was deemed dismissed for redundancy. Previously, it was determined by the application of a 'functional test' (what work the worker was doing at the time of dismissal) or a 'contract test' (what the worker's contract required the worker to do). This difference of approach has been resolved by the House of Lords in *Murray v Foyle Meats Ltd.*[78] There is no need to apply either of these tests. There is a redundancy dismissal if the dismissal of the worker is attributable wholly or mainly to a diminution in the employer's need for workers or a particular type of worker (irrespective of the terms of the contract or the function which the worker performed).

Reduction of the workforce

57   It is a dismissal for redundancy where it is

> wholly or mainly attributable to . . . the fact that the requirements of that business—
> (i) for employees to carry out work of a particular kind, or
> (ii) . . . to carry out work of a particular kind in the place where the employee was employed by the employer, have ceased or diminished or are expected to cease or diminish.[79]

This is where the employer reduces the workforce due to a downturn in business[80] or as the result of a rationalisation.[81] The particular worker's job either disappears or is absorbed by other workers.

.8–7.60   Finally, an employer may offer a redundant worker another worker's job. The other worker is then treated as dismissed for redundancy.[82] This process is known as 'bumping' and usually occurs in recognition of long service, though it occurs only rarely now.

77   *Lesney Products and Co v Nolan and Others* [1977] IRLR 77, CA.
78   [1999] IRLR 562.
79   ERA 1996 s139(1)(b).
80   *Association of University Teachers v University of Newcastle* [1987] ICR 317; [1988] IRLR 10, EAT.
81   *McRae v Cullen and Davison* [1988] IRLR 30, NICA.
82   *Gimber and Sons v Spurrett* [1967] ITR 308.

Redundancy payments

7.61   A worker dismissed on the ground of redundancy is entitled to redundancy pay if s/he has worked for the requisite period of time.[83] If the dismissal is also unfair, the worker will be awarded additional compensation for the unfair dismissal.[84]

Suitable alternative employment

7.62   If the worker unreasonably refuses an offer of suitable alternative employment, s/he will lose his/her entitlement to redundancy pay.[85]

What constitutes a valid offer?

7.63   The offer of alternative employment must be made before the old job ends and the new job must start immediately or within four weeks of the end of the previous employment. The offer need not be in writing, but it will be for the employer to prove that a suitable offer was made.[86] If the worker says s/he is not interested in receiving any alternative offer and the employer therefore does not make one, the worker will not be taken to have unreasonably refused a suitable offer and is entitled to a redundancy payment.[87] The offer must set out the main terms of the new job in enough detail to show how it differs from the old one[88] and the starting date should be clear.

The trial period

7.64   The worker can try out the new job, where it differs from the old one, for a trial period of up to four weeks.[89] The trial period starts on the date the worker begins the new job and ends four weeks later, by which time the worker must have decided whether to accept the new job permanently. If the worker works beyond the four-week period, s/he will lose the right to claim redundancy pay. However, an offer of a different alternative job will attract another four-week trial period. It

---

83   See para 14.13 below on remedies and para 11.80 on discrimination and redundancy pay.
84   See para 14.15 below for overlap.
85   ERA 1996 s141.
86   *Kitching v Ward* [1967] ITR 464; (1967) 3 KIR 322, DC.
87   Although different rules may apply to collectively agreed and other contractual redundancy schemes.
88   *Havenhand v Thomas Black Ltd* [1968] 2 All ER 1037; [1968] ITR 271, DC.
89   ERA 1996 s138.

is a strict time limit and can be extended only for the purpose of retraining the worker; such agreement must be in writing and specify a new date when the trial period will end.[90]

Unreasonable refusal of a suitable offer

7.65   The employer must prove both that the offer was suitable and that the worker's refusal was unreasonable. There is very little case-law guidance on what a worker may refuse and it depends on the particular situation. 'Suitability' tends to mean objective job-related factors such as pay, status, hours and location. The reasonableness of a refusal depends more on the worker's individual circumstances, eg, domestic factors and health. A very common form of alternative offer is of the same job but in a different location. Whether this is a suitable offer which the worker cannot reasonably refuse depends on a combination of factors such as extra travelling time and expense, childcare responsibilities, health, and status of the job (the higher the status, the more an ET would expect a worker to travel).

Unfair redundancy

7.66   A dismissal for redundancy may be unfair for one or more of the following reasons:

a) there was no genuine redundancy situation;
b) the employer failed to consult;
c) the worker was unfairly selected; or
d) the employer failed to offer alternative employment.

No genuine redundancy situation

7.67   If the employer maintains but cannot prove that the dismissal was wholly or mainly attributable to a redundancy situation,[91] s/he will have failed to show the reason or principal reason for dismissal and the dismissal will be automatically unfair. Employers frequently argue in the alternative, ie, that the dismissal was either for redundancy or for some other substantial reason. An employer would need to show which was the principal reason for dismissal[92] and justify it. An ET is more likely to be cynical over the true reason for dismissal

---

90 ERA 1996 s138(3).
91 *MacFisheries v Willgloss* [1972] ITR 57, NIRC.
92 *Smith v City of Glasgow DC* [1987] ICR 796; [1987] IRLR 326, HL.

where an employer appears uncertain by arguing in the alternative. Furthermore, it is rare for a single dismissal to occur in a genuine redundancy situation.

Failure to consult

7.68   The importance of consultation in redundancy dismissals has been recognised since the introduction of the unfair dismissal legislation. It is relevant to the fairness of the dismissal. As a separate right with different remedies[93] the employer is also obliged to consult where making collective redundancies.

7.69   Consultation requires the employer to consider options which would not involve making the worker redundant, including early retirement, seeking volunteers, alternative employment, lay-off and short-time working. The workers and their representatives should be involved in this process. Consultation means more than communicating a decision already made. The Industrial Relations Code of Practice,[94] which has been repealed, provided a good definition of consultation. It defined consultation as jointly examining and discussing problems of concern to both management and workers. It involves seeking mutually acceptable solutions through a genuine exchange of views and information.[95] Furthermore, the court has held that fair consultation involves consultation when the proposals are still at a formative stage, adequate information on which to respond, adequate time in which to respond, conscientious consideration by an authority of the response to consultation.[96]

7.70   The obligation to consult applies equally to unionised and non-unionised workers.[97] When making redundant unionised workers, the employer also has a statutory obligation to consult with the trade union at the earliest opportunity and to comply with the minimum notice periods, ranging from 30 to 90 days according to the number of workers being made redundant.[98]

7.71   The requirement to consult takes many forms. At one end of the spectrum it involves detailed discussions and meetings; at the other end it will entail discussions with individual workers who are likely to be made redundant.

---

93   See para 2.15.
94   1972 para 46.
95   *Heron v Nottingham City Link* [1993] IRLR 372.
96   *R v British Coal Corporation ex p Price* [1994] IRLR 72.
97   *Freud v Bentalls* [1982] IRLR 443; [1983] ICR 77, EAT.
98   TULR(C)A ss188 to 198. See paras 2.15 onwards on statutory consultation.

.72   Following fair procedures is extremely important and an employer will be able to justify failure to consult only if it would have been utterly futile or pointless to do so.[99] Given the various functions of consultation, this will rarely be the case.

Unfair selection

.73   The employer must show that the selection criteria adopted were objective and that they were fairly applied. The employer should usually take account of all matters which can be objectively assessed, eg, length of service,[100] productivity (if it can be objectively assessed), time-keeping, the worker's adaptability and the employer's future needs. The application of certain criteria, such as pregnancy, part-time working, flexibility or indeed length of service, may be directly or indirectly discriminatory.[101]

74   The lengths to which the ET expects an employer to go in drawing up and applying criteria will depend on the employer's size and administrative resources.[102] Usually the ET expects the medium or large employer to have adopted a methodical approach, awarding each potentially redundant worker with points against various criteria and dismissing those who score least.[103] This selection process, provided it is consistent and measured objectively, will in most cases justify the dismissal. However, even small employers must show that they used a fair selection method.

Failure to offer alternative employment

75   The employer must offer any available alternative employment which the worker is able to perform. The employer's duty is not limited to offering similar positions or positions in the same workplace. In rare situations, the employer is expected to have carefully considered 'bumping' another worker and offering the job to the redundant worker. This would be the case if such a procedure had been applied on a regular basis in the past.[104]

76   When offering alternative employment, the employer must give

---

99   See para 6.59 above on *Polkey v AE Dayton Services* [1988] ICR 142, HL.
100   *Bessenden Properties v Corness* [1974] IRLR 338; [1977] ICR 821, CA.
101   See para 11.107 below for redundancy and discrimination.
102   ERA 1996 s98(4).
103   *Williams and Others v Compair Maxam* [1982] IRLR 83; [1982] ICR 156, EAT.
104   *Thomas and Betts Manufacturing Co v Harding* [1980] IRLR 255, CA and para 7.60 above.

sufficient detail of the vacancy and allow (unless the job functions are obvious) a trial period. Failure to do so is likely to make the dismissal unfair.[105] It is up to the worker whether to accept the alternative employment, which might even involve demotion or a reduction in pay.[106] However, workers who unreasonably refuse a suitable alternative offer will reduce their chances of winning an unfair dismissal case or receiving full compensation if they do win. They will also lose their entitlement to statutory redundancy pay.

7.77   One of the main purposes of consultation is to consider other employment, eg, transfer to another workplace, as an alternative to dismissal.[107] The ET will consider what vacancies exist throughout the employer's operation and with any associated employer.[108] The ET will look at vacancies existing during the consultation period (regardless of whether there was actual consultation) and during the worker's notice period as well as at the time of dismissal itself.

Redundancy dismissals: Key points

- Even where there is a genuine redundancy situation the worker may have been unfairly dismissed.
- A worker who is dismissed on the ground of redundancy where there is no redundancy situation will have been unfairly dismissed.
- A redundancy dismissal is also unfair if there has been inadequate consultation by the employer or unfair selection for dismissal, or if there has been a failure to offer available alternative employment.
- The most important requirement is for the employer to consult adequately with the worker before dismissal. The only exception to this requirement is where such consultation would be utterly pointless or futile.
- Length of service is a common criterion but can be discriminatory. Larger employers will be expected to have more sophisticated selection criteria than small enterprises and they should be objective rather than subjective.
- The employer is expected to offer any alternative available

105 *Elliott v Richard Stump Ltd* [1987] ICR 579; [1987] IRLR 215, EAT.
106 *Avonmouth Construction Co v Shipway* [1979] IRLR 14, EAT.
107 Industrial Relations Code of Practice 1972 para 46(ii).
108 *Vokes Ltd v Bear* [1973] IRLR 363, NIRC.

employment which the worker is capable of doing. It is for the worker to decide whether to accept the offer, and not for the employer to make this decision.

- Watch out for direct and indirect discrimination against black workers, women and pregnant women, or discrimination related to disability, in the choice of worker or selection criteria.

General guide to useful evidence

- Get copies of all minutes, notes and memoranda of meetings at which the redundancy dismissal was discussed.
- Get a list of all workers who could have been selected for redundancy and discover when they started their employment, why they have been kept on, and how they met the selection criterion.
- Find out all vacancies available shortly before and after the dismissal (including the whole of the notice period) to see whether the worker could have done any of them.
- Find out from those workers who are still employed, what happened to the worker's job after the dismissal. Was the worker simply replaced? If so, find out who the new worker is, and get a copy of the job advert and the letter of appointment.

Statutory restriction dismissals

.78   There are very few cases where the employer relies on a statutory restriction as the reason for dismissal. The most common example is the loss of a necessary qualification for a job, eg, a van driver losing his/her driving licence. If the employer wrongly believes a statutory restriction applies, this will not be a potentially fair reason for dismissal, even if the employer was acting in good faith. The dismissal will then be justifiable only if it falls within one of the other potentially fair reasons for dismissal; usually for 'some other substantial reason'. The employer must show that the statutory restriction affected the work that the person was employed to perform and that no alternative employment was available. The larger the employer, the greater the duty to try to find an alternative to dismissal.[109]

---

109   *Appleyard v FM Smith (Hull)* [1972] IRLR 19, IT.

7.79   Consultation on the consequences of the ban and possible alternatives is very important.[110] Where a restriction does not prevent the worker from doing his/her job but makes it difficult, eg, a salesperson losing a driving licence, the employer should consult on what assistance may be possible. Even where continued employment of the worker would be unlawful, eg, where a GP has been struck off the medical register, the employer should still consult on the likelihood of the decision being reversed.

Dismissals for some other substantial reason (SOSR)

7.80   A dismissal which is not for one of the four potentially fair reasons may still be fair if it is for 'some other substantial reason of a kind such as to justify the dismissal'.[111] The most common SOSR dismissals are for reorganisation including variation of the contract of employment, in order to protect the employer's business interests or as a consequence of the transfer of a business. Note that a substantial reason is one which is not trivial or unworthy but one which would justify the dismissal.[112]

Dismissals due to reorganisation

7.81   It is sometimes hard to differentiate between a reorganisation and a redundancy situation. Employers usually try to claim that the dismissal is because of reorganisation, in order to avoid making a redundancy payment.

7.82   A worker may be dismissed because s/he cannot or will not accept a change in terms and conditions resulting from the reorganisation. If an employer cannot establish that the reorganisation (and the worker's refusal or inability to fit in with it) was a substantial reason such as could justify dismissal, the dismissal is automatically unfair.[113] In practice, it is fairly easy for the employer to meet this initial requirement.

7.83   An employer is entitled to reorganise the workforce and terms

---

110   *Sutcliffe and Eaton v Pinney* [1977] IRLR 349, EAT.
111   ERA 1996 s98(1).
112   *Gilham v Kent CC (No 1)* [1985] IRLR 16, CA.
113   ERA 1996 s98(1).

and conditions of employment so as to improve efficiency and to dismiss a worker who does not co-operate with the changes.[114] It is sufficient for the employer to show that the reorganisation is for sound business reasons requiring a change in the worker's terms and conditions.[115] The reorganisation need not be essential.

7.84   It is very hard for a worker at the ET to challenge the employer's reasons as not being sound and good. The employer needs only to demonstrate the benefits to the business of the reorganisation, perceived at the time of dismissal. If the employer cannot demonstrate the benefits and the importance attached to them at the time of dismissal, the dismissal will be unfair as the employer will not have established a 'substantial' reason for dismissal.[116]

The reasonableness test: ERA 1996 s98(4)

7.85   Although the ET should consider a number of factors when deciding whether it was fair to dismiss, it primarily looks at the situation from the employer's point of view, ie, whether a reasonable employer would make those changes to the worker's terms of employment.[117] The ET considers the competing advantages and disadvantages to the employer and the worker, but the main emphasis in reorganisation dismissals is on the employer's interests which are paramount. Nevertheless, there have been some recent ET decisions, endorsed by the EAT, indicating that an employer does not have a completely free hand.[118] A change in terms and conditions may also lead to a successful discrimination claim, eg, for indirect sex discrimination on an introduction of flexi-shifts.

7.86   Consultation now plays an important part in all types of dismissal, including reorganisation, after the *Polkey*[119] decision.

Dismissals to protect employers' business interests

7.87   There is an implied term of fidelity and good faith in every employment contract which lasts as long as the worker is employed. Some

114 *Lesney Products and Co v Nolan* [1977] IRLR 77, CA.
115 *Hollister v National Farmers Union* [1979] ICR 542; [1979] IRLR 238, CA.
116 *Banerjee v City and East London Area Health Authority* [1979] IRLR 147, EAT.
117 *Chubb Fire Security v Harper* [1983] IRLR 311, EAT.
118 *Interconnections Systems v Gibson* (1994) 508 IRLB 8, EAT; *Selfridges Ltd v Wayne and Others* (1995) 535 IRLB 13, EAT.
119 *Polkey v AE Dayton Services* [1987] IRLR 503; [1988] ICR 142, HL, and see para 6.59 above.

workers also agree to express terms which restrict their future employment in the same industry for a given period. These terms are known as restrictive covenants.

7.88   A worker dismissed for breaking the implied term of good faith and fidelity will be dismissed for SOSR and perhaps also misconduct. In addition, there may be a substantial reason potentially justifying dismissal if:

- a worker refuses to sign a restrictive covenant and the employer is genuinely seeking to protect the business interests;[120] or
- there is a genuine risk arising from a worker's relationship with a competitor.[121]

Other situations where a dismissal might be deemed to be for SOSR are where the interests of the business might suffer as a result of friction at work between two colleagues, or a worker is incompatible and does not fit in, or adverse publicity on any matter, eg, relating to a worker taking drugs[122] or having a criminal conviction.[123]

The reasonableness test: ERA 1996 s98(4)

7.89   Where dismissal is for refusing to sign a restrictive covenant, the ET will take into account the necessity of applying it, whether the industry usually requires employers to take this precaution and whether the worker's job was of sufficient importance. The ET will also consider the manner and method of the introduction of the clause and whether it was consistently introduced among other workers.

7.90   Where dismissal is due to a personal relationship with a competitor, the ET should take into account the nature of the relationship and its bearing on the work situation. The manner of the worker's dismissal and the degree of notice or warning of impending dismissal are also relevant.[124] Before an employer dismisses a worker for incompatibility, s/he should do all that is reasonable to try to remedy the problem, which might involve transferring the worker.[125]

---

120 *RS Components v Irwin* [1973] ICR 535; [1973] IRLR 239, NIRC.
121 *Skyrail Oceanic v Coleman* [1981] ICR 864, CA.
122 See para 7.47 above.
123 See para 11.90 below on discrimination against gay men.
124 *Skyrail Oceanic v Coleman* (n121 above).
125 *Turner v Vestric Ltd* [1980] ICR 528; [1981] IRLR 23, EAT.

Dismissals on transfer of an undertaking

.91 A dismissal of a worker on or after the transfer of an undertaking for an economic, technical or organisational reason entailing changes in the workforce of either the buyer (transferor) or seller (transferee) is treated as a substantial reason of a kind that can justify dismissal.[126–127]

.92   Dismissals at the time of a transfer usually arise out of the desire of the buyer or seller or both to reduce the workforce so as to make the business a more valuable asset. Any reduction in the workforce means a reduction in potential liability for wrongful dismissal, unfair dismissal and redundancy claims. For more detail, see para 6.108 above.

The reasonableness test: ERA 1996 s98(4)

.93 There is no presumption that the dismissal is fair just because it was for an economic, technical or organisational reason,[128] but if it is not, it is automatically unfair on transfer. The employer would be expected to justify the decision on the basis of sound, good business reasons.

'Some other substantial reason' dismissals: Key points

- The most common type of 'some other substantial reason' for dismissal is where the dismissal arises out of a reorganisation at the workplace.
- It is necessary for the dismissal to be for a substantial reason. The courts treat the interests of the employer as being more important than those of the worker. The dismissal of a worker who may prejudice the interests of the employer will generally be treated as substantial, and usually justifiable.
- Dismissals due to incompatibility with other workers will be for some other substantial reason.

126–127 Transfer of Undertakings (Protection of Employment) Regulations 1981 SI No 1794 reg 8.
128 *McGrath v Rank Leisure* [1985] ICR 527; [1985] IRLR 323, EAT.

> ## General guide to useful evidence
>
> - Any evidence to show that it was not prejudicial to the employer to continue to employ the worker will be valuable.
> - Find out if any other workers in a similar situation were dismissed.

Maternity leave

7.94   The rules regarding maternity leave have always been very complex. The Maternity and Parental Leave etc. Regulations 1999[129] issued under the ERA 1999 have simplified the law to some extent with regard to women whose expected week of childbirth begins on or after 30 April 2000.The regulations also grant new rights to parental leave for male and female employees. The law is very new, still complex and uncertain in some areas. The following is therefore only a general introduction.

7.95   Under previous law, a woman risked losing all her rights if she failed to take the correct steps before and after maternity leave. Even under the new law, there are important rules to comply with. A woman may also be able to claim that any refusal to allow maternity leave or permit her return is unlawful sex discrimination. There are advantages in claiming jointly under the ERA 1999 and the SDA where both apply, since the SDA can attract additional compensation and also enables use of the questionnaire procedure. In some cases, the woman may only be able to use the SDA, eg, because she has not followed the procedural requirements to obtain her rights under the ERA or she is not an employee.

7.96   There are now two main types of statutory maternity leave available to employees: ordinary maternity leave (OML) and additional maternity leave (AML). There is also a short period of compulsory maternity leave.

The right to ordinary maternity leave for all women

7.97   This right is available to all employees, regardless of length of service. The new law extends ordinary maternity leave from 14 weeks to 18

---

129   SI 1999 No 3312.

weeks in total. If necessary, it will be extended for the compulsory maternity leave period of two weeks after childbirth[130] (or for any period where there is a relevant statutory prohibition on the woman working).

7.98　OML starts on the date notified by the woman. It can start earlier, eg, if childbirth occurs or on the first day after the start of the sixth week before the EWC on which she is absent from work wholly or partly because of pregnancy.[131] This means that maternity leave could start automatically, even though the woman does not want it to, just because she is off work through pregnancy-related sickness for an isolated day. However, her employer may be prepared to make an agreement that her leave is not automatically triggered in this way.

The required notifications

7.99　The woman must give notice at least 21 days before she intends OML to start (or if that is not reasonably practicable, as soon as reasonably practicable afterwards) of:[132]

- her pregnancy;
- the expected week of childbirth (EWC);
- (in writing if her employer so requests) the date she intends her OML to start. This cannot be earlier than the eleventh week before the EWC.

Where the woman's OML is automatically triggered by a pregnancy-related absence in the last six weeks before the EWC (see above) or by childbirth itself, she must notify the employer (in writing if requested) as soon as reasonably practicable that she is absent due to pregnancy or childbirth. Otherwise she will lose her right to OML.[133]

.100　If requested by her employer, the woman must produce a certificate from a registered medical practitioner or midwife stating the EWC.[134]

.101　The EWC means the week, beginning with midnight between Saturday and Sunday, in which it is expected that childbirth will occur.[135]

130　ERA 1996 s72; SI No 3312 reg 8.
131　SI No 3312 reg 6.
132　Ibid reg 4(1).
133　Ibid reg 4(3).
134　Ibid reg 4(1).
135　Ibid reg 2.

The right to additional maternity leave (AML)

7.102   The right to additional maternity leave is available to a woman who has been employed for at least one year at the start of the eleventh week before the expected week of childbirth.[136] AML starts on the last day after the expiry of OML and continues until the end of 29 weeks beginning with the actual week of childbirth.[137]

The required notifications

7.103   The woman must make the same notifications as for OML. She need not state explicitly that she will be taking AML as it is presumed that she will do so if eligible.

Returning from ordinary or additional maternity leave

The return date

7.104   A woman does not need to give notice of her return date if she intends to return at the end of the OML or AML period (as applicable). However, if a woman is on additional maternity leave, an employer can ask her to notify the actual date of childbirth and whether she intends to return at the end of her additional maternity leave. As long as the employer makes the request in the appropriate form, the woman must respond. Otherwise she will lose her protection against detriment or automatic unfair dismissal due to her having taken AML (although depending on the circumstances, she may still have an ordinary unfair dismissal claim).The employer's request must be in writing and accompanied by a written statement explaining how the woman can calculate when her AML ends[138] and warning her of the consequence of failing to respond within 21 days of receiving the request.[139] The employer's request cannot be made any sooner than 21 days before the end of the woman's OML.

7.105   If a woman wants to return early from OML or AML, she must give at least 21 days' notice. Otherwise her employer can postpone her return for up to the 21 days (though not beyond the end of the relevant maternity leave period).[140]

---

136   Ibid reg 5.
137   Ibid reg 7(4).
138   Ie, under ibid reg 7(4).
139   Ibid reg 12.
140   Ibid reg 11.

7.106   If a woman is unable to return after her leave due to sickness, the normal sick-leave procedures at her workplace will apply. If the woman is dismissed during OML or AML, but before its expiry, the leave period ends at the time of the dismissal.[141]

Redundancy during maternity leave

7.107   Where – during OML or AML – it is not practicable due to redundancy for the woman's employer to continue to employ her under her existing contract of employment, the woman must be offered any suitable available vacancy with her employer or an associated employer.[142] The terms and conditions (including as to capacity and place) must not be substantially less favourable than had she continued under the previous contract.

.108   The offer must be made before the end of her existing contract of employment and must start immediately on the ending of her existing contract of employment.

Parental leave

109   Workers who are employees have a limited right to have leave for the purpose of caring for a child.[143] There is no definition in the regulations of what 'caring for a child' means. However, the DTI leaflet *Parental Leave: a short guide for employers and employees* defines it as leave taken to look after a child or make arrangements for the child's welfare.[144] Reasons for the leave need not be connected with the child's health. It could cover settling in a child at a new playgroup. Leave is unpaid, although income support may be available.

Who is entitled?

.10   Employees who have been continuously employed for at least one year and who have or expect to have responsibility for a child

---

141   Ibid reg 11.
142   Ibid reg 10.
143   Ibid reg 15.
144   DTI Guides are available on the DTI website at www.dti.gov.uk/ir/erbill.htm.

are entitled to parental leave.[145] The right applies in respect of children born on or after 15 December 1999 or adopted or placed for adoption on or after that date.[146] Generally there is no entitlement to leave requested after a child's fifth birthday, but there are exceptions:[147]

- until after the child's eighteenth birthday where s/he is entitled to a disability living allowance;
- where a child is placed with the employee for adoption by the employee, until after the fifth anniversary of the date placement began or the child's eighteenth birthday, whichever is earlier;
- where the default scheme applies and the employer postponed the requested leave.

Overall scheme: how the entitlement works

7.111   A worker is entitled to a total of 13 weeks leave in respect of each child. A part-time worker's entitlement is pro-rata.[148] The rules regarding terms and conditions during parental leave are the same as apply during AML (see below). Both parents are entitled to parental leave. The woman can take parental leave immediately after her statutory maternity leave if she wishes.

7.112   The government hopes that collective or workforce agreements will set out detailed rules regarding how a parental leave scheme will work and that such schemes will be incorporated into individual workers' contracts. A collective agreement or workforce agreement cannot agree less than the minimum entitlements, but can be more generous. It can also work out the precise rules as to how and when leave is taken. More generous terms, for example, could include allowing more than 13 weeks in total, allowing paid leave, allowing leave for children older than five years, or allowing leave to be taken in the form of reduced hours working.

7.113   If there is no such collective agreed scheme, a default scheme applies (see below). The default scheme may be less generous than a

---

145 SI 1999 No 3312 reg 13.
146 Ibid. The exclusion of children born before 15 December 1999 is currently under challenge as contrary to the Parental Leave Directive 96/34/EC.
147 Ibid reg 15.
148 Ibid reg 14.

scheme which could be negotiated by collective agreement. For example, a collective agreement could negotiate more flexible notice requirements than appear in the default scheme.[149]

The default scheme

7.114 The default scheme is set out in Schedule 2 to the Regulations. Better terms may be collectively agreed. The key elements of the scheme are as follows, though for exact details the Regulations should be checked.

7.115 Under the scheme, a worker cannot take more than four weeks in respect of an individual child during a particular year. The employee can only take the leave in one-week blocks (or part-time equivalent). The exception is for a child entitled to a disability living allowance. A worker is not entitled to the leave unless s/he produces, if requested, any evidence to the employer which is reasonably required to establish the employee's responsibility for the child, the child's date of birth or adoption date, or the child's entitlement to a disability living allowance.

7.116 The worker must give the correct notice. Except where a baby is yet to be born or adopted, the required notice must specify the dates the leave period will start and end, and give the employer at least 21 days' notice of the start. The employer can postpone this leave if the operation of the business would be unduly disrupted, provided the employer agrees a period of leave of equivalent length may be taken within six months, starting on a date determined by the employer after consulting the worker. The employer must give the employee written notice of such postponement, stating the reason for it and specifying the new dates. The notice must be given to the employee no more than seven days after the employee's notice was given to the employer.

7.117 If the worker is an expectant father, he need only specify the expected week of childbirth and the duration of the leave period. He must give the notice at least 21 days in advance of the EWC. If the child is to be adopted, the worker need only notify the expected week of placement, the duration of the required leave, and again must give notice at least 21 days in advance.

149 Ibid reg 16.

The job returned to after maternity or parental leave

Ordinary maternity leave

7.118   The woman is entitled to return to the job in which she was employed before her absence on no less favourable terms and conditions than had she not been absent.[150] Her seniority, pension rights and other rights must be as if she had not been absent.[151]

Additional maternity leave and/or parental leave

7.119   A worker who takes parental leave for four weeks or less (other than immediately after taking AML) is entitled to return to the job in which s/he was employed before his or her absence, in the same capacity and with the nature and place of work under his/her contract.[152] The same applies if s/he takes AML or more than four weeks' parental leave, except that if it is not reasonably practicable to return to the same job, the right is to return to another job which is suitable and appropriate for the worker in the circumstances.[153] Where parental leave of four weeks or less is added on to AML, the position is the same if it would also not have been reasonably practicable to return to the same job at the end of AML.[154] The position is different where a redundancy situation arises during maternity leave.[155]

7.120   Broadly speaking, the worker is entitled to return on terms and conditions (including as to remuneration) not less favourable than those which would have applied had s/he not taken any maternity or parental leave.[156] On return, the worker should therefore get any pay-rise awarded during his/her leave. Seniority, pension and similar rights must be treated as if the worker's period of employment immediately before the start of his/her AML or parental leave was continuous with his/her employment following his/her return to

---

150   ERA 1996 s71(4)(c); s71(7)(b).
151   Though subject to the rules on pension rights under Social Security Act 1999 Sch 5 para 5. ERA 1996 s71(7)(a).
152   SI 1999 No 3312 regs 2(1), 18(1).
153   Ibid reg18(2).
154   Ibid reg18(3).
155   See para 7.107 above and ibid reg 18(4).
156   For exact position, see ibid reg 18(5)(a)(c).

work. Pension rights continue to accrue during OML, but for AML see the requirements of Sch 5 of the Social Security Act 1989.[157]

Rights during leave

7.121 There is no statutory requirement that a woman receive her full pay during maternity leave, nor is it sex discrimination in itself, but she must on her return benefit from any pay-rise.[158] A woman on OML is entitled to the benefit of her terms and conditions except for remuneration (and is also bound by obligations) which would apply if she was not absent.[159] This includes non-contractual matters which are connected with her employment. 'Remuneration' only refers to sums payable as wages or salary.[160] This suggests that the woman will still be entitled to benefits in kind, eg, health insurance and company cars, and possibly to one-off cash payments such as bonuses.

7.122 During AML or parental leave, the worker is entitled to the benefit of the employer's implied obligation of trust and confidence and any terms and conditions relating to notice pay on termination; compensation in the case of redundancy; disciplinary or grievance procedures. The worker is bound by the implied term of trust and confidence; the obligation to give notice of termination; the obligation not to disclose confidential information and not to participate in any other business, and obligations regarding acceptance of gifts and benefits.[161]

7.123 The position regarding occupational pension contributions is complex and not dealt with in this book.

Contractual rights to maternity or parental leave

7.124 Where a worker is entitled to maternity or parental leave and also has a right under her contract of employment, she cannot exercise each right separately, but she may take advantage of whichever right is in any particular respect the more favourable.[162]

---

157 Ibid reg 18(5).
158 See chapter 11, pregnancy discrimination.
159 ERA s71(4)(5).
160 SI 1999 No 3312 reg 9.
161 Ibid reg 17.
162 Ibid reg 21.

Dependant leave

7.125   An employee is entitled to reasonable time-off to take action necessary for any of the following purposes:[163]

– to provide assistance on an occasion when a dependent is injured or assaulted, falls ill or gives birth;
– to make care arrangements for a dependant who is ill or injured;
– in consequence of the death of a dependant;
– because of the unexpected disruption or termination of arrangements for the care of a dependant;
– to deal with an incident involving the employee's child which occurs unexpectedly while the child is at an educational establishment.

To have this right, the worker must tell the employer how long s/he expects to be absent and the reason, as soon as reasonably practicable.[164]

7.126   A 'dependant' means a spouse, child, parent or person (other than a tenant, lodger or employee) who lives in the employee's household. In relation to the right to time-off to provide care for illness or injury, it also includes anyone who reasonably relies on the employee for assistance in those circumstances.[165]

7.127   A worker can complain to an ET within three months of any refusal of such time-off. The ET can award compensation which it considers just and equitable including for resulting loss.[166]

Detriments and automatic unfair dismissal

7.128   It is unlawful to subject a worker to a detriment for a number of reasons related to the fact that s/he has taken maternity, parental or dependant leaves. It is also automatically unfair dismissal to dismiss the worker for any of those reasons. See para 6.68 above for the reasons and exceptions.

163   ERA 1996 s57A(1).
164   Ibid s57A(2).
165   Ibid s57A(3).
166   Ibid s57A(4).

Suspension from work on maternity grounds

.129 The Management of Health and Safety at Work (Amendment) Regulations 1994[167] were passed to implement the health and safety provisions of the EU Pregnant Workers' Directive.[168] The Health and Safety Executive has issued guidance to employers on the known risks and what action should be taken.[169]

.130 As part of their general duty to carry out risk assessment in the workplace, where employees include women of child-bearing age and the work could involve a risk to the mother or baby, employers must include any risk which might be posed to a new or expectant mother.[170] Once the woman has notified her employer in writing that she is pregnant, has given birth in the previous six months or is breast-feeding,[171] the employer must alter her working conditions or hours of work to avoid the risk.[172] If it is not reasonable to do this or it would not avoid the risk, the employer should suspend the woman from work for as long as necessary.[173] This is the woman's entitlement to a health and safety suspension.[174] However, the woman is entitled to be offered any available suitable alternative work before being suspended.[175]

131 The woman is entitled to be paid during her suspension, unless she has turned down an offer of suitable alternative work for the relevant period.[176] The work must be of a kind which is both suitable in relation to the woman and appropriate for her to do in the circumstances, and on terms and conditions not substantially less favourable than her normal terms and conditions.[177] The woman must produce a medical certificate confirming her pregnancy within a reasonable time of any written request to do so by her employer.[178]

---

167 SI No 2865.
168 92/85/EEC.
169 *New and expectant mothers at work – a guide for employers*, available from HSE Books, PO Box 1999, Sudbury, Suffolk CO10 6FS.
170 Management of Health and Safety at Work Regulations 1992 SI No 2051 reg 13A(1) as amended.
171 Ibid reg 13C(1).
172 Ibid reg 13A(2).
173 Ibid reg 13A(3).
174 ERA 1996, s66.
175 Ibid s67(1).
176 Ibid s68.
177 Ibid s67(2).
178 SI 1992 No 2051 (see n170 above) reg 13C(2).

7.132   The risks covered may include nightworking[179] and any physical, biological or chemical agent which carries risk to the health and safety of a new or expectant mother, including the risks specified in Annexes I and II to the EU Directive on Pregnant Workers.[180] Physical risks include extremes of heat and cold, prolonged exposure to loud noise, manual handling of loads, regular exposure to shocks and low-frequency vibration, working in tightly-fitted workstations, excessive physical or mental pressure causing stress and anxiety, fatigue from standing and other physical work, travelling inside or outside the establishment. Steps to avoid risks could include ensuring available seating, granting longer and more frequent rest breaks, adjusting workstations, ensuring that hours and volume of work are not excessive and that, where possible, the woman has some control over how her work is organised.

7.133   It is too soon to know how this protection will operate in practice. The provisions regarding fatigue are particularly important, but their scope in practice is untested. An example would seem to be as follows: a woman may find that due to pregnancy-related fatigue, she is unable to work her full hours. Her employer must allow her to work reduced hours on full pay (or, if it sufficed, alter her duties so they were less tiring). If the woman became unable to work at all, she must be suspended on full pay. It would be automatically unfair to dismiss her for these reasons.

7.134   Where a woman is suspended without pay, she may claim her pay from an ET. Where she is on paid suspension but the employer has failed to offer suitable alternative work, an ET may award any sum it considers just and equitable, with no ceiling.[181] The time-limit is three months from the date the suspension started.[182] It is automatically unfair to dismiss a woman because of her entitlement to a medical suspension.[183] If a woman is injured as a result of the employer's failure to comply with the Management of Health and Safety at Work Regulations, she may sue for damages.[184]

179   Ibid reg 13B.
180   The annexed risks and ways to avoid them are set out in (1995) 60 EOR 35.
181   ERA 1996 s70.
182   Ibid s70(2).
183   Ibid s90.
184   SI 1992 No 2051 (see n175 above) reg 15(2).

Time off for ante-natal care

7.135   A pregnant employee must not be unreasonably refused time-off during her working hours to attend an appointment for ante-natal care, which has been made on the advice of a medical practitioner, registered midwife or registered health visitor.[185] Ante-natal care probably includes relaxation classes attended on medical advice.[186] Apart from on the first appointment, if her employer so requests, the worker must produce a certificate from one of the latter, confirming her pregnancy and a document proving the appointment has been made.[187] If the worker is allowed the time off, she is entitled to be paid for it.[188] If the employer unreasonably refuses the time off or allows it, but fails to pay, the woman can claim the pay for the time she should have been allowed. She must bring her ET claim within three months of the date of the appointment.[189]

---

185   ERA 1996 s55(1).
186   As accepted by an ET in *Gregory v Tudsbury Ltd* [1982] IRLR 267.
187   ERA 1996 s55(2), (3).
188   Ibid s56 sets out how the pay should be calculated.
189   Ibid s57.

Evidence in unfair dismissal cases

What kind of evidence is helpful?

Burden of proof

8.1   If dismissal is disputed, the burden is on the worker to prove that it occurred. Once dismissal is proved, the employer must show the reason (or if there is more than one reason, the principal reason) for the dismissal and that it was one of the potentially fair reasons set out in Employment Rights Act (ERA) 1996 s98.

Proving a disputed dismissal

8.2   If the worker seeks advice shortly after dismissal, it is essential to secure the written reasons for dismissal with which s/he may have already been provided. In any event the employer should be asked under ERA 1996 s92 for confirmation of the dismissal and the written reasons for it.[1] Where dismissal is during pregnancy, the employer should automatically supply such a statement, whether requested or not, but it is worth asking if s/he does not.[2]

8.3   If there is a dispute whether the worker was actually dismissed, supporting documents and witnesses will be needed. As early as possible, try to obtain a signed statement plus the name and address of any witnesses to the dismissal. If the employer decided to dismiss before the worker knew about it, any documentary proof will be helpful, eg, a copy of job advertisements which had already appeared for the worker's job.

8.4   If advising on a potential constructive dismissal claim where the worker must show a fundamental breach of contract, all contractual documents must be obtained. These may comprise a letter of appointment, statement of main terms and conditions, notices of variation of contract[3] and staff handbook.

Conduct and capability dismissals

8.5   It should be ascertained whether the worker has received any written or verbal warnings in the past, particularly concerning the matter for

---

1   ERA 1996 s92. Note that to found a claim for compensation for supplying false reasons, those reasons must have been supplied in response to a formal written request: *Catherine Haigh Harlequin Hair Design v Seed* [1990] IRLR 175.
2   ERA 1996 s92(4).
3   Under ERA 1996 s4.

which s/he was dismissed. Copies of the written warnings should be obtained. With verbal warnings, it is necessary to check when they were given, by whom and roughly what was said.

6   The relevant provisions of the contract of employment or staff handbook must be examined, in particular the notice provisions, the required disciplinary procedure and, if relevant, what offences are listed as disciplinary matters, particularly what amounts to gross misconduct. Ascertain whether the contractual procedures were in fact followed.

7   The worker should be asked what disciplinary hearings took place, who was present, whether s/he was advised s/he could bring a representative, how much warning was given of the hearing and whether it was known what it would be about in advance. All these are matters of procedural fairness. In particular, it should be asked at what point in the meeting s/he was told that s/he was dismissed. If the employer said something at the start of the hearing to indicate that the decision to dismiss had already been taken, this would be unfair. It is surprising how often the letter of dismissal has been typed prior to the disciplinary meeting, which is a strong indication that the hearing was a sham! Who took notes at the hearing and whether the worker has any should be ascertained. An effort should be made to get the worker's best recollection of the detail of the meeting and, in particular, what each person said as soon as possible, as important matters may be forgotten if there is a delay. In general, what is important is what the employer knew or ought to have known, had s/he properly investigated or consulted at the time of dismissal.

If relevant (eg, with fighting, alcohol or lateness dismissals), how the employer treated similar offences or problems in the past should be established. It is necessary to point to other similar cases prior to the decision to dismiss or during the appeal process, as an ET has to determine the fairness of the dismissal at the time of dismissal and during the appeal process but not at the time of the ET hearing. With sickness, injury or qualification dismissals, what other jobs the employer had available at the relevant time should be noted. The ET will expect serious efforts to be made to offer alternative employment.[4]

---

4   *P v Nottingham CC* [1992] IRLR 362.

Absenteeism and lateness

8.9   Discovery of the attendance record of similar workers should be sought to see whether the employer was acting consistently in deciding to dismiss. The names of the other workers will be needed so that their statutory sick pay or attendance records can be obtained from the employer to make this comparison. However, it will be for the employer to show the reason for the differential treatment.

8.10   To what extent the worker was made aware of the employer's dissatisfaction with his/her attendance should be ascertained and whether it was made clear that dismissal would follow a failure to improve. If there was only a verbal warning, given to a group of workers, it should be clarified from another of those workers what was said and whether it was clear that dismissal might ensue.

8.11   Whether the employer properly reviewed the worker's attendance record prior to giving any warning or dismissing should be checked. This should have involved consulting the worker as to the reasons for the absences or lateness. In general, it should be considered whether the employer approached the dismissal of the worker with sympathy, and understanding.

Prolonged sickness absence

8.12   If the employer obtained a medical opinion on the worker's state of health (no medical opinion could have been obtained without the worker's consent), a copy of any medical report should be obtained. Was the worker consulted in respect of the employer's medical report? If so, copies of notes taken of the meeting and a statement from the worker on what was said should be obtained. The worker should be asked whether s/he was offered the opportunity of getting his/her own medical report.

8.13   The importance of the worker's job and whether the employer could be expected to hold it open any longer should be considered. What arrangements were made during the worker's absence? What other short-term solutions were possible? How soon after the dismissal was the vacancy filled?

Injury

8.14   It should be clarified whether the injury was such as to make the performance of the job impossible. Could the worker, through retraining or the use of aids, have continued to do the job?[5] Was there any form of consultation with the worker on the medical prognosis and what s/he could do? If the worker seeks advice while still any form of consultation with the worker on the medical prognosis and what s/he could do? If the worker seeks advice while still employed, the employer may have a beneficial sickness retirement scheme in certain circumstances. It may also be worth considering whether the worker should take advice in respect of a personal injury claim if the injury occurred at work.

Qualifications

.15 It should be established whether the qualification was a term of the contract or otherwise a genuine requirement of the job. If not, the employer will find it hard to justify dismissal. If the employer has changed the requirement, why was the change necessary? Are there any other workers doing the same job who do not have the qualifications, and are new workers expected to be qualified? Also, whether other jobs were available which the worker was qualified to do at the time of dismissal should be ascertained. Finally, whether the requirement had a discriminatory effect on the worker should be considered (see para 9.51 below).

Redundancy dismissals

16 If relevant, the selection criteria adopted by the employer should be established. Were there other workers in similar jobs who were not made redundant, particularly any who had shorter service? To check whether it was a genuine redundancy, it should be established whether a new employee has simply replaced the worker in the same job. It is important to obtain all internal and external advertisements and vacancy lists relating to suitable vacancies at the time of dismissal and for a short period before and after. These are relevant both to the genuineness of the redundancy (advertisements for the same job) and to the availability of alternative jobs which should have been offered. The worker should be asked what other jobs s/he could and would have done for the employer and whether s/he was consulted about vacancies or doing any other work.

---

5 See chapter 13 below for any protection a worker may have if the injury causes a disability.

Part III

Discrimination

Discrimination on grounds of race and sex

The legal framework

9.1 The principal statute prohibiting race discrimination in employment is the Race Relations Act (RRA) 1976. The legislation prohibiting discrimination on grounds of sex or marital status is more complex and contained in several Acts of parliament. Similar provisions to those in the RRA are contained in the Sex Discrimination Act (SDA) 1975 as amended by the SDA 1986. However, sex discrimination in pay and other contractual terms is dealt with separately[1] under the Equal Pay Act (EqPA) 1970, amended by the Equal Pay (Amendment) Regulations 1983 SI No 1794.

9.2 A 'Code of Practice for the elimination of racial discrimination and the promotion of equal opportunity in employment' came into effect on 1 April 1984. The code of practice was made by the Commission for Racial Equality (CRE) under RRA 1976 s47. The Equal Opportunities Commission issued a similar 'Code of Practice for the elimination of discrimination on the grounds of sex and marriage and the promotion of equality of opportunity in employment' under SDA 1975 s56A, which was brought into effect on 30 April 1985.

9.3 The codes of practice lay down guidelines for good employment practice, but they are not legally actionable in themselves.[2] However, the codes are admissible in evidence at a hearing and the ET should 'take into account' any relevant provision in reaching its decision. In 1988 the Court of Appeal endorsed the importance of the Race Relations Code of Practice.[3]

9.4 The DfEE has published a Guide to the Sex Discrimination (Gender Reassignment) Regulations 1999.[4] Although this is not a code and has no special legal status, tribunals are likely to look at the Guide.

9.5 In 1998, the CRE submitted proposals to the Home Secretary for strengthening the RRA 1976.[5] Previous proposals have been ignored and it remains to be seen whether these are now taken up. The EOC also submitted detailed proposals for reform of sex equality laws in November 1998.[6]

---

1 Except where it is against transsexuals. See para 5.2 above for the ambit of the EqPA. Also note SDA 1975 s8.
2 RRA 1976 s47(10), SDA 1975 s56A(10).
3 *West Midlands Passenger Transport Executive v Singh* [1988] IRLR 186 at paras 15 and 25.
4 Available free from Prolog Ltd, tel: 0845 6022260.
5 Reform of the RRA 1976: Proposals from the CRE (1998) 80 EOR 40.
6 82 EOR 31.

EU legislation: sex discrimination

In some circumstances EU legislation applies to discrimination on grounds of sex and marital or family status. Originally the material legislation was:

(a) article 119 of the Treaty of Rome, which lays down the principle of equal pay for equal work;
(b) the Equal Pay Directive 75/117/EEC (EPD), which expands the principle set out in article 119; and
(c) the Equal Treatment Directive 76/207/EEC (ETD), which provides for equal treatment between men and women in their access to employment, training, promotion, working conditions and dismissal.

On 1 May 1999, the Treaty of Amsterdam came into force, which amended the Treaty of Rome in several important ways for employment law, including renumbering the articles. Article 119, now numbered article 141, is expanded to include for the first time a reference to the principle of equal treatment in employment generally (not just equal pay). It also allows national states to provide for certain positive discrimination measures.

The general position regarding the interaction between EU and national law generally is set out at paras 3.1 onwards, where it is explained when EU legislation and case-law can be relied on by individual workers in the UK. Broadly speaking, the sex discrimination position is as follows.

Equal pay

In almost all equal pay cases, a worker could claim the benefit of article 119 directly against private as well as state employers.[7] This is because of the status of the Treaty of Rome. In so far as the Equal Pay Directive merely interprets article 119, it can also be used directly against a non-state employer, but it cannot be used in so far as it establishes rights additional to those contained in article 119. The position remains unaltered after the Amsterdam Treaty's amendment and renumbering of article 119 as article 141. Article 141(1) states:

Each member state shall ensure that the principle of equal pay for

---

7 *Barber v GRE Assurance Group* [1990] IRLR 240, ECJ.

male and female workers for equal work or work of equal value is applied.

The Equal Treatment Directive

9.9   Until the implementation of the Amsterdam Treaty, the Equal Treatment Directive had no Treaty basis. The UK as a member state was supposed to implement the ETD into national law. Wherever possible, therefore, national law had to be interpreted consistently with the ETD and EU case-law. However, where an unimplemented part of the ETD gave rights which cannot be read into the SDA 1975 (or other national law), the position was more complicated. Individuals in ETs and other national courts could use the ETD, but only against any employer which is an 'emanation of the state'.[8] Where the employer was a private one, then probably the only option was to sue the government for damages for non-implementation of the ETD.[9] Now that the ETD is supported by the Treaty (ie, the amended article 141), the position may change although the effect of this change is unclear.

9.10   Article 141(3) now reads:

> The Council . . . shall adopt measures to ensure the application of the principle of equal opportunities and equal treatment of men and women in matters of employment and occupation, including the principle of equal pay for equal work or work of equal value.

EU legislation: race discrimination

9.11   There is as yet no specific EU legislation prohibiting race discrimination, although the new article 13 introduced by the Treaty of Amsterdam provides a legal basis for action to be taken in the future.[10] The Commission has now proposed two draft directives which include prohibitions on race discrimination in employment.[11]

9.12   Article 13 adds to the pre-existing article 12 (formerly article 6), which simply prohibits discrimination on the ground of nationality.

---

8   See para 3.11.
9   See para 3.9.
10   See para 3.7.
11   The drafts are available on the website of the Directorate for Employment and Social Affairs, www.europa.eu.int/comm/dgas/key_en.htm. See also para 3.7 above.

Article 39 (formerly article 48) whose content pre-dates the Amsterdam Treaty, requires freedom of movement for workers within the EU. Article 39(2) states:

> Such freedom of movement shall entail the abolition of any discrimination based on nationality between workers of the member states as regards employment, remuneration and other conditions of work and employment.

Article 39 has direct effect, which means that workers can rely on it.[12] On the whole, this is unnecessary because workers in the UK have access to the RRA 1976. However there are occasions when article 39 may give wider rights than the RRA 1976, for example in relation to the definition of indirect discrimination.[13-14]

Who is covered?

3   The RRA 1976 and SDA 1975 are wider in scope than the ERA. They protect job applicants, apprentices, employees, contract workers and those working on a contract personally to execute any work,[15] in relation to employment at an establishment in Great Britain.[16] Former employees may be unable to claim under the RRA 1976 in relation to incidents occurring after their employment ended.[17] Volunteers will be covered if in reality they work under a contract, as may be indicated by the level of their obligations and pay.[18]

4   The protection of contract workers is becoming increasingly important with the fragmentation of the labour market. Broadly speaking, contract workers are those who are employed by one organisation ('the employer') but supplied to do work for another ('the principal') under a contract between the two.[19] Precisely who can be considered as a contract worker depends on the facts but it will probably cover workers supplied by an employment agency to

---

12   *Van Duyn v Home Office* 1975 Ch 358, ECJ.
13–14 See para 9.55.
15   SDA 1975 s82(1), RRA 1976 s78(1).
16   Cf RRA 1976 s8 and SDA 1975 s10 for what is considered to be employment in an establishment in GB. See para 9.24.
17   Though see para 9.36 for full position.
18   See Feature (1998) 626 *IDS Brief* 14.
19   RRA 1976 s7, SDA 1975 s9.

work for a different company,[20] workers supplied by concessionaires to work for department stores in specific concessions, and workers employed in contracted-out services.[21] The importance of the protection is that it means a worker who is discriminated against by the principal, as opposed to his/her employer, still has a legal claim.

9.15   Employment agencies must not discriminate in their provision of services.[22] Any person providing or making arrangements for the provision of training facilities is also covered.[23] This protects trainees on work experience and work placement programmes.

9.16   Barristers must not discriminate against pupils or tenants, nor must anyone discriminate in which barristers they instruct.[24] Trade unions must not discriminate in access to membership or against members, for example, in the way they offer access to benefits or services.[25]

9.17   Employers are liable for the discriminatory acts of their employees carried out in the course of employment regardless of whether they knew or approved those acts, unless they took all reasonably practicable preventative steps.[26] The scope of employers' liability is a particularly important issue in claims of sexual or racial harassment.[27] Employers are also liable for the acts of their agents.[28] There are statutory provisions on where employers' liability lies in the case of the police.[29]

Sex Discrimination Acts 1975 and 1986

9.18   The SDAs prohibit discrimination against women, men or married persons. It is not prohibited to discriminate against an unmarried person although this may be unlawful under the ETD article 2(1).

---

20   *BP Chemicals Ltd v Gillick* [1995] IRLR 128, EAT.
21   The key case is *Harrods Ltd v Remick* [1997] IRLR 583; 76 EOR 41, CA. See also *MHC Consulting Services v Tansell* [1999] IRLR 677; 88 EOR 55, EAT under the DDA where the supply went through a third party (an agency).
22   RRA 1976 s14, SDA 1975 s15.
23   RRA 1976 s13 as amended, SDA 1975 s14 as amended.
24   SDA 1975 s35A; RRA 1976 s26A.
25   RRA 1976 s11, SDA 1975 s12.
26   RRA 1976 s32, SDA 1975 s41.
27   See para 11.41 below for more detail.
28   RRA 1976 s32, SDA 1975 s41.
29   RRA 1976 s16, SDA 1975 s17.

From 1 May 1999, the SDA 1975 was amended to include a prohibition on discrimination against a worker on grounds that s/he intends to undergo, is undergoing or has undergone gender reassignment.[30] Gender reassignment means any process or part of a process undertaken under medical supervision, but not necessarily surgery, for the reassignment of someone's sex by changing physiological or other characteristics.[31] Discrimination against gay and lesbian workers is not covered as such unless it amounts to gender discrimination.[32]

Race Relations Act 1976

19   The RRA 1976 prohibits discrimination on 'racial grounds' or against members of any 'racial group'. Section 3 defines 'racial' in these contexts as 'by reference to colour, race, nationality or ethnic or national origins'. For the purposes of the RRA, a particular racial group may comprise two or more distinct racial groups.[33] For example, a person of Cypriot nationality could claim s/he has suffered discrimination not only as a Cypriot, but as a non-British national or as someone not of EU nationality.[34]

20   A British national from Northern Ireland who is discriminated against on grounds of being 'Irish' is covered by the RRA.[35] English-speaking Welsh people are not considered a different racial group from Welsh-speaking Welsh people.[36] If a worker is discriminated against in England, for example, because s/he is from Scotland, Wales or Northern Ireland, s/he should probably claim race discrimination on grounds of national origin as opposed to nationality or ethnic origin.[37] However the definition of what 'national origin' really means could be problematic in practice.

---

30   SDA 1975 s2A(1). The SDA is amended by the Sex Discrimination (Gender Reassignment) Regulations 1995. SI 1999 No 1102, following *P v S & Cornwall CC* [1996] IRLR 347; 68 EOR 44, ECJ. The Regs are printed with a useful commentary plus extracts from the DfEE's Guide at (1999) 85 EOR 36.
31   SDA 1975 s82(1).
32   See paras 11.86–11.96 below.
33   RRA 1976 s3(2).
34   *Orphanos v Queen Mary College* [1985] IRLR 349, HL.
35   *Bogdenie v Sauer-Sundstrand Ltd* (1988) 383 IDS Brief 15, EAT.
36   *Gwynedd CC v Jones & Doyle* (1986) 336 *IDS Brief* 15, EAT.
37   *Northern Joint Police Board v Power* [1997] IRLR 610; 76 EOR 43, EAT. *Boyce v British Airways PLC* (1997) 581 IRLB 7, EAT.

Ethnic groups

9.21   There are seven essential characteristics which a group must have, to fall within the meaning of 'ethnic group' under the RRA 1976.[38] In summary, these are:

(1) a long shared history;
(2) its own cultural tradition;
(3) a common language;
(4) literature;
(5) religion;
(6) a common geographical origin; and
(7) being a minority or oppressed group within a larger community.

It does not matter if the size of a particular ethnic group has diminished due to intermarriage or lapsed observance, provided there remains a discernible minority.[39]

9.22   Jewish and Sikh people are covered by the RRA 1976, but unfortunately Rastafarian[40] and Muslim[41] people are not. 'Gypsies' in the narrow sense of 'a wandering race (by themselves called "Romany") of Hindu origin' are an 'ethnic group', although a prohibition against 'travellers' may refer to all those of a nomadic way of life and amount only to indirect discrimination[42] against those of Romany origin.[43]

Discrimination on the ground of religion

9.23   The RRA 1976 does not prohibit religious discrimination as such, but where there is discrimination in connection with religion, it may be possible to claim indirect discrimination against a racial group protected by the RRA 1976.[44] An employer who attacks a religious practice which is particularly associated with a worker's racial (ethnic or national) group is likely to discriminate indirectly. For example:

   – a rule against wearing turbans may indirectly discriminate against Sikhs;

---

38 *Mandla v Lee* [1983] IRLR 209; [1983] ICR 385, HL.
39 *CRE v Dutton* [1989] IRLR 8, CA.
40 *Dawkins v Department of the Environment* (1993) 49 EOR 377 and [1993] IRLR 284, CA.
41 *Nyazi v Rymans* (1988) EAT 6/88.
42 For indirect discrimination see paras 9.51 onwards.
43 *CRE v Dutton* [1989] IRLR 8, CA.
44 See paras 9.51 onwards for definition of indirect racial discrimination.

- imposing a short dress as uniform would indirectly discriminate against a Muslim female worker of Pakistani national origin;
- a requirement that a manager work on Saturdays may indirectly discriminate against Jewish workers;[45]
- a rule that no holidays are taken over summer peak periods and therefore not on Eid may indirectly discriminate against workers of Asian national origin;[46]
- an employer who refuses to employ a worker of Pakistani nationality or national origin because of his/her Muslim religion would indirectly discriminate against Pakistani workers.

Employment outside Great Britain

4   The RRA 1976 and SDA 1975 do not apply to those employed wholly outside Great Britain. People working on a ship or airline registered in the UK and operated by a person based in Great Britain are deemed to work in Great Britain unless they work wholly outside Great Britain.[47] It is not unlawful race discrimination for an employer specifically to train in Great Britain a non-Great Britain resident in skills which are to be exercised outside Great Britain.[48]

5   Under article 39 of the Treaty of Rome, there must be no discrimination on grounds of nationality against workers from the EU member states. This means that the RRA 1976 must be applied to protect such workers. For example, in one case[49] an Italian national living in Great Britain was not interviewed for an aircraft cabin crew job, based in Italy, due to his Italian nationality. As the job was not at an establishment in Great Britain, the RRA 1976 would not usually cover the claim. Nevertheless, due to EU law, the exclusion under the RRA 1976 was disapplied and the ET had to hear the claim.

Private households

26   The RRA 1976 does not apply to direct or indirect discrimination in employment in private households, although victimisation is covered.[50] Thus, if a worker in a private household complains about

---

45   *Tower Hamlets LBC v Rabin (1989) 406 IDS Brief* 12 EAT.
46   *J H Walker Ltd v Hussain* [1996] IRLR 11; (1996) 66 EOR 50, EAT.
47   SDA 1975 ss6 and 10, RRA 1976 ss4 and 8. Note amendments made by the Equal Opportunities (Employment Legislation) (Territorial Limits) Regulations 1999 SI No 3163.
48   RRA 1976 s6.
49   *Bossa v Nordstress Ltd* [1998] IRLR 284; 80 EOR 51, EAT.
50   RRA 1976 s4(3).

discrimination and is dismissed as a result, this is unlawful victimisation.

9.27   Workers in private households are usually domestic servants or private chauffeurs. Sometimes it is difficult to know whether the worker is employed for the purposes of a private household or not. For example, it will depend on all the facts whether a chauffeur, employed to drive a company director to and from work as well as the director and his/her spouse on leisure trips, may be employed by the company rather than in the director's private household.[51]

Crown employees

9.28   The RRA 1976 and SDA 1975 generally cover employment by the Crown save for statutory office-holders and Crown ministers.[52] Regulations also exist under the RRA 1976 permitting certain key posts in specified bodies, eg, the Bank of England, the House of Commons and the House of Lords, to be restricted to workers of particular birth, nationality or residence.[53]

The armed services

9.29   The RRA 1976 covers members of the armed forces. Originally the SDA 1975 did not cover employment in the armed forces and auxiliary services. However, following many successful claims under the ETD by women discharged by the armed services for being pregnant, the exclusion was removed save where the discrimination is done to ensure combat effectiveness.[54] Servicewomen can claim maternity rights under the unfair dismissal legislation.[55]

9.30   Under both Acts, it is necessary to go through an internal procedure save for claims related to recruitment.[56] The internal procedure must follow basic rules of fairness.[57]

---

51   See *Heron Corporation v Commis* [1980] ICR 713, EAT.
52   See RRA 1976 ss75–76, SDA 1975 ss85–86.
53   A list of the prescribed bodies is set out in the Race Relations (Prescribed Public Bodies) (No. 2) Regulations 1994 SI No 1986.
54   SDA 1975 (Application to Armed Forces etc) Regulations 1994 SI No 3276, implemented from 1 February 1995.
55   ERA 1996 s192.
56   RRA 1976 s75 and see Race Relations (Complaints to Employment Tribunals) (Armed Forces) Regs 1997 SI No 2161; SDA 1975 s85(9A–9E), and the Sex Discrimination (Complaints to Employment Tribunals) (Armed Forces) Regs 1997 SI No 2163.
57   *R v Army Board of the Defence Council ex p Anderson* [1991] IRLR 425, DC.

Police and prison officers

9.31 Members of the police force are generally covered but[58] discrimination in height requirements between male and female prison officers is allowed,[59] as are requirements for height, uniform or equipment within the police force.[60]

Ministers of religion

9.32 The SDA 1975 does not apply to employment for the purposes of an organised religion.[61]

Prohibited actions

9.33 Unlike the law on unfair dismissal, the law on discrimination covers all aspects of employment, including recruitment, promotion and dismissal. RRA 1976 s4 and SDA 1975 s6 prohibit discrimination in the arrangements made for determining who should be offered employment, in the terms on which employment is offered, in refusing to offer employment, and in access to opportunities for promotion, transfer, training or any other benefits, facilities or services. Whereas the RRA 1976 prohibits race discrimination in pay and contract terms, the SDA 1975 does not,[62] this being covered by the EqPA 1970. Finally, RRA 1976 s4(2)(c) and SDA 1975 s6(2)(b) prohibit discrimination 'by dismissing him/her, or subjecting him/her to any other detriment'. Under the SDA 1975, a 'dismissal' includes expiry and non-renewal of a fixed term contract and also constructive dismissal.[63] There is no equivalent definition of 'dismissal' under the RRA 1976, and in a constructive dismissal situation, the discriminatory acts complained of should be those leading to the worker's resignation.[64]

9.34 The law is not clear as to what amounts to 'subjecting' the worker to 'any other detriment'. Basically it means putting the worker at a disadvantage,[65] but a worker cannot bring a case in respect of dis-

58 RRA 1976 s16, SDA 1975 s17.
59 SDA 1975 s18.
60 SDA 1975 s17.
61 SDA 1975 s19.
62 Except as against transsexuals.
63 SDA 1975 s82(1)A.
64 *Harrold v Wiltshire Healthcare NHS Trust* (1999) 620 IRLB 15, EAT.
65 *Jeremiah v Ministry of Defence* [1979] 3 All ER 833; [1979] IRLR 436, CA. Here, men were required to work in a dustier part of the factory than women.

crimination on a trivial matter. The worker must show that 'by reason of the act or acts complained of a reasonable worker would or might take the view that he had thereby been disadvantaged in the circumstances in which he had thereafter to work'.[66]

9.35   The statutes do not expressly prohibit racial or sexual harassment and abuse, but this behaviour is covered if the worker is subjected to a 'detriment'.

9.36   Currently it seems that acts of racial discrimination against a former employee taking place after his/her job has ended are not covered, eg, in giving a reference or in the conduct of an appeal against dismissal.[67] However, post-dismissal victimisation is covered by the SDA 1975 and the ETD, at least where it results from complaints of sex discrimination originally made during the worker's employment.[68] It remains to be seen whether the RRA 1976 will now be interpreted in this way.

The meaning of 'discrimination'

9.37   There are three kinds of unlawful discrimination: direct discrimination, indirect discrimination and victimisation. Each of these has a precise legal meaning, which is set out below. In summary, the meaning of each form of discrimination is as follows.

(a) *Direct discrimination* is where one worker is treated differently from another because of his/her race, sex or marital status. Always ask the question, 'Had this worker been of a different race/sex, would the employer have treated him/her the same way?'

If different requirements are imposed on workers according to their race or sex, this is direct discrimination. Example: if an employer required all male workers to be over six feet and all female workers to be over five feet, a male job applicant of five feet five inches, who was therefore refused a job, would suffer direct discrimination.

There is no defence, although there are some exceptions for

---

66   *De Souza v The Automobile Association* [1986] IRLR 103; [1986] ICR 514, CA.

67   *Adekeye v The Post Office (No 2)* [1997] IRLR 105; 71 EOR 41, CA; *Nagarajan v Agnew* [1994] IRLR 61; (1994) 54 EOR 39, EAT. Although this has been doubted by the EAT in *Coote v Granada Hospitality Ltd (No 2)* [1999] IRLR 452; (1999) 87 EOR 53, EAT.

68   *Coote v Granada Hospitality Ltd* [1998] IRLR 656, ECJ, applied by the EAT in *Coote (No 2)* ibid.

genuine occupational qualifications and for positive action (see below).

(b) *Indirect discrimination* is where an apparently neutral requirement or condition is applied, but workers of a certain race or sex are less able to meet the requirement. Example: an employer requires all workers to be over six feet tall. Women would be disproportionately less able to meet this requirement. A female job applicant below six feet would suffer indirect discrimination.

Requirements which can be objectively justified are not unlawful indirect discrimination.

(c) *Victimisation* is when a worker is treated differently because s/he has previously complained of discrimination, given evidence for another worker in a discrimination case or done any other 'protected act'. Example: an employer sacks a worker because s/he complained of race discrimination.

The only defence for the employer is if the worker made a false allegation and did not act in good faith.

Direct discrimination

.38   This is the most obvious form of discrimination. It entails differential treatment on grounds of race, sex or marital status. The formal definition is in RRA 1976 s1(1)(a) and SDA 1975 ss1(1)(a), 2 and 3(1)(a). RRA 1976 s1(1)(a) states:

> A person discriminates against another if on racial grounds he treats that other less favourably than he treats or would treat other persons.

SDA 1975 s1(1)(a) is similar except that it prohibits discrimination against a woman 'on the ground of her sex'. Discrimination against men is also prohibited[69] and s3 prohibits less favourable treatment of a married person 'on the ground of his or her marital status' compared with an unmarried person of the same sex. It is not unlawful to discriminate against someone on the ground of their unmarried status.

39   Segregating a person on racial grounds is regarded as less favourable treatment under RRA 1976 s1(2).

40   Direct discrimination is best thought of in terms of comparative treatment. Comparisons between workers of different racial groups or of different sex or marital status must be made where the relevant

---

69   SDA 1975 s2.

circumstances are the same or not materially different[70] so that the comparison is significant. A worker will usually have a stronger case if s/he can point to an actual person of different race or sex who was treated more favourably in similar circumstances. However, it is not essential to find an actual comparator if it can be shown that the employer 'would have treated' someone of different race or sex more favourably.

9.41   A possible example of direct discrimination is where an employer does not appoint a woman with appropriate qualifications and experience for a job. If the woman was not appointed because she was a woman, then direct discrimination has occurred. This is so regardless of whether an actual man with similar qualifications and experience has applied and been appointed, although the woman would find it harder to prove her case if there was no actual comparable man.[71]

9.42   In certain cases it is hard to make a direct comparison with someone of the opposite sex, eg, unfavourable treatment of pregnant women[72] or cases concerning dress and appearance. Where women are not allowed to wear trousers or men are required to cut their hair, English ETs and courts have tended to say that there is no discrimination if workers of the opposite sex have been required to meet comparable or equivalent standards of smartness.[73]

9.43   Where there is more than one ground for an employer's action, it is sufficient if race or sex was 'an important factor'.[74]

Direct discrimination on grounds of gender reassignment

9.44   It is unlawful to treat a worker less favourably on grounds that s/he intends to undergo, is undergoing or has undergone gender reassignment.[75] The comparison is with the way the employer treats or would treat a worker who is not a transsexual. It would be dis-

---

70   SDA 1975 s5(3) and RRA 1976 s3(4).
71   See chapter 12 below for relevant evidence to prove direct discrimination.
72   See para 11.7 below.
73   See *Schmidt v Austicks Bookshops* [1977] IRLR 360; [1978] ICR 85, EAT; *Smith v Safeway plc* [1996] IRLR 456, CA, overturning the more liberal EAT decision. Note the different approach taken by the Northern Ireland High Court in *McConomy v Croft Inns Ltd* [1992] IRLR 561. In cases involving transsexuals, see the DfEE Guide to the Sex Discrimination (Gender Reassignment) Regs.
74   *Owen & Briggs v James* [1982] ICR 618; [1982] IRLR 502, CA; *Nagarajan v Agnew* [1994] IRLR 61, EAT.
75   SDA 1975 s2A(1).

criminatory to treat a worker's time off for gender reassignment less favourably than a routine sickness absence.[76] It may also be discriminatory to treat such absence less favourably than if the absence was due to some other cause, eg, paid or unpaid leave, but this depends on whether it is reasonable to do so.[77] The DfEE's Guide to the Regulations[78] suggests good practice for accommodating a worker's transition to the new gender including managing the timescale and time off.

Direct discrimination on grounds of someone else's race

9.45 Unlike the SDA, the wording of the RRA does not seem to require the discrimination to be on grounds of the worker's own race. It is therefore direct discrimination to discriminate against a worker due to the race of another. For example, where a worker is dismissed because s/he refuses to carry out a discriminatory instruction to exclude black customers, or,[79] presumably, a white worker is harassed because she has a black boyfriend or because she is friendly with a black member of staff. In some of these situations, the law on victimisation would more obviously apply (see below).

The employer's state of mind

9.46 Employers often tell the ET that they are not personally prejudiced and insist that they acted with the best of intentions in everything they did. This is irrelevant.[80] What counts is what the employer does, not what s/he thinks. If an employer in fact treats a black worker worse than s/he would treat a white worker, this is direct discrimination in any of the following situations:

- the employer intended to treat the black worker worse out of personal racial prejudice or malice;
- the employer intended to treat the black worker worse, but out of a non-malicious or even benevolent motive;

---

76 Ibid s2A(3)(a).
77 Ibid s2A(3)(b).
78 See para 9.4 and n4 above.
79 *Showboat Entertainment Centre Ltd v Owens* [1984] IRLR 7, EAT; *Zarczynska v Levy* [1978] IRLR 532, EAT; *Weathersfield Ltd t/a Van & Truck Rentals v Sargent* [1999] IRLR 94, CA.
80 The key cases on this are *R v Birmingham CC ex p EOC* [1989] IRLR 173, HL; *James v Eastleigh BC* [1990] IRLR 288, HL; *Swiggs v Nagarajan* [1999] IRLR 572; (1999) EOR 51, HL.

– the employer in fact treated the black worker worse but without realising it, ie, unconscious discrimination.

Examples of direct discrimination where the employer was not personally prejudiced are: where a headteacher refused to appoint a teacher because the pupils wished to be taught English by someone of English national origin;[81] or where a Pakistani worker was not re-employed because the employer feared industrial unrest among fellow Pakistani workers resulting from an earlier incident between him and a white foreman.[82]

9.47   Examples of discrimination outside the employment field are where a council offered free swimming to persons over state retirement age (ie, women from 60 and men from 65) in order to alleviate financial hardship of pensioners;[83] and where a council inherited a situation whereby there were more grammar school places for boys than for girls and therefore had to set higher entrance requirements for girls.[84]

9.48   Case-law has suggested that the 'but for' test should be applied to direct discrimination.[85] The question is whether the worker, but for his/her race or sex, would have been treated differently. The advantage of this test is that it focuses on actions not intentions and the ET need not try to assess the employer's state of mind.

9.49   Unconscious discrimination is hard to prove but it is a concept which the law recognises. The Court of Appeal has talked about the possibility of 'a conscious or unconscious racial attitude which involves stereotyped assumptions about members of that [racial] group'. The most explicit and enlightened guidance on this point was given only recently by the House of Lords in *Swiggs v Nagarajan*.[86] Although the case concerned victimisation, the guidance was intended also to apply to direct discrimination:

> All human beings have preconceptions, beliefs, attitudes and prejudices on many subjects. It is part of our make-up. Moreover, we do not always recognise our own prejudices. Many people are unable, or unwilling, to admit even to themselves that actions of theirs may be racially motivated. An employer may genuinely believe that the reason why he rejected an applicant had nothing to do with the applicant's race. After careful and thorough investigation of the claim, members

---

81 *Hafeez v Richmond School* (1981) COIT 1112/38.
82 *Din v Carrington Viyella* [1982] IRLR 281; [1982] ICR 256, EAT.
83 *James v Eastleigh BC* [1990] IRLR 288, HL.
84 *R v Birmingham CC ex p EOC* [1989] IRLR 173, HL.
85 Ibid and see *James v Eastleigh BC* (n83, above).
86 See n80 above.

of an employment tribunal may decide that the proper inference to be drawn from the evidence is that whether the employer realised it at the time or not, race was the reason why he acted as he did . . . Members of racial groups need protection from conduct driven by unconscious prejudice as much as from conscious and deliberate discrimination.

Unfortunately, many ETs fail to understand that much discrimination occurs due to unconscious stereotyping, for example, unconsciously undervaluing the performance or capability of a black worker. ETs repeatedly find that racial discrimination has not occurred because they believe in the 'honesty' of the employers' witnesses. Yet a manager who honestly believes a black worker is not fitted for promotion may nevertheless have reached a different 'honest' view of a white worker, when confronted with the same objective evidence. In some cases, it may now be worth explicitly drawing the above passage to the ET's attention at the outset of a hearing.

Defences to direct discrimination

An employer cannot claim that for some reason s/he was justified in directly discriminating. Only indirect discrimination can be justified. Direct discrimination is absolutely unjustifiable, although in certain specified circumstances it is permitted, eg, where authenticity is required for an acting role or to preserve privacy and decency between the sexes. These limited exceptions (which are basically common sense) together with positive action provisions are set out below in chapter 10.[87]

Direct discrimination: Key points

- Look for different treatment of the worker and of someone not of the worker's race, sex or marital status. If possible, find another worker for comparison, but a hypothetical comparison will suffice.
- The employer's prejudices, motives and intentions are irrelevant.
- If direct discrimination has occurred, it cannot be justified. However, there are exceptions for positive action or if the genuine occupational qualification defence applies.

---

87 There is also a specific defence available under the SDA 1975 where transsexuals are discriminated against in terms of time off. This may breach EU law.

General guide to useful evidence

- Evidence discrediting the employer's likely explanation of events.
- Indications of prejudice on the part of the relevant managers. (Although this is not legally necessary, it can strengthen the case.)
- Directly comparable examples within the workplace where workers of the same race or sex as the worker have been treated less favourably than those of a different race or sex.
- Statistics as to the position and treatment of workers, of the complainant's race or sex, generally within the workforce.

Indirect discrimination

9.51   This is a more difficult concept for practitioners and tribunals alike. The definition of prohibited discrimination was extended in the RRA 1976 to include indirect discrimination, as it was recognised that the law against direct discrimination did not go far enough to eliminate institutionalised disadvantage in the workplace. The great difficulty of indirect discrimination is that it is not always easy to detect and advisers need to be particularly alert.

9.52   Indirect discrimination occurs where there is apparently equal treatment of all groups, but the effect of certain requirements, conditions or practices imposed by employers has an adverse impact disproportionally on one group or other. For example, a requirement that all job applicants speak fluent English, while applied equally to everyone, would disproportionally debar persons born outside the UK from employment.

9.53   It is important to stress to ETs that the prohibition on indirect discrimination does not reduce standards or entail any kind of reverse discrimination. This is a common misconception. If a discriminatory requirement or condition can be justified, then it is not unlawful. The law simply prohibits unjustifiable requirements or conditions which have a discriminatory effect.

The definition

9.54   The definition of indirect discrimination under the RRA 1976 and SDA 1975 is recognised to be tortuous. It is set out in RRA 1976 s1(1)(b) and SDA 1975 ss1(1)(b) and 3(1)(b). The former reads as follows:

A person discriminates against another . . . if—(b) he applies to that other a requirement or condition which he applies or would apply equally to persons not of the same racial group as that other but—

(i)   which is such that the proportion of persons of the same racial group as that other who can comply with it is considerably smaller than the proportion of persons not of that racial group who can comply with it; and

(ii) which he cannot show to be justifiable irrespective of the colour, race, nationality or ethnic or national origins of the person to whom it is applied; and

(iii) which is to the detriment of that other because he cannot comply with it.

5   Put more simply, the following steps are necessary to identify indirect discrimination:

– there must be a requirement or condition which is applied to the worker;

– the particular worker bringing a case must be unable to comply with the condition or requirement and must suffer a disadvantage as a result;

– proportionally fewer people of the worker's race or sex than those not of the worker's race or sex must be able to comply with the condition or requirement; and

– the requirement or condition must be unjustifiable.

There is a wealth of case-law on the meaning of each part of the s1(1)(b) definition. The definition is simpler under EU law. The Directive on the Burden of Proof in Cases of Discrimination based on Sex (the Burden of Proof Directive)[88] is to be implemented by 22 July 2001 and states

indirect discrimination shall exist where an apparently neutral provision, criterion or practice disadvantages a substantially higher proportion of the members of one sex unless that provision, criterion or practice is appropriate and necessary and can be justified by objective factors unrelated to sex.

This definition broadly reflects EU case-law.

Identifying the requirement or condition

6   Not everything which an employer does is covered by s1(1)(b). The CRE in its proposals for reform of the RRA 1976 has suggested that

---

88   Council Directive 97/80/EC, applied to the UK by Directive 98/52/EC.

the wording be extended to cover any 'provision, criterion, practice or policy' involving an employee or job applicant. As things stand, however, it is only discriminatory requirements or conditions which are unlawful under the RRA 1976.[89]

9.57   Once the Burden of Proof Directive comes into force, the SDA 1975 must be amended to apply to any apparently neutral provision, criterion or practice.

9.58   A 'requirement or condition' bears its natural meaning and should not be narrowly construed.[90] It is not always easy to identify which is the relevant requirement or condition imposed by the employer. Formulating the requirement wrongly can make the difference between winning and losing a case.[91] Common requirements or conditions which may be discriminatory under the RRA 1976 are those requiring certain dress,[92] languages, qualifications, experience, duration or area of residence. Those under the SDA 1975 could relate to height, mobility, shift-working or full-time work. Length of service may be discriminatory against women and black workers.[93]

9.59   If an employer does not apply a condition absolutely but operates only a preference, this will not be covered by the definition of indirect discrimination.[94] This is a big loophole in the law.[95] It means that an employer can work to discriminatory preferences with impunity. For example, an employer might advertise a job stating 'English 'A' level preferred'. An applicant without English 'A' level may still be considered but will be at a disadvantage compared with a person who has the qualification. Nevertheless, the RRA will not apply.

9.60   In another example,[96] an employer used 12 informal criteria for shortlisting for the post of local government solicitor. Failure to meet any of the criteria did not bar candidates, but lowered their score for

---

89 Though see comments regarding EU law above.
90 *Clarke v Eley (IMI) Kynoch* [1982] IRLR 482; [1983] ICR 165, EAT. *Home Office v Holmes* [1984] IRLR 299; [1984] ICR 678, EAT.
91 *Francis v British Airways Engineering Overhaul* [1982] IRLR 10, EAT.
92 *Kingston and Richmond Health Auithority v Kaur* [1981] IRLR 337; [1981] ICR 631, EAT.
93 See appendix B for checklists on common discretionary requirements and circumstances where they may be applied.
94 *Perera v Civil Service Commission* [1983] IRLR 166; [1983] ICR 428, CA. *Meer v Tower Hamlets LBC* [1988] IRLR 399, CA.
95 And it is possibly a wrong interpretation of the legislation, but will stand until there is a HL decision. See the interesting SDA decision in *Falkirk Council v Whyte* [1997] IRLR 560; (1997) 75 EOR 44, EAT.
96 *Meer v Tower Hamlets LBC* [1988] IRLR 399, CA.

the purpose of shortlisting. One criterion was Tower Hamlets' experience. Mr Meer, who was of Indian origin, did not have such experience and indeed no Indian solicitors would have been able to fulfil such a condition. Nevertheless, because it was merely preferable and not essential that candidates could satisfy the criterion the case failed. Unfortunately it is common to find the 'person specifications' issued by large employers containing lists of 'essential' and 'preferable' requirements.[97]

.61   It is sometimes possible to win an indirect discrimination claim, even though the worker seems only to have been disadvantaged by the operation of a preference. For example, the employer may in reality be operating the preference as an absolute bar. This would be suggested if no one who fails to meet the preference for the job is shortlisted for a job. Alternatively, the employer may operate the preference differentially along racial lines so that, eg, white applicants are shortlisted even though they cannot meet the preference whereas black candidates are not. This would be direct discrimination.

.62   Similar problems arise where redundancy selection is made according to points scored on a number of criteria. A worker who scores badly on one criterion with discriminatory effect, eg, length of service, may be unable to claim indirect discrimination.[98] It would be different if an absolute bar applied, eg, all workers with less than five years' service are selected for redundancy first.

Ability to meet the requirement

.63   The relevant time at which a person's ability to comply with a requirement or condition must be measured is the same both for testing the particular worker's ability to comply and for measuring generally[99] whether others of the same and different racial or sexual groups can comply.[100] It is the date on which the worker suffered a detriment because s/he could not comply with the requirement and when the requirement or condition had to be fulfilled.[101] For example, a woman of Asian origin who qualified as a teacher in Kenya could

---

97 See appendix A for sample questionnaire.
98 *Hall v Shorts Missile Systems Ltd (1997)* 72 EOR 39, NI CA.
99 Though in some situations, it may be relevant to look over a wider period, *R v Secretary of State for Employment ex p Seymour-Smith and Perez* [1999] IRLR 253, ECJ.
100 *Clarke v Eley (IMI) Kynoch* [1982] IRLR 482, EAT.
101 Ibid.

not comply with a requirement for a clerical post of having English 'O' level. It was irrelevant that she had the ability to gain an 'O' level and could in the past or in the future have obtained one. At the time that the requirement was applied, she could not meet it.[102]

9.64   In another case,[103] part-timers were selected first for redundancy. At the time of the redundancy dismissals, Mrs Clarke was a part-time worker. It was irrelevant that she could have changed to full-time working several years ago once her children had grown-up, since she had not in fact done so and at the time of the selection, she was still a part-timer.[104]

9.65   The test is whether someone can in practice comply with the condition or requirement at the relevant time, not whether they could comply in theory.[105] For example, a Sikh could in theory comply with a requirement that he wear no turban. He need only take it off. However, in practice, he could not comply. The test is whether someone can comply 'consistently with the customs and cultural conditions of the racial group'.[106]

9.66   A civil service requirement that candidates for the post of executive officer must be under 29[107] does not in theory bar any more women than men. However, in practice, many women take career breaks to raise children, so that this requirement was held to discriminate indirectly against women.[108] The court said that it was relevant to consider 'the current usual behaviour of women in this respect, as observed in practice, putting on one side behaviour and responses which are unusual or extreme'.[109]

Comparing proportions who can and cannot comply with the requirement

9.67   A worker must show that within a 'pool' chosen for comparison, a considerably smaller proportion of those of the worker's own race or sex than those not of the worker's race or sex can comply with the

---

102   *Raval v DHSS and the Civil Service Commission* [1985] IRLR 370; [1985] ICR 685, EAT.
103   *Clarke v Eley (IMI) Kynoch* [1982] IRLR 482, EAT.
104   Though see paras 11.11 onwards regarding part-timers generally.
105   *Mandla v Lee* [1983] IRLR 209; [1983] ICR 385, HL; *Price v The Civil Service Commission* [1977] IRLR 291; [1978] ICR 27, EAT.
106   *Mandla v Lee* n105 above.
107   *Price v The Civil Service Commission* [1977] IRLR 291, EAT.
108   Ibid.
109   Ibid, but see para 11.19 below on *Clymo v Wandsworth LBC* [1989] IRLR 241; [1989] ICR 250, EAT on this point.

requirement. The Burden of Proof Directive (see above) refers to disadvantaging a 'substantially higher proportion' of one sex.

9.68 The question is within what section of the community does the proportionate comparison fall to be made?[110] For example, is the ability to comply measured among the total female and male population or only those in a particular town or a specific workplace or with appropriate qualifications?[111] The appropriate 'pool' will depend on the facts of each case and which section of the public is likely to be affected by the requirement.[112] In choosing the pool, people must be compared in the same, or not materially different, relevant circumstances.[113] In many cases, for example, the appropriate pool will be those who, apart from the discriminatory requirement, have the required qualifications for the post.[114]

9.69 Clearly the statistical outcome will vary according to the pool chosen. The ET's selection of the appropriate pool is a matter for its discretion.[115] However, the pool must not be such that it incorporates the act of discrimination. For example, in one case[116] only those who had been resident in the EU were eligible for lower college fees. It would have been misleading to choose as a pool, people who had actually applied to the college, because many would have been deterred from applying.

9.70 In another case,[117] lone parents who had never married were not eligible for grants. Ms Schaffter complained that this indirectly discriminated against women. The statistics showed that whereas 80 per cent of all lone parents were female, 20 per cent of the male lone parents and 20 per cent of female lone parents had never married. The court said that the appropriate pool for comparison was among all students with dependent children claiming grants and not among all lone parents who had never married. The latter pool was a 'trap' and would disguise the discrimination.

9.71 Indirect discrimination is concerned with whether a requirement or condition adversely affects one particular sex or racial group more than others. The law compares the proportions (fractions or percent-

---

110 Question 6 in *Raval v DHSS and the Civil Service Commission* (n102 above).
111 *Pearse v City of Bradford MC* [1988] IRLR 379, EAT; *Price v The Civil Service Commission* (n107 above).
112 *London Underground Ltd v Edwards* [1998] IRLR 364, CA.
113 RRA 1976 s3(4), SDA 1975 s5(3).
114 *Jones v University of Manchester* [1993] IRLR 218; (1993) 20 EOR 48, CA.
115 *Kidd v DRG (UK)* [1985] IRLR 190; [1985] ICR 405, EAT.
116 *Orphanos v Queen Mary College* [1985] IRLR 349, HL.
117 *R v Secretary of State for Education ex p Schaffter* [1987] IRLR 53, QBD.

ages) of people who can comply with the requirement, not absolute numbers. This makes a difference.[118]

9.72   For example, a Spanish worker may claim indirect discrimination because s/he cannot meet a potential employer's requirement for fluent English. The appropriate comparison is not the total number of Spaniards who can speak fluent English as against the total number of non-Spaniards who can speak fluent English. The proper comparison is the proportion of all Spanish people who can speak fluent English as against the proportion of all non-Spanish people who can do so. The calculation could be done as follows:

A = The total number of Spaniards within the chosen pool.
B = The number of Spaniards within the pool who can speak fluent English.
C = The total number of non-Spaniards in the pool.
D = The number of non-Spaniards in the pool who can speak fluent English.

Then B is divided by A and D is divided by C to get the fractions to be compared. Percentages can be calculated by multiplying each fraction by 100. Since many workers born in countries other than Spain also could not meet a fluent English requirement, looking at the statistics in this way may be misleading. It may be more accurate to describe the Spanish worker as 'non-English'[119] and compare the extent to which non-English workers, as opposed to English workers, could meet such a requirement. Note that the comparison cannot simply be made between Spanish workers and English workers: a comparison must be made between those of a particular racial group as against everyone else.

9.73   Taking a sex discrimination example: A hotel introduces a 24 hour rotating shift pattern for all managerial staff. A woman who cannot comply because of child-care obligations is dismissed. The proper comparison is B÷A compared with D÷C where:

A = The total number of female managers in the hotel.
B = The number of those women who can work full-time.
C = The total number of male managers in the hotel.
D = The number of those men who can work full-time.

---

118 Although the High Court in *Schaffter* said that it was relevant to the ETD if, in absolute numbers, substantially fewer women than men could comply with a requirement.
119 RRA 1976 s3(2). A racial group can comprise two or more distinct racial groups.

What amounts to a 'considerably smaller' proportion? The percentages should be looked at in terms of each other; it does not matter if the practice under attack has no relevance to the vast bulk of humanity.[120] Thus a difference of one per cent or two per cent with very small percentages would be no less significant than a difference between 30 per cent and 60 per cent.

4   A useful measure of what amounts to a significant difference used to be the '4/5th' or '80 per cent' rule, which was commonly used in the USA. If the smaller percentage is less than 80 per cent of the larger percentage, the difference is significant. There is alternatively a well-established statistical formula which determines whether a difference is statistically significant in accordance with the laws of probability as opposed to merely random.[121]

5   However UK courts have rejected the idea of following any rigid rule or formula, suggesting that ETs simply apply a common-sense approach in assessing what is a considerably smaller proportion.[122] In making this assessment, the meaning of the word 'considerably' should not be exaggerated.[123] The ECJ has said that the significance of statistical comparisons should be assessed by reference to factors such as the number of individuals counted and whether they illustrate purely fortuitous or short-term phenomena.[124] A lesser disparity which persisted over a long period could be sufficient.[125]

6   It does not defeat the claim if no one of the particular sex or racial group can comply.[126] Note that there will be special rules where part-timers are discriminated against, regardless of their sex or marital status.[127]

---

120 *Schaffter* (n 117 above). See table at para 9.91 for sample formulae.
121 For an explanation in the context of a Northern Ireland case under the Fair Employment (Northern Ireland) Act 1989, see 49 EOR 28.
122 *R v Secretary of State for Employment ex p Seymour-Smith and Perez* [1995] IRLR 464, CA; *McCausland v Dungannon DistrictCouncil* [1993] IRLR 583; (1994) 53 EOR 50, NICA. Most helpful is *London Underground Ltd v Edwards (No 2)* [1998] IRLR 364, CA.
123 *Seymour-Smith and Perez* (n122 above).
124 *Enderby v Frenchay Health Authority and Secretary of State for Health* [1993] IRLR 591, ECJ.
125 *R v Secretary of State for Employment ex p Seymour-Smith and Perez* [1993] IRLR 253, ECJ.
126 *Greencroft Social Club and Institute v Mullen* [1985] ICR 796, EAT.
127 See paras 11.11 onwards.

Is the requirement or condition justifiable?

9.77 The concept of justifiability is central to the law on indirect discrimination. In practice there are numerous, often hidden, requirements, conditions and practices with discriminatory effect in every workplace. The possibility of bringing a successful case often turns on whether the requirement or condition is justifiable.

9.78 Justifiability is very much a question of fact. It is difficult to gain guidance from past cases since tribunals have applied different tests for what is justifiable. At one time an employer needed to produce only what right-thinking people would consider were 'sound and tolerable reasons' for applying a requirement.[128] Now it is not so easy. What an ET would consider justifiable requires 'an objective balance between the discriminatory effect of the condition and the reasonable needs of the party who applies the condition'[129] An employer must show that:

- the requirement was objectively justifiable regardless of race or sex;
- the requirement served a real business need of the employer;[130] and
- the need was reasonable and objectively justifiable on economic or other grounds, eg, administrative efficiency; it is not sufficient that the particular employer personally considers it justifiable.[131]

The greater the discriminatory effect of the requirement, the greater the objective need an employer must show s/he has.[132] Under EU law, the discriminatory measure must be 'necessary, appropriate and proportionate to the aim pursued' – generalisations will not do.[133]

9.79 Examples of factors which may justify a discriminatory requirement are hygiene, safety, consistency of care, consistency of management and important economic and administrative considerations. Each case will depend on its precise facts and the principle of balance. Note that the Employment Act 1989 exempted turban-wearing Sikhs from any statutory requirements to wear safety helmets on constructions sites and declared that any requirement imposed by an

---

128 *Ojutiku and Oburoni v MSC* [1982] IRLR 418; [1982] ICR 661, CA.
129 *Hampson v Department of Education and Science* [1989] IRLR 69, CA.
130 *Bilka-Kaufhaus GmbH v Weber von Hartz* [1986] IRLR 317; [1987] ICR 110, ECJ; *Rainey v Greater Glasgow Health Board* [1987] IRLR 36; [1987] ICR 129, HL.
131 Ibid (NB these were equal pay cases); *Hampson* (n129 above).
132 *Hampson v Department of Education and Science* [1990] IRLR 302, HL. This is now the key case on what is justifiable. It imports the concept of 'proportionality' or balance from EU and US law.
133 *Küratorium für Dialyse und Nierentransplantation eV v Lewark* [1996] IRLR 637, ECJ. See also the Burden of Proof Directive at para 9.55.

employer to that effect would not be justifiable indirect discrimination.[134] Note also that the special treatment of lone parents participating in employment training is now permissible.[135]

80   Often employers lose sight of their aims when imposing discriminatory requirements. Where an employer seeks to justify a requirement, it is worth establishing first what business need the employer purports to have, and then examining whether the imposition of the requirement serves (or is necessary to serve) that need at all.

81   Once it is shown that there is a prima facie discriminatory requirement, the employer must prove it is justifiable.[136] This is often forgotten by ETs who expect workers to show why the requirement is not justifiable and to suggest alternative ways for employers to achieve needs. Obviously it is helpful if workers can show how employers could meet their needs by taking action with less discriminatory effect, but workers should not be required to provide such evidence.

Indirect discrimination: Key points

- Find the requirement, condition or if EU law applies, practice, which the worker cannot meet.
- The requirement, condition or practice must be such that people of the worker's race or sex are generally less able to meet it than other people.
- Consider whether the employer is likely to be able objectively to justify applying the requirement or condition.
- Note the special position regarding part-time workers.

General guide to useful evidence

- Statistics or other evidence showing that proportionally fewer people of the worker's race or sex could meet the requirement.
- Evidence showing that the worker cannot in practice meet the requirement.

---

134 Employment Act 1989 ss11 and 12. Note that the employers' liabilty for injury is, as a consequence, restricted.
135 SDA 1975 (Exemption of Special Treatment for Lone Parents) Order 1989 SI No 2140 and 1991 SI No 2813.
136 See para 12.5 below on burden of proof.

Victimisation

9.82 It is unlawful to victimise a worker because s/he has made a complaint of discrimination or done any other 'protected act' under the RRA 1976 or SDA 1975. This protection is particularly important for workers who risk dismissal by bringing up controversial issues, but do not have the requisite length of service to qualify for a claim of unfair dismissal. The law protects workers complaining about discrimination against themselves as well as workers speaking out on behalf of others. For example, a white worker must not be victimised for supporting a black worker who has brought a grievance of race discrimination. Similarly a trade union representative could claim victimisation if s/he is put under pressure by the employer when s/he takes up race or sex discrimination cases, but not for other types of case.[137]

9.83 Unfortunately, it is very hard to prove that victimisation has taken place. A worker must show three things:

(1) s/he has done a 'protected act', ie, an act within RRA 1976 s2(a)–(d) or SDA 1975 s4(a)–(d);

(2) s/he has been treated less favourably by the employer because s/he did the protected act. The comparison is with the way another worker who had not done the protected act would have been treated;[138] and

(3) the less favourable treatment is precisely because the worker's conduct was under or by reference to the RRA 1976, SDA 1975, EqPA 1970 or Pensions Act 1995[139] ss 62 to 65.[140]

It is not necessary to show that the employer was consciously motivated or influenced by the fact that the worker had done the protected act.[141]

9.84 It is unlawful under RRA 1976 s2 to treat people less favourably because they have done any 'protected act', ie, if they have brought proceedings under the RRA 1976 or have given evidence or information in proceedings (brought by themselves or anyone else) under the

---

137 S/he may also be able to claim discrimination for taking up trade union activities. See para 6.76.

138 *Chief Constable of West Yorkshire Police and Others v Khan* (2000) 638 IRLB 8, CA. *Aziz v Trinity Street Taxis* [1988] IRLR 204; [1988] ICR 534, CA.

139 Concerning sex discrimination in occupational pensions.

140 *Aziz* (n138 above).

141 *Swiggs v Nagarajan* [1999] IRLR 572; (1999) EOR 51, HL.

RRA 1976, or intend to do any of those things.[142] More generally, it is unlawful to treat people less favourably because they have done, or intend to do, anything under or by reference to the RRA 1976 or because they have alleged, or intend to allege, that anyone has committed an act which would in fact amount to a contravention of the RRA 1976.[143] It is also unlawful for an employer to victimise a worker because s/he suspects the worker has done or intends to do a protected act. SDA 1975 s4 grants similar protection in relation to the SDA 1975, the EqPA 1970 and the Pensions Act 1995.

The precise scope of doing anything 'under or by reference to' the statutes is uncertain. A Leeds ET thought that the activities of three local authority race trainers in pursuance of the authority's obligations under RRA 1976 s71 were protected acts under s2(c) and their dismissal when the authority changed hands was unlawful victimisation.[144] Other examples of 'protected acts' could be encouraging a colleague to take up a discrimination case; issuing a press statement referring to breaches of the RRA 1976 or SDA 1975; or approaching the CRE or a Race Equality Council.

Since a worker first has to prove that s/he has done a 'protected act', which s/he feels has led to victimisation, it is advisable that any complaint of discrimination or statement of intention to bring proceedings or give evidence should be put in writing at the time. If appropriate, such written statement should be accompanied by a reminder to the employers of the right not to be victimised under the appropriate sections.

As a matter of evidence, it is difficult to prove that the reason the employer has treated the worker unfavourably is because the worker has done a protected act. For example, an employer dismissing a woman because she has made an allegation of sexual harassment may purport to do so because her work is poor.

Employers often say they are not punishing the worker for doing the protected act, but for some other aspect of his/her behaviour. For example, in one case,[145] Mr Aziz was a taxi driver and member of TST, a company promoting the interests of taxi drivers in Coventry.

---

142 RRA 1976 s2(a), (b).
143 Ibid s2(c), (d).
144 *Grant v Knight and City of Bradford MC* (1990) 394 IRLIB 14, ET. Note, it would be necessary to prove the trainers were dismissed because they had done protected acts.
145 *Aziz v Trinity Street Taxis* [1988] IRLR 204, CA. This is a key case on the law of victimisation.

He made secret tape recordings of other TST members, as he felt he was being discriminated against. He later decided to make a race discrimination claim against TST. When the recordings were disclosed during the case, he was expelled from TST. Mr Aziz claimed that he was victimised by being expelled. He claimed that the protected act was making the tape recordings with a view possibly to bringing a race discrimination case. He lost his case because the ET found that the reason for his expulsion was the fact that the recordings were underhand and a breach of trust. The ET accepted that TST would still have expelled Mr Aziz even if the purpose of the recordings was nothing to do with the race relations legislation.

9.89   Victimisation by an employer is not always as obvious as dismissing or disciplining a worker who does a 'protected act'. It may take many less obvious and more subtle forms, for example:

- pressurising a worker to drop an allegation of discrimination;
- withdrawing or reducing trade union facilities to a shop steward who is gathering evidence for a discrimination or equal pay claim;
- refusing holiday leave requests at the time desired; or
- writing a poor reference while a worker is still in employment but looking for a new job.[146]

An employer has a defence to a victimisation claim in relation to a worker's allegation under the RRA 1976, SDA 1975, EqPA 1970 or Pension Act 1995, where such allegation was false and not made in good faith.[147] Therefore as long as the worker genuinely believes the discrimination of which s/he complains has occurred, even if the ET disagrees, s/he should be protected.

9.90   However, if the worker complains of discrimination which would not be covered by the relevant Acts even if s/he proved it happened, s/he will not be protected.[148] For example, a worker who is dismissed for complaining of a sexual assault taking place outside the course of employment (and therefore not covered by the SDA 1975) cannot complain of victimisation.[149]

---

146 See para 9.36 above for discrimination by the employer taking place after the worker has left.
147 RRA 1976 s2, SDA 1975 s4.
148 *Waters v Commissioner of Police of the Metropolis* [1997] IRLR 589; (1997) 76 EOR 40, CA.
149 Although she could claim direct discrimination if a man bringing an equally serious complaint would not have been dismissed.

As is apparent from all of the above, the difficulties in proving motive or causation severely limit the effectiveness of the victimisation provisions in practice. Victimisation is a major practical problem in the workplace, but tends to be overlooked as an industrial relations issue. It is remarkable how often equal opportunities policies and training deal with direct and indirect discrimination but fail to address victimisation.

INDIRECT DISCRIMINATION: FORMULAS FOR COMPARISON

$$\frac{\text{number of women (in pool) [who can meet requirement]}}{\text{total number of women (in pool)}} \quad v \quad \frac{\text{number of men (in pool) [who can meet requirement]}}{\text{total number of men (in pool)}}$$

$$\frac{\text{members of racial group (in pool) [who can meet requirement]}}{\text{all members of racial group (in pool)}} \quad v \quad \frac{\text{those outside racial group (in pool) [who can meet requirement]}}{\text{all those outside racial group (in pool)}}$$

[EXAMPLES:]

$$\frac{\text{number of women (managers at hotel) [who can work flexi-shifts]}}{\text{total number of women (managers at hotel)}} \quad v \quad \frac{\text{number of men [managers at hotel] [who can work flexi-shifts]}}{\text{total number of men (managers at hotel)}}$$

$$\frac{\text{Spanish people (of working age living in UK) [who speak fluent English]}}{\text{all Spanish people (of working age living in UK)}} \quad v \quad \frac{\text{non-Spanish people (of working age living in UK) [who speak fluent English]}}{\text{all non-Spanish people (of working age living in UK}}$$

$$v$$

[OR]

$$\frac{\text{non-English people (of working age, living in UK) [who meet requirement]}}{\text{all non-English people (of working age living in UK)}} \quad v \quad \frac{\text{English people (of working age living in UK) [who meet requirement]}}{\text{all English people (of working age living in UK)}}$$

Permitted race and sex discrimination

Genuine occupational qualifications

10.1   Under RRA 1976 s5 and SDA 1975 s7, discrimination is permitted in certain circumstances[1] where being of a particular racial group or gender is a genuine occupational qualification (GOQ) of the job. The GOQ defence may apply to discrimination in refusing to offer someone employment or in the arrangements made for determining who should be offered employment or in access to opportunities for promotion or transfer or to training for employment.

10.2   The GOQ defence is *not* available in the following circumstances:

- under the SDA 1975, where discrimination is against married persons;
- where discrimination occurs in the terms of employment offered or afforded to workers, or in access to benefits, facilities or services (other than promotion, transfer or training), or in dismissing someone or subjecting them to any other detriment;
- to the filling of a vacancy at a time when the employer already has workers of the particular race/sex who are capable of carrying out the duties in question, whom it would be reasonable to employ on those duties and who could carry out those duties without undue inconvenience to the employer.[2] For example, in *Etam plc v Rowan*,[3] a shop selling womens' clothes refused to employ a male shop assistant because the job was likely to involve contact with women in a state of undress.[4] The GOQ defence failed because the part of a sales assistant's job which involved contact with women in changing rooms could have been carried out by other (female) shop assistants without causing undue inconvenience to the employer.

For a full list of GOQs, it is important to read the wording of the sections. In summary, they are as follows.

10.3   Under the RRA 1976:

- for reasons of authenticity as an actor, entertainer, artist's or photographer's model;
- for reasons of authenticity, working in a place where food or drink is served to the public in a particular setting; or

---

1 RRA 1976 s5(1), SDA 1976 s7(1).
2 RRA 1976 s5(4), SDA 1975 s7(4).
3 [1989] IRLR 150, EAT.
4 SDA 1975 s7(2)(b)(i) and (ii).

- to provide personal services promoting the welfare of persons of the same racial group.

Under the SDA 1975:

- for reasons of authenticity as an actor or entertainer or for reasons of physiology (excluding physical strength or stamina);
- to preserve decency or privacy because of likely physical contact or contact with persons in a state of undress or using sanitary facilities or, where work is in a private home, because of close physical or social contact with someone living in the home;
- because it is necessary to live on work premises and there are no separate sleeping and sanitary facilities and it is not reasonable to expect the employer to supply these;
- where the work is in a single-sex establishment or part of an establishment for persons requiring special care, supervision or attention, eg, a hospital or prison;
- where the job is one of two to be held by a married couple; or
- to provide personal services promoting the welfare or education or similar services to persons of the same sex.

An employer can invoke the GOQ defence even where only some of the duties of the job are covered by the section,[5] although of course it is then more likely that the duties can be covered by other workers.

Transsexuals

4   GOQs also apply to permit discrimination against transsexuals in certain circumstances, but the position is more complex.[6] Again, it is advisable to read the precise wording but broadly speaking the position is as follows. The single sex GOQs[7] apply as set out above provided the employer can show the treatment is reasonable.[8] Unlike the usual position, the GOQ defence is also available where the employer dismisses a worker.[9] There are four supplementary GOQs[10] which also apply to dismissal as well as recruitment, promotion, transfer and training. In brief these are:

5   RRA 1976 s5(3), SDA 1975 s7(3).
6   See SDA 1975 ss7A and 7B and the EOR report on the new legislation at (1999) 85 EOR 36.
7   SDA 1975 s7 and listed above.
8   SDA 1975 s7A(1).
9   Ibid s7A(2).
10   Ibid s7B.

- where the job-holder may have to carry out intimate physical searches pursuant to statutory powers;[11]
- where work is in a private home, because of physical or social contact with someone living in the home;[12]
- because it is necessary to live on work premises and it is not reasonable to expect the employer to make alternative arrangements or equip the premises to preserve decency and privacy.[13] Unlike the above two supplemental GOQs, this GOQ only applies while the worker is currently undergoing gender reassignment;
- where the work provides vulnerable individuals with personal welfare or other services and in the reasonable view of the employer, these could not be effectively provided whilst the worker is undergoing gender reassignment.[14]

The exception to the single-sex GOQs where there are other employees who could reasonably carry out the relevant duties[15] does not apply to these supplementary GOQs.

Positive action

10.5   The codes of practice encourage positive action.

Personal services

10.6   The RRA 1976 s5(2)(d) says that being of a particular racial group is a GOQ where:

> the holder of the job provides persons of that racial group with personal services promoting their welfare, and those services can most effectively be provided by a person of that racial group.

SDA 1975 s7(2)(e) is similar in relation to gender except that it refers to personal services promoting 'welfare or education or similar personal services'. To gain the protection of the subsections the following must be satisfied.

- The job must involve wholly or partly the provision of 'personal

---

11   Ibid s7B(2)(a).
12   Ibid s7(2)(b).
13   Ibid s7B(2)(c).
14   Ibid s7B(2)(d).
15   Ibid s7(4) and above.

services'. The post-holder must be directly involved in the provision of the services,[16] ie, in face-to-face contact with the recipient. Purely administrative and managerial positions such as assistant head of a local authority housing benefit department[17] are not covered.

- Those services must be such that they are most effectively provided by a person of the same sex or racial group.[18] It is not necessary to show that the services can be provided only by a person of the same sex or racial group. It is recognised that 'where language or a knowledge and understanding of cultural and religious background are important, then those services may be most effectively provided by a person of a particular racial group'.[19]

- The EAT has said that the provider of services must be of a particular racial group which is the same group as that of the recipients and not simply black.[20] However, Balcombe LJ in the Court of Appeal suggested obiter that in some circumstances, eg, a health visitor, personal services may be most effectively provided to persons of 'a racial group defined by colour', eg, black people, by a person of the same colour, regardless of which ethnic group each person came from.[21]

- There must be no other workers already employed who could, without undue inconvenience, provide those services.[22]

Encouraging applications/offering training

.7   Under RRA 1976 s38 and SDA 1975 s48, an employer can:

- encourage people of only a particular sex or racial group to apply for jobs; and
- offer training only to people of a particular sex or racial group;

provided that in the previous 12 months the number of women or people of that racial group doing the work in question was compara-

16 *Tottenham Green Under Fives' Centre v Marshall* [1989] IRLR 147; [1989] ICR 214, EAT.
17 *Lambeth LBC v CRE* [1990] IRLR 231, CA.
18 *Tottenham Green* (n16 above).
19 *Lambeth LBC v CRE* (n17 above).
20 *Tottenham Green* (n16 above); *Lambeth LBC v CRE* (n17 above).
21 *Lambeth LBC v CRE* (n17 above). See also *Hartup v Sandwell MBC*, EAT 20 July 1993 (479/92), summarised at (1993) 504 *IDS Brief* 16, where the EAT accepted that 'a particular racial group' can compromise two or more distinct racial groups.
22 RRA 1976 s5(4), SDA 1975 s7(4).

tively small, either generally or in the employing organisation in particular.

10.8   Note that, although it is permissible to encourage job applicants who are women or of a particular racial group, it is not permissible to discriminate at the point of taking someone on. Employers can therefore place advertisements expressly encouraging applications from women and particular racial groups or ask job centres to tell such people that applications from them are particularly welcome, but it should be made clear that selection will be on merit, regardless of race or sex.

Special needs

10.9   It is not unlawful under RRA 1976 s35 to afford someone of a particular racial group access to facilities or services to meet his/her special needs in regard to his/her education, training or welfare.

Discriminatory advertisements

10.10   Under RRA 1976 s29 and SDA 1975 s38 it is unlawful to publish or have published an advertisement which indicates or might reasonably be understood as indicating an intention to discriminate, unless a GOQ or other exceptions apply.[23] Proceedings in respect of unlawful advertisements can only be brought by the Commission for Racial Equality or Equal Opportunities Commission, not by individuals.[24] However, a discriminatory advertisement may be evidence supporting an individual's claim of unlawful discrimination if a person goes on to apply for the job and is unsuccessful.

Statutory authority

10.11   RRA 1976 s41 excludes from the ambit of the RRA any discriminatory act done in pursuance of a statute or statutory instrument. It is now established that 'in pursuance of' is confined to acts done in necessary performance of an express obligation contained in a statute or statutory instrument and does not include anything done merely

---

23   See these sections for exceptions to liability.
24   RRA 1976 s63, SDA 1975 s72.

in the exercise of a power or discretion conferred by statute.[25] For example, the Secretary of State for Education was not protected by s41 when exercising his discretion under the Education (Teachers) Regulations 1982 SI No 106 to decide whether to grant qualified teacher status to an overseas teacher on the basis of his own non-statutory criteria.

12   The sex discrimination exemption is quite different and SDA 1975 s51 was significantly amended by the Employment Act 1989 s3. Discriminatory acts which are 'necessary' to comply with a requirement of any statute passed before the SDA 1975 are permitted, provided that the purpose of the provision was to protect women as regards pregnancy, maternity or any other risks specifically affecting women.[26] The Employment Act 1989 Sch 1 sets out specific health and safety legislation which is also excluded.

National security

13   Discriminatory acts done to safeguard national security are excluded from the RRA 1976 and SDA 1975.[27]

Pregnancy or childbirth

14   SDA 1975 s2(2) permits (but does not require) special treatment afforded to women in connection with pregnancy or childbirth.

---

25   *Hampson v Department of Education and Science* [1990] IRLR 302, HL.
26   SDA 1975 s51(2).
27   RRA s42, SDA s52

CHAPTER 11

Special situations

For complete chapter contents, see overleaf

11.1   **Pregnancy dismissals and discrimination**

Pregnancy dismissals and discrimination

11.1   Under ERA 1996 s99, it is automatically unfair to dismiss a woman for a number of reasons related to her pregnancy, maternity or maternity leave (see para 6.68 above). There is no minimum service requirement to claim unfair dismissal for those reasons. Additionally, it is unlawful to take action short of dismissal for any of those reasons. All women will also have a right to 18 weeks' maternity leave.[1] If a woman is unable to work for health and safety reasons, she may be entitled to paid medical suspension.

11.2   Linked to these rights, a woman is additionally entitled to written reasons if she is dismissed while pregnant or on maternity leave, regardless of her length of service.[2] Women may also claim that dismissal in such circumstances is unlawful sex discrimination contrary to the SDA 1975. Where possible, women should usually claim under both statutes, since a successful sex discrimination claim would lead to additional compensation. Claiming under the SDA also enables a woman to use the useful SDA questionnaire procedure to gather evidence.

11.3   Sometimes making a claim under the SDA will be the only legal option, eg, because she does not meet the other qualifying requirements for claiming unfair dismissal under the ERA 1996, for instance, because she is a contract worker and not an employee.

  It is impossible to understand how pregnancy discrimination fits within the law on sex discrimination without knowing the history of the case-law. It has always been difficult to prove that a dismissal or other discrimination due to pregnancy amounts to unlawful sex discrimination. Historically, tribunals and courts have been reluctant to say that pregnancy discrimination falls within the SDA.

11.4   Originally, the provisions of the SDA 1975 were applied rather literally so that discrimination against pregnant women was permitted. It was said that no comparison could be made for the purposes of s1(1)(a) because men could not be pregnant.[3] Similarly, under s1(1)(b), a requirement of not being pregnant could not be applied to men and women alike.

11.5   The next stage was the case of *Hayes v Malleable Working Men's Club and Institute* and *Maughan v North East London Magistrates'*

---

1 See para 7.97.
2 ERA 1996 s92(4). See para 16.8.
3 *Turley v Allders Stores* [1980] ICR 66; [1980] IRLR 4, EAT.

Courts Committee,[4] where the EAT interpreted the law more sensibly, noting:

> It will usually be the consequences of pregnancy, rather than the condition itself, which provides the grounds for dismissal; the general effect upon the employee's performance at work or the need to take time off for her confinement and for periods of rest before and afterwards.

The EAT went on to suggest that a pregnant woman employee could properly be compared with a sick male employee for the purposes of the SDA 1975. The problem with this approach is that it involves an artificial comparison which ignores the unique status of pregnancy.

The cases tend to concern dismissal. However, action short of dismissal may also be sex discrimination, eg, harassment or refusing maternity leave.[5] In applying the ETD, the ECJ took a more favourable view than the UK courts. In 1991 it said[6] that it is not necessary to make any artificial comparison with a man; thus a woman who is dismissed due to her pregnancy or the need for maternity leave suffers unlawful discrimination regardless of the way a man in comparable circumstances would have been treated. Equally, a woman who is not recruited because she is pregnant is discriminated against even though the person who gets the job is also a woman, who is not pregnant. Since pregnancy relates only to women, then it is automatically sex discrimination contrary to the directive.

There has been some uncertainty as to how far in time the *Webb*[7] principle extends. It now seems clear that it is sex discrimination to treat a woman less favourably due to her pregnancy at any time up to the end of her statutory maternity leave period.[8] However, where the discrimination occurs after the end of her maternity leave, a comparison with a man in a similar position is still necessary, eg, where a woman is dismissed due to a pregnancy-related illness occurring after her maternity leave period.[9] In such a case, a woman is entitled to be treated no worse than a man would be treated if sick for a

4 [1985] IRLR 367; [1985] ICR 703, EAT.
5 *Curl v Air (UK)* (1988) 22 EOR 44, ET.
6 *Handels og-Kontorfuntionaererenes Forbund i Danmark (acting for Hertz) v Dansk Arbejdsgiverforening* [1991] IRLR 31, ECJ; *Dekker v Stichting Vormingscentrum voor Jonge Volwassenen Plus* [1991] IRLR 27, ECJ.
7 *Webb v EMO Air Cargo (UK) Ltd* [1994] IRLR 482, ECJ.
8 *Brown v Rentokil Ltd* [1998] IRLR 445; 81 EOR 45, ECJ.
9 *Hertz* (n6, above); *Brown* (n8, above).

similar period disregarding the earlier period of absence during pregnancy and maternity leave.[10]

11.8   It is sex discrimination (without needing the male comparison) for a sick pay scheme to exclude pregnancy-related illness.[11] It is also discriminatory to fail to give a woman a performance-related pay assessment because she has been absent on maternity leave.[12] Similarly, a woman must be given the benefit of any pay rise awarded before or during maternity leave.[13] However, a woman cannot argue that she should be paid full wages during maternity leave purely because her absence is pregnancy-related.[14] This is because women on maternity leave are in a special position that affords them special protection, but which is not comparable with the position of other workers. The only requirement under EU law is that maternity pay must not fall below an adequate level, ie, that of statutory sick benefits.[15] This requirement is normally satisfied by the level of statutory maternity pay.[16]

11.9   Even where there is contractual sick pay, but no contractual maternity pay, a woman cannot claim sex or pregnancy discrimination.[17] The same applies if there is contractual pay for both sickness and maternity leave, but only the maternity pay must be repaid if the woman fails to return to work for a specified time after her absence.[18]

11.10   A woman who is dismissed because her replacement while she is on maternity leave is more efficient may claim sex discrimination because, had she not been absent. the unfavourable comparison would not have arisen.[19] Note that men cannot claim sex discrimination if an employer chooses to give special treatment to women in connection with pregnancy or childbirth.[20]

10 *Brown* (n8, above)
11 *Handels-og Kontorfunktionaerernes Forbund i Danmark acting on behalf of Hoj Pedersen v Faellesforeningen for Danmarks Brugsforeninger acting on behalf of Kvickly Skive*, C-66/96 [1999] IRLR 55; (1999) 83 EOR 43, ECJ.
12 *Caisse Nationale D'Assurance Vieillesse des Travailleurs Salaries (CNAVTS) v Thibault* [1998] IRLR 399, ECJ.
13 *Gillespie v Northern Health and Social Services Board* [1996] IRLR 214, ECJ.
14 *Gillespie* ibid.
15 *Gillespie*. ibid; *Gillespie v Northern Health and Social Services Board (No 2); Todd v Eastern Health and Social Services Board and Department of Health and Social Services* [1997] IRLR 410, NI CA.
16 But see *Banks v (1) Tesco Stores Ltd (2) Secretary of State for Social Security* (1999) 648 *IDS Brief* 9, EAT, where the woman was ineligible even for SMP.
17 *Gillespie (No 2)* and *Todd* (n15, above).
18 *Boyle v EOC* [1998] IRLR 717, ECJ.
19 *Rees v Apollo Watch Repairs plc* (1996) 563 *IDS Brief* 6, EAT.
20 SDA 1975 s2(2).

Pregnancy dismissals: Key points

- Dismissals for reasons connected with pregnancy, maternity, maternity leave or terms are automatically unfair. Action short of dismissal is also unlawful. There is no minimum qualifying service.
- Discrimination due to pregnancy and related reasons such as pregnancy-related sickness is usually unlawful sex discrimination in itself if it occurs during pregnancy or maternity leave.
- In limited circumstances, eg, pregnancy-related sickness occurring after maternity leave, a comparison with a man in equivalent circumstances may be necessary.

General guide to useful evidence

- Evidence proving that the dismissal was for pregnancy or a related reason as opposed to the reason put forward by the employer.
- If comparison with a man is necessary, evidence showing how a man would have been treated in comparable circumstances, eg, if he required sick leave.

Part-time working and job-shares

1 The Employment Relations Act 1999 states that the secretary of state will issue regulations to ensure equal treatment of part-timers with full-timers at work 'to such extent as the regulations may specify'.[21] This is to implement EU Directive 97/81/EC on the framework agreement on part-time work. At the time of writing, draft regulations have been issued for consultation (see para 11.14 below).

2 Until the Directive is implemented, there is no general right to work part-time or for part-timers to be treated equally with full-timers. Workers can only claim rights in this direction if they fall within sex discrimination law. The basic principle is that more women than men work part-time and wish to work part-time, by reason of child care responsibilities. Thus, any less favourable treatment of part-timers or any prohibition on part-time working is likely

21 ERA 1999 s19.

to have an adverse impact on women. Similar arguments can be made in respect of married persons as against unmarried persons. Unfortunately, the restrictive definition of indirect sex discrimination under the SDA 1975 has meant that many workers could not gain the necessary protection.

Protection of part-time employees generally

11.13   The Part-time Employees (Prevention of Less Favourable Treatment) Regulations 2000 in draft form prohibit less favourable treatment of part-time employees (men and women, married and unmarried) unless the treatment is objectively justified. The government intends the regulations to ensure part-timers have pro rata entitlements and are not unjustifiably discriminated against in pay-rates, pensions, sick-pay and leave etc. Part-timers will also have a right to written reasons for any treatment they consider less favourable under the regulations. They must not be subjected to a detriment because they have taken up these rights. The draft regulations do not explictly grant a right to move from full-time to part-time work and their effect is unclear in this respect.

11.14   Where they apply the regulations will be far simpler than claiming indirect sex discrimination, although an employer will still be able to claim the defence that it can justify treating a part-timer less favourably. Where possible, a worker should claim both under the ERA 1999 and the SDA 1975. Although more difficult to prove, the advantage of a sex discrimination claim is that the questionnaire procedure can be used in running a case. It may also attract additional compensation, eg, for injury to feelings, but that depends on the final form of the regulations.

Part-time working and sex discrimination

Is there a right to work part-time?

11.15   There is no absolute right in sex discrimination law to work part-time or to job-share. However, a number of cases have accepted that women are adversely affected when only full-time work is available and this can be unlawful as indirect sex discrimination. Even if an ET declares that insistence on full-time working in a particular case is discriminatory, an employer cannot be compelled to employ someone part-time and the only remedies are compensation for sex discrimination, victimisation or unfair dismissal.

1.16   The main case establishing that refusal to let women work part-time may be unlawful indirect discrimination was *Home Office v Holmes*[22] in 1984. The stages of proving indirect discrimination have been dealt with above.[23] Where a woman claims that an employer's insistence on full-time working is indirect discrimination, the following special considerations apply.

Is full-time working a requirement or condition?

1.17   It is now fairly well-established that an employer who insists on full-time work is imposing a requirement or condition within the meaning of the SDA 1975.[24] Once the Burden of Proof Directive comes into effect, this narrow wording will not apply in any event.[25]

Ability to work full-time

.18   Is the full-time working requirement to the worker's detriment because she cannot comply with it? In *Holmes*, the ET considered that the applicant could not comply with the requirement and that was to her detriment. It said that attempting to fulfil parental responsibilities and work full-time entailed excessive demands on Ms Holmes' time and energy.

.19   In *Clymo*,[26] the ET was less sympathetic. A senior branch librarian wished to job-share with her husband after returning from maternity leave. The ET thought that she could comply with the full-time requirement since the council had offered child-minding and she and her husband were earning enough to pay for it; she was merely exercising a personal preference to care for her child. The EAT agreed with this view,[27] revealing its attitude by stating: 'in every employment ladder from the lowliest to the highest, there will come a stage at which a woman who has family responsibilities must make a choice'. This seemingly contradicted the EAT's earlier comment that the librarian 'should not be coerced into a position of complying with a situation wholly alien to her womanhood or motherhood'. However,

22 [1984] IRLR 299; [1984] ICR 678, EAT.
23 See paras 9.54 to 9.81.
24 *Home Office v Holmes* [1984] IRLR 299, EAT; *Briggs v North Eastern Education and Library Board* [1990] IRLR 181, NI CA.
25 See para 12.6.
26 *Clymo v Wandsworth LBC* [1989] IRLR 241, EAT.
27 Despite the wide meaning of 'can comply' established by *Price v Civil Service Commission* (n28 below) and *Mandla v Lee* [1983] IRLR 209, HL (see para 9.65 above).

it does seem that the ET and EAT were influenced by the worker's relatively high status and income and the council's offer of childcare.

11.20　By contrast, in an earlier case the EAT stated quite clearly that although a woman 'is not obliged to marry, or to have children, or to mind children; she may find somebody to look after them', to say that for those reasons she can comply with a requirement to work full-time would be 'wholly out of sympathy with the spirit and intent of the Act'.[28]

11.21　If an ET takes an unsympathetic approach, a woman will be in difficulty if she has demonstrated in the meantime that she can in fact work full-time. On the other hand, she will not want to resign if there is a chance that the ET can help her. This is a good reason for asking the ET for an early hearing date on the ground that the woman's job is in jeopardy because she cannot continue working. Sometimes an employer may agree that she works part-time pending the result. If not, she may have to show the ET that her childcare arrangements could only be sustained in the short term and were causing great stress, expense or inconvenience. Ms Clymo tried to avoid this trap by using up her days off to work part-time in practice. Ms Holmes took six months' sick leave.

Is the requirement justifiable?

11.22　This depends on the facts of the particular case. In *Holmes*, the Home Office tried to justify the requirement by arguing that the bulk of industry, national and local government service was still organised on a full-time basis. The EAT was unimpressed with that argument and found the requirement unjustified.

11.23　In another case,[29] a health visitor was permitted to work part-time after maternity leave, provided her hours were spread over five days. The worker objected that this involved her in greater expenses for the same wage. Nevertheless, the EAT found the requirement justified because patients needed regular personal contact and health visitors should be available five days a week for consultation with doctors or social workers.

11.24　The introduction of more general rights for part-timers with the ERA 1999 suggests that it should be harder for employers than in the past to justify insisting on full-time working or treating part-timers less favourably.

28　*Price v Civil Service Commission* [1977] IRLR 291, EAT.
29　*Greater Glasgow Health Board v Carey* [1987] IRLR 484, EAT.

Common forms of discrimination against part-timers

5 The application of the redundancy selection criterion of part-timers first may well be unlawful sex discrimination.[30] Most difficulties facing part-time workers, however, concern less favourable terms and conditions, particularly indirect discrimination in 'pay' in its broadest sense. Because article 141 is binding on all employers, EU law has been very helpful in securing equality of pay, pension contributions,[31] sick pay, etc. Examples of indirect discrimination against part-timers or job-sharers include (subject to justification):

- requiring a longer period of part-time service than full-time service in order to be eligible for promotion;[32]
- on a job-sharer converting to full-time working, placing her on the incremental scale according to actual hours worked in post in the past, so that she is lower in the scale than had she worked the same number of years full-time.[33]

It may be direct sex discrimination if the employer is willing to allow a man to work part-time or to be flexible with his hours, but not a woman.

Shifts, flexible hours and mobility: sex discrimination

26 A requirement that an employee work shifts or flexible hours may indirectly discriminate against a woman because of childcare commitments. Similarly, an employer's attempt to alter a woman's hours (whether or not permitted to do so by her contract), even in a minor way, may be indirect discrimination if, for example, it interferes with her arrangements for collecting her children from school. Again, the main issue is likely to be whether the change is justifiable. Similar considerations apply with mobility requirements. In one case, where a lone parent was unable to comply with new flexi-rotas due to childcare, the EAT said that employers should consider carefully the impact which a new roster might have on a section of their workforce

---

30 *Clarke v Eley (IMI) Kynoch* [1982] IRLR 482; [1983] ICR 165, EAT; see para 9.64 above.
31 See para 11.81 regarding pensions.
32 Eg, see *Gerster v Freistaat Bayern* [1997] IRLR 699, ECJ.
33 *Hill and Stapleton v Revenue Commissioners and Department of Finance.* [1998] IRLR 466, ECJ.

and take a reasonably flexible attitude towards accommodating a worker's particular needs.[34]

11.27   Any assumption made by an employer that women will be less mobile or flexible is directly discriminatory. Interview questions concerning mobility or flexibility, if asked only of female candidates, are likely to lead to poorer interview performance and constitute direct discrimination in the arrangements made for determining who should be offered employment.[35]

Part-time working: Key points

- Under regulations soon to be finalised, part-timers (male or female) should be treated equally with full-timers (on a pro rata basis), unless an employer can justify not doing so.
- Refusal to permit a woman or married person to work part-time may also be unlawful indirect sex discrimination.
- It may also be indirect sex discrimination to treat part-time workers less well than full-timers. Where part-timers are given less favourable terms and conditions, including pay rates, EU law usually applies, as this may contravene article 141 and the Equal Pay Directive.
- The main issue on part-time working will usually be whether the employer can justify insisting on full-time working.

General guide to useful evidence

- Establish how the employers will try to justify their behaviour.
- Evidence to show why part-time working in the job will be satisfactory or even beneficial.

To claim sex discrimination:

- Evidence generally and within the appropriate pool showing that women more often work part-time and are less able to work full-time than men.
- Evidence showing that the particular worker cannot in practice work full-time.

---

34   *London Underground Ltd v Edwards (No 2)* [1997] IRLR 157; (1997) 72 EOR 46, EAT. Note that this case went to the CA on a number of different points.
35   SDA 1975 s6(1)(a)

Sexual or racial or disability-related harassment or abuse

Meaning of harassment

11.28 There is no express prohibition in the RRA 1976, SDA 1975 or DDA 1995 against harassment or abuse. If a worker wants to bring a claim solely about harassment, the treatment complained of must fall within the range of prohibited behaviour under RRA 1976 ss1 and 4, SDA 1975 ss1 and 6 or DDA 1995 ss4 and 5. The worker must prove:

– less favourable treatment on grounds of race or sex, ie, direct discrimination (RRA 1976 s1(1)(a), SDA 1975 s1(1)(a)) or related to the worker's disability (DDA 1995 s5(1)); and

– that the less favourable treatment took the form of a prohibited act under RRA 1976 s4, SDA 1975 s6 or DDA 1995 s4. Most commonly, the worker will claim s/he has been 'subjected to a detriment'.

It is confusing to think in terms of proving 'sexual harassment', which has certain non-legal meanings which are not relevant for proving unlawful sex discrimination. Two important cases have emphasised that the test is simply whether direct discrimination occurred. In *Strathclyde RC v Porcelli*,[36] the court said that the primary question was not whether there was sexual harassment, a phrase not found in the SDA 1975, but simply whether the worker was less favourably treated on the ground of her sex than a man would have been.

11.29 In *Bracebridge Engineering v Darby*,[37] a worker was sexually assaulted by two supervisors. The employer argued that a single incident could not be described as 'sexual harassment'. However, the EAT said 'whether or not harassment is a continuing course of conduct, there was here an act which was an act of discrimination against a woman because she was a woman'.

11.30 The test is the normal one for direct discrimination, ie, has the worker been less favourably treated on grounds of his/her sex than someone of the opposite sex has or would have been treated? Where the treatment is gender specific or based on stereotypical assumptions as to gender characteristics, then as a matter of fact, it will

36 [1986] IRLR 134; [1986] ICR 564, Court of Session.
37 [1990] IRLR 3, EAT.

almost certainly be less favourable treatment as between the sexes.[38] Where the treatment appears 'neutral', eg, the employer shouts at the worker or tears up his/her letters, then it will be harder to prove that a worker of a different sex would have been treated differently.

11.31　　In the *Porcelli* case (above), Mrs Porcelli was subjected to a campaign of sexual harassment by two male colleagues. The employer claimed that the way she was treated was not based on her sex but simply because she was disliked. However the harassment included comments which would not normally have been made to a man, eg, showing her a screw nail and asking her if she 'wanted a screw'. The court said it was irrelevant that an equally disliked male colleague would have been treated just as unpleasantly. It was not necessary to show that the treatment of Mrs Porcelli had any sex-related motive or objective:

> This particular part of the campaign was plainly adopted against Mrs Porcelli because she was a woman. It was a particular kind of weapon, based upon the sex of the victim, which would not have been used against an equally disliked man.[39]

Similarly, if a chosen insult is expressly racial, an employer cannot evade the RRA 1976 by saying that s/he would have been equally insulting to other workers.

11.32　　If the harasser continues or intensifies the harassment or otherwise punishes the worker after s/he complains to the harasser or to management of the harassment, this may be unlawful victimisation as well as further direct discrimination.

11.33　　In 1991 the European Commission adopted a *Recommendation on the Protection of the Dignity of Women and Men at Work*. Annexed to the Recommendation is a *Code of Practice on measures to combat sexual harassment*.[40] The exact legal effect of the code is unclear, but the ET should take it into account where relevant in sexual harassment cases.[41] The code covers the definition of harassment, preventative steps and handling grievances.

38　Though not inevitably so: *Smith v Gardner Merchant Ltd* [1998] IRLR 510; (1998) 81 EOR 49, CA.
39　[1986] IRLR 134, Court of Session.
40　Reproduced in full (1992) 41 EOR 38.
41　*Grimaldi v Fonds des Maladies Professionelles* [1990] IRLR 400, ECJ; *Wadman v Carpenter Farrer Partnership* [1993] IRLR 374, EAT.

'Any other detriment'

11.34 The act or acts of discrimination concerned must fall within the areas of behaviour covered by the RRA 1976, SDA 1975 and DDA 1995.[42] There is no difficulty where, for example, refusal to accept sexual advances leads to lack of promotion, dismissal or other discriminatory acts prohibited under SDA 1975 s6. Where harassment does not lead to such easily identifiable consequences, the question arises whether it is unlawful. In order to bring such a claim under the RRA 1976, SDA 1975 or DDA 1995, a worker would have to show that the harassment or abuse, in itself, amounted to 'any other detriment'.[43]

11.35 The courts have said that sexual harassment is legal shorthand for an activity which is easily recognised as subjecting the worker to any other detriment.[44] A 'detriment' simply means 'putting at a disadvantage'.[45] Several cases have dealt with how serious the detriment must be to amount to an unlawful act. For example, can a single racist insult amount to unlawful race discrimination, or the display of a pin-up calendar[46] amount to unlawful sex discrimination?

11.36 A single incident of harassment can amount to a detriment 'provided it is sufficiently serious'. A one-off racist or sexist 'joke' or remark is unlikely to be enough in itself, but the surrounding circumstances may make it so. For example, an offensive or demeaning sexual comment made by a junior employee to a supervisor in front of others could be unlawful.[47] Where there is a series of incidents, it is important not to look at each one separately, since there can be a cumulative effect which exceeds the sum of each incident.[48] Once unwelcome sexual interest has been shown by a man in a female employee, other incidents which would normally appear quite unobjectionable, eg, asking to look at personal photographs, can take on a different significance.[49]

11.37 The EC code defines sexual harassment as:

42 RRA 1976 s4, SDA 1975 s6, DDA 1995 s4 set out types of behaviour covered by the statutes.
43 RRA 1976 s4(2)(c), SDA 1975 s6(2)(b), DDA 1995 s4(2)(d).
44 *Wileman v Minilec Engineering Ltd* [1998] IRLR 144, EAT approved by CA in *Smith v Gardner Merchant Ltd* (n38, above).
45 *Jeremiah v Ministry of Defence* [1979] 3 All ER 833; [1979] IRLR 436, CA.
46 In *Stewart v Cleveland Guest (Engineering) Ltd* (1995) 57 EOR 48, the EAT said the display of nude pictures of women was not necessarily sex discrimination. This is criticised in the EOR report and feature at 57 EOR 24.
47 *Insitu Cleaning Co Ltd v Heads* [1995] IRLR 4, EAT.
48 *Reed and Bull Information Systems Ltd v Stedman* [1999] IRLR 299, EAT.
49 Ibid.

unwanted conduct of a sexual nature or other conduct based on sex affecting the dignity of women and men at work . . . a range of behaviour may be considered to constitute sexual harassment. It is unacceptable if such conduct is unwanted, unreasonable and offensive to the recipient. The essential characteristic of sexual harassment is that it is unwanted by the recipient, that it is for each individual to determine what behaviour is acceptable to them and what they regard as offensive.

Because it is for each individual to decide what she finds unwelcome or offensive, there may be cases where there is a gap between what an ET would find acceptable and what the individual in question was prepared to tolerate. However, ETs should be aware that it does not therefore follow that the case must lose.[50]

11.38   As it is so important to show that the behaviour was 'unwanted', the harasser sometimes argues that the worker did not complain for a long time and as soon as s/he did complain, the harasser stopped. The EAT has said that some conduct is obviously unwelcome unless invited. On the other hand, with less obvious behaviour, the question would be whether the woman by words or behaviour made it clear that she found the conduct unwelcome. She need not make a public fuss to indicate her disapproval; walking out of the room might be sufficient, provided that any reasonable person would understand her to be rejecting the conduct.[51]

11.39   Unfortunately it would seem that a woman's sexual attitudes are relevant. The EAT has said that evidence of a worker's mode of dress at work[52] and evidence showing that a woman talked freely about sexual matters to fellow workers[53] can be relevant both to whether she suffered a detriment and as to compensation for injury to feelings. Somewhat inconsistently, the EAT also acknowledged that 'a person may be quite happy to accept the remarks of A or B in a sexual context, and wholly upset by similar remarks made by C'.[54] These cases should be challenged as out of date, following the principles set out in 1991 EC Code.

11.40   The position regarding racial harassment, where there is no specific code, is more restrictive, although the principles and case-law relating to sexual harassment should generally apply. Under the RRA

---

50   Ibid.
51   Ibid.
52   *Wileman v Minilec Engineering* [1988] IRLR 144; [1988] ICR 318, EAT.
53   *Snowball v Gardner Merchant* [1987] IRLR 397; ICR 719, EAT.
54   *Wileman* (n52, above).

1976 it seems necessary to show that by reason of the harassment, the worker has suffered has suffered a disadvantage in his/her working circumstances. Unlike with sexual harassment, it does not appear to be a purely subjective test. In *De Souza v Automobile Association*,[55] a secretary claimed racial discrimination after she overheard a manager tell a senior clerk to give some typing 'to the wog'. The Court of Appeal said:

> Racially to insult a coloured employee is not enough by itself, even if that insult caused him or her distress; before the employee can be said to have been subjected to some 'other detriment' the court or tribunal must find that by reason of the act or acts complained of a reasonable worker would or might take the view that he had thereby been disadvantaged in the circumstances in which he had thereafter to work.

On the facts of *De Souza*, the court felt that the woman was not 'treated' less favourably, because it was not intended that she overhear the remark. For the same reason, she was not subjected to a detriment under RRA 1976 s4(2)(c). There was no evidence to show that both the woman and 'the reasonable coloured secretary in like situation would or might be disadvantaged in the circumstances and conditions in which they were working'. This is an astonishing decision, but it is important to be aware of the attitude the courts may take. It is to be hoped that in most cases involving such an explicit and offensive racist remark about a worker, an ET would realise the worker had indeed suffered a detriment. It is impossible to see how a worker who is racially insulted by a supervisor or manager cannot be disadvantaged in his/her working circumstances.

Employers' liability

41   Under RRA 1976 s32, SDA 1975 s41 and DDA 1995 s58, the employing organisation is legally responsible for any discriminatory action by one employee against another, provided that the action is carried out in the course of employment. This is often called 'vicarious liability'. The organisation is vicariously liable even if it did not instruct, authorise, approve or even know of the discrimination.

42   When is a discriminatory act carried out outside the course of employment? The most important case on this issue is *Jones v Tower*

---

55   [1986] IRLR 103, CA, at p107.

234 Employment law / chapter 11

Boot Co Ltd,[56] where Mr Jones was subjected to a number of horrific incidents of verbal and physical racial abuse. These took place in work time and on work premises. The employers argued that they could not be liable for such clearly unauthorised acts carried out by fellow employees.[57] The Court of Appeal disagreed, saying that the words 'in the course of employment' should be given their natural meaning. The whole point was to widen the net of responsibility beyond the guilty employees themselves, by making all employers additionally responsible.

11.43   Discrimination carried out in work time and on the premises by fellow employees therefore seems to be covered, even if it is extremely serious and wholly unrelated to the employment, eg, physical assault. But harassment often takes place out of work time or during rest-breaks. It will then be for each ET to decide on the facts whether it took place during 'the course of employment'.[58] An incident which occurs during a chance meeting between work colleagues at a supermarket, for example, would almost certainly not be covered.[59] Similarly, an incident when one employee visits another at her house outside work hours and on a purely social basis will probably not be covered.[60] On the other hand, harassment during business trips, office Christmas parties, organised leaving parties or a social gathering of work colleagues in the pub immediately after work, may well be 'in the course of employment'.[61]

The employer's defence

11.44   The employer is responsible regardless of whether s/he knew or approved of the unlawful act, unless s/he 'took such steps as were reasonably practicable' to prevent unlawful acts of discrimination.[62] It is for the employer to prove this defence.[63]

11.45   It is important to remember that the employer's responsibility is to take preventative action; it is not a defence that the employer acted promptly once s/he discovered the discrimination, eg, by sack-

56 [1997] IRLR 168; (1997) 71 EOR 40, CA.
57 Based on *Irving v The Post Office* [1987] IRLR 289, CA, and the concept of vicarious liability applicable in tort.
58 *Jones v Tower Boot Co Ltd* [1997] IRLR 168; (1997)71 EOR 40, CA.
59 *Chief Constable of the Lincolnshire Police v Stubbs* [1999] IRLR 81, EAT.
60 *Waters v Commissioner of Police of the Metropolis* [1997] IRLR 589, CA.
61 *Stubbs* (n59, above).
62 RRA 1976 s32(3), SDA 1975 s41(3), DDA 1995 s58(5).
63 *Enterprise Glass Co Ltd v Miles* [1990] ICR 787, EAT.

ing the harasser (although this may prevent liability for further discrimination).

.46   There are no rigid guidelines on the necessary level of preventative action, but this defence does not often succeed. A written equal opportunities policy is unlikely to suffice unless it is very actively implemented. As one ET put it when allowing the defence, 'Harassment [in the workplace] is a live issue, not a dead letter'.[64] A useful measure of adequate preventative action is contained in the recommendations of the EC Code on Sexual Harassment.

Employer's reaction to a complaint of harassment

.47   In some cases, particularly in small organisations, the perpetrator is in reality the employer and there is no one more senior for the worker to turn to. In many cases, however, the perpetrator is a colleague or intermediate manager and the worker may complain about his/her treatment to more senior management. As protection against victimisation, it would be wise to make the complaint in writing.

.48   The employing organisation will not only be vicariously liable for the harassment itself, but it may also be guilty of direct discrimination and/or victimisation in the way it reacts to the complaint. The discrimination could occur both in the way the complaint is investigated (or not investigated) and also in the subsequent reaction, eg, transfer or dismissal of the worker.

.49   To show that this is further direct race or sex discrimination, it is necessary to prove that a man (in sexual harassment cases) or white worker (in racial harassment cases) bringing an equivalent complaint would not have received the same reaction; for example, his complaint would have been treated more seriously and investigated more thoroughly and he would have been kept better informed. Further, he would not have been transferred or dismissed as a consequence.

.50   It is not necessary to have evidence of any such comparable incident in the past. As with any direct discrimination case, the ET can infer from the evidence generally that a complaint from a man (or white person) would have been dealt with in a more favourable manner.[65]

.51   The ETs have been undecided about what is a sensible actual or

---

64   *Graham v Royal Mail and Nicholson* (1994) 20 EOR DCLD 5, ET. Though see the research report on women in the Royal Mail during the 1990s referred to in (1999) 83 EOR 3.

65   *Sheppard v The Post Office* (1992) 462 IRLB 6, EAT.

hypothetical comparison. Is the question how the employer would have treated a man complaining of; (a) sexual harassment by a female colleague or manager, (b) sexual harassment by a male colleague or manager, (c) non-sexual harassment or violence by a male colleague or manager, or (d) any serious grievance? The first two do not seem helpful comparisons because of the relative rarity of such situations and because they ignore the usually greater physical and social power of the perpetrator. The third and fourth scenarios are a more logical comparison, but even then, it is not really comparable, as again there is usually less imbalance of power, and there is not the same stigma attached.

11.52   In a case under the DDA 1995, the worker needs to show that the employer's reaction to his/her complaint was related to the worker's disability.

11.53   Whether or not the employer can be accused of direct discrimination in its handling of and response to the complaint, his/her treatment of the worker may amount to victimisation, ie, penalising him/her for raising the issue. This only applies where the complaint relates to treatment which would, if proved, be covered by the RRA 1976, SDA 1975 or DDA 1995. For example, a woman who is sacked for complaining about a sexual assault which took place outside the course of employment probably cannot claim victimisation under the SDA 1975[66], although she may be able to claim direct discrimination if the employer would not have sacked a man who complained about an assault outside work by a colleague.

11.54   The employer's failure to take a complaint seriously may also entitle the worker to resign and claim constructive unfair dismissal (see para 11.56 below). In this case it is not necessary to show that a complaint from a man (or white person) would have been treated more favourably. It is simply necessary to show that the employer's handling of the matter was so dismissive or hostile that it amounted to a fundamental breach of trust and confidence.

Self-defence

11.55   A worker who has been subjected to racial (or other) harassment may engage in violence or other inappropriate behaviour as self-defence. An employer should not ignore the provocation. If, for example, a

---

66   *Waters* (n60, above). Although the assault may fall under the SDA 1975—see para 11.58 below.

black worker and a white worker become involved in a fight started by
the white worker on racial grounds, an employer should not simply
adopt an 'even-handed' approach and sack both. If the employer simply ignores the racial element in his/her investigation and appeals
procedure, this is itself 'race-specific conduct' and direct race discrimination, without the need to show that a person from a different
racial group would have been treated more favourably.[67]

Constructive dismissal

As well as any discrimination claim, if an employer commits a repudiatory or fundamental breach of contract, a worker may resign and
claim constructive unfair dismissal[68] provided s/he meets the unfair
dismissal eligibility requirements. What amounts to a repudiatory
breach is a question of fact, but in the key case of *Western Excavating
(ECC) v Sharp*,[69] Lawton LJ said that:

> Persistent and unwanted amorous advances by an employer to a
> female member of his staff would clearly be such conduct.

In *Bracebridge Engineering v Darby*,[70] the employer's failure to treat
seriously and fully investigate the worker's allegations of assault
clearly amounted to a repudiatory breach of the implied term of trust
and confidence and the obligation not to undermine the confidence
of female staff. In certain circumstances, the worker may be able to
claim automatic unfair dismissal (see para 6.72 above).

Harassment by the public

The employer is not vicariously liable under the RRA 1976, SDA 1975
or DDA 1995 for harassment by members of the public. Nevertheless
the employer may in some circumstances be responsible for direct
discrimination in 'subjecting' the worker to the discriminatory
behaviour of the member of the public. The case establishing this
was *Burton and Rhule v De Vere Hotels*,[71] where two casual waitresses
employed by the hotel worked at a dinner organised by the Derby
Round Table, which had booked Bernard Manning as a speaker. Mr

67 *Sidhu v Aerospace Composite Technology Ltd* (1999) 637 *IDS Brief* 3, EAT.
68 See paras 6.41 to 6.48 above.
69 [1978] IRLR 27; [1978] ICR 221, CA.
70 [1990] IRLR 3, EAT.
71 [1996] IRLR 596; 70 EOR 48, EAT.

Manning made sexually and racially offensive remarks to the women, who were very upset. Assistant managers were present, but did nothing until the waitresses complained. The next day, after a further complaint, the hotel manager also apologised. In general, the hotel behaved appropriately once the workers complained, but the EAT found they were guilty of direct race discrimination[72] in allowing them to work during Mr Manning's act and therefore subjecting them to racial harassment by him.

11.58   An employer will not always be responsible in this way for harassment by a member of the public. The real test is whether something was sufficiently under the employer's control that s/he could, by the application of good employment practice, have prevented or reduced the harassment. This means the employer must know or foresee that harassment is a real possibility and be able to do something about it. Here, the hotel manager, knowing Mr Manning's reputation, should have warned the assistant managers to keep a look-out and withdraw the waitresses if things became unpleasant.

11.59   It is important to note in this case that the hotel would have asked staff to work at the dinner whether they were black or white, male or female. The direct discrimination did not lie in the choice of staff to serve at the dinner, but in allowing racist behaviour by the public. The case may be important where employers fail to take preventative or remedial action in the face of racial or sexual abuse, for example by customers, patients or tenants. In many situations this is concretely foreseeable; certainly where an incident has happened once and is therefore likely to be repeated. More difficult is what level of preventative action an ET would realistically expect. Another problem is the solution suggested by the EAT in the *Burton* case. It is surely discriminatory in itself, and in any event, undesirable, to withdraw black or female staff from working in certain areas. A better option was suggested in another case[73] where a company provided entertainers for children's parties. After the employer refused to allow a worker to leave when she complained of sexual harassment by a parent, the parent went on to assault the worker. The EAT found the employer responsible for the assault, although not the original harassment as that could not have been anticipated. The worker should have been allowed to leave or the parent thrown out of the party.

11.60   The above concerns an employer's responsibility for the harass-

---

72   The complaint could equally have been brought under the SDA 1975.
73   *Go Kidz Go Ltd v Bourdouane* 70 EOR 49, EAT.

ment itself. However, the employer may also be responsible for direct discrimination in his/her response to an employee's complaint about such harassment. In addition, failure to take appropriate action may entitle an employee to resign and claim constructive dismissal.

Civil or criminal claims outside the SDA, RRA or DDA

1 Sometimes due to the limitations of the discrimination legislation, other legal claims may be appropriate. These can also apply where the harassment, eg, assault or general bullying, is not based on race, sex or disability. Usually an ET claim under the RRA, SDA or DDA is preferable.[74A] It offers a simpler and quicker procedure, with the benefit of the statutory questionnaire procedure. Where the worker is not eligible for legal aid or backed by a trade union or one of the equality commissions, the costs risk of losing in the county court makes it an unrealistic option. However, advisers may want to explore the option of a conditional fee arrangement with after-the-event insurance against costs risks. Furthermore, as an industrial court, the ET may be more willing than a county court to understand and believe the claim (although this may be too optimistic a view).

Common law claims

2 Where the harassment involves physical contact, particularly if there is a severe assault, the worker may have a claim for damages at common law either in civil assault against the perpetrator or negligence against the employer. The employer's failure to take action may also be in breach of an implied term to give reasonable support to an employee. Even where there is no physical contact, a tortious claim may be possible where the perpetrator intentionally inflicts injury (physical or psychiatric) by his words or actions.[74] Common law claims are an under-used remedy and the possibility should not be overlooked. The advantage of such claims is that they are heard in the civil courts where legal aid may sometimes be available and it is unnecessary to prove the assault was on grounds of race, sex or disability. Longer time limits also apply. It may also help if the assault was by a member of the public or otherwise outside the course of employment. The disadvantages are set out above.

---

74 *Burris v Adzani* [1995] 1 WLR 1373, CA.
74A Consider also the implications of *Sheriff v Klyne Tugs (Lowestoft) Ltd* [1999] IRLR 451, CA (para 15.20 below).

Protection from Harassment Act 1997

11.63   Although the Protection from Harassment Act (PHA) 1997 was not designed for employment situations, it can apply. Under the PHA 1997 s1 a person must not pursue a course of conduct which s/he knows or a reasonable person would know amounts to harassment of another person.[75] A 'course of conduct' means conduct on at least two occasions.[76] Harassment is not defined except to say that it includes alarming the person or causing the person distress and the conduct can include speech.[77]

11.64   The conduct is not unlawful if it was reasonable in the particular circumstances.[78] Presumably therefore reasonable disciplinary action, although causing distress, would be excluded. On the other hand, a series of unjustified warnings may on the facts amount to harassment.

11.65   Under PHA 1997 s4 it is also an offence to cause another person on at least two occasions to fear that violence would be used against him/her. There is an exception for reasonable self-defence.[79]

11.66   Breach of ss1 or 4 is a criminal offence liable to imprisonment or a fine.[80] A civil claim can also be made for damages for financial loss and anxiety.[81] The High Court or county court can also issue an injunction restraining the perpetrator from continuing to harass.[82]

11.67   The PHA 1997 may be very helpful where the harassment is not covered by the discrimination legislation, eg, because it cannot be proved that it is on grounds of race, sex or disability, or because it took place off work premises and possibly outside the course of employment, or was perpetrated by a member of the public. Indeed, sometimes a case which fails in an ET on one of these technical grounds, but makes the necessary fact findings of incidents of harassment, could provide a good foundation for a follow-up case under the PHA 1997. The other great advantage is the potential to obtain a restraining injunction, which is not available under the RRA 1976, SDA 1975 or DDA 1995 in the ETs. Although the time-limits are also longer,[83] it

75   PHA 1997 s1(1), (2).
76   Ibid s7(3).
77   Ibid s7.
78   Ibid s1(3)(c). There are also other exceptions.
79   Ibid s4(3). Together with other exceptions.
80   Ibid s2(2); s 4(4).
81   Ibid s3(2).
82   Ibid s3(3).
83   Advisers should check the exact position on this.

will usually be important to act quickly, especially if an injunction is sought.

8   The disadvantage of the PHA 1997, as with all non-ET claims, is the more formal procedure and the costs risks. The scope of the PHA 1997 for use in employment cases is still being tested. One of the uncertainties is whether a claim may only be made against individual perpetrators or whether the employing organisation will be vicariously liable for harassment by its employees or agents.

Criminal Justice and Public Order Act 1994

9   A person is guilty of a criminal offence if s/he, with intent, causes another person

> harassment, alarm or distress by using threatening, abusive or insulting words or behaviour, or by displaying any writing or sign or other visible representation which is threatening, abusive or insulting.[84]

It is a defence if the accused person's conduct was reasonable in the circumstances.

0   Although introduced to assist the police in dealing with serious racial harassment, the Act appears to cover harassment in the workplace. The advantage is that it is not confined to racial and sexual harassment and it is not necessary to prove the grounds for the harassment.

1   As with inviting the police to prosecute for criminal assault where physical harassment has taken place, there are difficulties in following this route. The facts are harder to prove due to the stricter rules of evidence and the criminal standard of proof. Moreover, the worker is simply a witness in a police action and loses control of the process. An unsuccessful criminal case is likely to jeopardise any parallel civil claim.

Bullying

2   Bullying or harassment which is not attributable to the worker's race, sex or disability is now recognised as a workplace problem in itself. If the bullying is carried out by the employer or if the employer fails to deal adequately with a complaint, a worker may be able to resign and claim constructive unfair dismissal.[85] If the bullying is serious, the worker may also be able to bring a civil or criminal claim as set out above.

---

84 Criminal Justice and Public Order Act 1994 s4A.
85 Subject to the usual rules.

Harassment: Key points

- Sexual, racial or disability-related harassment or abuse is not prohibited as such under the RRA 1976, SDA 1975 or DDA 1995. The worker must prove that the harassment amounts to direct discrimination in the usual way.
- The discrimination must amount to a disadvantage in the person's working conditions.
- The harasser's motive is irrelevant. What is relevant is the form that the harasser's action takes, eg, unwanted sexual advances or racial abuse.
- The harassment must be carried out in the course of employment.
- The employer may discriminate by subjecting a worker to harassment by a member of the public.
- The employer's failure to deal, or his mode of dealing, with an allegation of harassment may itself be a discriminatory act.
- The harassment, or the employer's failure to deal with a complaint about it, may also constitute fundamental breach of contract entitling the worker to resign and claim constructive dismissal.
- Other civil and criminal causes of action outside the RRA, SDA and DDA may exist, although none are easy.
- Bullying or harassment which is not attributable to the worker's race, sex or disability may also give rise to a criminal or civil claim. In some circumstances a worker may resign and claim constructive dismissal.

General guide to useful evidence

- Evidence proving that the harassment occurred, eg, visits to a GP.
- Evidence of any efforts to inform management and the response.
- Evidence of any substantial preventative measures taken by the employer, eg, equal opportunities training of staff.
- Compare what actually happened with the recommendations in the EC Code on Sexual Harassment.

Age discrimination, retirement and pensions

1.73 A worker cannot claim unfair dismissal or redundancy pay once s/he has reached normal retirement age.[86] Nevertheless s/he will retain contractual rights plus certain statutory rights. It is automatically unfair to dismiss a worker for a number of reasons, including asserting a statutory right, whatever his/her age (see paras 6.69 onwards).

.74 If an employer dismisses a worker on grounds of age at any time before his/her normal retirement age, the worker may claim unfair dismissal in the usual way. Considerations will often include the employer's reasons, the worker's capability to continue doing a heavy job, alternative employment and procedures generally.

.75 Britain's age profile is changing. By 2010, almost 40 per cent of the labour force will be aged 45 or over, while 16–24-year-olds will make up 17 per cent.[87] Despite evidence of widespread discrimination on grounds of age in employment,[88] no government has been prepared to legislate against age discrimination. The most the present government has been prepared to do is issue a voluntary Code of Practice on Age Diversity in Employment.[89] The Code has recommendations for good practice in recruitment, selection, promotion, training and development, redundancy and retirement. For example, it is recommended that employers should:

- avoid restricting age in job adverts, explicitly or implicitly, eg, 'young graduates';
- use mixed age interviewing panels and ensure all interviewers are trained to avoid prejudice and stereotyping;
- use objective job-related criteria for redundancy selection and ensure age is not a criterion.

The Code is accompanied by further Guidance and case-studies with good practice indicators, for example:

- monitoring statistics of job applicants, who is interviewed and who is appointed, according to age;
- maintenance of a balanced age profile across the workforce;
- on redundancy, retention of key skills for the future well-being of the organisation;

---

86 See para 6.22 above for definition.
87 Age Diversity in Employment: A Code of Practice.
88 See, eg, feature at (1998) 80 EOR 32 and Carnegie Report referred to at (1996) 69 EOR 7.
89 Available DfEE Publications. Tel: 0845 60 222 60; fax: 0845 60 333 60. Ref: Age2.

– more choice and flexibility regarding retirement.

The content of the Code has been described as 'embarrassingly banal' and even its legal status is unclear. As age discrimination is not generally unlawful in itself, the Code cannot have the status of the Codes regarding race, sex and disability discrimination. However it is likely that the ET will take account of any breaches of the Code in the context of unfair dismissal claims.

11.76 Under the new article 13 of the Treaty of Rome,[90] the EU will have power to introduce Directives to combat a variety of forms of discrimination including that based on age. On 25 November 1999, the Commission proposed a draft directive prohibiting discrimination on a number of grounds including age.

11.77 Some employers have equal opportunities policies which prohibit discrimination on grounds of age. Unless (unusually) the EOP is incorporated into the worker's contract of employment and the provisions on age discrimination give clear individual rights, its status will merely be as a policy statement which cannot be enforced by the worker.[91] Even if a prohibition on age discrimination does form part of the contract of employment, it does not apply to the imposition of a contractual retirement age.[92]

Discriminatory retirement age

11.78 An employer must not discriminate in either contractual[93] or statutory[94] redundancy pay. Both men and women are entitled to statutory redundancy pay up until 65 years of age or any earlier non-discriminatory retirement age.[95]

11.79 It is unlawful direct discrimination to make men and women retire at different ages[96] or to reduce a worker's status or refuse promotion, training or transfer because of a worker's proximity to a discriminatory retirement age.

90 Introduced by the Treaty of Amsterdam on 1 May 1999. See para 3.7.
91 See *Wandsworth LBC v D'Silva* [1998] IRLR 193, CA; *Grant v South West Trains* [1998] IRLR 188, QBD; *Taylor v Secretary of State for Scotland* (1999) 639 *IDS Brief* 5, CS for case-law regarding whether EOPs are contractually enforceable.
92 *Taylor* ibid.
93 *Hammersmith and Queen Charlotte's Special Health Authority v Cato* [1987] IRLR 483; [1988] ICR 132, EAT.
94 *Barber v GRE Assurance Group* [1990] IRLR 240, ECJ.
95 ERA 1996 s156(1).
96 SDA 1975 and EqPA 1970 as amended by SDA 1986. See para 6.22 for effect on what is the normal retirement age for unfair dismissal purposes.

30   In *Nash v Mash/Roe Group Ltd*,[97] an ET accepted that the statutory upper age limit of 65 for claiming unfair dismissal or redundancy pay was indirectly discriminatory against men, as a higher proportion of men than women were economically active after the age of 65 and therefore disqualified from the statutory rights. The ET's decision is to be tested on appeal.

Pensions

31 Originally the legislation did not prohibit all forms of discrimination in connection with retirement and pensions, so in many cases the only protection was under EU law. Partly as a result of different state pension ages, occupational pension schemes have tended to discriminate. A series of decisions by the ECJ under article 141 declaring such discrimination unlawful led to the Pensions Act 1995 and the Occupational Pension Schemes (Equal Treatment) Regulations 1995.[97A] It remains to be seen whether this legislation fully implements the requirements of article 141.

32 As well as providing for equal treatment between men and women in access to and terms of membership of occupational pension schemes (subject to certain exclusions), the Pensions Act 1995 provides for equal state pension age to be phased in from 2010 to 2020.

33 The legislation is modelled on the EqPA in that it imports an 'equal treatment rule' into a woman's pension where she is or was employed on like work, work rated as equivalent under a job evaluation scheme or work of equal value, unless the trustees of the scheme can prove a genuine material factor defence other than sex.[97B]

34 It would be unlawful to discriminate directly, eg, by refusing entry to women, or indirectly, eg, by unjustifiably excluding part-timers.

35 The law on equality of pensions (access, benefits and contributions), time-limits and retrospective claims is complex and undergoing change. Full guidance is beyond the scope of this book. Note also that occupational pensions may be adversely affected on the transfer of an employer's business, even if the Transfer of Undertakings (Protection of Employment) Regulations apply. It would be wise for workers to clarify at the time of any sale of the business the effect on their pension.

97   [1998] IRLR 168, CT.
97A SI No 3183 in force 1 January 1996.
97B Pensions Act 1995 s62.

Age, pensions, retirement: Key points

- Age discrimination is not unlawful in itself, but is discouraged by a voluntary Code.
- It is unlawful sex discrimination to apply different retirement ages to men and women
- Men and women are entitled to redundancy payments if made redundant before the age of 65 or any non-discriminatory retirement age.
- Men and women can claim unfair dismissal if dismissed before the age of 65 unless there is an earlier normal retirement age applicable equally to men and women.
- Men and women are entitled to equality in their occupational pension schemes.[98]

General Guide to Useful Evidence

- The Code of Practice on Age Discrimination
- Obtain documents relating to the contractual and/or normal retirement age of male and female workers,[99] eg, the worker's original contract, standard contracts of male and female workers and any subsequent memoranda purporting to amend the contractual and/or normal retirement age.
- Evidence/statistics on the age at which men and women in the workplace, particularly those with similar jobs to the worker, have retired in the past.

Discrimination against gay men and lesbians

11.86   In a TUC survey at the end of 1998 of 440 gay, lesbian and bisexual workers, 44 per cent said they had suffered discrimination at work because of their sexuality.[100] But although there is a desperate need, there is no legislation explicitly prohibiting discrimination on

---

98   As mentioned above, this area of law is complex and developing.
99   Although the contractual position is not conclusive.
100   (1999) 86 EOR 13.

grounds of sexual orientation.[101] The government has announced its intention to introduce a non-statutory code of practice on combating discrimination on the grounds of sexual orientation in the workplace.[102] Lesbian and gay workers may gain some protection from general employment law principles and particularly the law on sex discrimination and unfair dismissal. The European Court of Human Rights has declared the armed forces' ban on homosexuals to violate the European Convention on Human Rights.[103] It remains to be seen whether workers can benefit from this decision once the Human Rights Act 1998 comes into force.[104] The law prohibiting discrimination against workers who have undergone, are undergoing or intend to undergo gender reassignment is dealt with at para 9.44.

Unfair dismissal

11.87 There are very few reported cases above ET level concerning unfair dismissal on the ground of homosexuality. Those there are indicate a lack of understanding and, often, hostility towards gay workers. It is to be hoped that despite the AIDS hysteria which has become associated with gay men in particular, prevailing attitudes towards homosexuality will become more enlightened and in turn improve judicial attitudes. In the last few years, there have been signs of a more open judicial attitude in the higher courts.[105] However, as with cases of unlawful discrimination on grounds of race or sex, the prime difficulty is in proving that dismissal was connected with a worker's homosexuality.

11.88 In one case,[106] the EAT upheld an ET's decision that it was fair to dismiss a woman for refusing to remove a 'Lesbians Ignite' badge at work. A similar test as to issues of dress generally was applied. It was fair to dismiss because a reasonable employer 'on mature reflection' could reasonably have decided that the badge would be offensive to

---

101 See 'Equality for lesbians and gay men in the workplace' (1997) 74 EOR 20 for a useful survey of employers' voluntary policies.
102 (1999) 643 *IDS Brief* 19.
103 *Smith and Others v UK* [1999] IRLR 734; 88 EOR 49, ECHR.
104 See para 3.12 above.
105 In connection with cases brought for sex discrimination under the SDA 1975 or EC law.
106 *LM Boychuk v HJ Symons Holdings* [1977] IRLR 395, EAT.

customers and fellow workers. It was not necessary to wait and see whether the business was disrupted or damaged.

11.89   In another case,[107] an ET found it fair to dismiss a maintenance man from a children's camp because he was homosexual. The EAT agreed that dismissal was within the band of reasonable responses even though expert evidence had been called to the effect that homosexual men were no more likely to interfere with children than heterosexual men. The point was that there was a considerable body of popular opinion which took the contrary view, which was shared by the employer, who was entitled to dismiss regardless of whether that view had a proven foundation. The Court of Session refused to overturn the decision on the facts found and noted that the reason for dismissal was not solely for being homosexual. Presumably the court had in mind the employer's concern about the risk to children and anxiety of parents.

11.90   Much of the existing case-law concerns dismissal of gay men for holding criminal convictions for sexual offences. Many men plead guilty in the hope of minimising publicity so as not to risk losing their jobs, when their chances of acquittal by a jury may be high. Consequently, it is important to understand the context in which such convictions occur and not to take them at face value.[108]

11.91   In one case,[109] an ET found it fair to dismiss a drama teacher of boys aged 16 to 19 following two convictions for gross indecency with men in public lavatories. The EAT would not accept it as self-evident that someone who behaved as the teacher did would not be a risk to teenage boys in his charge; although there was a respectable body of opinion supporting that view. It was a highly controversial subject and an employer could not be said to have acted unfairly by concluding that there was some risk in continuing to employ the teacher.

11.92   Gay men wishing to work with children have particular difficulties because organisations which work with children often have access to information about potential employees from the police and other sources. Also, certain professionals, those working with young people under 18 and employees in the courts, police or prison service, are not protected by the Rehabilitation of Offenders Act 1974 and can be dismissed for failing to reveal a 'spent' conviction.

---

107   *Saunders v Scottish National Camps Association* [1981] IRLR 277, Court of Session.
108   See Phil Greasley, *Gay Men at Work* (Lesbian and Gay Employment Rights, 1986) and Paul Crane, *Gays and the Law* (Pluto Press, 1982).
109   *Wiseman v Salford CC* [1981] IRLR 202, EAT.

Sex discrimination

93 In some cases, it may be possible to invoke the protection of the SDA 1975, which of course covers detriments other than dismissal and has no minimum service requirement. Unfortunately it now seems clear that neither the SDA 1975[110] nor EU law[111] covers discrimination on grounds of sexual orientation as such. EU law does prohibit discrimination based on a worker's gender reassignment,[112] hence the amendment of the SDA 1995 to cover transsexuals,[113] but not discrimination based on a worker's sexual orientation.

94 Gay workers can therefore only claim sex discrimination if they can show a discriminatory element based on gender, eg, that the employer treats a gay man less favourably than s/he would treat a lesbian. The comparison is not with how the employer would treat a heterosexual woman. The reason for this is that under the SDA 1975 s5(3), any comparison must be made in the same, or not materially different, relevant circumstances. Here the 'relevant circumstances' are being homosexual.[114]

95 As different stereotyped ideas exist about each group, sex discrimination may sometimes be proved on this basis, but it is difficult. An example may be a comment to a gay man that 'he probably had all sorts of diseases and gay people who spread Aids should be put on an island'.[115–117] This comment is unlikely to have been made to a lesbian.

96 Unfortunately lesbians and gay men are often treated equally badly in the workplace and a sex discrimination claim would fail. There is an urgent need for the amendment of European and domestic legislation explicitly to prohibit discrimination of this kind. On 25 November 1999 the European Commission put forward a draft directive proposing to prohibit discrimination on a number of grounds including sexual orientation.

---

110 *Smith v Gardner Merchant Ltd* [1998] IRLR 511; (1998) 81 EOR 49, CA.
111 *Grant v South-West Trains Ltd* [1998] IRLR 206; (1998) 78 EOR 48, ECJ; *R v Secretary of State for Defence ex p Perkins (No 2)* [1998] IRLR 508, HC. Though see EOR commentary at (1998) 81 EOR 51.
112 *P v S and Cornwall CC* [1996] IRLR 347; (1996) 68 EOR 44, ECJ.
113 See para 9.18 above.
114 *Smith* (n110, above).
115–117 As alleged in *Smith* ibid.

Workers with HIV or AIDS

11.97   As with discrimination against gay men and lesbians, there is no specific legislation prohibiting discrimination against workers with AIDS or who are HIV positive. The DDA 1995 prohibits discrimination on grounds of 'disability' against workers once symptoms of the illness have emerged, but not before.[118] As far as possible, the ordinary unfair dismissal and race and sex discrimination provisions should also be used. AIDS and HIV-related discrimination is not a difficulty which affects only gay workers. For a variety of reasons, only a handful of cases concerning AIDS or HIV have reached the ETs,[119] so there is little indication of what approach an ET will take.

Unfair dismissal

11.98   HIV infection is not itself usually sufficient reason to justify dismissal.[120] Where the worker becomes ill, the usual rules as to dismissals for ill-health apply, including adequate consultation with doctors and the worker.[121] Because of the variable state of health of AIDS/HIV sufferers, proper consultation is particularly important.

11.99   In the rare event that a worker with AIDS/HIV constitutes a demonstrated health risk to others, dismissal for 'some other substantial reason' may be fair, although an employer should discuss with the worker the possibility of transfer to alternative employment. Where no health risk exists, but another worker harasses or refuses to work with someone with AIDS, the employer should make reasonable attempts at conciliation and to supply information on the transmission of AIDS in order to allay fears. If these steps fail and neither worker can be transferred, it may well be fair to discipline or even dismiss the employee who is refusing to work. An employer's failure to offer reasonable support to a worker being harassed could lead to a constructive dismissal claim.

11.100   If there are a large number of workers objecting, the employer may argue that it is impracticable to transfer or dismiss all of them

---

118   See chapter 13 above.
119   See Petra Wilson, *HIV and AIDS in the Workplace: An examination of cases of discrimination*, National AIDS Trust, 6th Floor, Eileen House, 80 Newington Causeway, London SE1 6EF.
120   See Department of Employment/Health and Safety Executive booklet, *AIDS and employment*.
121   See paras 7.8 to 7.18 above.

and it is therefore reasonable to dismiss the worker with AIDS. However, since an ET is not entitled to take account of a threat of industrial action in determining fairness,[122] it is arguable that it should not take account of pressure falling short of such a threat.[123]

.101   If there is customer pressure, the employer should again try to consult to allay fears. If that fails, and there is nowhere else to employ the worker, dismissal will probably be fair.

HIV testing

.102 It is probably a fundamental breach of contract (and therefore constructive dismissal) to require a worker to undergo an HIV test, even if there is a contractual right to do so, unless there is reasonable ground for suspecting that the worker is infected and that there may be a risk to the health and safety of others.[124] However, in the latter case, it is probably fair to dismiss a worker who refuses to have the test, provided that the employer has explained why the test is necessary and warned that a refusal will lead to dismissal.

.103   It is a breach of the implied duty of trust and confidence for an employer to disclose that a worker has AIDS/HIV without the worker's consent. In rare cases, disclosure may be permitted where it is only to persons who have a real need to know and it is in the public interest, for example, where health risks are concerned.

Discrimination

.104 Because of the popular misconception that only gay men are likely to have AIDS/HIV, male workers may be discriminated against solely because they are homosexual.[125] Therefore if men are treated adversely on the basis of assumptions about who is likely to have AIDS/HIV, this is probably contrary to the SDA 1975. Similarly, if an employer refuses to recruit job applicants from central African countries or requires only such applicants to undergo HIV tests (because AIDS is apparently more widespread in some of those countries), this is unlawful under the RRA 1976.

---

122 ERA 1996 s107.
123 See R A Watt, 'HIV, Discrimination, Unfair Dismissal and Pressure to Dismiss', *ILJ* Vol 21 No 4 Dec 1992.
124 See *Bliss v South East Thames Regional Health Authority* [1985] IRLR 308; [1987] ICR 700, CA, on requiring a surgeon to undergo a medical examination.
125 See para 11.95 above.

11.105   The difficulty is that any comparison for discrimination purposes must be in the same relevant circumstances. If the relevant circumstance is the worker's sexual orientation, then a gay man may successfully claim sex discrimination if a lesbian would not have been treated in the same way. However, if the relevant circumstance is membership of a high-risk group, the SDA 1975 may not help, as an employer might have treated a woman who was an intravenous drug user in the same way as s/he would have treated a gay man.

11.106   Any requirement imposed by an employer that, for example, a potential employee must not come from a high-risk group, may adversely affect men or people from certain countries and the issue will be one of justifiability.

Redundancy and discrimination

11.107 A worker who is made redundant may be able to claim unfair dismissal and/or discrimination on grounds of race, sex or disability as well as redundancy pay. Although there is a six-month time limit on redundancy pay claims, the time limit on unfair dismissal and discrimination claims is only three months.

Pregnancy/maternity dismissals

11.108 A redundancy dismissal due to pregnancy, maternity or a related reason is automatically unfair and no minimum qualifying service is required to make a claim. Where a woman is made redundant while pregnant or on maternity leave, but not due to that fact, the normal test of fairness applies. However, a woman made redundant on maternity leave must be offered any suitable available vacancy, however inconvenient for the employer. Failure to do this is automatically unfair dismissal.[126] Redundancy selection due to pregnancy or maternity may also be sex discrimination.[127]

Race discrimination – direct

11.109 In any case where a black worker has been selected for redundancy, it is worth checking that there has been no direct discrimination.

---

126   See para 6.68 above.
127   Ibid.

Indications may be the racial composition of those made redundant as compared with those retained. It is essential to ascertain why the employer says the worker has been selected. A common indicator of direct race discrimination is a selection criterion on which retained white workers score equally badly or worse. A questionnaire should be used to establish the selection criteria and whether they were consistently applied as between black and white workers.[128]

Indirectly discriminatory selection criteria

10 Criteria for selecting which workers are made redundant are frequently indirectly discriminatory. Criteria such as hours worked, flexibility, mobility, or attendance record could adversely affect women. Black workers may suffer from criteria based on conduct records, internal appraisals or customer complaints, if they have been subjected to direct discrimination in those areas. The selection of workers on short fixed-term contracts first may also be unjustifiable indirect race or sex discrimination.[129]

Last in first out (LIFO)

11 Length of service is still commonly applied as a means of redundancy selection. Although in many workplaces this requirement clearly disadvantages women and black workers, it is a traditional selection method which has often been found justifiable in the past. Where LIFO has an obvious adverse impact, the following approach should be taken to challenge its justifiability:

- The higher the proportion of black and women workers made redundant due to the application of this criterion, the stronger the necessary justification from the employer.[130]
- The employer must show that the use of LIFO serves a real business need. Nowadays employers' main concern is to retain a balanced and flexible workforce.[131] This need is unlikely to be served by over-emphasis on length of service.

---

128 See *RRA Questionnaires: How to use the Questionnaire Procedure* by Tamara Lewis. Available from the Central London Law Centre.
129 See also list of indirectly discriminatory requirements in appendix B.
130 *Hampson v Department of Education and Science* [1990] IRLR 302, HL.
131 IRS Employment Trends 504.

- Current working practices show that workers are employed increasingly on short-term and temporary contracts and little premium is placed on long service by employers.
- The mere fact that a particular requirement has been widely used in the past does not make it justifiable now. Nor should it be an objective justification that LIFO is or was preferred by certain trade union negotiators.
- It is helpful if other criteria can be suggested to the employer before any decision is reached.

Redundancy and disability

11.112 A disabled worker may be selected for redundancy due to a reason related to his/her disability. For example, s/he may not score well on selection criteria such as hours worked, flexibility, mobility, or sickness record. S/he may be unable to fulfil new flexible working practices or multiple duties. The employer will have to justify the dismissal, having made any reasonable adjustments. For example, it may be unjustified to hold it against a disabled worker that s/he has refused to work overtime in the past.

11.113 A worker could argue that any alternative duties should be modified for him/her or that she should be especially trained. The employer will be expected to take a more active role in seeking appropriate alternative employment than may be an employer's duties under ordinary unfair dismissal law.

Preventative action

11.114 In rare cases, it may be possible to prevent a public employer embarking on a discriminatory redundancy selection policy by means of judicial review in the High Court; it will be necessary clearly to establish that the policy definitely has discriminatory effect and on a fairly widespread basis.[132]

---

132   See *R v Hammersmith and Fulham LBC ex p NALGO* [1991] IRLR 249, HC.

CHAPTER 12

Evidence in race, sex or disability discrimination cases

The burden of proof in race and sex discrimination cases

12.1 The standard of proof in direct and indirect discrimination cases is the normal civil standard, namely whether, on the balance of probabilities (ie, 'more likely than not'), discrimination occurred. The ET should be reminded of this at the hearing.

12.2 The legal burden of proof is on the worker, who has to prove overall that discrimination happened. The main guidance on the approach which an ET should take was given by the CA in *King v Great Britain China Centre*.[1] An ET should bear in mind that it is unusual to find direct evidence of racial discrimination. Few employers will be prepared to admit such discrimination even to themselves. At the end of all the evidence, an ET should make findings as to what are the primary facts and should then draw inferences from those facts, bearing in mind the difficulties facing a person who complains of unlawful discrimination.

12.3 In many cases, the worker can identify another worker of a different race or sex who has been treated differently or more favourably in similar circumstances. If the employer cannot provide a satisfactory explanation, then it is legitimate for the ET to infer that the different treatment was on grounds of race or sex almost as a matter of common sense.[2] Even where there is no comparator, the worker may demonstrate a prima facie case which requires an explanation from the employer. For example, a woman who appears well qualified for a job is not even interviewed. Where there is a prima facie case and no credible explanation is put forward, an ET should not be reluctant to 'grasp the nettle' and find discrimination.[3]

12.4 Some employers argue at the ET hearing that it is not necessary for them to provide any explanation because the worker has not even made out a prima facie case. However, discrimination cases are best looked at as a whole. The ET will usually want to hear the employer's evidence and explanation and the worker should have the opportunity of questioning the employer's witnesses.[4]

12.5 In indirect discrimination cases, the burden of proof is on the

---

1 [1991] IRLR 513; [1992] ICR 516. Approved by HL in *Zafar v Glasgow City Council* [1998] IRLR 36.
2 *King* ibid.
3 *Grewal v Walsall MBC* (1995) 514 IRLB 19, EAT.
4 *JSV Oxford v DHSS* [1977] IRLR 225, EAT; *Laher v LB Hammersmith and Fulham LBC* (1995) 514 IRLB 4, EAT.

worker to show that there is a requirement or condition with discriminatory impact and which is to his/her detriment because s/he cannot comply with it. However, if the employer seeks to claim that a discriminatory requirement is justifiable, it is for the employer to prove it. If indirect race discrimination is proved, the burden is on the employer to show it was not intentional, so that damages may not be awarded.[5]

Article 4 of the EU Directive on the burden of proof in sex discrimination cases ('the Burden of Proof Directive'),[6] which is to be implemented by 22 July 2001 states that once a worker has established 'facts from which it may be presumed that there has been direct or indirect discrimination, it shall be for the respondent to prove that there has been no breach of the principle of equal treatment'. This should not change the current position regarding indirect sex discrimination, but should be an improvement as regards direct sex discrimination: it removes an ET's option to refuse to infer sex discrimination where a prima facie case exists, even though an employer's explanation has failed.

Helpful kinds of evidence in race and sex discrimination cases

Direct discrimination

In *King*,[7] the CA said that as direct evidence of discrimination is rarely available, the necessary evidence will 'usually depend on what inferences it is proper to draw from the primary facts'. In other words, the ET must look for clues and draw conclusions. The concept of the ET making 'inferences' is central to running a discrimination case. Since such an indirect approach is necessary, a wide range of evidence may seem relevant. Choosing which evidence to use in a case is important. A good case can become discredited by taking weak points. Excessive and inconclusive evidence clouds the real issues and lengthens the hearing, increasing the risk of a costs award if the claim fails (see below).

---

5 See para 15.22 below.
6 Council Directive 97/80/EC.
7 See n1, above.

Other acts of discrimination

12.8   Every act of discrimination within the three months prior to lodging an application to the ET may form the basis of a claim. However, acts of discrimination falling outside the time limit may be mentioned in the application purely as evidence in support of the discriminatory acts founding the claim.[8] It should be made clear which acts form the basis of the claim. Earlier alleged acts of discrimination will usually be helpful only if they took place relatively recently and relate to the same managers. Acts of discrimination or evidence of discriminatory attitudes occurring after the acts founding the claim are also admissible as supporting evidence of a tendency to discriminate.[9]

12.9   Where the worker mentions a number of out-of-time incidents as evidence supporting the claim, the ET should not look at each incident in isolation to decide if it was itself explicable on grounds of race or sex. In such a case, it is important to draw the ET's attention to the EAT's guidance in *Qureshi v (1) Victoria University of Manchester (2) Brazier*,[10] a case under the RRA 1976. The ET should find the primary facts about all the incidents and then look at the totality of those facts including the employers' explanations, in order to decide whether to infer the acts complained of in the IT1 were on racial grounds. To adopt a fragmented approach 'would inevitably have the effect of diminishing any eloquence that the cumulative effect of the primary facts might have on the issue of racial grounds'.

The employer's explanation

12.10   The employer's likely explanation for what has happened must be anticipated as it will have to be discredited. If, for example, a worker has clearly committed a dismissable offence or is obviously the least qualified and experienced for an appointment or promotion, then it will be extremely difficult to prove unlawful discrimination, even if it could be shown that the employer was generally prejudiced against workers of the same sex or racial group. The issue is less favourable treatment and if, for example, a man would similarly have been dismissed for the same offence, it is irrelevant that the employer was pleased to have the opportunity to dismiss a woman.

---

8   *Eke v Commissioners of Customs and Excise* [1981] IRLR 334, EAT; *Qureshi v (1) Victoria University of Manchester (2) Brazier* EAT/484/95.

9   *Chattopadhyay v Headmaster of Holloway School* [1981] IRLR 487, EAT.

10   EAT/484/95.

11   Where the alleged act of discrimination is dismissal, ETs often suspect that the case is an attempt to claim unfair dismissal for a worker without the necessary qualifying service. It must therefore be remembered that the ET is not interested in whether or not the dismissal was fair, but whether it was on the ground of race or sex.[11] Direct race or sex discrimination is not about unfair treatment. It is about different treatment. In some cases it can be argued that the dismissal was so patently unfair as to be irrational unless explained by hidden grounds. Even then, it is advisable to prove that the employer is not normally unreasonable with other workers or to show some further evidence indicating unlawful discrimination.

12   Discrimination cases are more than usually dependent on the quality of the employer's evidence at the hearing, which makes their outcome hard to predict. Much will depend on how well the employer's explanation stands up to cross-examination. Any contradiction between different witnesses for the employer or between the explanation given at the hearing and that in any contemporaneous document or in the defence or questionnaire reply may well lead the ET to infer race or sex discrimination. However, it will not usually be enough simply to discredit the employer's version of events; some other indication of unlawful discrimination may be required.

13   An ET should recognise that an employer may discriminate against one minority ethnic group even though it may not discriminate against another. The fact that a person is married to a black woman, for example, is not indicative as to whether he would racially abuse an Irish worker.[12]

Comparative treatment

14   The central concept in direct discrimination is that of actual or hypothetical comparative treatment. If a worker of a different sex or racial group can be identified who, in similar circumstances, was treated more favourably, then the case will be much stronger. Other variables should also be checked because these could provide an 'innocent' explanation for the different treatment. They include:

– relevant experience;
– relevant qualifications;
– age;
– status;

11 *Zafar v Glasgow City Council* [1998] IRLR 36, HL
12 *Robson v Commissioners of the Inland Revenue* [1998] IRLR 186; 77 EOR 46, EAT

- whether an internal or external candidate for a post;
- trade union membership.

In a recruitment case, if a job centre or recruitment agency was involved, it should be asked what job description the employer supplied. Where someone fails to gain a post after interview, despite having equal or better qualifications and experience than the person appointed, it is common for the employer to say that the successful candidate interviewed better. This is extremely difficult to contradict. All notes made by the interview panel in relation to each candidate during or after the interviews should be obtained. Also, while the interview is still fresh in his/her mind, the worker should note down the questions and answers as near verbatim as possible.

12.15   It may be relevant to know how the employer generally treats male and female workers or workers from different racial groups, in circumstances other than those of the alleged discriminatory act. It may be that an employer generally speaks more politely to white workers than to black workers, or that black workers are penalised for arriving late to work whereas white workers are not. In *West Midlands Passenger Transport Executive v Singh*,[13] the Court of Appeal said that evidence of discriminatory treatment against a group may be more indicative of unlawful discrimination than previous treatment of the particular worker, which may be due to personal factors other than discrimination. Sometimes it is appropriate, as in *Singh*, to request statistics showing comparative treatment of groups of workers.

12.16   It may also be helpful to show the worker has been treated differently from an expected norm, eg, the employers have not followed their own written disciplinary or grievance procedure on this occasion. Note that although it is helpful to identify an actual comparator, it is not essential. An ET may need reminding that it can infer from the surrounding circumstances that someone of a different race or sex would have been treated more favourably, even though there is no direct evidence of this.[14]

Statistics

12.17   The *Singh* case established the potential importance of statistical evidence in cases of direct discrimination. The Court of Appeal said:

---

13   [1988] IRLR 186, CA.
14   *Leeds Private Hospital Ltd v Parkin* EAT 519/89; *S v The Post Office* EAT 373/90; *Rosse v Paramount House Group Ltd* (1994) 524 *IDS Brief*, EAT.

Direct discrimination involves that an individual is not treated on his merits but receives unfavourable treatment because he is a member of a group. Statistical evidence may establish a discernible pattern in the treatment of a particular group.[15]

Mr Singh claimed racial discrimination in his failure to gain promotion to the post of senior inspector. The court said that if statistics revealed a regular failure of members of a certain group to gain promotion to certain jobs and an under-representation in such jobs, it may give rise to an inference of discrimination against members of the group.

.18   If statistical evidence is not available because, for example, an employer has not monitored the workforce and applications for employment and promotion, the ET could be invited to draw an adverse inference from this fact. Unfortunately, although monitoring is recommended by the Race Relations Code of Practice and encouraged by the higher courts,[16] most ETs will not draw an inference from failure to monitor. Nevertheless, with a large employer and particularly a public authority, it may be worth citing at the hearing the numerous public bodies who do now monitor,[17] so that it is clear that the particular employer is acting unusually.

Failure to follow the codes of practice

.19   The codes of practice are admissible in evidence and, under RRA 1976 s47(10) and SDA 1975 s56A(10), an ET must take into account relevant provisions of the codes in determining any question in the proceedings.[18] The codes make recommendations on good practice in recruitment and promotion procedures. In cases concerning discrimination in these areas, the employer's procedures should be examined to see whether the guidelines of the codes have been followed. The Court of Appeal has expressly referred to the importance of Race Relations Code of Practice para 1.13.[19] Questions in the questionnaire (see para 17.3) and requests for discovery (see para 17.41) should be aimed at establishing what procedures were adopted and these will be a matter for cross-examination at the hearing.

15 *West Midlands Passenger Transport Executive v Singh* [1988] IRLR 186 at p188.
16 Monitoring was approved by the CA in *Singh* (n15, above) and by the EAT in *Carrington v Helix Lighting* [1990] IRLR 6.
17 Some issues of *Equal Opportunities Review* and the CRE and EOC should have this information.
18 *Berry v The Bethlem & Maudsley NHS Trust* (1997) 31 EOR DCLD 1, EAT.
19 *Noone v North West Thames Regional Health Authority* [1988] IRLR 195, CA.

12.20   The Commission for Racial Equality's Code of Practice encourages record-keeping by employers and paras 1.22 and 1.23 recommend that in any disciplinary matter, the employer should consider the possible effect on a worker's behaviour of racial abuse or other racial provocation. Furthermore, any complaint of racial discrimination by a worker should not be treated lightly. The ET's attention should be drawn to those provisions, where the worker has complained of discrimination at some stage during his/her employment, including the final disciplinary hearing, and has been ignored.

12.21   An ET should not infer that discrimination has occurred purely from an employer's failure to follow his/her own equal opportunities policy,[20] but poor practice in recruitment procedures is likely to be a significant factor. It is also worth referring to the EC Code on Sexual Harassment for its definition and recommendations on preventative action and action in response to a complaint.[21]

Racist remarks/overt indications of prejudice

12.22   Although prejudice need not be present to prove discrimination,[22] it strengthens the case if it is demonstrably present. Difficulties often arise because it is only the worker's word and s/he can be accused of making up such remarks while giving evidence. It is therefore important that any crucial remarks are mentioned in the ET1 form from the start.

12.23   Another difficulty is that certain words, 'jokes' or actions may not be taken as indicative of a racist or sexist attitude by the ET. Even if they are, a tribunal will not automatically conclude that prejudiced attitudes lead to discriminatory treatment.[23] In an appointment or promotion case, an employer's comment that someone 'who would fit in' was wanted should be regarded as a danger signal.[24] In certain cases, racist comments may themselves constitute one of the acts of discrimination basing the claim (see paras 11.28 to 11.33 above).

---

20   *Qureshi v Newham LBC* [1991] IRLR 264, EAT.
21   *Grimaldi v Fonds des Maladies Professionelles* [1990] IRLR 400, ECJ; *Wadman v Carpenter Farrer Partnership* [1993] IRLR 374, EAT.
22   See para 9.46 above.
23   The Court of Appeal in *De Souza v Automobile Association* [1986] IRLR 103 felt able to draw this distinction.
24   *Baker v Cornwall CC* [1990] IRLR 194, CA at p198; *King v The Great Britain-China Centre* [1991] IRLR 513, CA.

Previous complaints of discrimination

.24 Recorded previous complaints of unlawful discrimination against relevant managers should constitute useful evidence, particularly if the employer has failed to investigate such allegations (see para 12.20). There are many and obvious reasons why a worker may not complain of discrimination while still employed. The EC Code specifically addresses this issue with regard to sexual harassment. Nevertheless, a worker who alleges that discrimination has been occurring for some time is likely to be heavily cross-examined on why s/he did not complain at the time, and should be prepared to answer this question at the hearing.

.25 Where a worker, during employment, seeks advice in respect of discrimination, proceedings will usually be regarded as a last resort. However, s/he should be advised of the risks of not registering the allegation in writing, should some issue of discrimination ultimately end up in the ET. According to the circumstances, the worker could make a formal complaint under the grievance procedure or write a low-key letter just putting the matter on record. If appropriate, the employer's attention could be expressly drawn to the prohibition on victimisation under RRA 1976 s2 or SDA 1975 s4.

Indirect discrimination

Proportions who can comply with the requirement

.26 Under RRA 1976 s1(1)(b)(i) and SDA 1975 s1(1)(b)(i) statistical evidence is almost invariably required. The ET can take account of its own knowledge and experience in determining whether a requirement or condition has disparate impact[25] and it is often undesirable to present elaborate statistical evidence. On the other hand, an ET may unexpectedly insist on evidential proof of apparently obvious facts. It is well-established that determining the correct pool for comparison of the proportions of people of different sexes or racial groups who can comply with a requirement is a question of fact for the ET.

.27 It may choose a pool not anticipated by the worker and catch him/her unprepared. It may be possible to avoid this difficulty by agreeing a pool with the employer prior to the hearing, by holding a preliminary hearing on the point or even adjourning the main hearing once the pool is decided if the necessary statistics are not available. How-

25 *Briggs v North Eastern Education and Library Board* [1990] IRLR 181, NI CA.

ever, it is wise to prepare statistics on all the potential pools. Clearly some pools will be more helpful than others and less helpful pools which the ET might choose should therefore be anticipated with, if possible, explanations as to why they are misleading or irrelevant, for example because they incorporate discrimination.

Where to find the statistics

12.28 As stated above, statistics need to be gathered to show adverse impact within every likely pool for comparison. The statistics must relate to those within and those outside the relevant race or sex group and within the possible pools. One of the difficulties with indirect discrimination cases is that statistics are rarely available to meet the exact purpose. Where directly relevant statistics are not available, other statistics or evidence, from which the relevant facts may be inferred, should be used.

12.29 Statistics on any workplace pool can be obtained on the questionnaire, eg, by asking how many of the existing workforce, by reference to sex and marital status, work part-time or full-time or how many women left after having children.

12.30 The CRE and EOC should be consulted as to what statistics can be obtained from various sources, eg, the Low Pay Unit, the Child Poverty Action Group, the TUC, trade unions and university research departments, libraries, the Joint Council for the Welfare of Immigrants and community groups. The EOC[26] and the CRE will advise on available reports and statistical sources. Both the CRE and Runnymede Trust have specialist libraries. The EOC publishes a useful annual booklet, *About Women and Men in Great Britain*.[27] See also the *LHS Historical Supplement* for labour market statistics 1994–98 and *Tracking people: a simple guide to survey data*.[28] The Department of Employment's *Gazette* summarises workforce surveys and is available in most libraries, as are the Labour Force Surveys and General Household Surveys which contain detailed statistics on patterns of full-time and part-time work by single and married men and women.[29] For a small fee, a market research company called

---

26 Publications catalogue available on request, tel: 0161 835 1637 or see the web site at www.eoc.org.uk.
27 Available free from EOC.
28 Each available from the Office of National Statistics, tel: 0171 533 6262.
29 The regional trends survey may show large regional variations in patterns of working women.

SPSS[30] provides detailed statistics on a range of subjects. Research reports or articles in specialist publications such as the *Nursing Times* on the position of black workers in the NHS, are useful for direct and indirect discrimination cases. The EOR is an excellent reference source with its own research features and detailed listings of recently published reports. Local authority social services should have statistics on childcare facilities and take-up.

12.31   Where there is no statistical or research evidence precisely on the point required, verbal evidence from 'experts' or respected members of the community may be useful.

Justifiability

2.32   Although the onus is on the employer to justify a condition or requirement, it seems that s/he is not required to produce evidence of the requirement's discriminatory effect, or at least no detailed statistical evidence.[31] As the greater the discriminatory effect, the better justification the employer needs, the worker should be prepared to supply such evidence. The type of evidence will be similar to that used to show the lesser proportion of women, etc, who could comply with the requirement at the relevant date.

2.33   Furthermore, the employer is under no obligation to prove that there is no other possible way of achieving his/her objective. If the worker thinks that there are reasonable alternative requirements with less discriminatory effect, s/he must put forward the suggestion and supporting evidence.[32]

2.34   The codes of practice[33] may provide guidance on what should be considered unjustifiable. For example, under paragraph 1.24 of the CRE Code, employers should consider whether it is reasonably practicable to adapt work requirements to enable workers to meet their cultural and religious needs.

Victimisation

.35   The worker first needs to prove that the 'protected act' took place. This may be difficult if his/her complaint of discrimination was made verbally. In order to show the worker was victimised as a result,

---

30   Tel: 020 7625 7222.
31   *Cobb v Secretary of State for Employment and MSC* [1989] IRLR 464, EAT.
32   Ibid.
33   See above.

it is useful to prove that the employer's behaviour towards the worker was different before and after doing the protected act. It is worth doing a chronology of the key facts. The timing of events is particularly revealing in victimisation cases.

Failure to respond to the questionnaire

12.36   Under RRA 1976 s65(2)(b) and SDA 1975 s74(2)(b), if the employer 'deliberately and without reasonable excuse' fails to answer the questionnaire within a reasonable time or answers in a way that is 'evasive or equivocal', the ET may draw an inference that the employer committed an unlawful act of discrimination.[34] The EAT has encouraged both the use of the questionnaire procedure[35] and ETs to draw inferences from vague or unsatisfactory replies.[36] It should be borne in mind when drafting the questionnaire that it should not be so onerous that an employer has a 'reasonable excuse' for not answering (see para 17.10).

Witnesses

12.37   The principles are the same as in other ET cases. However, there is little doubt that independent witnesses in discrimination cases (particularly if they are of a different sex or race to the worker) can vastly increase the chances of success. If witnesses are called on any point of detail, the adviser should check what they will say if asked whether they believe unlawful discrimination has taken place. Although this is only a matter of their opinion, it will harm the worker's case if his/her witness considers that discrimination has not occurred.

Helpful kinds of evidence in disability discrimination cases

12.38   The code of practice under the DDA 1995 is admissible in evidence and under s53(6) an ET must take into account any relevant provision.[37] The Guidance relating to the definition of disability must also

---

34   *King v Great Britain F1 China Centre* (n1 above).
35   *Carrington v Helix Lighting* [1990] IRLR 6.
36   *Berry v The Bethlem & Maudsley NHS Trust; Hinks v Riva Systems & Lumsden* (1997) 31 EOR DCLD 1, EAT
37   *Goodwin v The Patent Office* [1999] IRLR 4, EAT; *Clark v TDG Ltd (trading as Novacold)* [1999] IRLR 318; 85 EOR 46, CA

be taken into account.[38] Chapter 13 refers in detail to the provisions of the Code and Guidance.

39 Medical evidence[39] will usually be important and may be relevant to the definition of disability (whether the worker is covered by the DDA 1995), what reasonable adjustments may be made and compensation for future loss (see below). ETs often require evidence from specialists as opposed to simply GPs, though that would depend on the issues. When obtaining a medical report, ask the doctor directed questions according to the evidence you need to meet the legal requirements.[40] Specialist organisations will also suggest suitable adjustments.

40 The questionnaire procedure under the DDA 1995 is the same as under the SDA 1975 and RRA 1976. Under DDA 1995 s56(3)(b) if the employer 'deliberately and without reasonable excuse' fails to answer the questionnaire within a reasonable time or answers in a way that is 'evasive or equivocal', the ET may draw an inference that the employer committed an unlawful act of discrimination.[41] Evidence relating to victimisation will be similar to that necessary under the SDA 1975 and RRA 1976 above.

Injury to feelings, mitigation and other evidence

41 Sometimes other evidence may be wanted. For example, if the worker saw her GP because of stress, during or after her employment, a medical report could be useful to show 'detriment' and could also be relevant to the injury to feelings award.[42] In sexual harassment cases, an expert medical report may help convey the degree of distress suffered by the worker. General research reports and statistical evidence as to the level of sexual harassment of women at work and its effects may also be useful.[43]

42 If the discrimination has damaged the worker's health such that compensation can be claimed for personal injuries,[44] a medical report

38 DDA 1995 s3(3); *Goodwin* ibid.
39 See para 17.56 on expenses.
40 See p391 for a sample letter.
41 See para 17.3 below.
42 See the paras 15.11 to 15.19 below on remedies.
43 See, eg, *Mental Rape: The effects of sexual harassment*, available from City Centre, tel: 020 7608 1338, and various features in EOR over the years.
44 See para 15.20.

will be essential. Some ETs take pregnancy dismissal cases less seriously than other forms of discrimination. Again, a report from the worker's own GP plus any expert evidence that this can be a time when women feel particularly vulnerable, would be helpful. Women who are pregnant or with young babies, as well as black or disabled workers, will find it harder to obtain new employment. This can be relevant to the level of compensation in dismissal cases including unfair dismissal. As well as detailed evidence of the particular worker's attempts to find fresh employment, reference to the general problems of the subject group may be of assistance.[45]

12.43   EAT has said that compensation in discrimination cases where no upper limit applies cannot be dealt with briefly and informally. Careful preparation may be necessary for a remedies hearing. In cases under the DDA 1995, a medical expert may well be required as to the worker's likely future health, since this would be relevant to an assessment of future loss of earnings.[46]

---

45 Job centres are willing sometimes to write a letter on the general job prospects facing the worker.
46 *Buxton v Equinox Design Ltd* [1999] IRLR 158, EAT.

Discrimination on grounds of disability

The legal framework

13.1   In November 1995, the Disability Discrimination Act 1995 was at last passed after several unsuccessful attempts to bring in private members' bills prohibiting discrimination on grounds of disability. As with the RRA 1976 and SDA 1975, the DDA 1995 covers discrimination in relation to premises, education, goods, facilities and services and other areas as well as employment. There is to be a Disability Rights Commission, similar to the Commission for Racial Equality and the Equal Opportunities Commission.[1]

13.2   The employment part of the DDA came into force on 2 December 1996. Various regulations have been made giving more specific detail of legal requirements in certain areas.[2] Unusually, the DDA gives power to the government to issue such regulations modifying and explaining its provisions. Advisers must therefore be alert to developments. A *Code of Practice for the elimination of discrimination in the field of employment against disabled persons or persons who have had a disability* was issued under the DDA 1995 s53 and also came into effect on 2 December 1996.[3] As with the Codes under the RRA 1976 and SDA 1975, this Code must be taken into account by an ET on any relevant point, but it is not legally actionable in itself.[4]

13.3   The Code of Practice covers a range of matters, but is particularly useful regarding the scope of the employer's duty to make reasonable adjustments.[5] The other key document is the *Guidance on matters to be taken into account in determining questions relating to the definition of disability.*[6] The EAT has said that at least while the legislation is still relatively new, an ET should refer explicitly to any relevant provision of the Code or the Guidance.[7]

13.4   The DDA replaces the limited and ineffective requirements of the Disabled Persons (Employment) Act 1944, which required employers to employ a quota of registered disabled workers.[8]

13.5   Although the definition of discrimination under the DDA differs

---

1   Under the RRA 1976 and SDA 1975 respectively.
2   For example, the Disability Discrimination (Meaning of Disability) Regulations 1996 SI No 1455 (in force 30 July 1996) and the Disability Discrimination (Employment) Regulations 1996 SI No 1456 (in force 2 December 1996).
3   SI 1996 No 1986.
4   DDA 1995 s53(4)–(6).
5   See below.
6   SI 1996 No 1996. Issued under DDA 1995 s3.
7   *Goodwin v The Patent Office* [1999] IRLR 4, EAT.
8   DDA 1995 s61.

significantly from the definition in the RRA 1976 and SDA 1975, many other aspects of the scope of the legislation and ET procedure are identical. While the law is still developing, it may be useful in these other areas to cross-refer to the guidance on law and practice in running cases under the RRA 1976 and SDA 1975.

Which workers are covered?

As with the other discrimination legislation, the DDA protects job applicants, apprentices, contract workers[9] and those working personally on a contract to execute any work as well as employees.[10] With limited exceptions, employers are liable for the discriminatory acts of their employees or agents, regardless of whether they knew of or approved those acts.[11]

Trade organisations (eg, organisations of workers) must not discriminate in access to membership or in terms of membership.[12]

Which employers are covered?

If the employer had fewer than 15 employees, in the wide sense set out above,[13] at the time of the act of discrimination, s/he will be exempt from the DDA in relation to that act.[14] Workers at different locations working for the same employer would be included, but the DDA does not say that workers employed by an associated employer should be added in. There are special rules regarding firefighters, armed services personnel, holders of statutory office and certain categories of prison officer and police.[15] Service as a police officer may not be covered.[16]

---

9 DDA s12(1). See para 9.14 above, although the wording is slightly different to that under RRA 1976 s7 and SDA 1975 s9.
10 DDA s68.
11 DDA s58. See para 11.41 on the law on equivalent provisions under RRA 1976 and SDA 1975.
12 DDA ss13–15.
13 *Hidle v Hi-Drive Plant Services* (1990) 40 EOR DCLD 12, EAT.
14 The Disability Discrimination (Exemption for Small Employers) Orders 1998 SI No 2618. With effect from 1 December 1998.
15 DDA ss64, 66.
16 *Pearson v Central Scotland Police* (1999) 619 IRLB 18, S(EAT).

Statutory authority

13.9   A discriminatory act will not be unlawful if it is done in pursuance of a statute or statutory instrument or to safeguard national security.[17]

Charities and supported employment

13.10   Charities are permitted to discriminate in pursuance of their charitable purposes if those are connected with disability.[18] Providers of supported employment under the Disabled Persons (Employment) Act 1944 may treat a particular group of disabled workers more favourably than others.[19]

Prohibited actions

13.11   DDA s4 prohibits discrimination against a disabled person in the arrangements made for deciding who should be offered employment, in the terms on which employment is offered, in refusing to offer employment, in access to opportunities for promotion, transfer, training or other benefit, in contract terms or by dismissing the worker or subjecting him/her to any other detriment (including harassment).[20] Employment must be at an establishment in Great Britain.[21] The DDA contains special rules regarding discrimination in occupational pension schemes[22] and in insurance provided by the employer.[23]

The meaning of 'disability'

13.12   Except in obvious cases, one of the most important and difficult issues is whether a worker is covered by the DDA. The DDA effectively covers many workers with long-term ill-health, which would not conventionally be seen as a 'disability'. The most frequently claimed

17   DDA s59.
18   Ibid s10(1).
19   Ibid s10.
20   See para 11.28 for how harassment fits into the discrimination legislation.
21   DDA s4(6). Though see the Equal Opportunities (Employment Legislation) (Territorial Limits) Regulations 1999 SI No 3163.
22   Ibid s17.
23   Ibid s18.

disabilities in the first 19 months of the DDA were back or neck impairments, and depression.[24] It is dangerous to generalise as to when the DDA applies and each case will depend on a close examination of its facts. A worker with a back problem, for example, may or may not be covered by the DDA, depending on the duration and severity of the problem. It is necessary to go through the stages of the statutory definition set out below, taking into account the clarification in the Guidance.[25]

The DDA prohibits unlawful discrimination against a 'disabled person' in employment.[26] Section 1 defines a disabled person as a person who has a disability. Section 1(1) reads:

> Subject to the provisions of Schedule 1, a person has a disability for the purposes of this Act if he has a physical or mental impairment which has a substantial and long-term adverse effect on his ability to carry out normal day-to-day activities.

Each element of this definition should be separately considered.[27] Schedule 1 provides guidance, and further clarification can be found in the Disability Discrimination (Meaning of Disability) Regulations 1996[28] and in the *Guidance on matters to be taken into account in determining questions relating to the definition of 'disability'*. The Guidance should be looked at in deciding whether someone has a disability, but it should not be used as an obstacle if it is obvious that they do.[29]

Physical impairment

'Physical impairment' includes sensory impairment and severe disfigurement, although not tattoos or ornamental body piercing.[30] Provided all aspects of the definition are met, conditions such as ME (chronic fatigue syndrome),[31] asthma and back disorders can be covered. Seasonal allergic rhinitis, for example hay-fever, is expressly excluded.[32] Addictions to alcohol, nicotine or other substances are

24 (1999) 86 EOR 12.
25 See n6 above. See also the checklist on p388.
26 DDA s4.
27 See checklist on p388.
28 SI No 1455.
29 *Goodwin v The Patent Office* [1999] IRLR 4, EAT.
30 Disability Discrimination (Meaning of Disability) Regulations 1996 SI No 1455, reg 5.
31 *O'Neill v Symm & Co Ltd* [1998] IRLR 233, EAT.
32 Disability Discrimination (Meaning of Disability) Regulations 1996 SI No 1455, reg 4(2).

also not covered unless the addiction was originally the result of administration of medical treatment or medically prescribed drugs.[33] It is not necessary to consider how a physical or mental impairment was caused. So for example, liver disease resulting from alcohol dependency would count as an impairment.[34]

Mental impairment

13.15   'Mental impairment' includes learning disabilities.[35] It does not include mental illness unless that illness is clinically well-recognised, ie, recognised by a respected body of medical opinion.[36] This is very likely to include mental illnesses specifically mentioned in publications such as the World Health Organisation's International Classification of Diseases.[37] It may not be clear when a mental illness is covered in a particular case. Workers suffering from schizophrenia, manic depression or severe psychoses will usually be covered. Neurotic (as opposed to psychotic) depression is also recognised as a proper medical diagnosis. It is sometimes referred to as 'clinical' or 'reactive' depression[38] and its effects may include loss of concentration. It should be distinguished from a worker simply feeling fed-up. However this kind of ordinary depression may fail to meet other aspects of the definition of disability, eg, it may not have a substantial adverse effect for as long as 12 months. Certain personality disorders are specifically excluded, for example, a tendency to set fires or steal, to physical or sexual abuse, voyeurism or exhibitionism.[39] It also includes learning disabilities.

Affecting normal day-to-day activities

13.16   The impairment must affect one of the following normal day-to-day activities: mobility, manual dexterity, physical co-ordination, continence, ability to lift, carry or move everyday objects, speech, hearing or

---

33   Disability Discrimination (Meaning of Disability) Regulations 1996 SI No 1455, reg 3.
34   Guidance Part I, para 11.
35   Guidance Part I, para 13.
36   DDA Sch 1 para 1.
37   Guidance, Part I, para 15.
38   *Kapadia v Lambeth LBC* (1999) 625 IRLB 2, EAT.
39   Disability Discrimination (Meaning of Disability) Regulations 1996 SI No 1455, reg 4(1).

eyesight, memory or ability to concentrate, learn or understand, or perception of the risk of physical danger. Part C of the Guidance provides extremely useful guidelines and illustration as to what are 'normal day-to-day activities'. The activity must be one which is carried out by most people on a daily or frequent or fairly regular basis. Impairments which only affect ability to carry out particular hobbies (eg, piano playing) or sports are not covered. Similarly, inability to carry out a particular form of work is not covered, because no particular form of work is 'normal' for most people. For example, a worker who could no longer reach secretarial typing speeds, but who could still press key-board buttons at the speed normal for most people, would not be covered. In one case, a garden centre worker was unsuccessful because although he could not lift heavy bags of soil, he could still lift everyday objects.[40]

7   A worker may tell an adviser or the tribunal that his/her day-to-day life is unaffected by his/her disability. This can be misleading. A worker may play down the effect of his/her disability.[41] Or it may be that a worker has rearranged his/her life to avoid carrying out a certain activity and feels that s/he is coping. The focus should be on what the worker cannot do; or cannot do without difficulty, as opposed to what s/he can do.[42]

Substantial effect

8   The Guidance at Section A expands on the meaning of 'substantial' adverse effect. It is unnecessary that a worker is completely unable to carry out the activity, but the effect must be clearly more than trivial.[43] A substantial effect could include where a worker can carry out the activity, but only for short periods of time or more slowly than usual or only in a particular way or under certain environmental conditions. It may be that a worker can carry out the activity, but it is tiring or painful to do so. Alternatively, the worker may have been medically advised to refrain from the activity altogether. Section C of the Guidance gives examples linked to each of the listed day-to-day activities (above) where it is unclear whether an impairment has substantial effect. For example, it would be reasonable to regard as having substantial adverse effect:

40   *Quinlan v B&Q Plc* 614 *IDS Brief,* EAT.
41   *Goodwin v The Patent Office* [1999] IRLR 4, EAT.
42   Ibid.
43   Ibid.

- difficulty going up stairs;
- inability to use one or more forms of public transport;
- inability to handle a knife and fork at the same time;
- inability to carry a moderately loaded tray successfully;
- inability to ask specific questions to clarify instructions.

It would not be reasonable to regard as having substantial adverse effect:

- inability to travel in a car for more than two hours without discomfort;
- inability to thread a small needle;
- inability to carry heavy luggage;
- inability to converse in a foreign language;
- a minor lisp or stutter.

The Guidance should be looked at in full and advisers should always consider each case on its particular facts, rather than generalise from the examples.

13.19   Severe disfigurement is deemed to have 'substantial' adverse effect.

13.20   The fact that medical treatment or medication controls or corrects the impairment is irrelevant (except for someone whose sight impairment is corrected by glasses or lenses).[44] The effect without the correcting measures should be assessed. So, for example, a worker is still protected, even if his/her diabetes is controlled by insulin or his/her depression is controlled by counselling sessions with a clinical psychologist.[45] The EAT has suggested that an ET should consider both the effect of a worker's impairment while on medication and the 'deduced effects' but for the medication.[46] This is obviously difficult and medical evidence may be needed.

13.21   A worker with a progressive condition, eg, cancer or AIDS, is deemed disabled as soon as the condition has any effect on the worker's ability to carry out day-to-day duties, even if the effect is not yet substantial.[47] However, if the condition has not yet had any effect at all, eg, symptom-free HIV infection, s/he is not protected.[48]

---

44   DDA Sch 1 para 6.
45   *Kapadia v Lambeth LBC* (1999) 625 IRLB 2, EAT.
46   *Goodwin* above.
47   DDA Sch 1 para 8.
48   Ibid.

Long-term effect

22 The DDA does not protect those with short-term or temporary disability. To be considered long term, the effect of the impairment must have lasted or be likely to last at least 12 months or for the rest of the worker's life. In determining whether the effect of the impairment is likely to last 12 months, the ET will consider this (the adverse effect) up to and including the ET hearing.[49] If an impairment ceases to have substantial adverse effect but is likely to recur, it is treated as continuing. This covers workers with impairments with fluctuating or recurring effects, eg, rheumatoid arthritis or multiple sclerosis. Conditions which recur only sporadically or for short periods (eg, epilepsy or, presumably, migraine) can still apply, depending on the facts.[50] For the meaning of 'recurring and long-term effect' see the Guidance, Section B.

Deemed disability

23 For a transitional period of three years, workers registered under the Disabled Persons (Employment) Act 1944 s6 both on 12 January 1995 and on the date the DDA came into force will be deemed disabled.[51]

Past disability

24 A worker who has recovered from a past disability is protected if s/he is discriminated against in connection with that disability.[52] The DDA does not protect workers who are discriminated against because they are incorrectly perceived to have a disability.

The meaning of 'discrimination'

25 The definition of discrimination is different in important respects from the definition in the RRA 1976 and SDA 1975 and it is essential not to become confused. Whereas direct discrimination under the other Acts cannot be justified, there is no absolute prohibition against discrimination on grounds of disability. However, the DDA tries to

---

49 *Greenwood v British Airways plc* [1999] IRLR 600.
50 Guidance, para B3.
51 DDA Sch 1 para 7.
52 DDA Sch 1 para 2 and Sch 2.

restrict the employer's scope for justification. In addition, there is a positive duty on employers to make adjustments for disability. There are three kinds of unlawful discrimination under the DDA.

(1) Less favourable treatment for a reason related to the worker's disability.[53]

(2) Failure to comply with a duty to make reasonable adjustment in relation to the disabled worker.[54] Note that this can be an unlawful act of discrimination in itself. Many sets of facts will potentially amount to discrimination under both s5(1) and s5(2) and both should be claimed.[55]

(3) Victimisation.[56] This is when a worker is punished or treated differently as a result of complaining about discrimination or raising the issue or doing any other 'protected act'. It is the equivalent to unlawful victimisation under the RRA 1976 and SDA 1975 and the same case-law should apply to all three Acts.[57]

Less favourable treatment

13.26   DDA s5(1) states:

> An employer discriminates against a disabled person if –
> (a) for a reason which relates to the disabled person's disability, he treats him less favourably than he treats or would treat others to whom that reason does not or would not apply; and
> (b) he cannot show that the treatment in question is justified.

This definition replaces the concepts of direct and indirect discrimination, which are dealt with separately in the RRA 1976 and SDA 1975. Subject to the defence of justification, the following situations are examples of where an employer may discriminate:

– an employer refuses to employ a worker purely because the worker is disabled;

– a blind worker is not short-listed for a job involving computers because the employer assumes blind people cannot use computers;[58]

---

53   DDA s5(1).
54   Ibid s5(2).
55   See example ETI at p392.
56   DDA s55.
57   See paras 9.82 to 9.91 above.
58   See Code, para 4.6.

- an employer will not employ a wheelchair user because of access difficulties;
- a factory worker with learning difficulties is dismissed because her productivity is lower than that of other workers;[59]
- an employer specifies that a driving licence is required for a job which involves limited travelling. A candidate with cerebral palsy who cannot drive is excluded;[60]
- an employer prefers all employees to have a certain level of educational qualification, which is not in fact necessary for the job. A worker with a learning disability is turned down from a job because s/he does not have this qualification;[61]
- an employer wrongly assumes that a disabled worker will be unwilling or unable to attend a residential training course, instead of taking an informed decision.[62]

3.27 Some early cases suggested that to prove discrimination under s5(1), a comparison needed to be made with how the employers would have treated a non-disabled worker in similar circumstances. This is the appropriate comparison for cases of direct race or sex discrimination, but not for disability discrimination.[63] Under DDA s5(1), the worker need only show s/he has been less favourably treated than others, where the reason for the treatment is related to his/her disability, and that reason does not apply to the others. This approach is similar (in this respect) to that for pregnancy discrimination, where a comparison with the treatment of a sick man is not necessary.

3.28   For example, a worker is dismissed for sickness absence totalling three months, when the entire absence is due to disability. This is discrimination under s5(1) because the reason for the dismissal (the sickness absence) was related to the worker's disability. If the reason did not apply, ie, if the worker had no sickness absence, s/he would not have been dismissed. It is irrelevant that the employers would equally have dismissed a non-disabled worker with a three-month sickness absence.

.29   In order to discriminate for a reason related to a worker's disability, the employers need not know of the worker's disability, although

59 See Code, para 4.6.
60 See Code, para 5.3.
61 See Code, para 5.6.
62 See Code, para 6.6.
63 *Clark v TDG Ltd t/a Novacold* [1999] IRLR 318; 85 EOR 46, CA.

if the employers did not know, they may have lesser obligations to make reasonable adjustment, therefore, although workers may be reluctant to reveal they have a disability, it may be important to tell the employer, and in writing, to gain the protection of the DDA.[64-65]

13.30   The DDA does not prohibit positive discrimination in favour of disabled workers, as it is not unlawful to discriminate against a worker on grounds that s/he is not disabled. However, local government employers may be restricted due to the provisions of the Local Government and Housing Act 1989.[66]

The employer's defence

13.31   The employer can only justify his/her discriminatory treatment if the reason for it was both material to the circumstances of the particular case and substantial.[67] This means the reason must relate to the individual circumstances in question and not just be trivial or minor.[68] The ET must carry out a balancing exercise between the interests of the disabled worker and the interests of the employer.[69] For example, a general assumption that a disabled person will have a high level of sick leave, would be insufficient without looking at the individual's health record. A non-substantial reason might be if an employer moves a worker with mental illness to a different workplace solely because she mutters quietly to herself while she works.

13.32   If the employer's justification would not be sufficient had s/he complied with any duty to make reasonable adjustments, then the defence will fail.[70] For example, an applicant for a typing job may be genuinely unsuitable for the job because her typing speeds are too slow due to arthritis. However, she may be able to overcome this with an adapted keyboard. The Code of Practice, particularly at paragraphs 4.6 and 4.7, gives examples of what will, and what will not, be justified treatment.

64-65   *H J Heinz Co Ltd v Kenrick* [2000] IRLR 144, EAT, disagreeing with *O'Neill v Symm & Co Ltd* [1998] IRLR 233, EAT.
66   See commentary in (1996) 65 EOR 38.
67   DDA s5(3).
68   Code of Practice, para 4.6.
69   *Baynton v Saurus General Engineering Ltd* [1999] IRLR 604.
70   DDA s5(5).

Failure to make reasonable adjustment

33 DDA s5(2) states:

> An employer also discriminates against a disabled person if –
> (a) he fails to comply with a s6 duty imposed on him in relation to the disabled person; and
> (b) he cannot show that his failure to comply with that duty is justified.

Under DDA s6, an employer has a duty to make reasonable adjustments to avoid placing a disabled worker or job applicant at a substantial disadvantage due to any arrangements made by the employer or any physical feature of the premises. The steps which it is envisaged the employer may have to take include adjusting premises, acquiring equipment, providing interpreters, modifying instructions and assessment procedures, adjusting hours and allowing time-off for care, arranging training, reallocating duties.[71]

34   There is no open-ended duty to make adjustments; the duty is owed in relation to a particular employee or job applicant whom the employer knows to have a disability and is likely to be disadvantaged.[72] A worker who fails to get a job or who is not promoted or trained or who suffers any other detriment as a result of the employer's failure to make reasonable adjustments may bring a discrimination case.[73] Strictly speaking, the s6 duty does not apply to the decision to dismiss. However, failure to make adjustments during employment which would prevent dismissal will be covered and an ET can award compensation for the resulting loss of a job.[74]

35   Factors which are particularly relevant in deciding whether it was reasonable for the employer to have made the necessary adjustment are the extent to which the adjustment would prevent the disadvantage, the practicability of the employer making the adjustment, the employer's financial and other resources, the availability of financial or other assistance to make the adjustment, and the cost and disruption entailed.[75]

36   The Code of Practice clarifies further when the duty to make adjustments may arise. The following are a few examples of possible

---

71 Ibid s6.
72 Ibid s6(5), (6).
73 Ibid ss5(2), 6.
74 *Clark v TDG Ltd t/a Novacold* [1999] IRLR 318, CA.
75 DDA s6(4); see Code 4.21–4.32.

adjustments from the Code. Note that whether it is reasonable to expect the employer to make such adjustments will depend on all the facts of the case. Possibilities are:

- allowing the worker to work flexi-time to enable additional breaks to overcome fatigue or changing the worker's hours to fit with the availability of a carer or to avoid travel on public transport during rush hours;
- adapting training so it is suitable for a disabled worker, eg, allowing more time or using modified equipment;
- providing a support worker or help from a colleague, in appropriate circumstances, for a worker whose disability leads to uncertainty or lack of confidence;
- giving a newly disabled employee time to adjust, eg, by initially working from home; a gradual build-up to full-time hours; or additional training or job coaching.

The EAT has said an employer may be under a duty to make physical arrangements for the worker to go to the toilet or to accommodate an external carer to help the worker do so. However, this does not go as far as a duty actually to provide the carers to attend to a worker's personal needs.[76]

13.37   Research suggests that adjustments are not necessarily expensive.[77] There may also be financial assistance available, eg, grants under the Access to Work Scheme as well as advice and information from specialist bodies, eg, the RNIB and the Employment Service's Placing Assessment and Counselling Teams.[78] Special rules exist where an employer may need to alter premises which s/he occupies under a lease.[79]

13.38   In *Morse v Wiltshire County Council*,[80] the EAT sets out the steps which an ET should take in considering whether an employer has met any duty of reasonable adjustment. The ET must apply an objective test. Although it should scrutinise the employer's explanation, it must reach its own decision on what steps were reasonable and what was objectively justified.

---

76 *Kenny v Hampshire Constabulary* [1999] IRLR 76, EAT.
77 See the evidence quoted in Brian Doyle, *Disability, Discrimination and Equal Opportunities* (1995), chap 9.
78 For practical advice, ideas and sources of help see article 'Adjusting the Workplace: Employers' duty under the DDA' (1995) 61 EOR 11.
79 DDA s16.
80 [1998] IRLR 352, EAT.

39   The employer is under no duty to make reasonable adjustment if s/he does not know and cannot reasonably be expected to know that the worker or job applicant is disabled and likely to be substantially disadvantaged.[81] A worker does not have to tell an employer that s/he is disabled, but if s/he needs adjustments to be made, s/he would be wise to tell the employer clearly in writing that s/he is disabled and any adjustment s/he knows would help. Although an employer has a duty to make reasonable enquiries based on information given to him/her, there is no absolute onus on the employer to make every enquiry possible.[82] Early cases suggest, rather alarmingly, that employers do not always need to take a very pro-active approach in finding out.

The employer's defence

40   Again, the employer can only justify his/her discriminatory treatment if the reason for it was both material to the circumstances of the particular case and substantial.[83] It is unlikely that an employer could justify failure to make a reasonable adjustment because of ignorance or wrong information about appropriate adjustments or the availability of help with making the adjustment. The employer would need to show s/he had made a reasonable effort to obtain good information from a reputable source.[84] In deciding whether the employer's behaviour was justified, the ET should not look purely at the employers' interests, but should balance these with the interests of the disabled employee.[85]

---

81   DDA s6(6); see paras 4.57 and 4.61 of the Code.
82   *Ridout v T C Group* [1998] IRLR 628; (1998) 82 EOR 46, EAT; *O'Neill v Symm & Co Ltd* [1998] IRLR 237; *Hanlon v University of Huddersfield* (1998) 619 *IDS Brief* 6, EAT.
83   DDA s5(4); Code, para 4.34.
84   Code, para 4.34.
85   *Baynton v Saurus General Engineers Ltd* [1999] IRLR 604, EAT.

Part IV

Procedures

Unfair dismissal remedies

14.1 An ET, having found that a worker has been unfairly dismissed, must make a declaration to this effect. It must explain what would occur if an order for reinstatement or re-engagement was made, then ask the worker whether s/he wants to be re-employed and if not make an award of compensation.[1] If neither of the re-employment orders is practicable or desired by the worker, the ET will make an award of compensation.[2]

14.2 It was envisaged when ETs were first introduced that re-employment orders would be the primary remedy. It is, however, unlikely for the parties to want to work with each other again after the conclusion of an ET hearing, making re-employment orders rare. Nevertheless, ETs must explain this option.[3]

14.3 Even if an employer is prepared to make a payment equal to or in excess of the maximum compensatory award, the worker is still entitled to go to court to obtain a declaration that s/he has been unfairly dismissed without fear of having to pay costs unless the employer concedes the unfairness of the dismissal as well.[4]

Reinstatement

14.4 Reinstatement is where the ET orders that the worker returns to his/her old job, whereas re-engagement is where the worker returns to a similar job either with the employer or an associated employer. The ET is under a statutory duty to ask the worker after the hearing whether s/he wants to be reinstated even if no mention of it was made on the ET1 form (the application to the tribunal). If the worker wants reinstatement or re-engagement, s/he should indicate this on the ET1 form. In determining whether it is reasonably practicable to reinstate or re-engage a worker who has been unfairly dismissed, an ET must disregard the employment of any replacement worker if reinstatement or re-engagement has been requested on the ET1 form.[5] It is therefore important to put the employer on notice. Otherwise the employer might be able to avoid an order (see below).

---

1 *Cowley v Manson Timber Ltd* [1995] IRLR 153; [1995] ICR 367, CA.
2 ERA 1996 s112(4).
3 *Cowley v Manson Timber Ltd* (see n1).
4 *Telephone Information Services Ltd v Wilkinson* [1991] IRLR 148.
5 ERA 1996 s116(5).

When making a reinstatement order, the ET decides the date when the worker will return to work and the amount of the missing wages and benefit that the employer must pay for the period between dismissal and reinstatement, including restoring any rights that the worker would have acquired during the period of absence.[6] The terms of employment cannot be less favourable than those previously enjoyed.[7]

Whether reinstatement is practicable involves consideration of a number of issues. The factors which the ET must consider are: the worker's wish to be reinstated; whether it is practicable for the employer to comply with the order (the job may no longer exist);[8] and whether the worker caused or contributed to some extent to the dismissal.[9] The ET must not take into consideration the fact that the employer has employed a permanent replacement unless the worker has delayed in putting the employer on notice that s/he wanted to be reinstated, or if it was not practicable for the employer to have the work carried out on a temporary basis.[10]

The ET must consider each case on its own merits, and decide whether such an order is capable of being put into effect with success.[11] Factors that should be taken into account include whether the reinstatement of the worker is going to cause problems with the other workers, the size of the employer,[12] and the workability of such an order.[13] ETs are encouraged to adopt a common sense approach and to avoid treating it as a technical exercise.

Finally, the ET must consider whether the worker has to some extent caused or contributed to his/her dismissal and, if s/he has, whether it is just to make an order for reinstatement.[14] It might be that, although the dismissal was unfair, subsequent information implicated the worker or demonstrated that there had been a degree of contributory fault.[15] The ET in the circumstances can refuse to make an order for reinstatement, although it may make a re-engagement order instead if it would be just to do so.

6 ERA 1996 ss114 and 115.
7 *Artisan Press v Srawley and Parker* [1986] IRLR 126; [1986] ICR 328, EAT.
8 *Boots plc v Lees* [1986] IRLR 485.
9 ERA 1996 s116.
10 ERA 1996 s116(5).
11 *Coleman and Stephenson v Magnet Joinery* [1974] IRLR 343; [1975] ICR 46.
12 *Enessy Co SA v Minoprio* [1978] IRLR 489, EAT.
13 *Nothman v LB Barnet (No 2)* [1980] IRLR 65, EAT.
14 ERA 1996 s116(1)(c).
15 *W Devis and Sons v Atkins* [1977] IRLR 314; [1977] ICR 662, HL.

Re-engagement

14.9   Re-engagement is where the worker returns to a similar job either with the employer, a successor or an associated employer on such terms as the ET may decide,[16] being comparable or suitable employment.[17] The ET must, in making a re-engagement order, state the identity of the employer, the nature of the employment (including any rights or privileges which must be restored), the rate of pay, and the amount of the arrears of pay and loss of other benefits for the period when the worker was not employed by the employer.

14.10   In deciding whether to make an order for re-engagement, the ET must again take into consideration the worker's wishes, the practicability of such an order, contributory fault, whether it is just to make an order and, if so, on what terms.[18] The statutory provisions entitle the worker to put forward his/her own views on the terms of the order; the investigation by the ET is thereby made more flexible and conciliatory than with reinstatement.

14.11   The non-compliance with a reinstatement or re-engagement order will lead to an additional award being made against the employer of not less than 26 weeks pay and not more than 52 weeks pay.[19]

Compensation

14.12   Compensation consists of two elements: the basic award and the compensatory award.

The basic award and redundancy payment

14.13   The basic award was introduced to compensate workers for the loss of job security following dismissal.[20] It has been described as the 'paid-up insurance policy' against redundancy. The basic award is calculated broadly in the same way as a redundancy payment. The only difference between them is that the redundancy payment does not recognise any service below the age of 18.

14.14   The basic award is calculated by reference to the period ending

---

16   ERA 1996 s115.
17   Ibid.
18   Ibid s115(2).
19   Ibid s117(3)(b)
20   Employment Act 1975.

with the effective date of termination (see para 16.15 above) during which the worker has been continuously employed. It allows for one-and-a-half weeks' pay for each year of employment in which the worker was not below the age of 41, one week's pay for each year of employment when the worker was not below the age of 22, and half a week's pay for each year of employment below the age of 22. A maximum of 20 years' employment will be counted. A table allows easy assessment of the number of weeks of entitlement (see appendix E). A minimum basic award applies in certain cases, eg, dismissal due to trade union membership or activities, duties of a health and safety representative, trustee of an occupational pension scheme, or employee representative.

16.5   A week's pay is subject to a maximum figure which is index linked (to the retail price index) for September of each year. The figure is presently £230.[21] If there are fixed working hours, a week's pay is the amount payable by the employer under the contract of employment. If the worker's pay varies with the amount of work done ('piece rate') the amount of a week's pay is calculated by reference to the average hourly rate of pay over the last 12 weeks of employment,[22] and where there are no normal hours, a week's pay will be the average weekly pay over the last 12 weeks of employment. The basic award may be reduced if the worker:

- behaved before the dismissal or before the notice was given in such a way that it would be just and equitable to do so;[23]
- received a redundancy payment, whether paid under statute or otherwise;[24]
- received an ex gratia payment which is expressly or impliedly referable to the basic award;[25]
- unreasonably refused an offer of reinstatement, in which case the ET will reduce the basic award by such amount as it considers just and equitable;[26] or
- is 64, in which case the basic award is reduced by 1/12th for each completed month of employment during that year.[27]

---

21 ERA 1996 s227(1). £230 applies to a basic award where the effective date of termination was on or after 1 February 2000.
22 Ibid s222(3).
23 Ibid s122(2).
24 Ibid s122(4).
25 *Chelsea Football Club v Heath* [1981] IRLR 73; [1981] ICR 323, EAT.
26 ERA 1996 s122(1).
27 Ibid s119(4) and (5).

The compensatory award

14.16   The compensatory award recompenses the worker for the financial loss suffered as a result of being dismissed, including expenses incurred and loss of benefits.[28] Although ETs enjoy wide discretionary powers in assessing the compensatory award, it has been made clear that the object is to compensate fully, but not to award a bonus.[29] The ET should approach the calculation as follows:[30]

(1) calculate the loss which the worker has sustained in consequence of the dismissal, and insofar as the loss is attributable to action taken by the employer;

(2) in assessing that loss, full credit should be given for all sums paid by the employer as compensation for the dismissal but excluding at this stage any contractual severance payment to the extent it exceeds the basic award. Sums earned by way of mitigation should also be deducted as this stage;

(3) any *Polkey* reduction should then be made; this determines that proportion of the loss for which the employer is responsible;

(4) any reduction for contributory fault is then made in relation to that loss as established;

(5) from that sum it is necessary to deduct any contractual redundancy payment to the extent it exceeds the basic award as well as any severance and ex gratia payments;

(6) if the sum calculated in accordance with the above is in excess of the statutory ceiling (currently £50,000), the final stage is to reduce it so as to bring it down to the statutory maximum.

The *Polkey* reduction is reflected as a percentage chance that, had the correct procedures been followed, the worker would have been fairly dismissed. The amount of the percentage reduction is a matter for the ET to determine. If the ET decide that the dismissal is substantially rather than procedurally unfair it will not make a percentage reduction under (3) above[31] (see para 14.25 below).

Loss the worker has sustained

14.17   Loss of wages is calculated from the effective date of termination (see para 16.15) until the hearing date and thereafter until the ET decides

28   ERA 1996 s123.
29   *Norton Tool Co v Tewson* [1972] IRLR 86; [1972] ICR 501, NIRC.
30   *Digital Equipment Co Ltd v Clements (No 2)* [1997] IRLR 140.
31   *King v Eaton Ltd (No 2)* [1998] IRLR 686.

that the loss would have stopped or it becomes too speculative to award any further loss. This sum is calculated net of tax and National Insurance contributions. It consists of the amount the worker would have earned, including regular overtime and bonuses.[32] However, if the employer can show that such overtime would have diminished or ceased, the award will be reduced accordingly.[33] Where the worker was dismissed without notice or payment in lieu of notice, s/he will be awarded the net wages to which s/he would have been entitled during the notice period less any net earnings from a new job.[34]

Evidence of loss of earnings

18 The worker must provide evidence of his/her loss and likely future loss. The ET will estimate how long it thinks the worker will remain unemployed as a result of the dismissal and how much the worker would have earned had s/he remained in the old job. If the worker has obtained a new job at a lower rate of pay, the ET will estimate how long s/he is likely to be earning less, and award the difference. Once a new job is secured which is as well or better paid the compensation calculation will stop at that point.[35]

19 If the worker has not found a new job, the ET, in assessing how long s/he is likely to remain unemployed, will take into consideration the worker's age[36] and personal characteristics,[37] the availability of work in the locality,[38] and the likely duration of the lost job.[39] Owing to the speculative nature of this part of the award, it is important to present compelling and persuasive evidence; this should include the opinion of the local job centre or other job agencies and the efforts made to secure employment.

20 In assessing what the worker would be earning, the ET must take account of anticipatory wage increases, including anticipated overtime payments.[40] The award will be greater where the increase is certain rather than probable. Backdated pay increases may be included in the compensatory award.[41]

32 *Mullett v Brush Electric Machines* [1977] ICR 829, EAT.
33 *Everwear Candlewick v Isaac* [1974] ICR 525; [1974] ITR 334, NIRC.
34 *Tradewinds Airways v Fletcher* [1981] IRLR 272, EAT.
35 *Dench v Flynn & Partners* [1998] IRLR 653.
36 *Isle of Wight Tourist Board v Coombes* [1976] IRLR 413, EAT.
37 *Fougere v Phoenix Motor Co* [1976] IRLR 259, EAT.
38 *Eastern Counties Timber Co v Hunt* (1976) EAT 483/76.
39 *Penprase v Mander Bros* [1973] IRLR 167, IT.
40 *York Trailer Co v Sparks* [1973] IRLR 348; [1973] ICR 518, NIRC.
41 *Leske v Rogers of Salcoates* (1982) EAT 502/82.

Loss of fringe benefits

14.21   The compensatory award includes an element for the loss of benefits in respect of both the immediate and the future loss period. The following have been taken into consideration by ETs:

- pension entitlement and/or pension contributions;
- entitlement to holiday pay;[42]
- tips or other gratuitous payments which would have been earned during the compensatory period;[43]
- the loss of a company car, which is usually assessed by reference to the AA annual guidelines;[44]
- cheap loans (ie, the value in comparison with bank loans);[45]
- accommodation, if it is free or subsidised;[46] and
- medical insurance, which is assessed by reference to the cost to the worker of acquiring the same medical protection.[47]

Loss of statutory rights

14.22   Loss of long notice entitlement, maternity rights and the right to claim unfair dismissal should be reflected in the compensatory award. The loss of right to claim unfair dismissal is usually compensated at £200[48] and the loss of long notice entitlement which is based on a figure of half of the entitlement to statutory notice calculated as a net sum.[49]

Loss of pension rights

14.23   This is by far the hardest to quantify but at the same time can be the most valuable. In order to attach a realistic value to the loss of pension rights there have been a number of guideline documents. The ETs, for a number of years, have used the Government Actuary Department's guidelines which were first produced in 1980 and

---

42 *Wilson v Tote Bookmakers* (1981) COIT 15570/81.
43 *Palmanor v Cedron Ltd* [1978] IRLR 303; [1978] ICR 1008, EAT.
44 *AA schedule of estimated standing and running costs of vehicles.*
45 *UBAF Bank v Davis* [1978] IRLR 442, EAT.
46 *Butler v Wendon & Sons* [1972] IRLR 15; [1972] ITR 418, IT.
47 *Ross v Yewlands Engineering Co Ltd* COIT 17321/83/LN.
48 *Head v SH Muffet* [1986] IRLR 488; [1987] ICR 1, EAT. The EAT at the time said £100 was the going rate; the going rate is now £200.
49 *Daley v Dorsett (Almar Dolls)* [1981] IRLR 385; [1982] ICR 1, EAT.

revised in 1989.[50] There have been two recent guidelines which are now being applied. The most relevant has been drawn up by a committee of ET chairs and is entitled *Compensation for Loss of Pension Rights*. As with all guidelines, it is speculative and so the ETs have been encouraged to adopt a 'broad brush' approach when assessing loss of pension rights. As long as one of the guidelines has been followed, this will normally be sufficient. As pensions differ, so does the approach to the best manner in assessing the loss. Pensions are usually money purchase schemes (pension directly related to the contributions made by the employer and worker) or final salary schemes (determined by the length of service, age and final salary). Under a money purchase scheme, the loss to the worker is the employer's contributions which can be calculated during the period of loss determined by the ET. Under a final salary scheme, the loss, as identified by the *Compensation for Loss of Pension Rights* guidelines, is under three headings: (1) loss of pension rights from the date of dismissal to the date of the hearing; (2) loss of future rights; and (3) loss of enhancement of accrued pension rights. The calculation of a final salary scheme should be assessed by reference to the guidelines in the *Compensation for Loss of Pension Rights*. As this loss is often a valuable loss it might be advisable to secure the services of an expert to determine this loss.

Reduction of the award

24   The compensatory award can be reduced on account of contributory fault if the worker's conduct was culpable or blameworthy.[51] The decision to reduce the award and the degree of contribution is discretionary and can only be challenged before the Employment Appeal Tribunal if it is legally perverse (ie, that no ET properly directing itself could have reached the same decision). Such a challenge is very difficult to succeed with.

25   So-called '*Polkey* reductions' are fairly common. If the dismissal was unfair, purely due to the employer's failure to comply with the procedural requirements, but s/he can demonstrate at the hearing that a reasonable employer would certainly have dismissed the worker after following the appropriate procedure, the compensatory award can be reduced to a few weeks' pay to reflect the period that the

---

50   A suggested method for assessing loss of pension rights under an occupational scheme following a finding of unfair dismissal by an employment tribunal.
51   ERA 1996 s123; *Nelson v BBC (No 2)* [1979] IRLR 346; [1980] ICR 110, CA.

procedural requirements would have taken to perform.[52] Alternatively, if the ET thinks, for example, that there was a 50 per cent chance of dismissal had the employer followed correct procedures, then compensation can be reduced by 50 per cent.[53] Some ETs have been too ready to cut down compensation on these grounds. No such reduction should be made where the unfairness, while apparently procedural, is in reality substantive.[54] The distinction is not always clear.

14.26   The award can be further reduced if the worker has failed to mitigate his/her loss, eg, by trying to get a new job. In applying this rule the ET must identify what steps should have been taken, the date when they should have been taken and the likely consequence. For example, if the ET thinks the worker should have obtained a job, although at a lower wage, by a certain date, the ET will award the difference in pay from that date onwards.[55] In deciding the worker has failed to mitigate, his/her personal characteristics and circumstances (eg, age and poor health) must be taken into account.[55A] It is important to note that it is for the employer to prove a failure to mitigate, not the worker.[56]

14.26A   An ET can reduce the compensatory award by up to two weeks' pay (taking account of all the circumstances and the chances of an appeal succeeding) if a worker chooses not to appeal, having been given written notice that an appeal procedure is available and its details. The notice must be given at the time of dismissal or within a reasonable period afterwards.[57] Equally, if an employer provides an appeal procedure, but prevents the worker from using it, the ET can award up to two weeks' additional compensation to the worker, again, depending on the likely chances of success.[58]

14.27   The maximum compensatory award is presently £50,000.[59] This figure is applied after the calculation of the compensatory award,

52 *Polkey v AE Dayton Services* [1987] IRLR 503; [1988] ICR 142, HL; *Abbotts and Standley v Wesson-Glynwed Steels Ltd* [1982] IRLR 51.
53 *Hough and APEX v Leyland DAF Ltd* [1991] IRLR 194.
54 *Steel Stockholders (Birmingham) Ltd v Kirkwood* [1993] IRLR 515, EAT.
55 *Gardiner-Hill v Roland Berger Technics* [1982] IRLR 498, EAT.
55A *Fougere v Phoenix Motor Co Ltd* [1978] IRLR 66, EAT.
56 ERA 1996 s123(4). See *Bessenden Properties Ltd v Cornes* [1974] IRLR 338, CA; *Fyfe v Scientific Furnishings Ltd* [1989] IRLR 331, EAT.
57 ERA 1996 s127A.
58 Ibid.
59 ERA 1996 s124. There is no upper ceiling for dismissals for health and safety or whistleblowing reasons under ERA 1996 ss100 and 103A.

including any deduction for ex gratia payments made, contributory fault, failure to mitigate, or percentage reduction for the uncertainty as to what would have occurred had a proper procedure been adopted; not *before* any such reduction is made[60] (see above).

4.28 For example, the ET determines that the worker has lost £43,136 as a result of his/her dismissal. The worker received £20,865 contractual severance payment over and above the statutory redundancy entitlement and the ET decides there should be a 50 per cent deduction to reflect the uncertainty that had a proper procedure been adopted the dismissal may have occurred anyway. The calculation would be as follows:

£43,136 × 50% − £20,865 = £883 (rather than £43,136 − £20,865 × 50% = £11,225[61])

This is in order to allow the employer to get full credit for payments made over and above the statutory basic award.

4.29 In all other calculations the more generous assessment is applied.[62] Had the facts been that the worker had lost £43,136 as a result of his/her dismissal, that during the period of loss s/he had earned £20,865 by way of salary and social security benefits, and that there was a 50 per cent deduction to reflect the uncertainty that had the proper procedure been adopted the dismissal may have occurred, the calculation would be as follows:

£43,136 − £20,865 − 50% = £11,225.

The additional award

4.30 If a reinstatement or re-engagement order is made and the employer fails to comply with it, either entirely or partially, the ET must make an additional award unless the employer can satisfy the ET that it was not practicable to comply.[63] The additional award will be between 26 and 52 weeks' pay subject to a weekly maximum of £230.

Recoupment

4.31 If the ET makes a compensatory award, where the worker has received income support or jobseeker's allowance, these should not

60 *Walter Braund (London) v Murray* [1990] IRLR 100, EAT.
61 *Digital Equipment Co Ltd v Clements (No 2)* [1998] IRLR 134.
62 *Ministry of Defence v Wheeler* [1998] IRLR 23.
63 *Port of London Authority v Payne and Others* [1994] IRLR 9, CA.

be set off against the employee's loss.[64] This is because the secretary of state may first recoup an amount in respect of social security benefits which s/he finds have been paid to the worker. The recoupment notice must be served by the secretary of state on the employer within 21 days of the conclusion of the hearing. The employer only pays over to the worker the award of compensation minus the recoupment figure. If no recoupment notice is served, the recoupment must be paid to the worker. If the worker was receiving a large amount of income support, his/her claim could be worth very little. However, if the case is settled before the hearing, the recoupment provisions do not apply. It is therefore in the interests of both parties to settle and to reach an agreement as to compensation, bearing in mind that there will no recoupment on this settlement.[65] However, the adviser should be careful that the settlement is for a single figure and does not itemise the specific claims that are being settled such as notice pay, holiday pay, wages, etc, as the recoupment provisions may well then be applied.

Interest

14.32   Interest is payable on ET awards which remain unpaid 42 days after the decision on compensation is promulgated, ie, recorded as sent to the parties.[66] Where there is an appeal which does not affect the level of compensation, the interest still accrues from that date. Where the appeal alters the award of compensation, interest runs on the altered award but still from 42 days after the original decision was promulgated. Unfortunately, if an ET has only made a decision on liability, which is appealed by the employer, no interest can run until a decision on compensation is made, usually not until the appeal has been disposed of.

14.33   Interest runs on a daily basis on unpaid parts of the award and the rate is that applicable from time to time under the Judgments Act 1838 s17.[67]

---

64   Employment Protection (Recoupment of Jobseeker's Allowance and Income Support) Regulations 1996 SI No 2349.
65   Where the worker has claimed mortgage interest relief, recoupment may swallow most of the award and settlement is very advisable.
66   Industrial Tribunals (Interest) Order 1990 SI No 479.
67   On 1 April 1993 the rate was reduced from 15% to 8% – Judgment Debts (Rate of Interest) Order 1993 SI No 564 (L2).

CHAPTER 15

Race, sex and disability discrimination remedies

15.1   When an ET has made a finding of unlawful discrimination, it may make such of the following as it considers just and equitable:[1]

- a declaration of the rights of the parties in respect of the matter to which the complaint related;
- a recommendation;
- an order for compensation, although not for unintentional indirect race discrimination.

Recommendations

15.2   The ET may recommend that, within a specified period of time, the employer take action to obviate or reduce the adverse effect of the act of discrimination proved.[2] If 'without reasonable justification' the employer fails to comply with the recommendation, the ET can award compensation or additional compensation, save where the act concerned was unintentional indirect race discrimination.[3] The ET cannot insist on a recommendation being carried out.

15.3   Examples of recommendations are that the employer makes a full written apology to the worker, that s/he removes discriminatory documents, warnings, adverse reports, etc, from the worker's personnel file, or that s/he notes on it that the worker has been discriminated against previously. It seems that the ET is hampered in what it can recommend. In *Noone v North West Thames Regional Health Authority (No 2)*,[4] the ET recommended that if another post of consultant microbiologist became available, the health authority should seek the secretary of state's permission to dispense with the normal NHS advertising requirements and offer the post to Dr Noone. The CA rescinded the recommendation because it undermined fair recruitment procedures to the detriment of the NHS, the professions concerned with it, the public and would-be applicants for the post.

15.4   Two other recommendations proposed by the health authority

---

1 RRA 1976 s54, SDA 1975 s65, DDA 1995 s8.
2 RRA 1976 s56(1)(c), SDA 1975 s65(1)(c), DDA 1995 s8(2)(c).
3 See para 15.22 below regarding compensation for indirect race or sex discrimination.
4 [1988] IRLR 530; (1989) 23 EOR 46, CA.

were substituted. These were that the health authority draw to the attention of any future appointments committee considering an application by Dr Noone the provisions of the RRA 1976 and remind them that Dr Noone's previous application had failed on the ground of race. This case probably means that, whatever the industry, an ET cannot recommend that the worker be given the next available vacancy.

5.5   Note that the ET cannot make general recommendations as to good practice in the workplace, for example, that an equal opportunities policy is introduced or that there is monitoring or training of staff. Neither can it recommend a pay rise as this should be covered by an award of compensation.

5.6   Sometimes settlement can be negotiated as to action which an employer is willing to undertake. Not only will this not be subject to the above limitations, but it will also be enforceable.

The award of compensation

.7   There used to be an upper limit on the compensatory award,[5] but unlike for unfair dismissal, this no longer exists. Although the ET may select which of the three remedies it orders, according to what is 'just and equitable', if it does make a financial award, this must not be limited by such considerations.[6] An award of compensation should comprise all reasonably foreseeable loss[7] arising from the act of discrimination including past and future loss of earnings, loss of opportunity and injury to feelings.[8] In sex discrimination cases, the overriding principle laid down by the ECJ is that compensation must enable the loss and damage actually sustained as a result of the discrimination to be made good in full in accordance with the applicable national laws.[9]

8   Loss of earnings may be claimed where appropriate, eg, the discrimination is dismissal or refusal to promote to a higher paid post. Where a candidate is not short-listed for interview, an ET may award compensation representing loss of opportunity, so that the potential

---

5 Until 1993/4.
6 *Hurley v Mustoe (No 2)* [1983] ICR 422, EAT.
7 Ie, the measure of damages ordinarily payable in tort. RRA 1976 s56(1)(b), SDA 1975 s65(1)(b), DDA 1995 s8(3).
8 RRA 1976 s57(4), SDA 1975 s66(4), DDA 1995 s8(4).
9 *Marshall v Southampton AHA (No 2)* [1993] IRLR 445, ECJ.

loss of earnings will be reduced by a percentage representing the likelihood of the candidate actually obtaining the job had s/he not been discriminated against. Where the act of discrimination also amounts to unfair dismissal, the basic and additional awards apply as normal.

15.9   Where there are findings of discrimination against individually named respondents as well as against an employing organisation, the ET can make orders of compensation specifically against the individuals. It is becoming increasingly common for ETs to make the major award against the employer, but to order a smaller additional sum, eg, £500 to be paid by the named individuals.[10]

15.10   Large ET awards following dismissal may be taxable where they exceed a certain sum.[11] If the award comprises past and future loss of earnings, which have been calculated net of tax by the ET, the worker is in effect taxed twice on the same sum. To compensate the worker properly, it is arguable that the ET should award a grossed up figure.[12]

Injury to feelings

15.11   Unlike in unfair dismissal cases, an ET may make an award for injury to feelings where it finds unlawful discrimination. This often includes extra compensation for 'aggravated damages', ie, where a worker's sense of injury is 'justifiably heightened by the manner in which or motive for which' the employer did the wrongful act.[13]

15.12   At one stage, an ET could also award 'exemplary damages' which did not relate to the worker's feelings, but were purely punitive against the employer. However, these are no longer awarded as there is a real doubt whether they are lawful.[14] Nevertheless, particularly bad behaviour by the employer is likely to upset the worker more. Indeed, in *Alexander*, the Court of Appeal said:

> compensatory damages may and in some cases should include an element of aggravated damages where, for example, the defendant

---

10 This is one reason to name individuals in the ET1. See para 17.38.
11 Recently £30,000.
12 As the ET did in *Kirker v British Sugar PLC LA Update November 1999*, although it is believed this point has not been tested on appeal.
13 *Alexander v The Home Office* [1988] IRLR 190, CA.
14 *Deane v Ealing LBC* and *Crofton v Hackney LBC* [1993] IRLR 209; (1993) 49 EOR 39, EAT, relying on *AB v South West Water Services Ltd* [1993] 1 All ER 609, CA. *MOD v Meredith* [1995] IRLR 539; (1995) 62 EOR 41, EAT, says there is no right to exemplary damages under the ETD.

may have behaved in a high-handed, malicious, insulting or oppressive manner in committing the act of discrimination.

In practice, ETs have awarded compensation under this head in a range of circumstances (see below).

The size of the injury to feelings award

.13   The size of the award is largely in the ET's discretion. Prior to the lifting of the upper limit on the compensatory award in 1993,[15] case-law suggested the injury to feelings element should not be disproportionately high. However, this reasoning is no longer applicable and the level of ET awards has rapidly increased. At the time of writing, awards for injury to feelings together with aggravated damages (see below) in the more serious cases of discrimination and harassment are occasionally reaching £20,000 to £30,000. In one extremely serious case under the RRA, an ET awarded £45,000 for injury to feelings including £10,000 aggravated damages.[16] £41,500 has been awarded for injury to health and to feelings under the SDA to a police detective retired on ill-health grounds after lengthy sexual harassment.[17]

14   ETs have an enormous amount of discretion in how much they award and the EAT will rarely interfere. It is, therefore, very hard for advisers to predict the size of an award as, for example, one ET may legitimately award £10,000 where another would award double on the same set of facts. The key case to go to the EAT, *(1) Armitage (2) Marsden (3) HM Prison Service v Johnson*[18] merely illustrates when an ET is entitled (if it chooses) to make a high award. Mr Johnson, a black prison auxiliary, was awarded £20,000 for injury to feelings for a campaign of racial harassment lasting 18 months plus £7,500 aggravated damages for the employer's rejection of his grievance and putting it down to a character defect. The employer's investigation, instead of providing a remedy for the wrongs suffered by the worker, added to his injury. £500 was also awarded against two prison officers personally. The EAT decided the ET was entitled to award £28,500 (even if it was a little on the high side) for such a serious (although not the worse possible) case of discrimination. The EAT said that, in general, injury to feelings awards should bear some broad similarity

---

15   For SDA claims; 1994 for RRA claims.
16   *Yeboah v (1) Crofton (2) Hackney LBC* (1999) 86 EOR 21.
17   *Stubbs* (1999) 41 EOR DCLD.
18   [1997] IRLR 162; (1997) 71 EOR 43, EAT.

to the range of awards in personal injury cases. It should also relate to the value of the sum, in terms of purchasing power or earnings, in real life.

15.15   The EAT refused to overturn another large ET award of £20,000 for injury to feelings and £5000 aggravated damages in *Chan v Hackney LBC*.[19] Mr Chan was forced into medical retirement after months of sustained pressure. The EAT said it was legitimate to take into account the treatment of Mr Chan outside the time limit as context for the impact on his feelings of the acts of race discrimination within the time limit.

15.16   So far, the highest awards have been in race discrimination and sexual harassment cases. Factors which lead to high awards tend to be a long period or numerous incidents of discrimination, a particular vulnerability of the worker, eg, due to age or work environment, and most importantly, evidence of severe injury to health and feelings. Aggravating factors may be victimisation, ignoring or mishandling a grievance or a character attack on the worker. The employer's behaviour in the ET proceedings will also be relevant.

15.17   There is clearer case-law guidance regarding the minimum suitable award. The key case, again prior to the lifting of the ceiling, is *Alexander v The Home Office*,[20] where a black prisoner was deprived of work in the prison kitchen on the ground of his race. The Court of Appeal increased the county court judge's award from £50 to £500, saying that:

> For the injury to feelings, however, for the humiliation, for the insult, it is impossible to say what is restitution and the answer must depend on the experience and good sense of the judge and his assessors. Awards should not be minimal, because this would tend to trivialise or diminish respect for the public policy to which the Act gives effect. On the other hand . . . to award sums which are generally felt to be excessive does almost as much harm.[21]

Since the Court of Appeal relied on the judge's finding that Mr Alexander 'had not suffered any substantial injury to his feelings', £500 should be regarded as the absolute minimum appropriate award for injury to feelings. This view has been confirmed by the EAT in *Sharifi v Strathclyde Regional Council*.[22] See also the views of the EAT in a SDA

19   EAT/120/97; (1997) November LA 15, EAT; May LA 10, ET.
20   [1988] IRLR 190, CA.
21   Ibid, May LJ at 193.
22   [1992] IRLR 259; (1992) 44 EOR 36, EAT.

case, *Murray v Powertech*,[23] where the ET's award was increased to £1,250.

It is surprising in the light of these cases, that awards as low as £1,000–£2,000 or less are still made. It is advisable not to take it for granted that the ET will appreciate the likely impact of the discrimination on the worker's feelings, but to give explicit evidence on this from the worker and other witnesses including medical evidence where appropriate. It is also wise to point out that £500 was considered a minimum award, ie, where there is in reality little or no injury to feelings (a very unusual situation) and at a time before the lifting of the ceiling. Many years have passed and the value of money has increased even since the *Murray* case.

Unfortunately ET practice in the size of injury to feelings awards is extremely variable and difficult to predict. Some ETs clearly believe they are awarding a large sum when they award, say, £5,000 for serious injury. It is therefore important to draw the ET's attention to the higher awards, especially in comparable cases. It is not at all helpful to look at reports of average awards,[24] as these tend to keep the figures low and ignore the factors in the particular case. The employment law updates in Legal Action[25] report sample awards around the country with determining factors.[26] Media reports are highly misleading as they often report settlements rather than ET awards and in any event tend to include figures for the entire compensatory award, which may consist primarily of loss of earnings.

Injury to health (personal injuries)

In a case with potentially disastrous implications, the Court of Appeal has said that the ET can award compensation for any personal injury caused by the tort of racial discrimination.[27] The same would apply in sex or disability discrimination cases. This means that if the discrimination has seriously damaged the worker's health, physically or psychiatrically (and not solely his/her feelings), a claim for personal injuries damages (ie, injury to health) must be added to any discrimination case which is brought. Examples could include nervous breakdown or post-traumatic stress syndrome. If a worker

23 (1992) 44 EOR 35, EAT.
24 Such as in EOR.
25 Every May and November.
26 See also the EOR DCLD.
27 *Sheriff v Klyne Tugs (Lowestoft) Ltd* [1999] IRLR 481; 88 EOR 51, CA.

omits to add such a claim, but his/her discrimination case is decided by the ET or settled, s/he will very probably be unable to make any future personal injuries claim arising from the discriminatory actions by the employer.[28] This is because the issue could and should have been argued at the same time in front of the ET.

15.21   The problem is that ETs as well as advisers may be experienced in employment and discrimination law, but not in the different principles governing the measure of personal injuries awards (where legal aid has traditionally been available). Moreover, a formal medical report is likely to be essential for making such a claim. Note that the ET can only deal with the personal injury claim where it is attached to a discrimination claim. If the worker brings no discrimination claim, s/he would take his or her claim for personal injuries in the county court or High Court in the usual way.

Indirect race discrimination

15.22   No award of compensation may be made in respect of indirect race discrimination if the employer proves that the requirement or condition was not applied with the intention of treating the worker unfavourably on grounds of race.[29] The equivalent provision under the SDA 1975 was removed with effect from 25 March 1996, probably due to its incompatibility with EU law.[30]

15.23   There is case-law regarding the meaning of 'unintentional' indirect discrimination under both the RRA 1976 and the SDA 1975. In one case,[31] a single parent train operator resigned when London Underground imposed a new flexible rostering scheme in order to save costs. This was found to be intentional indirect discrimination because although the employer did not introduce the scheme with the intention of discriminating against women, it did insist on the worker complying with it, while knowing of the unfavourable consequences for her.

15.24   In another case,[32] to increase efficiency, a company decided no holidays could be taken during the May to July peak period. When Eid fell in June 1992, the company refused to make an exception to its

---

28   Ibid. Advisers should read *Sheriff* for its implications.
29   RRA 1976 s57(3).
30   Sex Discrimination and Equal Pay (Miscellaneous Amendments) Regulations 1996 SI No 438.
31   *London Underground Ltd v Edwards* [1995] IRLR 355; (1995) 62 EOR 39, EAT.
32   *J H Walker Ltd v Hussain* [1996] IRLR 11; (1996) 66 EOR 50, EAT.

policy, even though its Muslim employees offered to work extra hours to compensate. The discrimination was found to be intentional, even though the motive was purely to increase efficiency, because the employer wanted to bring about the state of affairs constituting the adverse treatment and knew that one racial group (ie, Asians) would be disproportionately affected.

Compensation for pregnancy discrimination

5 Many cases have been brought against the MOD by servicewomen formerly discharged on grounds of pregnancy. Compensatory awards have tended to be very high, mainly because they refer back to many years of lost earnings and concern unique difficulties for wives of service personnel in finding fresh employment. A few cases have laid down some guidelines applicable to assessing compensation, including the MOD cases specifically and pregnancy discrimination cases generally.[33]

6 Points made by the cases include the following.

- In awarding compensation for loss of earnings after birth, an ET should consider the chance that a woman would not have returned to work anyway, taking account of work and family demands.[34] It would not be exceptional or even unusual to assess the chance of a woman's return as 100 per cent.[35] Evidence as to what the woman did in fact do, having been dismissed, does not necessarily mean she would have done the same had she not been dismissed.[36]

- The order of deductions where a woman mitigates her loss by obtaining new employment at lesser pay is first to deduct her new earnings from the sum she would have received had she remained in her original employment and then to make any deduction assessed to reflect the chance she would not have returned to her original employment.[37]

---

33 See *MOD v Cannock* [1994] IRLR 509; (1994) 57 EOR 51, EAT, as improved and modified by a different EAT in *MOD v Hunt* [1996] IRLR 139, EAT. Also see *MOD v Wheeler, Donald, Nixon & Joslyn* [1998] IRLR 23, CA.
34 *MOD v Cannock* (n33, above).
35 *MOD v Hunt* (n33, above).
36 Ibid.
37 *MOD v Wheeler, Donald, Nixon & Joslyn* [1998] IRLR 23, CA.

- Concerning the duty to mitigate,[38] a woman must actively seek employment six months after the birth of her child if she wishes to obtain compensation for loss of earnings after that date.[39] However, expectations of what a worker should do to find work should not be unreasonable, as s/he is the wronged party.[40] Furthermore, an ET is entitled to take into account its own knowledge and experience of difficulties in the labour market facing women with young children.[41]
- The burden of proving failure to mitigate is on the person alleging it, ie, the employer. If no evidence is given as to failure to mitigate, eg, as to what steps should have been taken and when, the ET cannot fill the gap by making assumptions as to when the worker could have found fresh employment.[42]
- An ET should not allow a woman to be questioned on whether the pregnancy was planned or unplanned.

Interest

15.27   An ET has a discretion whether to award interest, although arguably the decision in *Marshall v Southampton AHA (No 2)*[43] requires interest to be awarded for sex discrimination. The rules are complicated and should be referred to for the precise calculation method.[44] However, broadly speaking, interest on an injury to feelings award runs from the date of the discrimination and, for any financial loss, runs from a date midway between the act of discrimination and the date of calculation by the ET. An ET must consider whether to award interest, even if it is not invited to do so, and in its written reasons must set out how interest was calculated or, if none has been awarded, explain why not.

15.28   Interest on unpaid awards runs from the date of the award unless full payment of the award is made within 14 days of the relevant decision day.[45]

---

38   See para 14.26.
39   *MOD v Cannock* (n33, above).
40   *MOD v Hunt* (n33, above), at para 11.
41   Ibid at para 85.
42   Ibid at para 2. Though it is still wise to bring evidence of efforts to mitigate.
43   [1993] IRLR 445, ECJ.
44   Employment Tribunals (Interest on Awards in Discrimination Cases) Regulations 1996 SI No 2803.
45   Ibid reg 8.

Costs

29 Costs may be awarded against either party on the same basis as in unfair dismissal actions. However, costs are far more frequently awarded against unsuccessful workers in discrimination cases than against unsuccessful employers, even though it must almost always be unreasonable for an employer to defend proceedings where s/he has knowingly discriminated and certainly in cases of sexual harassment.

Running an unfair dismissal case

For complete chapter contents, see overleaf

Preliminary steps

1   At the outset it should be established what the worker wants to achieve. If the worker wants his/her job back or a good reference or payment of outstanding wages, holiday or notice pay, it is not advisable to commence a claim for unfair dismissal. Nothing is more likely to annoy the employer. However, commencing a claim might induce a settlement which incorporates the monies owing and includes an agreed reference (see para 16.85).

2   If the priority is to get the worker's job back, negotiations with the employer should start immediately, possibly with the intervention of an ACAS conciliation officer[1] or some other party, eg, another worker. The greater the delay in starting negotiations, the less likelihood of success. If a worker simply wants a good written reference or payment of monies owed, a telephone call or polite letter should be the first step. Only if the employer refuses should the worker threaten ET proceedings.

3   As soon as a worker comes for advice, the adviser should work out and diarise the last day for lodging an originating application (ET1). The worker should also make a note. Once ET proceedings are started, they move very quickly. It can take as little as two months from the date the ET1 is lodged to the hearing. If information and documents need to be gathered, this must be started immediately. All time limits and dates for chasing up requests made to the employer should be scheduled.

Collecting information before lodging the ET1

4   Before starting the claim, the adviser should get all relevant documents in the worker's possession, eg, a statement of the main terms and conditions of employment and/or contract of employment, staff handbook, works rules, letter of appointment, letter of dismissal, P45 (which should state the last date worked), pay slips, warning letters and appraisal reports. There may well be other relevant documents.

5   It is very important to obtain all documents which may form the employment contract (see para above). If the worker signed any statement, document or letter during employment, it is essential to see this prior to lodging the ET1 if at all possible. Usually employers get workers to sign statements only if they contain terms favourable

1   ETA ss18 and 19.

to the employer, eg, a mobility clause (the right to move the worker to another workplace) or a flexibility clause (the right to alter a worker's hours or shifts).

16.6   The terms of the contract will be particularly vital in relation to a constructive dismissal claim (see para above), where the worker must show a significant and fundamental breach of contract. If, eg, the worker relies on a change of workplace as such a breach but the contract contains a mobility clause, there will be no breach of contract and the claim will fail. Once all the worker's documents are gathered, the adviser should take a full statement of all the material facts, concentrating on the reason for dismissal and the events immediately preceding it. The final disciplinary hearing leading to dismissal is usually very important and the adviser should obtain a near verbatim account while the worker's memory is relatively fresh. Probe the worker on the facts, particularly on the weaknesses. The names and addresses of possible witnesses to significant incidents and in relation to any warnings should be collected. It is usually easier to establish names and addresses at an early stage than months later when a witness order is needed.

16.7   The worker should sign and date the statement and keep a copy. It should be explained that the statement is only for private use as the adviser's working document. The statement is useful when negotiating, as an understanding of the facts, and thereby the issues, allowing negotiation from a position of strength. If and when the case goes to a full hearing, the adviser will probably prepare a 'witness statement' for the tribunal and to exchange with the employer's statements.[2] It will be easier to write the witness statement if there is a framework from the initial statement taken from the worker.

Written reasons for the dismissal: ERA 1996 s92

16.8   Before starting the claim, the worker should write to the employer requesting written reasons for the dismissal (see below) and copies of relevant documents which the worker does not have. When a worker has no contractual documents, it is sometimes uncertain whether any exist. The employer should therefore be asked at least for a statement of the main terms and conditions of employment which ought to have been given to the worker and copies of the relevant procedures.

2 See para 16.53.

9   The first letter to the employer is important. As well as requesting information which will be instrumental in the conduct of the case and its final outcome, it creates an initial impression on the employer which may encourage settlement later on. Every worker who qualifies to claim unfair dismissal is also entitled to receive on request an adequate and truthful statement of the reasons for dismissal.[3] The employer must supply the reasons within 14 days of the worker's request. In order to prove that a request was made, it is best to make it in writing and send it by recorded delivery.

.10   If the employer unreasonably refuses to supply written reasons within 14 days or supplies reasons which are inadequate or untrue, the worker is entitled to compensation of two weeks' gross pay.[4] There is no limit on a week's pay. An employer who fails to supply reasons within 14 days due to a genuine oversight, but supplies them when s/he realises the oversight will not be held to have unreasonably refused.[5] It is not enough for an employer to acknowledge the request within the 14 days and supply reasons later unless, for example, the person taking the decision to dismiss was on holiday. No compensation can be claimed unless the employer has been requested to provide reasons (except where the woman was dismissed while pregnant or on maternity leave).

.11   The written reasons must be adequate so that it is clear to the worker and to anyone else why the worker was dismissed and upon which of the potentially fair reasons under ERA 1996 s92 (see chapter 6) the employer relies.[6] The purpose of the right is to make the employer state truthfully the reason for dismissal. Any statement given by the employer is admissible in unfair dismissal proceedings and will be important in determining the fairness of the dismissal.[7] In deciding whether to award compensation, the ET is not concerned as to whether the reasons given were intrinsically good or bad.[8] If the reason was bad, the dismissal will be unfair, but there will be no award under ERA 1996 s93.

.12   The time limit for a claim for failure to supply adequate and true reasons is the same as for unfair dismissal. Even if reasons are supplied within 14 days, a s92 claim should always be added to the unfair

---

3 ERA 1996 s92.
4 Ibid s93(2)
5 *Ladbroke Entertainments v Clark* [1987] ICR 585, EAT.
6 *Horsley Smith & Sherry v Dutton* [1977] IRLR 172, EAT.
7 ERA 1996 s9(5).
8 *Harvard Securities v Younghusband* [1990] IRLR 17, EAT.

dismissal claim. One can never be sure what will emerge during the unfair dismissal hearing as to the truth of the reasons given.

16.13   Women dismissed while pregnant or on maternity leave will be entitled to written reasons, whether or not they request them, and regardless of their length of service.[9] This is because they can claim unfair dismissal for reasons related to pregnancy or maternity, even if they do not have the necessary length of service for ordinary unfair dismissal claims. If the reasons are not supplied, a claim should be made as in usual cases. Even though it is not necessary, it is probably worth asking the employer for reasons where they are not volunteered.

The originating application (ET1)

16.14   The time limit for lodging an unfair dismissal claim is within three months from dismissal, which is far shorter than that for any other civil claim. The time limit is strictly enforced with an extension only in exceptional circumstances.

16.15   The period of three calendar months runs from the effective date of termination (EDT). If the EDT is 20 May, the claim must be presented on or before midnight on 19 August.[10] The application should be sent to the relevant ET in good time, and if it has not been acknowledged within the time limit, a check should be made before the expiry of the time limit with the relevant Employment Tribunal office to confirm that it has arrived. It is possible to fax the ET1 to the Employment Tribunal office. For time limit purposes, the EDT means:

– when the contract is terminated by notice, the date that the notice expires;[11]

– when the contract is terminated without notice, the date on which termination takes effect.[12] With a summary dismissal for gross misconduct, this will be the last day worked. However, where there is no gross misconduct and notice is required, if the employer pays money in lieu of notice, the EDT can be ambiguous. Either the employer has terminated the contract of employment with immediate effect and paid in lieu of notice, or the

9   ERA 1996 s92(4).
10 *Post Office v Moore* [1981] ICR 623, EAT.
11 ERA 1996 s97(1)(a).
12 Ibid s97(1)(b).

employer has terminated the contract as from the end of the notice period, but does not require the worker to attend work in the interim.[13] The dismissal letter may indicate which is the case. Usually when the employer pays in lieu of notice, the EDT is the last day actually worked[14] and it is safest when calculating time limits to work from this date.

A useful rule of thumb is to present the claim within three months of the last day actually worked. By doing this, the claim will always be in time.

Late application

5.16 Exceptionally, the ET will admit a late claim provided it was not reasonably practicable to present the claim in time, and it was presented within such further period as the ET considers reasonable.[15] It is for the worker to show that it was not reasonably practicable to present the claim in time.[16] Ignorance of the law or of facts will be an acceptable excuse only if, tested objectively, 'a reasonable worker' would not be expected to know of the law[17] or be put on enquiry because of the facts.[18] It is getting increasingly difficult to make claims out of time.

.17 If the worker is pursuing an internal appeal s/he must still lodge the claim in time, even if the internal appeal remains unresolved. It is no defence that the worker's adviser, whether legally qualified or not, failed to tell the worker the time limit. The worker's remedy is then against the adviser for negligence. This is so whether the adviser is a solicitor,[19] trade union official[20] or Citizens Advice Bureau worker.[21] Even if the worker shows that it was not reasonably practicable to present the claim in time, s/he must do so within a further reasonable period. The worker must act promptly once s/he discovers that the claim is out of time.[22]

---

13 *Adams v GKN Sankey* [1980] IRLR 416, EAT.
14 *Dixon v Stenor* [1973] ICR 157; [1973] IRLR 28, NIRC.
15 ERA 1996 s111.
16 *Porter v Bandridge* [1978] ICR 943; [1978] IRLR 271, CA.
17 Ibid. Though see *Biggs v Somerset CC* [1996] IRLR 203, CA.
18 *Churchill v A Yeates & Sons* [1983] ICR 380; [1983] IRLR 187, EAT.
19 *Dedman v British Building & Engineering Appliances* [1973] IRLR 379; [1974] ICR 53, CA; *London International College Ltd v Sen* [1993] IRLR 333, CA.
20 *Times Newspapers v O'Regan* (1976) 11 ITR 259; [1977] IRLR 101, EAT.
21 *Riley v Tesco Stores and GLCABS* [1980] IRLR 103; [1980] ICR 323, CA.
22 *Golub v University of Sussex* (1981) 13 April, unreported, CA; *James W Cook & Co (in liquidation) v Tipper and Others* [1990] IRLR 386, CA.

Presentation of the ET1

16.18   The ET1 should be sent to the regional Employment Tribunals office, local to where the worker worked. The addresses are attached to the standard ET1 form. It is not necessary to use the standard ET1 form. A letter would do if it contains the necessary information. It should be addressed to the Secretary to the Employment Tribunal. It is permissible to fax a claim to the ET. Future correspondence will be with the regional office and addressed to the Regional Secretary of the Tribunals.

Drafting the ET1

16.19   ET1 forms can be obtained from the Department of Employment, job centres and most advice centres. The ET1 form need not be used for the originating application as long as all the necessary information is contained in a letter or statement namely:

- the worker's name and address. The worker is called the 'Applicant';
- the employer's name and address. The employer is called the 'Respondent'; and
- the grounds of the application and particulars of the relief sought. The worker must state why s/he thinks s/he has been unfairly dismissed. An extensive statement is not necessary as long as sufficient detail is given for the employer to resist the claim.[23]

It is important to remember that the ET1 will be the first document read by ET members before the hearing starts and will give them an important early impression of the merits of the case which can be difficult to shake afterwards. It is therefore foolish to write only a very brief statement. A well-written ET1 can also assist the case preparation to run more smoothly, eg, by making a pre-hearing review less likely, eliciting a more detailed ET3, making it easier to obtain interlocutory orders from the tribunal and improving the chances of settlement. The ET1 should state fully all the material facts (without going into laborious detail). If there are obvious weaknesses in the case, they cannot be hidden and it is best to refer to them in the ET1 and offer as convincing an explanation as possible.

16.20   It is unnecessary to refer to the law in the ET1, but it helps when completing the form to bear in mind the relevant law and therefore

23   *Burns International Security Services v Butt* [1983] IRLR 438, EAT.

what issues are relevant or irrelevant. For example, if the employer is a large company, this should be stated in the ET1, since the tribunal must consider fairness in the light of the employer's size and administrative resources (see para 6.57 above). If the employer is small, this will not help the worker and should not be mentioned in the ET1.

6.21　　It is best to complete the ET1 bearing in mind what the employer must do for a dismissal to be fair. The worker can then draw attention to what the employer ought to have done but did not. For example, in a conduct case, it is of little assistance to focus on the worker's innocence of the misconduct or to refer to matters occurring after dismissal, eg, the police's decision to drop charges. What is relevant is the employer's genuine and reasonable belief at the time of dismissal, the extent of the investigations into the worker's guilt and the opportunity afforded to the worker to offer an explanation. The ET1 should focus on these points. For the above reasons, it is almost always better for an adviser who understands the law to write the ET1 rather than ask the worker to write his/her own, even if the adviser intends to amend it.

6.22　　If the adviser puts himself/herself down as representative, s/he will receive all correspondence from the ET or employer and must keep the worker informed. If no representative is noted on the form, correspondence goes to the worker, who must be forewarned to keep in close touch, even if nothing happens for four or five weeks. An adviser can later take over the running of a case, simply by writing to the ET and to the employer to notify them of this.

The employer's defence (ET3)

6.23　　The Employment Tribunal sends the employer a copy of the ET1 and the employer replies, usually on an ET3 form. The ET sends the ET3 on to the worker. In the ET3, the employer must indicate whether s/he intends to resist the claim and, if so, on what grounds.[24] The employer must prove that dismissal was for one of the potentially fair reasons and that it actually was fair to dismiss for that reason.[25] The employer must give sufficient particulars of the grounds for the

---

24　Employment Tribunals (Constitution and Rules of Procedure) Regulations 1993 SI No 2687 (ET Regs) Sch 1 r3.
25　ERA 1996 s98.

defence[26] and if no grounds are set out in the ET3, a letter should be written to the ET pointing this out.

16.24   The ET3 should be supplied by the employer within 21 days of receiving the copy ET1, but the late submission of an ET3 does not affect the ET's jurisdiction. In practice therefore, the time limit is very loosely enforced. An employer will not be allowed to defend the action if s/he has submitted no ET3 by the time of the hearing. If an employer first produces an ET3 at the hearing itself or very shortly before, the ET has a discretion whether to allow it in. Quite often the tribunal will give leave for the late ET3 but grant an adjournment of the hearing, ordering the employer to pay the worker the wasted costs caused by the late adjournment.

16.25   When the ET3 is received, all the information in it should be checked, listing what points are not accepted. For example, it may be necessary to get another worker to give evidence on length of service, or bank statements to prove wages, if these are in dispute. If the employer's reasons for justifying the dismissal are vague or unclear, it may be wise to ask for more particulars and for relevant documents.

Interlocutory matters

16.26   Interlocutory matters are those concerned with the case preparation, eg, collecting information and documents from the other side, fixing hearing dates, etc. In non-discrimination cases, this preparation is usually dealt with in correspondence direct between each side and the ET is asked for an order only if agreement cannot be reached. In discrimination cases or other cases which are particularly large or complex, the ET usually holds one or more interlocutory hearings, where these matters are dealt with orally in front of a duty Chair.

16.27   Some ETs now send out standard letters with the ET3 giving 'directions' (which are usually suggestions rather than orders), eg, as to when documents should be shown to the other side, whether witness statements should be prepared and when trial bundles should be agreed. Regardless of whether there has been a standard letter, on receiving the ET3, the adviser should write to the employer asking for any particulars and documents which s/he particularly requires

26   See n24.

within a specified time limit, usually 14 days.[27] It is a good idea to send a copy of the letter to the ET in case the employer later denies having received it. If the employer fails to comply with the request, the ET should be asked, in writing, for an order. The employer should always be asked to supply the particulars voluntarily first.

The ET will usually order the employer to supply some or all of the requested particulars and documents within a further time limit. If the employer fails to comply with the order, the ET should be informed. It has power to strike out all or part of the ET3, which will prevent the employer from defending the claim or the relevant part of the claim.[28] It can also order costs for unreasonable conduct.

A request for an order will be considered by the duty Chair at the ET. The ET tends to be reluctant to order too many particulars and frequently amends the request. So the temptation to ask for too much should be avoided unless it is necessary because of the vagueness of the ET3. An ET may also refuse to order disclosure of all the documents a worker requests. An ET's refusal to make an order is not appealable unless the worker's case is clearly prejudiced. Remember that this procedure can be adopted in reverse against the worker. Failure by the worker to comply with any order made to supply particulars or documents may carry penalties.

Interlocutory orders, as with other ET correspondence, are contained in letters signed by administrative officers. The Chair who made the decision is not identified. Although some regions are willing to identify who made the decision, most are not. The EAT has stated very firmly that in future all judicial orders made by ET Chairs, whether interlocutory or otherwise, should identify the Chair and be signed by him or her.[29]

Further particulars of the ET3

The ET can order the worker and employer to supply further particulars of the ET1 or ET3 respectively.[30] The ET can make an order on its own initiative or at the request of either party.

All that can be asked for is more details or 'particulars' of the

---

27 See sample at p421.
28 ET Regs Sch 1 r4(7).
29 *Ilangartne v The British Medical Association* EAT/508/98; see (1999) November *Legal Action* 17.
30 ET Regs Sch 1 r4.

employer's defence as set out in the ET3.[31] The questions are to clarify the text of the ET3 and the respondent's case. For example, if the respondent says, 'We warned the Applicant on numerous occasions as to her conduct at work' a relevant request would be, 'Please state in respect of each warning the date when the Applicant was warned, by whom, and the nature of the warning given'. Clarification on essential points should always be requested, in order to be fully prepared. Where the worker needs information which cannot be obtained on the restrictive definition of 'further particulars', s/he can use the more general question and answer procedure (below). In practice, the letter to the employer may request particulars and interrogatories under a combined heading.

The question and answer procedure (interrogatories)

16.33   When the ET Rules were amended in 1993 an additional provision was introduced known as the question and answer procedure.[32] These are sometimes called 'interrogatories'. The worker can ask the employers a series of questions which will clarify any issue likely to arise for determination or if the information is likely to assist the ET in dealing with the claim. If the employer fails to provide a reply to the questions asked, the worker can apply for an order for this information. It would be permissible to ask of the employer in a dismissal case involving fighting at work, 'What action was taken against the other person involved in the fight and in the last five years have there been other incidents of fighting at work? If so, when, who was involved and were they dismissed; if not, what action was taken against them?'[33] However, the ET is unlikely to allow lengthy and detailed questioning. The aim is not to conduct the whole case on paper, cross-examination is usually reserved for the full ET hearing.

Discovery

16.34   'Discovery' is the method by which the worker can obtain documents which are in the employer's possession. Strictly speaking, an order for discovery only obliges the employer to produce a list of the requested documents. This is combined with an order for inspection,

---

31   See sample request at p421.
32   ET Regs Sch 1 r4(3).
33   See p406 for a sample request.

which allows the documents to be seen and copies taken at the worker's expense. In practice, the ET often simply asks the employer to send copies to the worker. This is useful as it saves copying costs and the employer can always be asked to bring the originals to the hearing. Note that the ET does not in fact have the power to order that copies be sent.

Which documents?

15 All courts prefer documents to witnesses and the ET is no exception. This is particularly true of contemporaneous documents. Cases are often won or lost on the strength of the documents before the ET and it is essential that all relevant documents are available at the hearing. Unlike with other civil litigation, the parties are under no duty to produce all relevant documents in their possession. Even the standard directions letter sometimes sent out by the ET (see above) only requires disclosure of documents which each side intends to use. An adviser must therefore specifically ask for what s/he wants and thinks that the employer has. The employer does not have to produce documents which will help a worker's case unless withholding certain documents in the light of a specific request would mislead the worker as to whether they existed.[34]

16 The ET is more ready to order discovery than particulars although it will not allow wide-ranging and speculative requests. The test is whether the documents are relevant for the fair disposal of the case or in order to save costs.[35] A document is relevant if it advances the worker's case or damages the employer's case.[36] The case-law on what documents are relevant is particularly developed in relation to discrimination cases.[37]

17 In unfair dismissal cases it is usually relevant to seek discovery of all contractual documents or statements of terms and conditions and any personnel file and written warnings relied on. It is always a good idea to request, 'any other relevant documents on which the employer will rely at the hearing'. The ET will usually order this category of documents and it prevents the employer surprising the worker with unseen documents on the day of the hearing. Letters between the parties or to ACAS concerning possible settlement of the

34 *Birds Eye Walls v Harrison* [1985] IRLR 47; [1985] ICR 278, EAT.
35 County Court Rules Order 14 r8.
36 *Compagnie Financiére du Pacifique v Peruvian Guano Co* (1882) 11 QB 55, CA.
37 See para 17.41 below.

claim must not be disclosed on discovery or put before the ET unless the party concerned expressly agrees.[38]

Witness orders

16.38   A worker can apply for a witness order requiring the attendance of any person as a witness if that person can give relevant evidence which is necessary (because it is disputed) and s/he will not attend voluntarily.[39] A request for an order should be sent to the ET in good time for the hearing, setting out the name and home or work address of the witness. It should very briefly summarise why the evidence is relevant and necessary and state that the witness is not prepared to attend the hearing voluntarily. The ET will then serve the witness order direct on the witness and send a copy to the worker and/or his/her representative. There is a financial penalty if the witness fails to attend, unless the witness successfully applies to the ET before the hearing for the order to be set aside.

16.39   An order should be obtained only if the witness is co-operative, but does not want to attend without an order (usually so s/he can tell his/her employer that s/he is not attending the hearing voluntarily). A witness who does not want to attend at all or is forced to do so is invariably a bad witness. It will also be hard to get a statement from an unwilling witness in advance of the hearing, so there is no certainty as to what s/he will say. The letter sent to the ET asking for a witness statement is not seen by the other party.

Hearing dates and adjournments

16.40   Usual practice is for the ET to send each side a notice of hearing, setting the hearing dates. Each party must receive at least 14 days' notice of a hearing date unless s/he agrees to less. ETs used to consult over convenient hearing dates, but this is now very rare, although sometimes the parties are asked how long they think the case will last. If the date is inconvenient, an adjournment should be requested immediately.

16.41   It is extremely hard to get an adjournment, even with both parties' consent, unless, eg, a key witness is ill or not enough days have been allocated. The ET is usually unsympathetic if a representative is

---

38 Or otherwise waives privilege.
39 *Dada v Metal Box Co* [1974] IRLR 251; [1974] ICR 559, NIRC.

unavailable, stating that another representative can surely be found. This is most unreasonable with small voluntary sector organisations and also fails to recognise the realities of how trade union representation is organised. The person who suffers is usually the low-paid worker who cannot afford to pay for representation and whose case will suffer from losing the adviser who has been involved from the beginning. There have been a few successful appeals against such refusals in discrimination cases where law centres and other voluntary advice centres have been involved.[40] To improve the chances of persuading an ET to grant a postponement in these circumstances, or a successful appeal otherwise, it is important generally to conduct the case promptly and efficiently, to request any necessary postponement as soon as the problematic date is notified, to explain fully in a letter to the ET why the postponement is needed and why it will harm the worker's case if the representative is unavailable. If the adviser knows in advance of any notice of hearing, that there will be problems with certain dates, s/he should write and inform the ET before the dates are set. Finally, if the ET refuses without giving reasons, the adviser should ask for full reasons if s/he intends to appeal. It may also be revealing to ask which Chair made the decision.[41]

42   If a request for an adjournment of the hearing is needed, an attempt should be made to get the employer's consent first. The ET will contact the employer in any event and the chances of a postponement are better if there is no objection.

Directions hearing

43   This is an informal hearing before an ET Chair sitting alone, attended by each party or its representatives, at which the preparation of the case is moved on. A directions hearing is not common in straightforward unfair dismissal cases, but can be requested at any time by either party or initiated by the ET itself, to deal with all or any outstanding procedural issues that are not being resolved in correspondence, eg, disclosure of documents, fixing hearing dates, or ordering that cases be heard together. A number of ETs will

---

40   *Christou v Morpheus and Symes* EAT/498/99; (1999) November *Legal Action* 17; *Yearwood v Royal Mail* EAT/843/97, LA Update May 1998; *De Souza v British Telecom and Lyon* (1997) 588 IDS Brief 15, EAT.
41   See para 16.30 above.

automatically have a directions hearing in respect of discrimination hearings.

Consolidation

16.44   Where similar issues of fact or law are concerned, the ET may order that cases be considered together. The ET can do this of its own accord or on application by either party. Each party will have the opportunity to argue for or against consolidation and consideration should be given to whether tactically it would help the individual cases. The commonest instances of consolidation are for multiple redundancy or equal pay claims.

Preliminary hearing

16.45   This can be requested by either side or ordered by the ET on its own initiative. It is a full hearing, usually with witnesses, to deal with a preliminary issue, normally on an issue of jurisdiction. Preparation is as for a full hearing, except that the evidence is collected relating to the preliminary issue alone. Preliminary hearings are held where there is a dispute over whether the worker has been employed for one continuous year, was an employee, worked under an illegal contract, commenced proceedings within three months of his/her dismissal, etc. Many of these hearings can be quite lengthy and complex, particularly if they concern TUPE issues, although hearings concerning late claims and time limits tend to be shorter and more informal, relying mainly on the arguments put by the parties' representatives rather than being dependent on a dispute over what happened.[42]

Pre-hearing reviews

16.46   Either of its own accord or at the request of either party, the ET may hold a pre-hearing review. This is an informal hearing before a full ET panel or a Chair sitting alone, where each party's representative may make oral or written representations. The ET will decide, solely on the basis of the representations and the ET1 and ET3, whether there are reasonable prospects for the success of the claim (or defence).

16.47   If the ET thinks that there are no reasonable prospects of success,

42   ET Regs Sch 1 r6.

it will require a deposit of up to £150 from a party as a condition of proceeding further.[43] The ET must take reasonable steps to determine the worker's ability to pay and it is therefore subject to means. This deposit will be used as security against costs being awarded to the other party at the hearing.

48   Since verbal and documentary evidence is not allowed at the pre-hearing review, the ET will rarely require a deposit if evidence in dispute is clearly central to the case and there is a substantial dis-agreement over what happened. This should be borne in mind when attending a pre-hearing review. Whether or not a deposit has been required, any costs ultimately ordered can exceed £150. Costs may be awarded against an unsuccessful party even if there has been no pre-hearing review (see para 16.76).

Preparation for the hearing

49   If possible a joint bundle of documents should be agreed with the employer. Four copies of the bundle should be produced for the ET's use (three ET members and the witness table). If agreement cannot be reached on the bundle, the worker's representative should prepare his/her own bundle. The bundle should be numbered on each page and indexed at the front.

50   The worker should bring to the hearing details of all efforts made to secure new employment, eg, letters, copies of advertisements, details of employment agencies contacted and expenses. If the work-er wins, and wants compensation only, the ET will want to know that s/he has made genuine efforts to obtain another job and mitigate his/her loss (see para 14.26 above). The ET clerk will also want to know details of the unemployment benefit office where the worker has signed on. Where it has been particularly hard to gain new employ-ment due to the way dismissal took place, a doctor's report may help or a report from an employment agency. If other factors caused dif-ficulties, eg, the worker's age, disability, race or having a young child, specialist evidence and reports will be useful.

51   Each witness should also be told where and when to attend the ET and statements should have been obtained from each of them. The adviser should prepare for his/her role as representative and in particular note down the key points on which s/he wants to

43 Ibid r7(3).

cross-examine the employer's witnesses. S/he ought to be able to anticipate what the employer will say at the hearing.

Before the hearing

16.52   If an adviser has not run a case before, it is a good idea to visit another ET hearing to see what happens. The worker may find this useful too. Arrive before 10 am when the hearings start and ask the clerk at reception what would be the most relevant case to watch. The clerks are usually very helpful if asked for assistance.

Witness statements

16.53   Increasingly ETs expect the parties to provide written 'witness statements' for their witnesses. The idea is that each witness will read out his/her evidence in chief. Advisers can usually ask a few supplementary questions and interrupt to draw the ET's attention to relevant pages of the trial bundle. The witness will then be cross-examined in the usual way. The procedure originated in the High Court and county court. The purpose of this approach is to speed up the proceedings and to let the parties know in advance what the evidence is going to be.

16.54   Usually there has been some agreement between the parties or suggestion (or an order) by the ET that the witness statements should be exchanged 7 or 14 days in advance of the hearing. It may be proposed in an ET standard letter or otherwise the adviser could suggest this at the time of requesting particulars and documents. It is useful both for forewarning the worker and preparing cross-examination to obtain the statements in advance. However, with a weak case where the worker is hoping for a last minute settlement, the disadvantage of exchange is that it reveals the worker's entire case and how few witnesses s/he may have.

16.55   If providing a witness statement will cause problems, inform the ET if it wants them done. The ET has specific power to make advisers provide such a statement although they should not do so in every case particularly when the parties are not legally represented[44]. Where the adviser is not using witness statements, s/he will still need a clear written note of the worker's evidence in a sensible order, from which s/he will ask questions at the hearing.

44   *Eurobell Holdings plc v Barker* [1998] ICR 299.

How should a witness statement be written?

56   Ideally a witness statement should be set out clearly, with typed and numbered short paragraphs and sub-headings to break up the text. Wide margins and double-spacing enables annotations to be made by the ET panel and representatives as evidence is given during the hearing. Dates and names should always be stated in full. The witness's evidence should be written in a logical order, usually explaining background details first and then telling the story chronologically. Care should be taken with accuracy and consistency of detail. Always bear in mind what are the relevant legal and factual issues, and provide the evidence which is relevant to those. For example, in an unfair dismissal case, always draw attention to poor procedures and the reason that led to substantive unfairness. In a discrimination case, always draw attention to different treatment.[45] If there are problem areas, as a matter of tactics it may be useful to lessen the impact of cross-examination by dealing with those areas in the statement.

57   Ensure the worker fully agrees with the content of the statement, that s/he understands all the words used and can easily read them. Most people stumble when reading under stress. Short words and sentences make reading easier. Try to use the words and expressions that the worker usually uses him/herself to describe the events. It is unwise to ask the worker to write his/her own statement with a view simply to tidying it up. The statement will probably be poorly structured, include irrelevant information and exclude relevant information.

58   If the worker cannot read or cannot read English, but can definitely understand English and the content of his/her statement, then the ET should be asked whether the statement can be read out by the adviser, with the worker indicating his/her understanding at regular intervals.

Expenses

59   The parties, their witnesses and certain unpaid representatives may claim expenses for attending ET hearings. Claims must be submitted within one month. The amounts and types of expenses covered are complicated and do change, so it is advisable to check direct with the

---

45   See pp393–396 for sample extracts.

ET office.[46] The current position appears to be roughly as follows. The first £5 of any travel expenses will not be covered unless the person was ordered to attend by a witness order. Taxi fares are only paid in exceptional circumstances, eg, the person has a medical condition which prevents him or her using public transport. Travel from overseas may be covered if the ET agrees it is in the interests of justice. Loss of earnings up to a maximum of £45 per day will be reimbursed if the employer certifies the loss has occurred; paid or annual leave is not covered. Overnight expenses are paid subject to certain limits, which may be exceeded if there are special requirements for people with a disability. There are child and adult care allowances of up to £5 per hour with a discretion to pay more for special needs. Reasonable charges for professional helpers, attendance of essential medical witnesses or production of reports, and the cost of helpers for people with medical needs are also covered.

On the day of the hearing

16.60   On the day of the hearing, arrive early and visit the employer in the respondents' waiting room to sort out any last-minute problems and to see what witnesses are there. The worker's representative should give the employer's representative copies of any cases that will be discussed in the closing speech. On arriving at the ET, the clerk must be given the name of the applicant's witnesses and, if asked, the clerk will say who are the employer's. The names and references of any cases to be referred to in closing should also be given to the clerk. S/he will probably ask whether the witnesses will swear or affirm when giving evidence. If witnesses require any holy book other than the New Testament, the clerk should be told at this point.

16.61   The time before the hearing starts can be used to clear up last-minute queries and to calm the worker and witnesses. Cases often settle on the morning of the hearing, so the representative should have in mind terms of settlement. If part of the settlement would be an agreed reference, which is common, a draft should have been prepared in advance.

---

46   See also DTI Press Notice P/99/87 dated 1 February 1999 confirming the expenses as set out below.

The hearing

52   The original intention was for the hearing of unfair dismissal claims
to be expedient, simple and informal. The rules encourage the ET to
avoid formality and strict rules about evidence.[47] Unfortunately ETs
vary enormously in their practice, from far too informal to the strict
formalities of civil courts. As an ET has a wide discretion to conduct
hearings as it likes, there is not much that can be done except be
prepared for anything! Always call the Chair 'Sir' or 'Madam' and
remain seated.

53   If the worker's claim is prejudiced by the ET's conduct, eg, continuous interruptions from the panel or refusal to allow certain evidence to be called, this can be a ground of appeal. You should object
at the time and ask the ET to note your objection. When you appeal,
the Chair's notes if relevant will be ordered. An appeal can also be
made if it is felt that the ET is biased or any member has a conflict of
interest, eg, has some connection with the employer. If it is intended
to appeal on any of these points, an objection must first be raised in
the ET. Only object if it is felt that it is really necessary, as it will
alienate the ET and appeals are difficult when concerning the conduct of ETs.

54   At the start of the hearing, the ET will deal with any preliminary
matters such as arguments about the documents or matters of jurisdiction, although the latter will usually have been resolved at a separate preliminary hearing. The ET usually informs the parties at this
stage as to how it wants the hearing conducted.

The order of events

65   If there is a dispute over whether there was a dismissal, the worker
goes first. Otherwise the employer starts.[48] The party starting will not
usually be allowed to make an opening statement. Assuming the
employer starts, s/he will call his/her witnesses first. The employer
(or employer's representative) will then ask questions of the first
witness. The representative must not 'lead' the witness, ie, must not
ask a question in such a way that it tells the witness what the answer
should be. However, if the facts to be established are not in dispute by
the other side, the representative can lead. Whether there are any

---

47   ET Regs Sch 1 r9(1).
48   See burden of proof at para 8.1.

facts that can be agreed should be checked with the other side before the hearing. If this has been done, it is wise to indicate to the ET that leading questions are being put because the facts are agreed.

16.66   If a witness statement has been prepared, most of the evidence will consist of the statement. Usually the witness reads this out, but occasionally the ET may read the statement to itself. By way of introducing the statement, the adviser asks the witness if it is his/her statement and if its contents are believed to be accurate and true. The adviser can ask some supplementary questions.

16.67   The witness's evidence to his/her own representative is called 'evidence-in-chief'. After it is finished the worker's representative can then ask questions. This is called cross-examination. After that, the employer's representative can ask a few more questions, simply clearing up anything that arose in cross-examination. This is called re-examination. The ET panel then usually questions the witness.

16.68   The same process is followed with each witness. After all the employer's witnesses have given evidence, the worker is immediately called to give evidence and then any of the worker's witnesses. It is useful to prepare in advance of the hearing a list of the important dates, the names of the main characters particularly those who will be giving evidence together with their job title.

The closing speech

16.69   Each party has a right to make a closing speech.[49] Normally, the party which started addresses the ET last. The length of the speech depends on the complexity of the case, but the ET should not be bored. The main point of the closing speech is to relate the key points of evidence to the relevant law. If the employer's representative has the last word, the worker's should anticipate and deal with the employer's strong points in his/her closing speech.

16.70   The ET should be reminded of the main issues and related evidence. Where there is a conflict of evidence, it can be suggested why the ET should prefer the worker's witnesses. To ensure that the ET addresses its mind to certain key issues, it should expressly be invited to make findings of fact on those matters. It may even be helpful to circulate a skeleton argument, ie, a list of the main legal and factual issues which are expanded in the closing speech, eg, breaches of

49 ET Regs Sch 1 r9(2).

the procedures by the employer and obvious weaknesses in the employer's evidence.

6.71   If any reported cases are referred to, remember that only the decision of the most senior court on a particular issue is important. On the whole, it is not necessary to read extracts from the case-law unless there is an unusual or difficult legal issue. The ET will be familiar with the main cases and legal principles and a key authority may just be referred to by name. If references are made to reported cases, advisers should make sure that they fully know and understand them.

The decision

6.72   The ET's decision is usually unanimous, although it may be by a majority.[50] The ET must give full written reasons in cases under the RRA 1976, SDA 1975 and 1986, EqPA 1970, DDA 1995 or related to trade union activities, but otherwise may choose whether to give full or summary reasons. It says at the top of the decision which it is. Full written reasons are necessary for an appeal. Therefore be careful to ask for full reasons at the end of the hearing or within 21 days of the summary reasons being sent.[51]

6.73   Most often the ET hears and decides whether the dismissal was unfair and holds a subsequent hearing on the question of compensation. Sometimes the ET adjourns the hearing after announcing that the worker is successful and suggests that the parties reach agreement on compensation. This may happen immediately, with the parties talking in the waiting rooms. To make any agreement binding if no one authorised to draw up a compromise agreement is present, the ET should be asked to make an order in the finally agreed terms. Alternatively, the ET may send the parties away, on the basis that settlement discussions will take place outside the ET on another day. ACAS can be asked to conciliate at this stage if desired. As long as the ET reached a final decision on liability, ie, that the worker was successful, then it should only be the compensation which is settled. In some circumstances, this may prevent the original decision being appealed. Time should not be allowed to drift. If no agreement can be achieved, then the applicant can simply write to the ET asking the case to be

---

50   For a discussion of the role of lay members and why decicions are usually unanimous, see Linda Dickens, *The industrial tribunal system* (Blackwell, 1985).
51   ET Regs Sch 1 r10(4).

relisted for a hearing on compensation. Delays in fixing the compensation hearing can cause financial distress to the worker and may also deprive him/her of the benefit of interest on an unpaid award.

Appeals and reviews

16.74   Any appeal must be made within 42 days of the date when the decision was sent to the parties. The ET may also be asked to review its decision within 14 days on specified grounds,[52] eg, because a crucial new case has just been reported, because the ET made a mathematical error in calculating compensation or the interest of justice requires it.

16.75   Workers often cannot understand that they may not automatically appeal when they lose. An appeal to the EAT is not a fresh rehearing of the entire case. It is a legal argument between the representatives for each party, largely based on the pleadings and the ET's decision on the facts. Normally the ET's notes of oral evidence will only be glanced at by the EAT, if at all. The appeal is confined to errors of law. Where there is no legal error, the worker must show that the ET's decision on the factual evidence was legally perverse, ie, that no reasonable ET could possibly have come to the same decision. It is very hard to show this and the EAT is reluctant to interfere with the ET's general discretion.

Costs

16.76   Unlike most civil courts, the ET does not usually order that the unsuccessful party pays the costs of the winner.[53] However, the ET may order costs if:

- the hearing was adjourned at the request of one party, when it can order costs of the adjournment;[54] or
- a party has acted frivolously, vexatiously, abusively, disruptively or otherwise unreasonably in bringing or conducting the proceedings.[55]

---

52 Ibid r11(1).
53 Ibid r12.
54 Ibid r12(4).
55 Ibid r12(1).

Costs may or may not be awarded regardless of whether or not there was a pre-hearing review or costs warning.

7   The ET may order one party to pay some or all of the other party's costs. If the worker is ordered to pay the employer's costs, the amount of costs the employer claims to have incurred must be taxed if above £500, ie, independently adjudicated by the county court, unless agreed.[56] The employer's estimate of his/her costs should not be agreed unless it seems very low. The ET must also take account of the worker's means when ordering costs.[57]

8   In practice costs tend to be awarded against a party who withdraws at the last moment without any explanation or who fails to attend the hearing without notifying the ET in advance. Costs may also be awarded if the case turns out to be completely hopeless and unreasonable or if the worker's or employer's representative greatly prolongs the hearing by bringing up entirely irrelevant matters.

9   A worker has an absolute right to have his/her unfair dismissal claim decided. An ET therefore should not award costs simply because the worker has turned down an open offer of compensation which turns out to equal or exceed the eventual ET award.[58] The position may be different if the employer concedes unfair dismissal.

Settlement[59]

30   An ACAS officer is attached to every claim for unfair dismissal or unlawful discrimination and has a statutory duty to promote a settlement. The ACAS officer usually contacts each party by telephone and one can choose whether to use him/her as an intermediary or negotiate direct with the employer. To find out which ACAS officer is allocated to the case, telephone the ACAS central office with the case number.

31   The ACAS officer has no duty to advise on the merits of the claim and there is no need to enter a discussion. There is also a risk that what is said to ACAS about the worker's case may be passed on to the employer's representative. There are many advantages in settling a claim, as it avoids the risk of losing, the unpleasantness of the

---

56   Ibid r12(3).
57   *Wiggin Alloys Ltd v Jenkins* [1981] IRLR 148, EAT.
58   *Telephone Information Services v Wilkinson* [1991] IRLR 148, EAT.
59   For more detail, see N O'Brien and T Kibling, 'Settling industrial tribunal claims' August 1988 *Legal Action* 9.

hearing, the recoupment provisions and may be the only way to negotiate a good reference as a term of the settlement.

16.82   A settlement agreement reached through ACAS is binding and
effective even if it is not recorded on the COT3 form.[60] It is essential
to have clear instructions from the worker as to whether to settle and
on what terms and to be absolutely clear to ACAS when any discussion is subject to final confirmation. The COT3 form is used to
record the settlement terms and is signed by the worker and
employer or their representatives. If a settlement is reached in direct
negotiation with the employer's representative, both must inform
ACAS. The ACAS officer then notifies the ET. If the hearing date is
very close, check that ACAS has done this and it may even be wise to
write to the ET to confirm that an ACAS settlement has been
reached.

16.83   Usually a settlement is not binding in respect of ET claims unless
it is agreed through ACAS. However, ACAS need not be involved
where there is an agreement reached between the parties which is in
writing, relates to the worker's complaint before the ET and states
that the worker has received independent advice from a qualified
lawyer (a solicitor holding a practising certificate or a barrister who is
covered by professional indemnity insurance), officers, officials or
workers of an independent trade union who have been certified by
the trade union as competent to give advice or an advice centre worker or volunteer who has been certified as competent to give advice. In
these circumstances it will be a binding settlement.[61] This is known
as a compromise agreement.

16.84   Care should be taken that the worker fully understands the implications and meaning of any settlement before an agreement is concluded. If possible, only the particular ET claim should be settled. In
practice, many employers insist on a wider settlement, ie, that in
return for payment of the specified sum, the worker waives any other
claim arising out of the contract of employment or its termination. As
well as explaining to the worker precisely what a 'full and final'
settlement means, it is safest to ask explicitly whether money is
owing in respect of wages, bonuses and commission, notice pay, or
holiday pay and (in the case of a nurse), whether there is any outstanding clinical grading appeal. One should ensure that any industrial injury claims and pension benefits are expressly excluded from

---

60 *Gilbert v Kembridge Fibres* [1984] IRLR 52, EAT.
61 ERA 1996 s203.

such a settlement.[62] ACAS officers usually suggest this exclusion in their standard wording.

It is advisable to specify in the COT3 or settlement agreement a date for payment. The actual wording of an agreed reference should be incorporated as well as the basis on which it will be supplied. The following considerations should be taken into account.[63]

–   Does the worker wish to ask for an open reference as well as asking the employer to write a reference in the agreed terms on request.

–   Does the worker wish to suggest that if the employer is asked for a verbal reference, s/he will only provide a written reference, or that s/he will respond verbally with the same content and spirit and without addition.

–   Does the worker wish to suggest that if the employer is asked for a reference which asks specific questions, s/he may not answer at all, or s/he may answer if asked, or only with the worker's prior written consent, or that s/he will answer with the same spirit and content as the agreed terms and without addition. What should the employer say if asked for more information.

–   It should be specified that the reference will be supplied on headed notepaper and duly signed. The worker may wish to specify who should or who should not deal with reference requests.

It should be remembered that an employer cannot be asked to lie in a reference and can only be controlled so far. Often it is important to preserve some remnants of goodwill to improve the chances of fair behaviour when reference requests are granted. Alternatively, it may focus the employer's mind, if s/he has asked for confidentiality, for example, to state that if the spirit or content of the reference agreement is not adhered to, then the worker will no longer be bound by confidentiality.

Employers often propose lengthy and complex settlement agreements with onerous and unsuitable terms. It is essential to understand what these mean and ensure the worker understands and consents.

---

62   But see para 15.20 if settling a discrimination case where health was damaged.
63   See appendix C, p426, for an example.

Running a case: Key points

- Winning unfair dismissal cases is mostly about the quality of the evidence. In running a case, advisers should try to obtain as much relevant evidence as they can, particularly if it is in documentary form, including witnesses.

- ETs are frequently persuaded by contemporaneous documentary evidence. Witnesses are often treated with suspicion as they are considered to be more unreliable than documents.

- If there is a potentially good witness, an order can be obtained from the ET to have that witness at the hearing.

- It is essential that there is a detailed written statement taken from the worker as soon after the dismissal as possible. Once the statement is completed it should be dated and signed.

- In most cases it is important to get further and better particulars of the employer's case (including the use of the question and answer procedure, see para 16.33) and inspection of the employer's documents before the hearing.

- It is crucial for the worker to detail all efforts made to look for new employment, and to keep a list of all expenses incurred. The duty is on the worker to take all reasonable steps to get another job as soon as possible even if it is not as well paid.

- Every case is allocated an officer from ACAS. Most of what is told to this officer will get back to the other party. The ACAS officer is there to try to settle the case and will get in touch in respect of a possible settlement.

- There are a number of advantages in settling claims. The most important is that the settlement can, and should, include an agreed written reference. This reference should be set out in writing as part of the settlement. A settlement also has the advantage of avoiding the recoupment of benefits by the DSS (see para 14.31).

- Remember, if an adviser is representing a worker at the ET and his/her name is on the record, everything will be sent to the adviser and not to the worker, including the hearing date. Remember to keep the worker informed.

- At the hearing, always make a note of the questions asked by the ET members and make sure that they are dealt with during the hearing and also in the closing speech. This is particularly true of the questions asked by the Chair of the ET.

CHAPTER 17

Running a race, sex or disability discrimination case

For complete chapter contents, see overleaf

In running discrimination cases, the basic principles are similar to those of unfair dismissal, dealt with in chapter 16 above. This chapter should be read in conjunction with that and highlights the procedural and technical differences that arise in cases under the RRA 1976, SDA 1975 and DDA 1995. An ET can hear claims based solely on EU law[1] and, in general, procedures applicable to cases under the SDA 1975, will apply,[2] although see below on time limits.

Occasionally the acts of discrimination will have damaged the worker's health such that damages can be claimed for personal injuries.[3] This may lead to additional requirements in case preparation, eg, obtaining an early medical report.

The questionnaire

Effective use of the special questionnaire procedure under RRA 1976 s65, SDA 1975 s74 and DDA 1995 s56 offers an important opportunity to obtain information from which inferences may later be drawn.[4] It is very hard to win a discrimination case where no questionnaire has been submitted. It is particularly necessary to gather evidence which is not contained in documents and therefore cannot be obtained on discovery. There are also several advantages of the procedure over the more limited potential of a request for further and better particulars of the ET3:

- any questions can be asked, not those limited to clarification of what is already in the ET3;
- questions may concern matters of evidence; and
- a questionnaire submitted at a very early stage can help decide whether a case should be pursued at all and, if so, how it should be formulated.

---

1 *Secretary of State for Scotland and Greater Glasgow Health Board v Wright and Hannah* [1991] IRLR 187, EAT.
2 *Livingstone v Hepworth Refractories plc* [1992] IRLR 63; (1992) 42 EOR 46.
3 See para 15.20.
4 For detailed guidance on the questionnaire procedure and precedents, see *RRA Questionnaires: How to use the Questionnaire Procedure* and *SDA Questionnaires: How to use the Questionnaire Procedure* by Tamara Lewis. Available from the Central London Law Centre.

Time limits

17.4   A questionnaire must be served on the employer within three months after the act of discrimination, unless an ET1 has already been presented, in which case the questionnaire must be served within 21 days of the date of presentation.[5] The ET has a discretion to grant leave for service of a questionnaire out of time,[6] but it may refuse to do so or take the opportunity to reduce the permissible questions.

17.5   Provided the time limits are adhered to, the questions and answers are admissible as evidence at the hearing. It is arguable that answers to a questionnaire served out of time without leave would be admissible as evidence in any event, although only of weaker hearsay value unless containing admissions contrary to the employer's interests. However, it is most unlikely that an adverse inference would be drawn from failure to answer a late questionnaire where there was no leave.

17.6   The EAT has said that it is a 'sensible and necessary part of the procedure that a worker can ask leave to serve a follow-up questionnaire after the initial one, provided that notice is given to the employer of the request for leave so that s/he can argue that any question is "unnecessary or too wide or oppressive" '.[7] It may also be possible to elicit follow-up information via a request for further particulars of the ET3 or discovery.

Procedure

17.7   Questionnaires are best submitted on the standard forms,[8] although in emergencies it is sufficient to accompany the questions with a statement of the alleged unlawful treatment on a letter headed, as appropriate, 'Race Relations (Questions and Replies) Order 1977 SI No 842', 'Sex Discrimination (Questions and Replies) Order 1975 SI No 2048' or 'Disability Discrimination (Questions and Replies) Order

---

5   Race Relations (Questions and Replies) Order 1977 SI No 842; Sex Discrimination (Questions and Replies) Order 1975 SI No 2048; Disability Discrimination (Questions and Replies) Order 1996 SI No 2793.
6   1977 SI No 842 art 5(b); 1975 SI No 2048 art 5(b); 1996 SI No 2793 art 3(b).
7   *Carrington v Helix Lighting* [1990] IRLR 6, EAT. See also *National Grid Co v Virdee* [1992] IRLR 555 paras 44 and 46, EAT.
8   RR65, SD74, DD56, obtainable from the Department of Employment or relevant Commissions.

1996 SI No 2793. The questionnaire should be sent by recorded delivery to the employer.

8   Unlike with particulars and discovery, the ET cannot make an order compelling the respondent to answer the questionnaire. Many employers do not realise this and it is worth fostering the illusion by requesting an answer within 14 days of service. The only sanction is the ET's ability to draw an inference from the failure to reply or from an evasive reply. If the employer does not reply after a chasing letter or if s/he replies selectively, an open letter should be written, stating that the failure to reply adequately will be drawn to the attention of the ET which will be invited to draw an adverse inference.

Drafting the questionnaire

.9   The questionnaire form contains two standard printed questions, but the main point is to think of additional questions, which can be set out at (or attached to) the standard paragraph 6. Broadly speaking, questions fall into three categories:

a) those concerning the facts and circumstances of the particular treatment of the worker bringing the claim;

b) questions to discover how other workers have been treated in similar circumstances and, in particular to find out comparable details of any comparator and how s/he has been treated and

c) general (normally statistical and procedural) questions about the workplace in general revealing how the employer treats other workers.[9]

As a general rule, it is useful to ask in the case of any major decision affecting a worker (eg, dismissal), who made the decision, when and for what reasons.

.10   Since an ET may draw an inference only if the employer had no reasonable excuse for failing to answer a questionnaire adequately and if it is just and equitable to do so,[10] it is important not to hand the employer an easy excuse by drafting an unclear or unreasonable questionnaire. Employers often say they cannot answer the questions because they do not understand in what way they are alleged to have discriminated. This objection is illogical and runs counter to one of the main purposes of the procedure: to assist in the formulation of

---

9   See appendix A for examples and tips on drafting questionnaires.
10   RRA 1976 s65(2)(b); SDA 1975 s74(2)(b); DDA 1995 s56(3)(b).

the claim. Unfortunately it is an objection which frequently wins sympathy in the ET and therefore the statement at paragraph 2 of the questionnaire form should clarify the allegations as far as possible.

17.11   The grounds set out eventually in the ET1 should normally be identical to para 2 of the questionnaire. Certainly no key facts should be omitted from either statement as the worker is likely to be cross-examined on any difference between the statements and any difference between either statement and his/her oral evidence. If the information requested in the questionnaire is too wide-ranging and/or difficult to collate, it will irritate the ET and provide an easy excuse for the employer not to answer. Either the extent of the requested statistics should be confined from the outset to the minimum necessary, or at a later stage the employer can be offered the opportunity of providing more limited information if s/he raises this objection. In particular, it should be carefully considered over what period, at what intervals and within what geographical or departmental area to request statistics.

17.12   Where the employer objects that statistics are not kept, s/he can be asked whether information is kept on computer or, with smaller employers, suggest a head-count. Either at the outset, or after an employer objects that certain information is confidential, it should be agreed that names and addresses of other workers be deleted.[11]

17.13   Race and colour are vague concepts which usually require clarification. To avoid misunderstanding or deliberate evasion in response to questionnaires under the RRA 1976, it should be specified under which 'racial categories' information is to be provided. For example, where there is any doubt as to whether the employer discriminates solely against African/Caribbeans or against all non-whites or only against workers born abroad, the questions should cover all the options.

17.14   A worker can choose whether to send the questionnaire to the employer before or after s/he has started an ET case. It is usually best to send the questionnaire long before lodging the ET1. This forces employers to answer before they can counter-attack by asking the worker to particularise his/her ET1. In general, sending the questionnaire as early as possible enables the worker to keep the initiative on the case and ensures there is time before the hearing to follow up the information provided. Also, if an ET is to draw an adverse inference from an employer's failure to answer a lengthy questionnaire

---

11 See para 17.41 below for confidentiality in relation to discovery.

adequately, it should be served sufficiently in advance of the hearing for the employer to be expected to collate the information. The other advantage of an early questionnaire is that the reply should be received before the deadline for starting a tribunal case. This enables the worker to make a more informed decision on the chances of success and whether to go ahead.

The originating application (ET1)

The time limit

15   The ET1 must be presented within three months of the act of discrimination. Earlier incidents can be referred to as supporting evidence.[12] If further discrimination takes place against a worker who is still employed after s/he has started an ET case, s/he should lodge a new ET1 and ask for the two cases to be considered together.

.16   The act of discrimination is not always easy to identify, so advisers must be alert about the time limit. Time usually runs from when a decision not to promote or appoint is made or communicated, or from when a warning is given, and not from the end of any appeal or grievance procedure. However, if the failure of the grievance procedure or appeal was itself on grounds of race or sex or related to disability, then that is a further act of discrimination from which another three-month period runs. It is unwise to rely on this extension, however, as usually it is the original action which constituted the discrimination, not the decision on appeal, which tends to be a rubber-stamping exercise. Also, if the appeal was against dismissal and took place after the termination date, the appeal will probably not be covered by the RRA 1976 and DDA 1995 at all.[13] Therefore if there is a lengthy appeal or grievance process, it is important not to allow the original incident to fall out of time.

.17   In recent years, the EAT has been reluctant to treat claims as out of time where the only reason for delay is the worker's attempt to resolve the matter internally. In one case the EAT said that, provided the outcome of the grievance or appeal was kept within the time limit, the original matter to which it related could also be taken as in time.[14] Even if this argument does not work, it should be just and

---

12   *Eke v Commissioners of Customs and Excise* [1981] IRLR 334, EAT.
13   For the sex discrimination position, see para 9.36 above.
14   *Ford Motor Ltd v Shah* EAT 350/95.

equitable to allow in a late claim in such circumstances.[15] Unfortunately, it is still unclear how reliable these cases are as they appear to depart from established principles.

17.18   In some situations, discrimination continues over a period of time, sometimes up to the date of leaving employment. The time for lodging an ET1 then runs from the end of that period.[16] The common, although technically inaccurate name for this is 'continuing discrimination'. Advisers should be careful if relying on showing continuing discrimination for time limit purposes as it is sometimes hard to distinguish it from a single act of discrimination with continuing effects. For example, a failed promotion attempt resulting in continued employment at a lower grade and wage is not in itself continuing discrimination.[17] If a worker is out of time, s/he should make another attempt at promotion on which it may be appropriate to base a claim provided this latest failure also appears discriminatory on the facts. On the other hand, if an employer maintained a rule that only workers of a particular race or sex would be promoted to certain posts, that would be continuing discrimination.

17.19   In *Calder v James Finlay Corporation Ltd.*,[18] a woman was twice refused a mortgage subsidy from her employer which was available to men. The EAT said that although the unsuccessful requests took place more than three months prior to her claim, the rules of the scheme barring women constituted a discriminatory act extending throughout Mrs Calder's employment until she left. Similarly, in *Barclays Bank v Kapur*,[19] the employer kept in force 'a discriminatory regime' throughout the workers' employment in that their past service in banks in Africa was not credited towards their pensionable service. The ET had jurisdiction to hear the claim even though the workers entered the discriminatory scheme several years earlier, which was when the decision not to include their service was taken.

17.20   The *Calder* and *Kapur* cases concerned formal rules which were discriminatory. This principle was taken further in *Owusu v London Fire and Civil Defence Authority*.[20] Mr Owusu, a clerical worker, complained of the failure to regrade him at any stage since his transfer

---

15 See below and *Aniagwu v Hackney LBC & Owens* [1999] IRLR 303; 82 EOR 48, EAT.
16 RRA 1976 s68(7); SDA 1975 s76(6); DDA 1995 Sch 3 s3.
17 *Amies v ILEA* (1976) 121 SJ 11; [1977] ICR 308, EAT.
18 [1989] IRLR 55, EAT.
19 [1989] IRLR 387, CA; [1991] IRLR 136; (1991) 36 EOR 33, HL.
20 [1995] IRLR 574, EAT.

several years earlier and the failure to let him act-up when such opportunities arose (all of which had arisen more than three months before he lodged his tribunal claim). The EAT accepted there could be a continuing act of discrimination if the worker proved a discriminatory policy, rule or practice (however informal) which, when followed or applied, excluded the worker from regrading or acting-up opportunities. However, it would be necessary to prove a linking practice as opposed to a series of one-off decisions, even if they were each discriminatory.

21   The *Owusu* case was approved of by the CA in *Cast v Croydon College*,[21] which confirmed that there could be a continuing policy or regime, even if it was not formal or written, and even if it was only confined to one post or role. Mrs Cast asked her line manager before she went on maternity leave whether she could return to work afterwards on a part-time or job-share basis. He refused, even though the College had a written policy generally receptive to job-sharing at all levels. Mrs Cast unsuccessfully repeated her request to her manager twice after her return. A few months later she resigned. Subsequently she lodged her ET claim. The ET said that the time limit was three months from the first refusal, before Mrs Cast even went on maternity leave. Mrs Cast's claim was therefore well out of time. The CA disagreed. It said that the several refusals of Mrs Cast's request indicated the existence of a discriminatory policy in relation to her post (manager of the College's information centre). This policy continued until Mrs Cast left and her claim was therefore in time, regardless of the date of any particular request and refusal.

.22   The CA also considered the position if there had not been a continuing policy or practice, but simply a succession of independent refusals. Any refusal within the last three months would be in time provided it was the result of a fresh consideration by the employers (even if it was a decision made by the same manager and on the same facts). On the other hand, if the employers simply referred back to their previous decision or expanded on their reasons, this would not be a fresh consideration, and time would run from the earlier decision. Mrs Cast therefore had an alternative argument that the time limit should be counted from the last (and not the first) of her line manager's refusals.[22]

21 [1998] IRLR 318; 80 EOR 49.
22 See also *Akhtar v Family Services Unit* (1996) 70 EOR 56, CA and the slightly different approach in a non-employment case, *Rovenska v General Medical Council* [1997] IRLR 367, CA.

17.23   Note that a close sequence of discriminatory actions, eg, a series of threats, warnings and abuse, as is common in harassment cases, does not in itself necessarily constitute continuing discrimination in the legal sense (although arguably there may be an underlying discriminatory regime). Strictly speaking, the ET claim should be lodged within three months of each incident. In practice, it is usually enough if the most serious incidents (and those easiest to prove) are in time. The other actions can still be referred to as supporting evidence. In this kind of case, the ET is also likely to be sympathetic to exercising its discretion to allow in late claims; even more so if there is medical evidence of the worker's distressed state of mind.

17.24   In harassment cases, time limits are often missed because, for example, the worker goes off sick and then resigns. No further acts of discrimination are likely to have occurred during the worker's absence, but an adviser may mistakenly calculate the three months from the resignation rather than from the last incident at work. Another trap into which advisers can fall occurs where the harassment stops once the worker complains, but the employer takes some time to investigate and the longer-term outcome is unsatisfactory. By the time the worker realises s/he is unhappy with the solution, three months may have passed.[23]

17.25   The case-law on time limits and on out-of-time claims (below) shows a current reluctance by the higher courts to be rigid about time limits. This attitude has not always filtered down to the ETs, who can seize the opportunity to free up overcrowded ET schedules by rejecting apparently late claims. Employers tend to argue fiercely that as many incidents as possible are out of time. Although several of the above cases may come to the rescue where a worker seems to be out of time, it is still far easier to run and prove a case where the relevant incidents occurred within the last three months. For example, the concept of continuing discrimination may seem to rescue a situation, but in fact it is much harder to prove that there is a linking practice, than that discrimination occurred on separate occasions.

---

23   Continuing failure to implement promised remedial measures may amount to continuing discrimination, thus extending the time limit: *Littlewoods Organisation plc v Traynor* [1993] IRLR 154; (1993) 49 EOR 35, EAT. The ambit of this decision is unclear and advisers should still be careful.

Claims outside the time limit

6 An ET may allow a claim outside the time limit if it is just and equitable to do so.[24] This is a wider and therefore more commonly granted discretion than for unfair dismissal claims. The ET must weigh up the reasons for and against extending time and explain its thinking.[25] The ET should consider whether the employer is 'prejudiced' by the lateness,[26] ie, whether the employer was already aware of the allegation and so not caught by surprise, and whether any harm is done to the employer or to the chances of a fair hearing by the element of lateness. An ET should normally find it just and equitable to extend time where the delay is because the worker first tried to resolve the matter through use of an internal grievance procedure.[27] If the delay was because the worker tried to pursue the matter in correspondence before rushing to an ET, this should also be considered.[28] Other factors which an ET will consider are the reason for the delay, the degree of lateness and the apparent strength of the case. The ET is entitled to take it into account if incorrect legal advice caused the delay.[29]

27 Where a claim is outside the time limit because a material fact emerges much later, eg, the job for which a black worker applied is filled several months later by a white person with lesser qualifications or experience, an ET should consider whether it was reasonable of the worker not to realise s/he had a prima facie case until this happened.[30] Alternatively, it could be argued that the claim is not out of time at all because the act of discrimination has not 'crystallised', ie, finally taken place, until the eventual appointment.[31] This is rather an unusual argument and should not be relied on.

28 The ET should also be reminded that discrimination is a particularly serious issue and a worker should not lightly be deprived of a hearing; where a time limit is missed due to an adviser's negligence, financial compensation from suing the adviser cannot compensate for the lost opportunity of having a finding of discrimination.

---

24 RRA 1976 s68(6); SDA 1975 s76(5); DDA 1995 Sch3 s3(2).
25 *Osaje v Camden LBC* (1997) EAT/317/96; *Legal Action* November 1997, 6.
26 *Osaje* ibid.
27 *Aniagwu v Hackney LBC & Owens* [1999] IRLR 303; 82 EOR 48, EAT.
28 *Osaje* (n25 above).
29 *Hawkins v (1) Ball and (2) Barclays Bank PLC* [1996] IRLR 258, EAT.
30 *Clarke v Hampshire Electro-Plating Co Ltd* [1991] IRLR 490, EAT.
31 Ibid.

17.29   It is often worth trying to get in an out-of-time claim, if the above factors are persuasive, as some ETs are prepared to exercise their discretion favourably. In particular, where there are several discriminatory acts, with only the most recent in time, the ET may well grant leave to allow in the earlier acts. This is especially so where the earlier acts will be raised in the case anyway as matters of evidence supporting the latest claim.[32] In this type of case, the ET1 should be clearly drafted so that it is plain that the earlier discriminatory acts are meant to be claims in their own right and not just supporting evidence.

17.30   It is also wise expressly to ask permission in the ET1 for the earlier claims to be allowed in under the ET's discretion. However, whether or not this request is made in the ET1 itself, it should be sought by the worker's representative at the very latest at the start of the hearing. The onus is on the worker's representative to seek permission. The ET is not obliged to offer to use its discretion and if nothing is said, the earlier acts may be treated purely as evidence.[33] Frequently, however, the question will already have been dealt with during the preparation of the case.

17.31   At an interlocutory hearing, the ET may order the worker to set out which of the claimed incidents of discrimination are in time. (See appendix A for a checklist and sample written submission on time limits.) The ET may also order a preliminary hearing to make decisions as to whether part or all of the claim is in time. However, if the main incident is in time and the earlier incidents will be heard as evidence anyway, a preliminary hearing is unnecessary as it will make no difference to the ground covered by the final hearing.[34] The ET can decide after it has heard all the evidence at the final hearing whether to allow in the earlier incidents as grounds of the claim.

Time limits on EU claims

17.32–34 Complex questions arise with regard to time-limits where a worker can claim directly under EU law. The rules differ according to whether the law concerned is an article with direct effect, eg, article

---

32 See chapter 12 on relevant evidence, para 12.8 on other acts of discrimination.
33 *Dimtsu v Westminster City Council* [1991] IRLR 450, EAT.
34 The EAT in *Sutcliffe v Big C's Marine* [1998] IRLR 428 and the CA in *Smith v Gardner Merchant Ltd* [1998] IRLR 510 at 512 have both commented against the general desirability of having preliminary hearings.

141 or a directive which has never been implemented or only after
a delay. A discussion of the legal position on this is beyond the scope
of this book.[35-38]

Drafting the ET1

.7.35 Provided the originating application claims 'race discrimination', any
claim under the RRA 1976 will be covered, whether it is direct discrimination, indirect discrimination or victimisation.[39] Nevertheless
it is helpful if the nature of the claim can be clarified at the outset or
as soon as possible, eg, after receiving a reply to the questionnaire.
Unfortunately many ETs take an excessively formalistic approach,
requiring very detailed and legalistic particularisation of discrimination claims. This approach does not seem to be required on other
types of case and does defeat the objective of accessibility and infor-
mality in the ET system.

7.36 If unfair dismissal is being claimed in addition to discrimination,
this should be added in a separate paragraph specifying in which
way the dismissal was unfair, to clarify that it is recognised that
it is a different issue.[40] All key matters on which the worker will
rely should be mentioned concisely in the grounds of application
with dates. It is important to include any racist or sexually offensive
remarks. If victimisation is claimed, the protected act should be
cited. In indirect discrimination claims, because of the uncertainty
as to which requirement/condition and which pool the ET will
approve, it is probably best to express the claim in broad or alternative
terms.

.37 It is very important to be sure about the extent of the worker's
claim and set it out correctly from the outset. The ET may not allow
any amendments of the ET1 later, especially to add entirely new
grounds. Even if the ET does allow an amendment, the original version of the ET1 will still be visible and any significant changes will
damage the worker's credibility.

35–38 Although, useful cases to consider are *Emmott v Minister for Social Welfare*
[1991] IRLR 387; [1993] ICR 8, ECJ; *Biggs v Somerset CC* [1996] IRLR 203, CA;
Preston and Others v Wolverhampton Healthcare NHS Trust and Others [1998]
IRLR 197; [1998] ICR 227, HL and pending reference to ECJ.
39 *Quarcoopome v Sock Shop Holdings Ltd* [1995] IRLR 353; (1995) 62 EOR 45, EAT.
40 See para 16.19 above for drafting an ET1 in unfair dismissal claims.

Naming individual respondents

17.38 In the questionnaire and in the ET1, individuals may be named as respondents, as well as the employing organisation. The latter should always be named, but whether the former are added depends on several considerations.

– Naming individuals ensures that the claim succeeds against somebody if the employing organisation might escape liability because the employer took all reasonably practicable steps to prevent the discrimination happening (see para 11.44). If the claim succeeds against the employer and named individuals, the award will usually be enforceable in its entirety against any of the respondents. This is the most obvious reason for naming individuals. Therefore if during the course of the case, the employing organisation accepts vicarious liability for any discriminatory actions of the discriminator, the ET often puts pressure on the worker to withdraw the claim against individuals. However, as set out below, there are other powerful reasons why the individuals should remain as respondents. An ET should not be allowed simply to strike out the case against individual respondents at an interlocutory hearing without the worker's consent: this is a judicial decision which should be handled appropriately and would require grounds.[41]

– It usually ensures that the named individuals will give evidence at the hearing, so the desirability of their attendance must be considered.

– In harassment cases, it is possible that the employer will require the individual to obtain separate representation in case there is a conflict of interest. The worker may gain useful additional or conflicting information from separated sources.

– In harassment cases, it ensures the individual perpetrator is personally accountable and unable to hide behind the employer. An element of compensation (or part of any settlement) may also be awarded (or agreed) against the perpetrator.

– Where there has been deliberate and malicious discrimination, costs may be awarded against an individual respondent for unreasonably defending the proceedings.[42] This is valuable

---

41 See para 17.48 below re ET's powers to strike out parts of the claim.
42 Employment Tribunals (Constitution and Rules of Procedure) Regulations 1993 SI No 2687 (IT Regs) Sch 1 r12.

because, where, as is common, the employer supports and funds the individual's case, it can be implied that s/he has underwritten the individual's costs,[43] including those ordered against the individual. However, where the individual is not joined as respondent, unless it can be argued that the principle in RRA 1976 s32, SDA 1975 s41 and DDA 1995 s58 extends to vicarious liability for the conduct of proceedings, the employer could avoid a costs order by claiming that s/he was entitled to rely on statements from the individual that s/he (the individual) had not discriminated.

- If the employing organisation is likely to go into liquidation with no funds for unsecured creditors, it ensures that the claim can proceed[44] and that there is a likelihood of recovering money, assuming the named individual has any assets.
- Individuals should be named as respondents only if there is a strong case against them, as the ET will be reluctant to make a specific finding against them. Caution should be used in naming more than one individual since ETs react badly to any suggestion of a conspiracy.

Written reasons for dismissal

9 Where the alleged act of discrimination is dismissal, a worker should usually request written reasons under the ERA 1996 s92 provided s/he had sufficient service (see para 16.8 above).[45] In discrimination cases this may be a particularly significant piece of evidence. Even if the reply is received within the 14 days, one should always add a s92 claim to the ET1 since, if the discrimination is proved, the worker is very likely to receive an award for untrue reasons.

Interlocutory matters

Further particulars of the ET3 and Interrogatories

10 The considerations and procedure are the same as for unfair dismissal. However, in discrimination cases it is especially important to secure as much information as possible of the employer's defence

---

43 *Bourne v Colodense* [1985] ICR 291; [1985] IRLR 339, CA.
44 Leave from the High Court may be necessary to proceed against a company in liquidation, depending on the type of liquidation.
45 Note also the position with pregnancy dismissals, para 11.2.

and this opportunity should not be lost. Although questions cannot be as free-ranging as on the questionnaire (see above), the advantage is that the ET can be asked to order the employer to reply.

Discovery

17.41 Discovery is a crucial part of the information-gathering process in most discrimination cases. The ET will not permit wide, trawling exercises for helpful evidence or a general request for all relevant documents and what will be relevant and useful needs to be thought out (see sample at p386 below). If documents are necessary for disposing fairly of a case or for saving costs, the ET should order their disclosure, even if they are confidential.[46] Where there is a problem about confidentiality, the ET can look privately at the documents to see if they are necessary and to decide whether the same information can be obtained in any other way.[47]

17.42 If an ET refuses discovery of something important, one should write asking the same Chair to review the decision, quoting the relevant test.[48] It may be best to request an oral hearing and to give notice to the employer of the request.

17.43 The ET can order disclosure of relevant statistics provided that they do not relate solely to the question of the employer's credit, but go to an issue in the case, eg, whether the employer, intentionally or otherwise, operated a discriminatory policy which manifested itself on other occasions and may have manifested itself in respect of the present complaint.[49]

17.44 Discovery is concerned with disclosure of documents. However, for the sake of convenience, the ET can order that the employer supply a digest of information contained in bulky documents. In this way, information generally only available from a questionnaire can be made the subject of an order for discovery. However, where the statistical information is known to the employer but is not contained in existing documents, the ET cannot order the employer to draw up such a schedule.[50]

---

46 *Nassé v Science Research Council; Vyas v Leyland Cars* [1979] IRLR 465; [1979] ICR 921, HL.
47 Ibid.
48 Ibid.
49 *West Midlands Passenger Transport Executive v Singh* [1988] IRLR 186; [1988] ICR 614, CA.
50 *Carrington v Helix Lighting* [1990] IRLR 6, EAT.

45   Original documents should always be inspected, as tampering is
not uncommon in discrimination cases, and a request should also be
made that the originals be brought to the hearing.

Interlocutory hearings

46   ETs usually propose interlocutory hearings in discrimination cases.
Their purpose is normally to clarify the issues, sort out what discovery and particulars should be ordered, decide on exchange of witness statements, estimate the length of hearing and fix dates. The
request for discovery and particulars should be served well before the
interlocutory hearing, so that an order can be requested. Depending
on tactics, it may also be useful to mention any unanswered items in
the questionnaire, since, although the ET cannot make an order, the
Chair may well encourage the employer to reply.

47   Many employers take the opportunity to seek clarification of the
case against them and the adviser should go prepared for some tricky
questions. The ET may insist on knowing whether direct or indirect
discrimination is being claimed or on the worker setting out every
incident of discrimination on which s/he relies. The latter can be very
awkward as, although the major incidents will have been pleaded in
the ET1, quite often the worker will come out with additional, more
minor, examples of less favourable treatment during the main hearing. If taken by surprise at the interlocutory hearing, do not attempt
to answer on the spot and ask for 14 days to supply voluntary particulars. The worker or adviser may find that statements or explanations
made casually at an interlocutory hearing find their way into the
ET's subsequent order or account of the hearing and cause problems
later.

48   Sometimes an ET at an interlocutory stage tries to strike out some
of the worker's supporting allegations on grounds that they are
irrelevant. This would mean the worker cannot deal with those matters at the full hearing and will be unable to obtain related discovery
at the preparatory stages. The EAT has said that an ET should be
careful not to overstep the line between legitimate case management and over-simplifying the case by striking out proper claims
because it would be quicker to deal with.[51] Although it may be
desirable that cases should be kept within proper bounds, the

51   *Hambly v Rathbone Community Industry Ltd* (1999) 617 IRLB 10, EAT/746/98.

worker must not be prevented from putting his or her full case.[52] If the ET does have a good reason to disallow some of the allegations, it must follow the correct procedure.[53] It cannot strike out claims under its general power to give directions. It can only do so on grounds that the claims are scandalous, frivolous or vexatious,[54] and the worker must have been given the chance to argue against the striking out.[55]

Restricted reporting orders

17.49   In a case involving allegations of 'sexual misconduct' (eg, a sexual harassment case) the ET has power at any time up to the promulgation of its decision to make a restricted reporting order, which specifies that certain parties must not be identified by the press.[56] It can also revoke the order at any time. The parties are entitled to an oral hearing if they wish, before the ET makes any order.[57] The order can cover the person making the allegation or anyone affected by it[58] This may include direct witnesses of the misconduct, but should not usually include those less directly involved, eg, managers conducting an investigation, or the employing organisation itself.[59] The order also should not be too wide-ranging in terms of which incidents are covered.[60]

17.50   Where there are allegations of a 'sexual offence', the ET must delete from the public record any information likely to lead members of the public to identify any person affected by or making such allegation.[61] Similar rules apply in the EAT.[62] The precise meanings of 'misconduct' and 'offence' are uncertain, but the latter probably

---

52   Ibid.
53   Ibid.
54   Employment Ttibunals (Constitution and Rules of Procedure) Regulations 1993 SI No 2687 Sch 1 r13(2)(d).
55   Ibid r13(3).
56   Employment Tribunals (Constitution and Rules of Procedure) Regulations 1993 Sch 1 r14; Employment Tribunals Act 1996 s11.
57   ET Regs Sch 1 r14(2).
58   ETA 1996 s11(1)(a).
59   *R v London (North) Industrial Tribunal ex p Associated Newspapers Ltd* [1998] IRLR 569, HC; *Leicester University v A* [1999] IRLR 352, EAT.
60   *R v London (North) Industrial Tribunal* ibid.
61   Ibid r13(6).
62   Employment Appeal Tribunal Rules 1993 (EAT Rules) SI No 2854 r23; Employment Tribunals Act 1996 s32.

refers to a criminal offence. ET hearings are open to the public and reporters are in regular attendance in some tribunals,[63] often arranging for photographers to ambush unwitting applicants as they leave the building. As there is no power for an ET to exclude the public or the press and as the restricted reporting order is effective only until the decision is issued, the protection is of limited value. However, the inability to identify the parties while the hearing is taking place will certainly deter a proportion of the daily reporters.

51   Ironically, although the reporting restrictions were brought in with a view to protecting complainants of sexual harassment,[64] it is very often the perpetrators who seek and obtain an order against the applicant's will. Many applicants have experienced heavy-handed attempts from their employers to silence them from the moment they raised the allegations, as well as intimidation from the harasser not to speak out. By the time they reach an ET, they wish the matter to be out in the open.

52   A restricted reporting order may also be made under the DDA 1995 where evidence of a personal nature is likely to be heard.[65] Unlike in cases of sexual misconduct, only the applicant or the ET (but not the respondent) can request a restricted reporting order.

Preparation for the hearing

Witness statements

53   It is increasingly common for the evidence of witnesses to be put into written 'witness statements', which are usually exchanged 7–14 days before the hearing.[66] Well-written witness statements can be very effective in helping to win discrimination cases. The following tips are useful in writing statements.

    – If the worker is likely to be the first witness, explain important background at the start of the statement, eg, how the workplace is structured, the hierarchy, and the worker's job.

---

63 For example, London North at Woburn Place.
64 See parliamentary debate in *Hansard*, 16 June 1993, p 951.
65 ET Regs Sch 1 r14(1A). ETA 1996 s12.
66 See paras 16.53–16.58 above.

– The worker's evidence should usually be set out clearly and in chronological order. Sub-headings are useful.
– If possible without destroying the sense and logical order, indicate some of the discriminatory elements early in the statement. For example, in a race discrimination case, draw attention to a white dominant work hierarchy or to any racist remarks early on.
– Ensure the worker understands and agrees with the content of his/her statement. Try to use his/her normal way of speaking and avoid jargon. If the worker fully understands English but cannot read it, it will be necessary to explain this to the ET at the hearing and ask to read the statement for him/her. If the worker's English is very limited, a statement will probably be unsuitable.
– Draw attention to legally relevant facts. For example, in a case of direct race discrimination, always point out where the employer's behaviour is different from the norm.[67–68] In direct discrimination cases, different treatment is more relevant than unfair treatment.
– In a DDA case, a worker may face difficult questioning related to the definition of 'disability'. The worker may not answer properly under the stress of a hearing. It is also well-known that some people play down the effect of their disability. A well-written witness statement addressing each aspect of the definition, having discussed the matter carefully with the worker when s/he is not under the pressure of cross-examination in a public forum, may be crucial.

Preparing the worker

17.54   It should be clearly explained to the worker what has to be proved and that the issue is not fairness. In particular, it should be stressed that it is necessary to prove that the reason for what happened was the worker's race, sex or related to disability. Advise the worker to keep to the relevant incidents, not to quote weak examples or accuse irrelevant people of racism or sexism. Certain cross-examination techniques are very common and the worker should be warned. In particular, s/he is likely to be asked in respect of all key persons for the employer whether they are racist or have discriminated. Explain the legal significance of saying that someone may have discriminated and that it is not the same as saying that someone is prejudiced. If the legal issues are not explained, the worker may find that as a result

67–68 See sample extracts from RRA witness statement at pp393–396.

of being pinned down at the outset, s/he unwittingly makes concessions or gives evidence which (wrongly) appears to contradict how the case has been set out. On the other hand, be careful not to confuse the worker.

55   Most discrimination hearings are traumatic experiences, whatever the results, so the worker should bring along a friend or relative, especially where s/he may otherwise be the only woman or black person in the room. Sexual harassment cases will be particularly unpleasant and the worker should be warned about possible lines of cross-examination (see para 11.39 above). Particularly if the worker has a disability, find out if s/he has any particular needs while attending the ET, eg, for regular breaks.

Expenses

56   The ET will pay reasonable charges for professional interpreters, including for deaf or blind workers, as well as for interpretation into different languages. It is usually unhelpful to use an unofficial interpreter, especially one known to the worker. The costs of a helper accompanying a witness because of a medical condition are covered as well as reasonable charges for the attendance of medical professionals or the production of medical reports where that is essential to the case.[69] As the rules on which expenses are covered and in what circumstances often change, it is essential to check the latest position with the ET itself before relying on getting costs fully covered.[70]

The hearing

Start of hearing: preliminary issues

57   Sometimes the ET will decide certain issues relating to jurisdiction immediately before starting the full hearing. This is the time to ask leave to allow out-of-time claims if such leave has not previously been requested.[71] It is advisable to warn the employer's representative in advance if this is intended. Otherwise, if there is a need to adjourn because the employer is taken by surprise, the costs of the adjournment may be awarded against the applicant.

69   DTI Press Release P/99/87, 1 February 1999. Reported in (1999) 612 IRLB 6.
70   See also para 16.59 above on travel and other expenses.
71   *Dimtsu* (see para 17.30 above).

Opening

17.58 As the burden of proof is on the worker, usually the worker's witnesses go first and his/her representative has the advantage of giving an opening speech. Many ETs have deep reservations about the concept of discrimination and the proper role of the law. The opening speech may be the best opportunity to address any misconceptions, either as to the law or as to the extent of discrimination in society. It may also be a useful tactic briefly to remind the ET of some of the research findings on the extent of discrimination in employment. The closing speech is too late.

17.59 In most direct discrimination cases, it is worth reminding the ET at the outset that in order to succeed, prejudice need not be demonstrated, nor need unlawful discrimination be a conscious or intentional act. It could also usefully be reminded that the standard of proof is only the balance of probabilities. Even though it is serious to allege discrimination against an employer, it is equally serious to fail to find discrimination where it has occurred.

17.60 Where a discrimination claim is combined with one of unfair dismissal, it is unclear who should start and the ET has the right to govern its own procedure. For the reasons set out above, it is usually worth arguing for the right to start. Sometimes, however, it may be best to let the employer start, for example, where the worker will make a bad witness but the employer has clearly breached procedures. If the worker starts in such a case, the ET may form an adverse view early on which distracts it from the employer's conduct.

Strategy

17.61 Employers' representatives frequently object at the beginning of a hearing that they do not know what case they have to meet and in what way they are alleged to have discriminated. ETs sometimes go along with this approach and require workers' representatives to commit themselves to precise allegations, even when the case is clearly pleaded and no request for clarification has been made at interlocutory stages. The adviser should therefore be prepared to answer the following sort of question put at the start of the hearing.

  – Is it alleged that the worker was discriminated against because s/he is of African national origin or because s/he is black?

- Precisely who are you alleging discriminated against the worker? In promotion cases, which members of the selection panel are you alleging discriminated?
- In what way did the employer discriminate? What is every matter relied on?

The difficulty with the last question is that the worker will be confined to every matter that s/he can remember to list at the outset. In respect of the first two questions, the issues should be kept open by putting matters in the alternative. Some ETs recognise that in a promotion case, for example, the worker cannot know how a decision was made, who influenced whom, who may have been prejudiced, who may have unconsciously discriminated, etc, and permit the worker simply to say it was some or all of the panel. If an ET insists on the worker saying which of a selection panel discriminated, unless one panel member clearly had a decisive influence, it may be best to name all panel members, reserving the right to drop the allegations against some. The worker's representative may also wish to register a formal protest against being forced to take a position, to safeguard the possibility of a later appeal.

12   As a general rule, it is best to run cases in a low-key way. Fierce cross-examination and use of emotive words such as 'racist' will usually alienate the ET. In the opening speech, the ET's expectations should not be needlessly raised. It may be planned to reveal overt prejudice, but legally this need not be shown, so do not promise more than may be possible to deliver. The ET may find it easier to accept that senior managers have acted with benevolent motives or through a desire to have someone who 'fits in' rather than through racial or sexual hostility.

13   In most cases, it is not certain whether the act of direct discrimination was conscious or unconscious, intended or not. The ET must not be relied on to understand what unconscious discrimination is or that it can happen. Many ETs still look for indications of deliberate discrimination (whether the motives were good or bad) and focus on the honesty and sincerity of the employer's witnesses. This issue must be taken on explicitly. It should be explained that an employer may not be aware that s/he has discriminated and that the proper approach for the ET to take in determining direct discrimination or victimisation cases, ie, whether inferences can be drawn from the primary facts (see para 12.2 above), does not require it to make a

finding as to whether the unlawful discrimination was conscious or not.[72]

17.64   On the whole, the fewer people that have to be proved discriminatory or prejudiced, the better, except where the main point is that a whole workplace was hostile towards workers of a particular race or sex. Unless there is extremely strong evidence, probably in the form of a direct witness, any suggestion of a conspiracy or policy in the employing organisation to discriminate should be avoided. As a final note of caution, in running the case, be careful not to lose sight of the main issues in a mass of detail.

Dismissals

17.65   Where an unfair dismissal claim is also before the ET, it usually entails quite different considerations, unless the claim is purely that the dismissal was unfair by reason of being discriminatory. The issues should be kept separate in the opening and closing speeches.

17.66   Where the worker does not have sufficient service to qualify for claiming unfair dismissal, ETs tend to be very suspicious, seeing the discrimination claim as an attempt to circumvent the qualifying period under the ERA 1996. Great care must be taken when running such a case not to deal with issues which relate solely to fairness.[73] Constantly draw attention to differences from the norm. Even so, in some circumstances it may be appropriate to argue that matters such as the employer's failure to follow disciplinary procedures, inadequate grounds for dismissal, failure to consult, etc, are also matters from which an inference of less favourable treatment may be drawn.

No case to answer

17.67   At the end of the evidence of the worker and his/her witnesses, the employer may ask the ET to reject the case at that stage on the basis that the worker has not made out a prima facie case for the employer to answer. The ET should be reminded of the decision in *Laher v Hammersmith and Fulham LBC*,[74] that only in the most exceptional

---

72   See paras 9.46 and 9.49 above.
73   Particularly after *Zafar v Glasgow City Council* [1998] IRLR 36, HL. See para 12.11 above.
74   (1995) 514 IRLB 4, EAT. See also *JSV Oxford v DHSS* [1977] IRLR 225, EAT and see paras 12.1–12.6 above on the burden of proof.

cases should the employer not be called to give an explanation. If the ET dismisses the case at that stage, there is a likely basis for appeal.

8   Some ETs deal with the matter instead, by warning the worker as to costs of proceeding further. Regardless of whether the ET actually gives a costs warning, workers' representatives should be aware of the danger of an ultimate award of costs if the ET seems sympathetic to the suggestion that there is no case to answer.

Costs

9   Costs are awarded on the same basis as in unfair dismissal cases although they seem to be awarded more readily against unsuccessful workers in discrimination cases. Because of the greater length of the latter, costs tend to be larger. There is little that can be done about this except to keep the issues within reasonable bounds and to be aware that if a case is clearly going badly, points should not be laboured. If a costs award has to be argued, point out the matters which called for an explanation from the employer and could only be obtained in the forum of an ET hearing.

0   Costs can be awarded regardless of whether there was a previous costs warning. In fact costs warnings are infrequent in discrimination cases and many ETs are reluctant to hold pre-hearing reviews because they recognise that discrimination is overwhelmingly a matter of evidence, which can be tested only at hearing.

APPENDICES

ET1—conduct
ET1—capability
Assessment of compensation for unfair dismissal
Case study

B   **Indirect race or sex discrimination: possibly discriminatory requirements**

Race discrimination
Sex discrimination

C   **Unfair dismissal case study**

D   **Glossary**

E   **Redundancy payments table**

Running ET cases: checklists and samples

TIMETABLE FOR THE BASIC PROCEDURE

1 Interview worker, take statement, check all documents, check time limits.

2 If appropriate, request written reasons for dismissal and await reply.

3 In case under RRA 1976, SDA 1975 or DDA 1995 send employer a questionnaire, before or within 21 days after case is started. Send chaser letters if there is a delay in answering or answers are inadequate.

4 Start case by sending ET1 to the relevant Regional Office of the Employment Tribunals (see addresses on ET1). ET1 must arrive within the time limit.

5 The ET will send an acknowledgement with a case number. From then on, correspondence with the ET goes to the Assistant Secretary at the regional office.

6 The ET will send the ET1 to the employer and will send a copy of the employer's ET3 to the worker's representative. Expect this two to three weeks after the acknowledgement. (Time-limits apply.)

7 When the ET3 is received, write to the employer asking for further particulars of the ET3, interrogatories (answers to specific questions) and for discovery. Set a time limit, usually 14 days. Send a copy to the ET for information.

8 If the information is not received, write to the ET and ask for an order. The ET will send any order it makes to the employer and a copy to the worker's representative.

9 If the employer does not supply the information as ordered, write to the ET asking that the employer be requested to show cause why the ET3 should not be struck out.

10 Optional: At stage 7, write to employer suggesting a mutual exchange of witness statements 7 to 14 days before the hearing.

11 Some ETs send out standard 'directions' letters with, or soon after, the ET3 setting time-scales for discovery, exchange of witness statements etc. This does not replace the need to make any specific requests. (Stages 7–10 may still apply.)

12 At any time, the ET will notify each side of the hearing date. Minimum 14 days' notice must be given. Inform ET immediately if the date is unsuitable.

13 An ACAS officer will be allocated to the case at the start and will contact the worker's representative and the employer. Negotiation can be through ACAS or direct with the employer. Once an agreement is

concluded, it becomes binding if each side has confirmed it verbally with ACAS. ACAS then tells the ET that the case has been settled. (Check ACAS has done this.) Alternatively, a binding settlement is reached when authorised representatives sign a compromise agreement.

14   If using ACAS, the officer will send a COT3 form for signature. This contains the agreed terms of settlement. Make sure that the worker at all stages knows the terms. If there is no settlement, the case will go to hearing. Any settlement agreed on the day of the hearing does not go to ACAS, but the ET should be asked to make an order in the agreed terms.

15   In good time for the hearing, write to the ET to request any witness orders that are wanted.

16   Prior to the hearing, prepare trial bundles, preferably in agreement with the employer. Each page of the bundle should be numbered.

17   If it has been ordered or there is agreement to do so, exchange witness statements with the other side.

18   At the end of the hearing, the ET will give its decision or reserve judgment and write to the parties later.

19   The ET will either hear evidence relating to liability and compensation all at once or, more usually, will hear just liability and then have a hearing on compensation if the worker wins. Be prepared for both.

20   Remember time limits for review and appeal after the decision if unsuccessful. If successful, interest runs on compensation not paid within 42 days of the decision.

Variations:

a)   The ET may hold a pre-hearing review, usually at an early stage, at which a deposit may be required.

b)   The ET may hold a preliminary hearing on issues of jurisdiction at an early stage which is prepared for and conducted like a full hearing except that it is confined to the preliminary issue.

c)   The ET may hold a hearing for directions with the representatives at any stage, just to sort out what needs to be done, eg, whether an order should be made for further particulars, discovery of documents.

d)   Equal value cases under the EqPA 1970 – similar, but procedure relating to the independent expert, if appointed, is different. In particular, a preliminary hearing is usually held prior to the appointment of the expert.

INITIAL INTERVIEW WITH WORKER SEEKING ADVICE ON DISMISSAL

1   Check what worker wants.

2   Check whether correct contractual/statutory notice was given or pay in lieu (unless gross misconduct).

3   Check whether any outstanding wages or holiday pay due.

4   Check date of dismissal and time limits for possible ET claims. Inform worker and diarise. Where there is a claim of discrimination, prepare a brief chronology, note and diarise the time limit of the last act of dis-

crimination, if it is a continuing act of discrimination, and the earliest act of discrimination if it is a discrete act or acts.

5 Check whether worker qualifies for unfair dismissal (continuous service, status as employee, whether s/he was 'dismissed').

6 If applicable and if worker qualifies, consider redundancy pay claim.

7 Check possibility of unlawful discrimination (no continuous service required).

8 Where likely, eg, where there is a sex discrimination issue, check for unequal pay under EqPA 1970.

9 Check pay-slips. If worker was given none, consider claim for failure to give itemised pay statements. Ask tax authorities and DSS to investigate contributions record so that credited contributions can be requested if necessary. Consider risk of illegal contract.

10 Obtain all relevant documents from worker and take full statement.

11 If appropriate, write initial letter to employer requesting written reasons for dismissal, P45 and monies due.

12 Consider whether anything can be done immediately to secure a good open reference.

13 Check whether worker has appealed.

INTERVIEW OF WORKER WITH RACE OR SEX DISCRIMINATION CLAIM

The following list suggests points that should be established by an adviser when interviewing a worker with a potential race discrimination claim. It can be adapted for sex discrimination cases. The suggestions are for guidance only and must not be followed rigidly. In each case, the facts and what needs to be proved must be carefully considered.

– Ask the worker why s/he thinks s/he was dismissed/disciplined/not promoted or appointed. This helps establish whether the worker believes it is race discrimination, although it may be necessary to ask more overtly. It also helps draw out any non-discriminatory explanation for the employer's conduct.

– Establish what is the worker's nationality or national origin (as relevant under the RRA 1976); what 'racial' group it is that the employer is discriminating against.

– Ask what makes the worker think s/he has been discriminated against. Explain that this is a good question to draw out evidence indicating discrimination. Ask whether there is a direct comparison with a white worker on the relevant incident.

– Establish all acts of discrimination within the last three months (eg, failed promotion applications; unfair appraisals; warnings; dismissal). These can be the basis of the claim.

– Establish all acts of discrimination or evidence of prejudicial attitudes throughout the worker's employment. (Although these cannot form the basis of a claim if more than three months ago, they can be supporting evidence for the main claim.)

- Expressly ask the worker whether any racist remarks were made by any relevant manager, either directly to the worker or in his/her hearing. Ask whether relevant managers demonstrated prejudice in any other way, eg, by differential treatment of staff according to their 'race'.
- Ask whether the worker ever alleged race discrimination and whether that can be proved. Ask for details and the employer's reaction. (This is relevant to credibility of the worker, and of the employer if no action was taken, and to any victimisation claim.)
- Establish who made the relevant decisions and what is the decision-making hierarchy; establish whether any discriminatory patterns among the workforce can be attributed to the same decision-makers (eg, the expression of prejudice by a senior manager is relevant only if that manager has some control over this worker's fate). Avoid 'conspiracy theories', ie, accusing too many senior managers and staff of racism.
- Assess whether there are non-racial explanations for events, eg, the person promoted above the worker was better qualified or was married to the appointing officer, or the worker was unpopular for reasons unconnected with his/her 'race'.
- Try to establish patterns. Patterns in the way the worker has been treated by certain persons in the past compared with how white staff are treated, and in the way other staff of the same 'racial' group are treated and their position in the workforce.
- Establish now rather than later if there are any holes in the patterns, eg, if the managers accused have in the past made senior appointments of persons in the same 'racial' group as the worker, or if black workers are generally highly placed in the employing organisation. Also look at who appointed/promoted the worker in the past and why, if the same manager is now discriminating.
- Ask if the employer has an equal opportunities policy.
- Establish whether direct or indirect discrimination or both is possible.
- Establish whether victimisation took place, ie, whether the worker alleged discrimination in the past and/or during incidents leading to dismissal and/or in any disciplinary hearing prior to dismissal.
- Watch out for sex discrimination – in addition to or instead of race discrimination.
- Establish evidential strength – witnesses, documents, and matters from which inferences could be drawn.
- Establish what information could be usefully obtained on a questionnaire. Ask worker about distribution (and treatment – promotions/ dismissals, etc) of workers of different racial groups in the workforce.
- Establish what the worker wants (particularly if still employed).

INTERVIEW OF WORKER WHO HAS BEEN MADE REDUNDANT

A worker who has been made redundant may only seek advice about the level of redundancy pay. However, s/he may have other rights. The following list suggests suitable areas for exploring.

1 Reasonable time off with pay during notice period to look for fresh employment.
2 Redundancy pay:
 • Check worker is eligible for statutory redundancy pay.
 • Check the calculation.
 • Check if s/he has a greater contractual entitlement.
 • May s/he lose the right to redundancy pay because s/he unreasonably refuses an offer of suitable alternative employment made before the expiry of her contract?
 • May s/he lose the right to redundancy pay if s/he has left before the expiry of her notice period?
  NOTE: there are rules as to the procedure to be followed if the member wants to leave early without losing her pay.
3 Unfair dismissal:
 • Check worker is eligible to claim. Be careful to check a dismissal has taken place as opposed to an agreed termination, eg, in some early retirement/voluntary redundancy situations.
 • Would the worker win? A redundancy dismissal may be unfair if:
  – there was no genuine redundancy situation.
  – unfair selection criteria were used or they were unfairly applied.
  – the employer did not consider alternative employment.
  NOTE: If the worker is made redundant while on maternity leave, s/he must be offered any suitable vacancy.
  – poor procedures were followed and there was no consultation with the individual or Union.
 • How much compensation is the worker likely to receive?
  NOTE: If the worker received a large contractual or voluntary redundancy payment or if s/he obtained a new job very quickly, her unfair dismissal claim may be worth little or nothing.
4 Was the worker selected for redundancy for an automatically unfair reason?
5 If the worker was dismissed for a reason related to pregnancy or maternity, this may be automatic unfair dismissal, which does not require her to have had any minimum length of service.
6 Unlawful discrimination:
 • Check eligibility. (Much wider than for unfair dismissal or statutory redundancy pay.)
 • Has the worker been selected for redundancy due to his/her race or sex or because she is pregnant?
  – have objective criteria been used and objectively applied?
  – would the worker have been selected if s/he had been of a different race or sex?
 • Has the worker been selected on an indirectly discriminatory criterion which cannot be justified, eg, LIFO; part-timers first; 'temps' or 'casuals' first, where these groups are disproportionately black or female.
 • Has the worker been selected for a reason related to her disability which cannot be justified, eg, attendance record?

- Has the worker been selected for redundancy because of recent complaints about discrimination or harassment which have upset the employer? This would be victimisation.
7   Redundancies on a transfer:
- Consider whether or not the Transfer of Undertakings Regulations apply.
- Consider whether claim should be made against new or old employer.
8   Trade Union or employee representatives' consultation.
- For collective redundancies.
- Where the Transfer of Undertakings Regulations apply.
NOTE: Any claim for breaking consultation rules is brought by the Trade Union or appropriate employee representatives on behalf of the workers.

INITIAL INTERVIEW OF WORKER WITH POSSIBLE SEXUAL HARASSMENT CLAIM

This is a sensitive area, with difficulties of law, evidence and the worker's feelings. The checklist below suggests the information which needs to be obtained to make an informed judgement about whether the worker can bring a legal case (or even risk speaking out). It may be best not to ask all the questions in the first interview, but to fix another meeting the next day or very soon after, to speak in more detail. The last part of the checklist suggests how such an interview should be conducted. The same questions will not always be appropriate. The adviser must be thorough in his/her questioning and listen carefully to the answers. This is to ensure that the worker is consistent throughout any grievance and ET case which s/he may take.

1   Questions to find out background information:
- The harasser's job title and working relationship with the worker.
- The nature of the working day. How often the worker has contact with the harasser.
- The general office situation, lay-out and presence of other workers.
- The worker's start date and disciplinary record. [This is sensitive: explain the question about the worker's record is only to see how vulnerable s/he is if management raise the issue.]
2   Questions about the harassment:
- When the harassment started.
- Details and dates of the harassment (verbal and physical). [This requires a sensitive approach as the worker may be embarrassed, particularly with a male representative.]
- Establish what is normal acceptable office behaviour and where the line is drawn.
- Witnesses? Has the worker kept a diary? Has s/he seen/told her GP?
- Has the harasser done the same thing to other workers? Have others complained to management?
- Has the worker said explicitly to the harasser or made it clear in any other way that s/he does not welcome the behaviour?

[Many kinds of behaviour are obviously unwelcome and it is not essential that the worker has said as much to the harasser, but it is helpful if s/he has. Note that although this is important information to know, it is extremely sensitive as the worker may feel s/he is to blame if s/he has not said anything to the harasser. Therefore, do not ask this question until late in the interview when confidence is built. This also gives the worker time to raise it his/herself, which is preferable. If it is necessary to raise the issue first, be sure to give prior reassurance that it would be understandable if the worker had not felt able to say anything.]

- If the worker did tell the harasser, how and when did s/he do so and what was his/her reaction?
- Has the worker raised the matter with anyone in management or told anyone else before? [This question also needs prior reassurance.]

3 Action:
- What does the worker want to do? [This is the most important question of all, and however bad the situation is it is not up to the representative to impose a solution.] [Discussion of options including taking a grievance, going to the ET plus time-limits, informal approach to the harasser, doing nothing but keeping a diary.]

4 Taking a sensitive approach:
- Take the matter seriously and give it the necessary time.
- Be friendly and supportive but formal. Do not be authoritarian or too informal. Both could replicate the harasser's behaviour.
- Take a clear role and explain why sensitive questions are asked before asking them.
- In the first interview, allow the worker to give a broad picture before going back (in this interview or a subsequent interview) to ask for more detail.
- Do not try to get all the information in the first interview – focus on building confidence (although you must find out enough to ensure you do not miss a legal time-limit). Ask more sensitive questions and deal with possible counter-allegations in later interviews after confidence in the adviser has been established.
- To maintain confidence, arrange swift follow-up interviews at the first interview. This is also essential before memories fade and witnesses lose interest.
- In case the worker is embarrassed, offer the opportunity to write down what has happened before discussing it. [*NOTE:* this is not a substitute for spending time talking to the worker.]
- If possible, where the adviser is male, offer the worker the chance to talk to a female adviser. [*NOTE:* this must not be seen as if the representative is not interested or concerned about the matter.]
- Provide reassurance that the worker is entitled to feel upset, that the harasser has behaved unacceptably and that the worker has done nothing wrong.
- Reassure the worker on confidentiality and that nothing will be done

without his/her permission. It is important to take notes, but ask permission first.

- Discuss various options, taking account of what the worker wants, offering appropriate support whatever s/he decides. Take a participative and consultative approach. Address any fear of reprisals.
- Raise with the worker his/her feelings and health and direct him/her to sources of support. The adviser should not attempt to act as an amateur counsellor or suggest the worker needs counselling/psychiatric help in a way which could be understood as meaning the adviser thinks there is something wrong with the worker. Suggestions of sources of support are not an alternative to concrete remedial action.

DO NOT:

- Make assumptions.
- Suggest the worker could be to blame in inviting the harassment.
- Blame the worker for not confronting the harasser or telling the union or management earlier.
- Suggest the worker may be misinterpreting events or being over-sensitive.
- Express any view as to the effect on the harasser or the harasser's wife/partner if the worker makes an allegation.
- Pressurise the worker into taking any form of action.
- If the adviser is a union representative, s/he should not say s/he knows the harasser and is surprised s/he has acted in that way, or express concern that the harasser is a worker of the same union.

INTERVIEW OF WORKER DISMISSED FOR POOR WORK, WITH A VIEW TO ASSESSING POTENTIAL CLAIMS FOR (A) UNFAIR DISMISSAL, (B) DISMISSAL IN FACT BECAUSE SHE IS PREGNANT, AND (C) DISMISSAL IN FACT BECAUSE S/HE IS BLACK

The following list suggests areas for questioning common to many dismissals on grounds of capability or conduct and is designed to highlight the additional questions necessary where discrimination due to pregnancy or race is suspected. Note that questions concerning discrimination are designed to find out if the worker has been treated differently, not just unfairly. The list is for guidance only.

Unfair dismissal:

1 Questions to test eligibility, eg, length of continuous service, whether the worker is an employee.
2 Questions to establish the sequence of events and disciplinary process followed leading up to dismissal.
3 Obtain documents worker has: contract of employment, disciplinary procedure, dismissal letter, other letters relating to the events leading to dismissal, previous warning letters, previous appraisals.
4 Questions to establish the worker's previous work record: previous disciplinary hearings, warnings (alive or lapsed), verbal criticisms, appraisals, compliment letters.

5   The worker's job and duties. The hierarchy and other staff in her department.

6   The nature of the allegations against the worker and his/her response – in the disciplinary hearing and, if different, to you.

7   If relevant, any training the worker has had. Has s/he recently been promoted? If so, what was his/her experience prior to promotion and is s/he being given support and guidance?

8   Dates of all relevant facts plus date of dismissal. (Relevant to show the pattern of events but also for time limits.)

9   What does the worker want to do?

Pregnancy dismissal – extra questions to unfair dismissal list

1   Does worker think dismissal was due to her pregnancy? If so, what makes the worker think that? (This is a useful question, but explain that it is useful to know what she has in mind and that she is not being disbelieved.)

2   Questions to establish whether and when the employer and relevant manager knew the worker was pregnant, eg:
    – when is the baby due?
    – when did the worker tell the employer she was pregnant? who did she tell? was it verbal or in writing?
    – has the worker had time off for pregnancy related ill-health? if so, when and who did she tell?
    – has the worker had time off for ante-natal care? have there been discussions about maternity leave or benefits? with whom? when?

3   Questions to establish if the employer or relevant manager is hostile towards the worker's pregnancy, eg:
    – in any of the above discussions or at any other time, has the employer expressed any irritation about time off or any other aspect of the pregnancy?
    – what did the employer say when the worker first told them of her pregnancy?
    – has there been any problem getting time off for ante-natal care?
    – has the employer/manager's behaviour or attitude towards the worker changed in any way since s/he found out she was pregnant?
    – what is the employer's general attitude towards pregnant workers? what about the particular manager(s) the worker is now dealing with?

4   Questions to establish either that the worker has not performed poor work at all or that other non-pregnant workers have performed equally poor work (or done worse things), yet have not been dismissed. Also ask:
    – how readily does the employer usually discipline or dismiss workers?
    – what sort of offences are usually considered dismissable?
    – compare the disciplinary procedure applied to the worker with any written procedure and with the normal practice adopted by the employer.

5   Where the pregnancy discrimination falls short of dismissal, eg, disciplinary action or non-promotion, ensure the worker seeks advice on

maternity-related matters, eg, how to preserve her right to return after maternity leave, maternity benefits, rights to time-off for ante-natal care, if relevant, rights to health and safety suspension.

6 Regarding what the worker wants to do, will she want to return to work there after her maternity leave? (This may affect how the matter is handled.)

7 *NOTE:* adverse treatment due to pregnancy may also be sex discrimination. For this a worker need not be an employee. Also watch for dates of all adverse treatment as time limits for sex discrimination will run from each detrimental act.

Race discrimination – extra questions to unfair dismissal list

1 Note that the worker need not be an employee to claim race discrimination.

2 Does the worker believe s/he has genuinely been dismissed for poor work or for some other reason?

3 Does the worker think s/he would have been dismissed if s/he was white? If so, what makes the worker think that? (This is a useful question, but explain that it is useful to know what s/he has in mind and that s/he is not being disbelieved.)

4 Questions regarding the ethnic breakdown of the workforce and particularly of the relevant managers.

5 Questions to compare the general treatment of black and white workers, eg, as to the level of disciplinary action and dismissals; recruitment; promotion; general day-to-day behaviour by management. Has anyone else complained of race discrimination previously?

6 Questions to establish either that the worker has not performed poor work at all or that other white workers have performed equally poor work (or done worse things), yet have not been dismissed. Also ask:
  – how readily does the employer usually discipline or dismiss workers?
  – what sort of offences are usually considered dismissable?
  – compare the disciplinary procedure applied to the worker with any written procedure and with the normal practice adopted by the employer.

7 Questions as to the previous treatment of the worker, eg, has the worker been subjected to different or racist treatment or remarks? Has the worker previously alleged race discrimination? If so, when and what happened?

8 Dates of all material incidents because the race discrimination time limit runs from each act of discrimination.

QUESTIONNAIRES – DRAFTING TIPS

The questionnaire procedure is often wasted by asking vague, unimportant and discursive questions. Some sample questionnaires are below, but the following areas of questioning should normally be adopted (particularly in a direct discrimination case):

- Analyse the strengths and weaknesses of the case, noting important facts which are unknown or where it is uncertain whether the employer will agree with or dispute a significant fact. The questionnaire can be used to find out the unknown facts and establish the employer's position.

- Regarding every important decision made by the employer, ask who made the decision, when, who was consulted, and the reasons for the decision.

- Ask questions to find out statistical patterns of discrimination in the workforce, eg, employees according to status, disciplinaries, dismissals, appointments and promotions (as relevant) by reference to race, sex and marital status (as relevant).

- Identify the actions of the employer towards the worker which may be discriminatory or indicate that the worker is being treated differently from others. Ask questions to test whether the employer has treated other workers (by reference to race or sex) differently in similar circumstances. For example:
  - If the worker was disciplined for a certain level of sickness, what is the sickness level of other workers and have they been disciplined?
  - If the employer has refused to allow the worker to take three weeks holiday at one time, how much holiday at one time have other workers been allowed over the last few years? Has anyone else asked for three or more weeks at one time and been refused?
  - If the employer has not shortlisted the worker for a job because s/he lacks a certain qualification, what are the qualifications of other candidates by reference to whether they were shortlisted?
  - If the worker has never been put on any training courses, what courses have other workers doing the same job been offered?

- Anticipate possible innocent explanations by the employer for treating a worker of a different race or sex more favourably. For example:
  - Another worker with a worse sick record than the applicant may not have been so severely disciplined. An obvious reason would be a significant difference in the nature of the illness. Therefore, the question could ask not only the number of days' sickness of other workers and whether disciplined, but the nature of sickness in each case.
  - Regarding training, the explanation may be that other workers have been employed for a longer period and have therefore received more training. Therefore, ask in each case not only what training they have received, but when, and their start date.

- Do not ask excessive questions. The more incidents relevant to the case, the more questions are likely to be necessary. It is dangerous to generalise, but questionnaires involving more than 25 questions are probably too long.

For further guidance, see 'RRA Questionnaires: How to use the Questionnaire Procedure' and 'SDA Questionnaires: How to use the Questionnaire Procedure' by Tamara Lewis. Available from Central London Law Centre, 19 Whitcomb Street, London WC1H 7HA.

RRA QUESTIONNAIRE – FAILED JOB APPLICATION/PROMOTION

Sample questionnaire questions under paragraph 6 in case of direct or indirect race discrimination in failed job application after interview. These questions would not be suitable for a small informal employer.

1   Please supply full details of the job for which the Complainant applied, including duties, responsibilities and pay. Please supply a copy of the job description and contract.

2   Please state the criteria for the selection of an appointee to the post for which the Complainant applied and, in respect of each of these, please state:
    a)   when it was devised or agreed and by whom;
    b)   whether it was put in writing and, if so, when;
    c)   whether it was mandatory that applicants should comply with the said criterion or simply a factor taken into consideration.

3   Please state in detail your procedures for advertising the said post and where and when advertisements appeared.

4   Please list all applications received for the said post, by reference to race,* academic qualifications, previous experience and whether internal or external candidates.

5   Please denote which of those listed at 4 above were:
    a)   shortlisted,
    b)   interviewed, and
    b)   offered the job.

6   Please state who was responsible for shortlisting and the criteria applied.

7   Of each of those interviewed including the Complainant, please state:
    a)   the date of the interview;
    b)   the name and position of each member of the interview panel;
    c)   whether each member of the panel had at any stage received equal opportunities training and, if so, what and when;
    d)   the name and position of each person making the decision whether or not to appoint and whether there was any difference of opinion;
    e)   precisely why the application failed or succeeded as the case may be.

8   Please give the name of any other person consulted in any way or advised of the decisions to appoint or not to appoint interviewees, and please state their role.

9   Why was the Complainant's application unsuccessful?

10   Were there any notes or standard interview forms completed by each appointment committee member at every interview? If yes, please forward copies of all notes and forms relating to all interviewees including the Complainant.

11   Please state by reference to race* and job title the number of employees of the respondents as at [appropriate date].

12   Please state by reference to race,* job title, date of appointment and place of work, the number of persons in the respondent company appointed from outside or promoted from within, to the position for which the Complainant applied or above, within the five years prior to the date of this questionnaire.

13   Please denote which of the above appointments/promotions were made by panels including any of the members of the Complainant's interview panel. Please identify which panel member.
14   Please state whether the respondents operate an equal opportunities policy and, if so, please supply a copy.

Note
*   For 'race' please state under the following categories: (a) colour, (b) nationality, and (c) national and ethnic origin.

RRA QUESTIONNAIRE – DISCIPLINARY DISMISSAL
Sample questionnaire in case of direct discrimination or victimisation in dismissal. Paragraph 2 could also stand as the grounds of an ET1.

Paragraph 2
1   I started working for the respondents in their West End branch on 6 January 1998. I was promoted to manager in April 1998. Throughout my employment, I received no warnings of any kind.
2   On 11 May 1999, I was dismissed. I believe this was discrimination. The reason I was given for my dismissal was that I had claimed taxi fares during the train strike without permission.
3   In the past I had been given travel fares in difficult travel circumstances and I had also given out fares to others. I understood this was in accordance with company policy. There was no secrecy involved, the petty cash slips were signed by myself and sent to head office, and the money was given to me by the chief cashier.
4   A new area manager was appointed in March 1999. On several occasions he told me to get more white staff in the shop. My deputy manager and I were both of Asian background. About half of the remaining staff were white. I told the area manager that I was not prepared to discriminate. When vacancies arose, I could only appoint the best applicants.
5   In April 1999, my deputy manager was suddenly demoted to the position of salesman. Then on 9 May 1999 I was called to a disciplinary hearing regarding my claim for taxi fares. The disciplinary was conducted by the area manager and personnel. I told them I believed this was race discrimination. On 11 May I received a letter notifying me of my dismissal. I subsequently appealed to the regional manager. Again I told him I believed it was race discrimination. My appeal was rejected on 20 May 1999.
6   I believe I have been unlawfully discriminated against contrary to s1(1)(a) and s2 of the Race Relations Act.

Paragraph 6
1   Please state each and every reason why I was dismissed.
2   Please state who took the decision to dismiss me and on what date. Please state anyone else consulted and when.
3   Please state each and every reason why the appeal was upheld.
4   Please state all investigations made into my allegation of race discrimin-

ation (a) during my disciplinary hearing, and (b) during my appeal. In each case, please state what investigation was made, by whom and when, and what was the finding.

5   Please confirm in relation to the allegation against me regarding claiming taxi fares:

   a)   that it is accepted I only claimed taxi fares on train strike days;
   b)   whether it is contended that I was not entitled to the fares at all or whether it is contended that I needed permission;
   c)   if the latter, whether permission would have been granted had I asked;
   d)   please clarify any other respect in which I allegedly broke company policy over claiming the fares;
   e)   please state whether the said policy is verbal or written. If written, please supply a copy. If verbal, please state how and when it was communicated to me;
   f)   please state what is the company's policy regarding when travel can be claimed and the mechanisms. Please include who has authority to give fares to each level of staff.

6   Please state all members of staff who have been given taxi fares on any occasion (i) during the transport strikes in 1999, or (ii) for any other reason, by reference to (a) race,† (b) job title and location, (c) on whose authorisation, and (d) the reason for using the taxi.

7   Please state all staff dismissed from London branches since 1 March 1997. In each case please state: (a) race,* (b) job title and location, (c) nature of offences leading to dismissal, and (d) date of dismissal.

8   Please state all disciplinary action, short of dismissal, taken against London staff since 1 March 1997. In each case, please state: (a) race,* (b) job title and location, (c) date and level of action, and (d) nature of offence.

9   With regard to the demotion of my deputy manager, please state (a) who took the decision and for what reasons, and (b) who was consulted and their views.

10   Please state all staff taken on since 1 March 1997 in London branches by reference to: (a) race,* (b) job title, (c) location placed, and (d) date taken on.

11   Please state all employees as at 11 May 1999 above the level of branch manager in the company by reference to: (a) race,* (b) job title, (c) start date, and (d) location.

12   Please state why the area manager thought there should be more white staff at my branch.

13   Does the company operate an Equal Opportunities Policy? If so, please provide a copy.

Note

†   For 'race' please state under the following categories: (a) colour, (b) nationality, and (c) national and ethnic origin.

RRA QUESTIONNAIRE – REDUNDANCY

Sample questionnaire questions under paragraph 6. The statement of facts is not written in a form appropriate for paragraph 2 or the grounds of an ET1.

Facts

The worker was one of 200 engineers employed across three sites in the Council's maintenance department. On 10 April 1999, he was made redundant together with 15 other engineers across all the sites. He was not individually consulted and does not know how the redundancy selection criteria were applied to him or to other workers. He does not know exactly who was selected for redundancy and whether they were black or white. However, the worker is suspicious because on what he knows about the selection criteria, he would not have expected to be chosen. The worker also has not been redeployed.

Paragraph 6

1. Please state the redundancy selection procedure adopted for the April [*year*] redundancies including the dates of all decisions and consultations and the persons involved.
2. Please state when it was first considered that redundancies might be a possibility.
3. Please state the redundancy selection criteria used, stating in the case of each criterion:
   a) when it was decided to use that criterion and by whom;
   b) the reason for using that criterion;
   c) how the criterion was to be measured and by whom;
   d) how the criterion was weighted.
4. Please state whether a decision was made in advance as to how many engineers should be made redundant. If so, when and by whom.
5. Please list all engineers employed by the Council immediately before the redundancy selection procedure. For each engineer, please state:
   a) their race;*
   b) their job-title, grade and location;
   c) their start date;
   d) whether or not they were made redundant;
   e) the reasons why they were or were not selected for redundancy;
   f) their score on each of the redundancy selection criteria;
   g) whether they applied for redeployment;
   h) details of any job offers made to them for redeployment;
   i) whether or not they were in fact redeployed and if not, why not.
6. Please state specifically with regard to myself:
   a) who decided I would be selected for redundancy and when?
   b) who else was consulted, when and what were their views?
   c) why was I made redundant?
   d) how did I score on each criterion?
   e) why was I not redeployed?‡

Note

‡ If the worker identified a specific redeployment opportunity which he was not offered, ask who decided he could not have that position and why not.

7   Please list all technical or engineering vacancies from 1 January this year to date by reference to job-title, grade, location, date vacant, date filled.

8   Please list all staff taken on to work as engineers for the three years prior to the date of this questionnaire by reference to:
a)   their race;* b)their start date;
c)   their job-title, grade and location.

9   Please state all staff dismissed from (a) the Engineering and Maintenance Department, and (b) the rest of the Council in the three years prior to the date of this questionnaire by reference to:
a)   their race;*
b)   their job-title, grade and location;
c)   the dismissal date;
d)   the reason for dismissal.

10   Please provide details of your Equal Opportunities Policy.

Note

*   Race – please state by reference to (i) black/white; (ii) national or ethnic origin; and (iii) nationality.

SDA QUESTIONNAIRE – RETIREMENT
Questionnaire in case of sex discrimination, by reason of dismissal, of a woman at an earlier retirement age than a man.

Facts
Date of dismissal:	1 December 1998
Age of complainant:	60 years as at 1 December 1998
Occupation:	Accounts clerk in a large company

Questions under paragraph 6
1   Please state by reference to (a) job title, and (b) sex, all staff employed by the respondents as at 1 December 1998 in the following departments:
a)   accounts department;
b)   other departments.

2   Of the above, please state:
a)   the date when employment with the respondents commenced;
b)   the date of birth, or, where unknown, the age of all staff of the age of 59 and above as at 1 December 1998.

3   Please state by reference to (a) job title, (b) sex, (c) date of birth, (d) commencement date, and (e) termination date, all staff whose employment terminated between 1 December 1993 and 1 December 1998 at the age of 59 or above.

4   Please state the normal retirement age, if any, for (a) men and (b) women staff.

5   Please state the contractual basis for requiring the complainant to retire at the age of 60.

6   Please state who made the decision to terminate the complainant's employment at the age of 60. Please name anyone else consulted.
7   Please state whether the respondents operate an equal opportunities policy. If so, please give details.

SDA QUESTIONNAIRE – PREGNANCY
Questionnaire in case of dismissal of a pregnant woman, ostensibly on grounds of capability/conduct, but suspected to be due to pregnancy.

Paragraph 2 questionnaire
1   I have worked as Assistant Manager for Winfield Shoes in their Nottingham Branch since 12 October 1997. Throughout my employment, I received no warnings from my employers, written or verbal.
2   On 20 October 1998, I informed my manager, Tessa Hennessy, that I was pregnant. On 21 November 1998, I was off sick. I telephoned Jane Baxter of personnel and explained that I would not be in because I felt sick due to my pregnancy.
3   On 24 November 1998 I was sent a letter requiring me to attend a disciplinary hearing on 26 November 1998. This came out of the blue and was a complete shock to me.
4   At the disciplinary meeting held on 26 November 1998 I was dismissed. The reasons given to me were poor supervision of staff, poor time-keeping and taking too many personal phone calls. These allegations were untrue. My appeal to the managing director on 3 December 1998 also failed. I believe I was dismissed due to my pregnancy.

Paragraph 6 questionnaire
1   Do you accept that I told Tessa on or about 20 October 1998 that I was pregnant? If not, when does Tessa say she first found out I was pregnant and how does she say she found out?
2   Do you accept that I told Jane Baxter on 21 November 1998, when I telephoned in sick, that I was pregnant? If not, what does Jane Baxter say I told her?
3   Please list every person within the company who knew before my dismissal that I was pregnant. In each case, please state when and how they had found out.
4   In respect of the decision to dismiss me, please state:
    a) who took the decision and when;
    b) who was consulted and what were their views;
    c) every reason for my dismissal.
5   In respect of the decision to reject my appeal, please state:
    a) who took the decision and when;
    b) who was consulted and what were their views;
    c) every reason for rejecting my appeal.
6   Please set out every alleged instance with dates of (a) poor staff supervision, (b) poor time-keeping, and (c) receiving personal telephone calls.
7   Please set out the company policy regarding taking personal telephone calls.

8   Do you have an equal opportunities policy? If so, please provide details.
9   Please state all dismissals and disciplinary action by the company since 1 January 1995, stating in each case (a) job title and location of person dismissed, (b) age of any children under five years, (c) sex of person dismissed and whether pregnant or on maternity leave at the time, (d) date and nature of disciplinary action, and (e) nature of offence.

Notes

With reference to questions 1 to 3: In post-dismissal correspondence, the managing director denies that the company knew the applicant was pregnant prior to her dismissal. If this happens or if it is possible that the company will deny knowledge, then questions should be asked to pin down its position.

It will not always be appropriate to ask such blunt questions, but on these facts, it is possible that early questions will get a truthful answer. If there has been no prior indication from the employer that it will deny knowledge, it may be better not to encourage denial by such questions. Instead, if the statement at paragraph 2 sets out when the complaint did tell the employer, then the employer's response should contain any denial.

SDA QUESTIONNAIRE – SEXUAL HARASSMENT

Paragraph 2 questionnaire

The applicant worked for the respondent council in their Homeless Persons Unit. From September 1997, she was sexually harassed by her supervisor, Mr Briggs. [*Cite incidents.*] On 13 February 1999, the applicant informed personnel of the harassment. An investigation was carried out, during which the applicant was instructed to remain off work. On 1 March 1999, the applicant was told that the outcome of the investigation was inconclusive.

On 9 April 1999, the applicant was required by Mr Briggs to attend a disciplinary hearing for poor work performance. She was issued with a final written warning. The applicant believes that this was victimisation contrary to SDA s4 because she had accused him of sexual harassment. Furthermore, the applicant believes the harassment carried out by Mr Briggs constituted unlawful direct discrimination contrary to SDA 1975 s1(1)(a).

Paragraph 6 questionnaire

1   Please state clearly and in detail which parts of para 2 are admitted and which are denied.
2   Please state all steps taken to investigate my allegations including all meetings and interviews with dates and persons involved.
3   In relation to every member of staff spoken to as part of the investigation, please state:
   a)   their name;
   b)   who spoke to them and on what date(s) and time(s);
   c)   whether anyone else was present;
   d)   what they were told about the allegations;
   e)   what they were asked and what they responded;
   f)   whether statements were made and their dates. (If so, please supply copies.)

4   Please state fully every finding of the respondents as a result of the investigation, indicating who made each finding and on what basis and on what date.

5   If any of my allegations were disbelieved, please state which and give reasons.

6   Was any action taken against Mr Briggs or any advice given to him following the investigation? If so, please specify.

7   Please state when Mr Briggs was first informed of my allegations and by whom.

8   Please state whether Mr Briggs was suspended during the investigation and if so, when.

9   With regard to Mr Briggs, please state (a) his start date, and (b) his job title and location throughout his employment with dates.

10 Please state all warnings or other disciplinary action taken against Mr Briggs at any stage in his employment including any informal counselling, giving in each case:
    a) its date;
    b) the level of warning;
    c) who decided upon it;
    d) the offence to which it related.

11 Please state all grievances, formal or informal, taken against Mr Briggs by any member of staff during his employment, in each case giving (a) the date, (b) the nature of the grievance, (c) whether male or female complaining, and (d) the outcome of the grievance.

12 Please state whether any other allegations of sexual harassment have been made by any Council employee in the last six years, formally or informally. If so, please state (a) the date, (b) the name of the alleged perpetrator, (c) whether the perpetrator was disciplined, (d) the job title and location of the employee making the allegation, and (e) whether she remained with the council. If not, when did she leave and why. (Please also give details if she was transferred to another job within the council.)

13 Please state the number of staff in the department as at 1 March 1999 by reference to (a) gender, and (b) job title and grade.

14 Please state all staff in the department in the last five years who have resigned, been disciplined or dismissed. In each case please state:
    a) whether male or female;
    b) whether resignation, dismissal or disciplinary action and date;
    c) if resignation, reason given;
    d) if dismissal or disciplinary action, nature of offence.

15 With regard to the decision to issue me with a final written warning, please state:
    a) who made the decision and when;
    b) whether anyone else was consulted. If so, when and what were their views;
    c) every reason for the warning;
    d) in relation to the criticism of my work, please specify precisely what was wrong with my work, giving dates and details.

16   Does the council operate (a) an equal opportunities policy, and (b) a harassment policy? If so, please provide a copy and details.

RRA REQUEST FOR DISCOVERY

Sample request for discovery in a case of alleged race discrimination in promotion or job application where the complainant failed to obtain a post after interview.

1   All notes made at any time by the members of the shortlisting and interview panels relating to the candidates who applied for and were appointed to the post.
2   All documents including application forms which were before the short-listing and interview panels for the said post.
3   Any memorandum or report written to or by any member of the interview panel relating to each of the said appointments.
4   All references written on behalf of the applicant and the successful candidate.
5   Any other notes, memoranda, letters or documents relating to the selection process for the post, including job description and person specification.
6   The advertisements placed for the post.
7   Any rules or regulations governing procedures for the appointment of employees of the respondents.
8   Any documents relating to the respondents' equal opportunities policy.
9   All other documents on which the respondents intend to rely at the hearing.

SAMPLE LETTER CHASING QUESTIONNAIRE REPLIES

Address the letter to the employer's representative, if known, and otherwise to the chief executive or managing director.

Dear Madam/Sir,

Thank you for your reply to the questionnaire dated 21 January, seven weeks after it was sent to the Health Authority.

I am concerned that the Health Authority has not answered questions 13 to 15 inclusive. It must be possible from conducting a simple 'head count' to answer question 13. Matters raised in question 14, and certainly in question 15, must be within the memory of senior staff, at least in part.

I would remind you of the provisions of section 65 of the Race Relations Act 1976. The employment tribunal is entitled to draw an adverse inference from a late or evasive answer to a questionnaire. I will be drawing this letter to the attention of the tribunal at the hearing and I would ask the Authority to reconsider its position.

Yours faithfully,

UNFAIR DISMISSAL *AND* DIRECT AND INDIRECT RACE DISCRIMINATION

ET1 grounds of application

1 The respondents operate a chain of fast-food restaurants in central London. The applicant worked as manager at various branches since his engagement in 1992. At the time of his dismissal, the applicant was working at the Piccadilly branch.

2 The applicant is of Algerian national origin.

3 On 5 November 1998, the applicant was told that his employment would be terminated by reason of redundancy on the closure of his branch on 17 November.

4 The applicant was not consulted at any time prior to his dismissal as to the possibility of employment at any of the respondents' other restaurants. Other staff in the applicant's branch who were white and of British national origin were redeployed within the respondents' organisation.

5 During a conversation in September 1998, the respondents' area manager told the applicant that the respondents had started to 'professionalise' their operation and bring in managers with catering qualifications from recognised UK colleges.

6 Having regard to the size and administrative resources of the respondents, the applicant's dismissal was unfair. The applicant was unfairly selected for redundancy. Furthermore, the respondents failed to consult with the applicant concerning the possibilities of alternative employment and failed to offer such employment.

7 Furthermore, the applicant was dismissed on the ground of his race contrary to Race Relations Act 1976 s1(1)(a).

8 Further or in the alternative, the applicant was subjected to indirect discrimination in his dismissal contrary to Race Relations Act 1976 s1(1)(b) in that the respondents applied a condition of retaining his services that he hold a UK catering qualification.

Questionnaire questions under paragraph 6

1 Why was the applicant dismissed?

2 Who took the decision to dismiss the applicant and when?

3 When did the respondents take the decision to close the Piccadilly restaurant?

4 In relation to all staff employed at the Piccadilly restaurant as at 1 November 1998, please state their race,* job title, date of engagement by the respondents, whether dismissed on closure of the branch, and if redeployed, where.

5 Please provide a list of all the respondents' branches as at 17 November 1998.

6 Please list all vacancies within the respondents' organisation in the posts of manager, deputy manager, assistant manager or supervisor, between 1 September 1998 and 1 March 1999.

7   Please state all dismissals from 17 November 1995 to date by reference to (a) race,* (b) job title, and (c) reason for dismissal.

8   In relation to all appointments or promotions made to the posts of branch supervisor and above from 17 November 1995 to date, please state (a) race,* (b) job title, (c) whether external appointment or internal promotion, (d) branch to which appointed, and (e) academic and catering qualifications held.

9   In relation to all existing employees as at 17 November 1998 in post as supervisor or above, please state their (a) race,* (b) job title, (c) date of engagement, and (d) any catering qualifications held.

10   When was it decided that branch managers should have catering qualifications and by whom and for what reasons?

11   Do the respondents have an equal opportunities policy? If so, please supply a copy.

Note

*   For 'race' please state under the following categories: colour, nationality, and national origin. Please indicate which are Algerian.

CHECKLIST ON THE DEFINITION OF 'DISABILITY' UNDER THE DDA 1995

NOTE: Unless the worker is obviously covered by the DDA, it will be important carefully to interview him/her with the following checklist in mind.

• Check whether the worker was registered disabled on the relevant dates and therefore deemed to be disabled.[1] The remainder of this Checklist applies to workers who are not deemed to be disabled.

• Check the worker has an 'impairment' which is either physical or mental.

• If it is a mental impairment which results from or consists of a mental illness, check whether that illness is clinically well-recognised.[2]

• Check none of the excluded conditions apply.[3]

• Check that the impairment has adverse effects on the worker's ability to carry out one or more of the following normal day-to-day activities:[4]

    – mobility;
    – manual dexterity;
    – physical co-ordination;
    – continence;
    – ability to lift, carry or otherwise move everyday objects;
    – speech, hearing or eyesight;
    – memory or ability to concentrate, learn or understand;
    – perception of the risk of physical danger.

Notes

1   DDA Sch 1 para 7; Guidance Part I, para 9; para 13.23 above.
2   DDA Sch 1(1); see Guidance Part I, paras 13–15 and para 13.15 above.
3   Part I, para 8 of the Guidance; para 13.14 above.
4   DDA Sch 1 para 4(1).

- Check the affected activity is a 'normal' activity as opposed to, for example, a specialised hobby or particular form of work.[5]
- Remember that the worker may have adopted coping strategies to avoid carrying out the affected activity. Therefore, it may not immediately be obvious that such normal activity is affected.[6]
- The focus should be on what the worker cannot do, not on what s/he can do.[7]
- Check whether the worker's ability to carry out the normal activity is 'substantially' affected, ie, the effect is clearly more than trivial.[8]

    It is unnecessary that the worker is completely unable to carry out the activity. For example:
    - the worker can only carry out the activity more slowly than usual;
    - the worker cannot sustain the activity due to depression;[9]
    - the worker can only carry out the activity in a particular way;
    - it is tiring or painful to carry out the activity;[10]
    - the worker has medical advice not to attempt the activity.[11]
- Remember that the worker may have 'played down' the true effect of his/her disability on his/her daily life, or may have adjusted his/her life to avoid the need to carry out the activity.[12]
- Remember that if the worker has a progressive condition, s/he is protected as soon as that condition has any adverse effect, even if that effect is not yet substantial.[13]
- Consider whether the worker can only carry out an activity without substantial adverse effect due to medical treatment or an aid (except for glasses correcting eye-sight).[14]
- *Note:* if the worker has a severe disfigurement, it is treated as having substantial adverse effect on normal day-to-day activities, unless this is a tattoo or ornamental body-piercing.[15]
- Consider whether the effect of the impairment on the activity is long-term, ie, for 12 months or the rest of the worker's life.[16]
- Remember that impairments with recurring substantial effects may be

---

Notes

5 See Part II, section C of the Guidance.
6 *Goodwin v The Patent Office* [1999] IRLR 4, EAT; see also the Guidance, section A7–8.
7 *Goodwin v The Patent Office* (see above).
8 See the Guidance, Part II, Section A; *Goodwin v The Patent Office* (see above).
9 Guidance, section C7.
10 Guidance, section C6.
11 Guidance, section C6.
12 *Goodwin v The Patent Office* (see above).
13 DDA Sch 1 para 8; Guidance, Part II, section A15; para 13.21 above.
14 DDA Sch 1 para 6; Guidance, Part II, section A11–14; para 13.20 above.
15 DDA Sch 1 para 3; Guidance, Part II, section A16–17.
16 DDA Sch 1 para 2(1).

covered, even though the effect is only for a short period at any one time.[17]

- Consider whether it is necessary to seek medical advice or obtain medical evidence on the above matters.[18]

DDA 1995 – OVERALL CHECKLIST

Note: this checklist cannot cover every aspect of the law.

- Is the worker eligible to claim under the DDA.
  - Check whether the employer is covered by the small employers' exemption.
  - Check the worker has a disability under the DDA.[19]
  - Check the worker's condition is not specifically excluded.[20]
- Has the employer treated the worker less favourably for a reason related to his/her disability?[21]
  - Pin down the employer's reason, ideally in writing.
  - Is it related to the worker's disability?
- Can the employer justify his/her treatment of the worker?
  - Is the justification relevant to the worker's own case?
  - Is the justification a substantial reason or a minor or trivial one?
  - Has the employer complied with any duty of reasonable adjustment?
- Has the employer discriminated by failing to comply with a duty of reasonable adjustment?[22]
  - Does the employer owe a duty of reasonable adjustment?
  - If the worker was dismissed, are there reasonable adjustments which the employer should have made prior to dismissal?
  - Can the worker prove the employer knew or should have known that the worker has a disability and that an adjustment may be required?
  - Consider possible adjustments which may assist the worker.[23] (Discuss with the worker, the worker's GP and any relevant specialist organisation.)
  - Is it reasonable to expect the employer to make the adjustment?[24]
- Can the employer justify failing to make a reasonable adjustment?
- Has the worker been victimised, eg, discriminated against for complaining of discrimination under the DDA?[25]
- If so, can the employer defend a claim by showing the worker's allegation was false and made in bad faith?

Notes

17　DDA Sch 1 para 2(2); Guidance, Part II, section B3–B9; para 13.22 above.
18　See sample letter below.
19　See Checklist above.
20　See Checklist above.
21　DDA s5(1).
22　DDA s5(2).
23　Check list of suggestions at DDA s6; para 13.33 above.
24　Consider factors in DDA s6(4); para 13.35 above.
25　DDA s55.

- Overall consider what medical and other evidence may be necessary.
- Can the cost of medical evidence be covered?
- Is the worker willing and able to bring an ET case?
- What outcome would the worker want?
- Note time-limits.
- Consider writing a Questionnaire.
- Does the worker have any other legal claims, eg, unfair dismissal?
- When writing the ET1, if the facts allow, state the case as under s5(1) and/or under s5(2).[26]

DDA 1995 – SAMPLE LETTER TO GP

NOTE that this is not a standard letter. The letter would vary according to the facts and how obvious the worker's disability and symptoms are. In some cases, it will be appropriate to write a shorter letter focusing on very specific points of concern.

Dear Dr . . . .

  I am advising A regarding a potential claim against her employers under the Disability Discrimination Act 1995. In order for me to assess whether A is covered by the Act, I should be grateful if you would write a Report concerning her condition and covering the following points.

1. Please could you specify the nature of the impairment from which A suffers.
2. Please could you comment on whether A's ability to carry out day-to-day activities in any of the following respects is adversely affected to a substantial degree:
   a) mobility;
   b) manual dexterity;
   c) physical co-ordination;
   d) continence;
   e) ability to lift or move everyday objects;
   f) speech, hearing or eyesight;
   g) memory or ability to concentrate, learn or understand;
   h) perception of the risk of physical danger.
   Please could you confirm that any such effect is substantial as opposed to trivial or minor.
3. If A's condition is controlled by medication or aids, please could you also state how A's abilities under the above categories would be affected were she not taking any medication.
4. The Act protects workers where the effect of the impairment has lasted at least 12 months or is likely to last for 12 months or for the rest of A's life, if less. Recurring effects are also covered, ie, if the effect lasts less than 12 months but is likely to recur. Please could you clarify when the substantial adverse effects started to apply to A and when they ceased or, if they have not yet ceased, when they are likely to cease.

Note

26 See sample below.

5. A has told me that she has particular difficulties with mobility. Could you please especially address this point and let me know whether you would expect her:
    i)   to have difficulty using public transport;
    ii) to be able to travel a short journey in a car;
    iii) to have difficulty going up or down stairs.
    Would the position be any different if she were not taking medication?

6. Do you have any suggestions as to adjustments to A's working conditions which may be of assistance to her?

I enclose A's written authorisation for you to disclose the above information to me. Please feel free to telephone should you wish clarification.

Yours sincerely,

NOTE: Where the adviser is aware of an area of difficulty for A, s/he may wish to guide the doctor further, eg, by reference to the examples in the Guidance from C14 to C21. Paragraph 5 is an example of this. Alternatively, if the worker is suffering from a mental illness, it may be necessary to ask whether the doctor considers it is well-recognised clinically.

If the GP's letter is to be shown to the employer, the worker must think carefully about its implications. If the letter suggests that the worker cannot do the job at all, but no adjustments are feasible, this could lead to difficulties.

DDA 1995 – ET1

Grounds of application where a discriminatory dismissal can be pleaded under both s5(1) and s5(2) of the DDA 1995.

1   I worked as a messenger for my employers from 17 May 1989 until my dismissal on 12 May 1999. I was dismissed because I reached 30 days sickness absence in each of my last three years of employment under the Sickness Monitoring Procedure. However, nearly all my sickness absences were due to bronchial asthma.

2   My employers were a large company employing over 1,000 members of staff. There were ten other messengers who did the same job as I did. If any messenger was absent through sickness, the others would cover the work on overtime. There was also an agency which supplied workers at short notice in emergencies.

3   The messengers were based in a small office with poor ventilation. I told my employers several times that this aggravated my asthma.

4   Apart from my sickness, I have had no warnings throughout my employment. Indeed, I have often been complimented on my good work.

5   I believe I have been discriminated against contrary to s5(1) of the Disability Discrimination Act 1995 in that I was dismissed due to my attendance record, which was almost entirely related to my disability (asthma).

6   Further or alternatively, I have been discriminated against contrary to s5(2) of the Disability Discrimination Act 1995 by my employers' failure to make adjustments in the terms and arrangements on which I was employed, for example, by (i) basing me in an office with better ventilation, and/or (ii) discounting my disability-related absences when applying the Sickness Monitoring Procedure to me, and/or (iii) any other reasonable adjustment.

SAMPLE WITNESS STATEMENT IN RACIAL HARASSMENT CASE

In reality, an applicant's witness statement may be longer than the following example. A description of the applicant's duties should also be added. The following, however, gives an idea as to style and content. Note how the statement draws attention to the differences in his treatment before and after the main discriminator (Ricky Johnson) started and also compares his treatment in detail with that of a white comparator (Peter Scholar). In discrimination cases, different treatment is more significant than unfair treatment.

SAYED MEGALI: WITNESS STATEMENT

Background

1   I was born in Egypt and I grew up there. I came to England in 1974. I have British nationality. I was employed as a room service waiter in Herberts Hotel for 16 years. I was promoted to supervisor after three years. Then after another three years I became senior supervisor. I never had any disciplinary action taken against me nor did I take any grievances.

2   In 1990 I left the job to return to Egypt for family reasons. When I came back to England in 1991, I started working as security guard for various agencies. On 15 October 1993, I started work as security guard for Matts Hotel.

3   I was already well-known in the hotel. I had worked as a casual waiter since 1991. I got on well with everyone. The hotel asked about me in the catering department before they took me on in security.

4   Robert Keen started one week before me as Chief of Security. Before Ricky Johnson started, I used to get on well with Robert Keen. Ricky Johnson started in July 1997 as Assistant Chief Security Officer. Ricky Johnson and Robert Keen are both white and English.

Ricky Johnson

5   Ricky Johnson was hostile and abusive from the beginning. If there was any news story about the Middle East or Arabs or if there were Arab guests in the hotel, he used to say, 'Fucking Arabs'.

6   Gradually Robert Keen became more and more hostile to me. For example, Robert Keen kept saying, 'I am fed up with you. Why don't you go back to Egypt?' He never used to talk like that before.

7   Before Ricky Johnson came, Robert Keen was helpful when I wanted to

pray. He even said, 'Sayed, I will be in the office for a while, you can go and pray.' He also let me take Fridays as one of my off-days so I could go to the mosque. After Ricky Johnson came, all this stopped, but Robert Keen gave Ricky every Saturday off so he could watch football.

8   One day in August or September 1997, I saw a PG Tips card with a picture of a monkey put up on the wall where we make tea. Ricky Johnson used to buy the tea. I took it down and threw it away, but a few weeks later, when a new packet of tea was bought, a new monkey card was put up. I asked Ricky Johnson if he put it there. He denied it, but I believe it was him. It never happened before he came.

9   On 30 October 1997, I wrote to the hotel manager (Frank Alexander) taking out a grievance for race discrimination against Ricky Johnson. Mr Alexander acknowledged my letter on 2 November 1997 and said that his secretary would contact me to arrange an appointment to meet.

10   On 14 November 1997, I received a letter from personnel calling me to a disciplinary the next day. I had worked in security for four years and as a casual waiter for the hotel since 1991. This was the first time I had been called to a disciplinary.

11   The letter said that the disciplinary was because Ricky Johnson said I had shouted and sworn at him. I told personnel at the disciplinary that this was not true. I said that he had made the accusation because I had taken out the grievance of race discrimination. At the end of the disciplinary, personnel decided to take no action.

12   I met Mr Alexander on 28 November 1997 to talk about my grievance. The meeting was for about one hour. Mr Alexander said he would investigate and come back to me, but he never did come back to me about it afterwards.

The new security guard

13   In January 1998, a new security guard, Peter Scholar, was recruited. Peter was white/English. Peter was very young, about 22 years old. He had not worked in Security for as long as I had. I knew Peter Scholar. He had worked at the hotel for six months in 1997 for an independent security company employed by the hotel's building contractors. His main job was to stop the builders using the staff entrance. He had to search the builders when they went out with a bag. He also patrolled the hotel to keep an eye on the builders.

14   Right from the start, Peter Scholar was treated better than I was in many ways. He was paid more than I, even though we were supposed to be doing the same job. Then in April 1999, he was given a rise and I did not get a rise.

15   In the first week Peter Scholar started, Ricky Johnson took him to a hotel management meeting. All the senior hotel managers go to that meeting every Friday. I have never been taken to it. The previous day I had heard Ricky tell Peter he would take him to the meeting so that he could cover if Robert Keen or Ricky Johnson were not there.

16   Before Peter Scholar started, the hotel's internal telephone directory

only listed Robert Keen and Ricky Johnson by name under Security. After Peter started, his name was put on the list too. I was still not named. I was just 'Back Door Security'.

17   When there is an important function in the ballroom, sometimes they need extra security. I was never given a chance to do this. It was always Robert Keen or Ricky Johnson or outside security. I was not asked. But in his first or second week, Peter Scholar was allowed to do a ballroom function.

18   I saw Ricky Johnson show Peter Scholar how to use the computer several times in his first few weeks. Ricky spent more time with Peter than he spent showing me.

19   In February 1999, the number of the safe in the security office was changed. Peter Scholar was given the new number, but I was not. I asked Robert Keen why he changed the safe number. He said it was because there were important papers there. He would not give me the number. This had never happened before. Later he told Mr Alexander he changed the safe number because of an electronic fault, but he did not say that to me and he did not give me the new safe number until Mr Alexander intervened.

20   In April 1999, Peter Scholar received a pay-rise. Most of the other hotel staff also received a rise – though some did not. Robert Keen and Ricky Johnson also received a rise, so the whole security department except me got a rise. I had received a rise every April since I started. This April I did not get a rise.

21   I have continued to be harassed by Ricky Johnson. [*Give full dates and details of incidents.*] Robert Keen has also started to criticise my work and threaten me with disciplinary action. [*Give full dates and details of incidents.*] Until Ricky Johnson started, Robert Keen had never made any serious criticisms of my work or threatened disciplinary action.

22   Until all this happened, I was never off sick from work, even for one day. All the pressure and harassment for so long have damaged my health. On 5 May 1999, my doctor told me I was not fit for work due to depression. I was off sick for four weeks.

23   I really did not want to go to the tribunal. I wrote so many letters. I told the hotel I would prefer to sort it out. But in the end they gave me no option. I have found it very hard to go to work over the last few years. Every day I wondered if I was going to get a letter accusing me of doing something wrong or a disciplinary. It is very stressful. In the end, I became very depressed. I have never been depressed before. I am not that kind of person.

SIGNED . . . .

DATED . . . .

EXTRACTS FROM SAMPLE WITNESS STATEMENT OF TRADE UNION OFFICIAL IN SUPPORT OF APPLICANT'S RACE DISCRIMINATION CASE

As well as establishing the facts and events in which the official was involved, this statement draws attention to all the ways in which the employers' behaviour differed from what normally occurs (with white staff). In discrimination cases, it is more relevant to highlight different behaviour than unfair behaviour. The statement also establishes the basis of experience from which the official is able to generalise and draw distinctions.

1   I am Branch Secretary of the [*name*] trade union, based at [*name*] Council. I have held that position for approximately four years. I have been a member of the local trade union committee since 1991. I have been involved in a multitude of investigations and disciplinaries of Council staff as their trade union representative.

2   The housing department, where the applicant works, comprises 120 members of staff. Although approximately one-third of the staff are black or from minority ethnic groups, nearly all the managers are white. The trade union has taken up equal opportunities issues with management on several occasions. [*Describe incidents revealing management in a bad light on equal opportunities policies.*]

3   I was involved in the events concerning the applicant from the beginning. My first involvement was on [*date*] when A was notified of disciplinary action.

4   [*Describe sequence of events with dates, official's role and how much information was given to the official and/or the member by management.*]

5   It is very unusual to have a disciplinary hearing without a prior investigation. Normally the investigation is carried out first and the accused person is told about the investigation and what the allegations are. The disciplinary then takes place if and when the investigation reveals there is enough to justify it. It was also extraordinary not even to know the allegations against the applicant until just before the disciplinary hearing.

6   Another unusual aspect was [*Describe all procedural irregularities which took place*].

7   [*If official has anything useful to say regarding the disciplinary allegations themselves, insert here.*]

WRITTEN SUBMISSION TO ET REGARDING DISCRIMINATION TIME-LIMITS

Discrimination cases often concern a number of incidents, some or all of which apparently occurred more than three months before the tribunal claim was lodged. The adviser may need to make verbal or written arguments to the tribunal at a preliminary hearing or at the full hearing as to why the incidents should be allowed in time as grounds of the claim. The following model may be useful, though advisers should watch out for more case-law developments on time-limits.

Grounds of application
[*NOTE: This does not draw attention to time-limit issues at this stage.*]

1   On 11 January 1999, the applicant failed in his attempt for promotion on grounds of his poor sick record. The applicant is black. As the successful candidate's sickness record was only two days less than the applicant's, and the applicant was otherwise more experienced and qualified for the post, the applicant believed this was due to direct race discrimination.

2   The applicant immediately lodged a grievance complaining of race discrimination, which was heard and rejected on 10 February 1999. Moreover, the applicant was informed that he could not apply for any other promotion vacancies until he achieved a clean sickness record for 12 months. The applicant believes this was direct discrimination and/or victimisation.

3   On 12 February 1999, the applicant appealed against the outcome of his grievance. Due to delays by his employers, the appeal was not heard until 28 April 1999. The applicant was not informed that his appeal was unsuccessful until 5 May 1999. The applicant believes that the delays and refusal of his grievance were further acts of discrimination and/or victimisation.

Written submissions regarding time-limits
[*NOTE: These submissions should not normally be included in the grounds of application, but are for any preliminary hearing or the full hearing, when the issue may arise.*]

The law

A   The applicant's contention will be that:
   a)   the grounds of his claim are not in fact out of time;
   b)   if the tribunal believes that any such grounds are out of time, the tribunal is asked to exercise its discretion to allow them in as a late claim;
   c)   in any event, the applicant will refer to such matters as are out of time as supporting evidence for those grounds which are in time (*Eke v Commissioners of Customs & Excise* [1981] IRLR 334, EAT).

B   In deciding whether or not the applicant's claims are in time, the tribunal is asked to consider the legal principles in the following cases:
   a)   Where a grievance procedure is initiated in response to a discriminatory act, the original discriminatory act is within time until three months from the final outcome of the grievance (*Ford Motor Co Ltd v Shah EAT*/530/95).
   b)   A discriminatory act extends over a period of time if it takes the form of some policy, rule or practice, in accordance with which decisions are taken from time to time (*Owusu v LFCDA* [1995] IRLR 574, EAT; approved by CA in *Cast v Croydon College* [1998] IRLR 318).

C   The tribunal is asked to exercise its discretion to allow in any out of time matters on the following grounds:
   a)   As the tribunal will be aware, the legal test for whether it should allow a late claim is wider than for unfair dismissal cases. The test is

not whether it was reasonably practicable for the applicant to have started his claim in time. The test is whether it is just and equitable in all the circumstances to allow a late claim.

b) Any out of time incidents will need to be dealt with as supporting evidence in any event. The issues before the tribunal will therefore be the same and will need to be resolved in any event. There will be no additional time or cost for the respondents.

c) The respondents have been aware from the outset of all the matters in dispute, they form a continuous sequence of events. The respondents have dealt with such matters in grievances. There is therefore no problem in having to remember facts unexpectedly raised from the past.

d) The EAT has encouraged the use of internal procedures in an attempt to resolve matters prior to resorting to the law. The applicant should not be penalised for taking this course and an ET should usually view it as just and equitable to allow an extension (*Aniagwu v Hackney LBC & Owens* [1999] IRLR 303, EAT; *Osaje v Camden LBC* (1997) EAT/317/96).

e) For the above reasons, the respondents have not been prejudiced by the fact of any delay in starting these proceedings. By contrast, the applicant would be severely prejudiced by not having the very serious matters he raises adjudicated upon.

The grounds in this case

The applicant's originating application was faxed to the Employment Tribunal on 10 July 1999.

1   *Ground*: Refusal of promotion on 11 January 1999.
This refusal is in time because the tribunal claim was lodged within three months of the final outcome of the grievance related to the promotion (*Ford v Shah*). Alternatively, the ET is asked to exercise its discretion to allow in a late claim on the principles of *Aniagwu* and *Osaje*. The respondents are not prejudiced by any delay in starting the tribunal case as they have known about the issues throughout.

2   *Ground*: Refusal of grievance on 10 February 1999.
See comments at 1 above.

3   *Ground*: Application of ban on promotion applications.
This act of discrimination continued into the three months prior to the lodging of the tribunal claim and is therefore not out of time (*Owusu v LFCDA*).

4   *Ground*: Refusal of grievance appeal.
This occurred within three months before the tribunal claim was lodged.

5   *Ground*: Delays in hearing the grievance appeal.
These delays continued until the final notification of the outcome of the appeal (*Owusu*). Alternatively, it is just and equitable to allow in a late claim (*Osaje*; *Aniagwu*).

ET1 – CONDUCT

Grounds of application

1   The applicant commenced employment on 1 February 1993 as a kitchen porter at the respondent's restaurant situated in London WC2. The applicant was promoted on three separate occasions and at the time of his dismissal he was employed in the capacity of head chef.[1]

2   At no time during the currency of the applicant's employment did he receive any written or verbal warnings as to his conduct or capability.[2]

3   On 26 August 1999 at about 3 pm the applicant had cause to complain to a waitress about an order which was not removed from the service lift. This service lift is the method by which food prepared in the kitchen can be transferred from the basement to the restaurant on the ground floor.

4   The applicant had told the waitress 'not to leave the bloody food in the service lift'. This was not said in an aggressive, loud or offensive manner and such language was commonplace among the staff and managers in the restaurant.[3]

5   The assistant manager overheard the conversation and told the applicant not to speak to other members of staff in this manner. There was no apparent explanation for the assistant manager's intervention which was both offensive and abusive. At the conclusion of this conversation the assistant manager left the kitchens.

6   In or about January the previous year (when the menu prices were increased in the respondent's restaurant), the applicant sought an increase in his salary. The applicant repeated this request thereafter on a number of occasions. As a consequence of these requests, the respondent's management, and in particular the assistant manager, subjected the applicant to similar demonstrations of capricious and arbitrary conduct as set out in paragraph 5 above.[4]

7   At about 5.50 pm on 26 August the manager came down to the kitchen and told the applicant that he was being dismissed for being abusive to the assistant manager. The applicant endeavoured to discuss the incident with the manager but was told that there was no point as he had been dismissed. The applicant asked the manager to speak to two of the

---

Notes

1   If the worker has been promoted or commended during his/her employment, state this.

2   If there have been no warnings during the worker's employment, state this.

3   Anticipate the employer's case, and do not avoid dealing with awkward or difficult matters of evidence. If this is done, it reflects badly on the case. If abusive language was used, try to put it into context.

4   If there is some explanation or motive for the employer's conduct this should be stated here and/or dealt with at the hearing. The members of the tribunal have to decide at the hearing whom they believe, and motive is crucial in this decision.

other members of the kitchen staff who had been present in the kitchens on 26 August but he refused to do so.[5]

8   The applicant was told to leave the restaurant immediately, that he had been dismissed and not to return to the restaurant.

9   The applicant's dismissal was unfair in that:[6]
   a) The respondent did not have reasonable grounds for believing that the applicant had been in fundamental breach of contract.
   b) The respondent failed properly or adequately to investigate the applicant's dismissal and refused him any opportunity to advance an explanation for the conversations which ensued, contrary to the requirements of the rules of natural justice.
   c) In the circumstances, no reasonable employer would have dismissed the applicant.

ET1 – CAPABILITY

Grounds of application

1   The respondent operates some 30 hotels throughout the United Kingdom. In addition to the respondent's centralised personnel department, each of the hotels has a personnel department which forms part of the respondent's administrative resources.[7]

2   The applicant commenced employment on 1 January 1984 at the respondent's Pepys Hotel situated in Sartor Road, London W1 as a porter and remained employed in this capacity until his dismissal on 23 November 1999.

3   On 23 November 1999, without prior warning or consultation, the applicant was notified of his summary dismissal by letter dated 22 November 1999 sent to his home address. The reason given for his dismissal in this letter was his 'prolonged absence from work on account of sickness'.

4   The applicant wrote to the respondent appealing against his dismissal in accordance with the respondent's disciplinary and grievance procedure. The respondent notified the applicant by letter dated 1 December 1999

Notes

5 Failure to consult and to discuss properly, or adequately with the worker the reasons for dismissal, prior to dismissal, is contrary to the rules of natural justice and will in the majority of cases render the dismissal unfair. The employer is required to have reasonable grounds for dismissing after carrying out a proper investigation, which will involve discussions with the worker and all the material witnesses. (See para 7.25 above and *British Home Stores v Burchell* [1978] IRLR 379.)

6 Set out each of the considerations which the tribunal has to address in determining the fairness of the dismissal. Never under-estimate the tribunal's capacity to get the law wrong.

7 Under ERA 1996 s98(4), the tribunal must take into account the size and administrative resources of the employer's undertaking, when determining the fairness of the dismissal. Therefore, if the employer is a large company, ensure that this is stated in the application to the tribunal.

that there was no point in having a meeting as the decision had been made 'at the highest level'.[8]

5 The applicant's dismissal was unfair as the respondent failed to:

a) take all reasonable steps as was necessary to ascertain the applicant's true medical condition and in particular the likely date of his return to work;[9]

b) consult and discuss fully with the applicant his medical condition and the consequence for his future employment;[10]

c) consider and/or discuss with the applicant the possibility of alternative employment elsewhere within the respondent company;[11]

d) allow the applicant access to the respondent's disciplinary and/or grievance procedure contrary to the rules of natural justice and in breach of contract.

6 The applicant seeks an order for reinstatement and/or re-engagement.

ASSESSMENT OF COMPENSATION FOR UNFAIR DISMISSAL

Ben Hugh was dismissed on 9 April 1999 for being persistently late for work. He had been with the company for seven years and at the time of dismissal was aged 35. His gross pay was £200 per week and his average take-home pay £155. He also received free meals at work.

He received six weeks' net pay in lieu of notice (£930) and an ex gratia payment of £1,400. Owing to the nature of his dismissal, his unemployment benefit has been suspended and he is not entitled to income support.

Ben accepts that he is partly to blame for his dismissal and therefore that his award will probably be reduced by 25% due to contributory fault.

Ben's case is due to be heard in the ET on 15 July 2000. He has two letters from local job agencies informing him that, based on their data, he is unlikely to secure similar employment for at least two years from that date, or although he will be able to secure a job paying him £75 a week take-home after one year.

Notes

8 The failure to allow the worker to operate the contractual disciplinary and grievance procedures will usually render the dismissal unfair. (See para 6.13 above and *West Midlands Co-operative Society v Tipton* [1986] IRLR 112.)

9 The employer must take the necessary steps to form a balanced view of the worker's medical condition and this will involve the obtaining of medical evidence. (See *Patterson v Messrs Bracketts* [1977] IRLR 137.)

10 See para 7.15 above and *East Lindsey DC v Daubney* [1977] IRLR 181.

11 The tribunal might expect a large employer to consider alternative employment before dismissing. (See *Carricks (Caterers) Ltd v Nolan* [1980] IRLR 259.)

Unfair dismissal: Compensation checklist

[*NOTE: This checklist refers to the most common elements comprising unfair dismissal compensation, but does not refer to all the variables.*]

1   **Basic award** (see paras 14.13–14.15)
   a)   Calculate according to age, whole years' service, gross weekly pay subject to current weekly maximum;
   b)   make any deductions for:
      i)   unreasonable refusal of an offer of reinstatement;
      ii)   misconduct before dismissal;
      iii) redundancy payments made;
   c)   check if dismissal was for a reason where a minimum basic award must be made.

2   **Compensatory award** (see paras 14.16–14.31)
   a)   subject to overall ceiling of £50,000 with some exceptions;
   b)   immediate loss of earnings (from dismissal to ET hearing or earlier if the worker has or should have obtained a new job at the same or greater pay);
   c)   future loss of earnings (from ET decision until a date when the ET thinks the worker should obtain a new job at the same pay);
   d)   earnings are calculated net of tax and include regular overtime, bonuses, fringe benefits (value of company cars, free meals and accommodation, etc) plus any likely pay rises;
   e)   reasonable expenses for job-hunting;
   f)   off-set any payment in lieu of notice;
   g)   off-set any earnings in new job (if a new job pays the same or higher pay, the loss is the net loss from dismissal to start of the new job. See para 14.18 n35);
   h)   loss of pension rights (see para 14.23);
   i)   loss of statutory rights (see para 14.23);
   j)   make any percentage or other deductions, eg, for contributory fault or on the *Polkey* principle;
   k)   deduct any ex gratia payment (usually) or sum by which a redundancy package exceeds the basic award;
   l)   remember that recoupment may apply to an award for any immediate loss of earnings, although in any settlement it would not apply;
   m) add or deduct for failure to appeal or allow appeal (see para 14.26A);
   n)   consider correct order of making deductions and applying ceiling (see para 14.28 and case-law).

3   **Additional award** (see para 14.20)

4   **Other legal rights**
   Extra compensation may be paid for other rights claimed at the same time in the tribunal, eg, discrimination (see below) or failure to give written reasons for dismissal under ERA 1996 s92 (two weeks' pay).

Race, sex or disability discrimination: Compensation checklist

1) A single compensatory award with no upper ceiling applies.
2) Financial loss resulting from the discrimination, eg, loss of earnings on dismissal or lack of promotion, loss of pension. (Similar principles to unfair dismissal but may be longer-term future loss of earnings if severity of discrimination has damaged worker's confidence or health.)
3) Compensation for injury to feelings including aggravated damages and compensation for damage to health.
4) Interest.
5) Note that an ET can make recommendations and award extra compensation for failure to comply with them.

THE BASIC AWARD

(£200 × 7)			£1,400
Less:	(a)	Unreasonable refusal of reinstatement	–
	(b)	Conduct before dismissal	–
	(c)	Redundancy payment	£1,400
(a) Net basic award			–

COMPENSATORY AWARD (maximum award £50,000)

Loss of wages to date of hearing (14 × £155)	£2,170
Less earning/money in lieu of notice	£ 930
(b) SUB TOTAL	£1,240

Loss of earnings from hearing date to date when it can be said that the applicant would have secured employment as well-paid as the job he was dismissed from.

104 weeks × £155	£16,120
Loss of benefits (free meals) £20 × 104	£ 2,080
Loss of statutory rights	£ 200
Loss of pension rights	–
Expenses looking for employment	£ 200
Compensation for failing to provide written reasons	–
Sub total	£18,600

LESS

52 weeks × £75	£ 3,900
(c) SUB TOTAL	£14,700
Add (a), (b) and (c)	£15,940
DEDUCT 25% (Contributory fault)	£11,955
TOTAL LOSS	£11,955

Case study
IN THE EMPLOYMENT TRIBUNAL

BETWEEN:

JOE VILLA

applicant

– and –

TAMWORTH HIGH SCHOOL

respondent

ORIGINATING APPLICATION

1   The respondent operates a secondary school with 1,800 pupils and a staff complement of 98 which includes a Personnel Manager. The budget for the school for the academic year 1999/2000 was £2.8m.

2   The applicant, who is black, commenced employment on 9 September 1996 as the respondent's Head of Science and remained continuously employed thereafter in this capacity until his dismissal on 1 June 1999.

3   The applicant has been employed as a teacher for 26 years during which time he has secured promotion on a number of occasions. At no time during his teaching career has he received any oral or written warning as to his conduct and/or capability.

4   The respondent's Science Department comprises nine teaching staff, including the applicant. Apart from the applicant, all the teaching staff in the Science Department were white. They had all commenced employment with the respondent before the applicant. At the time of the applicant's appointment Howard Bennett was acting Head of Science. Howard Bennett was unsuccessful in his application for the permanent post.

5   Throughout the applicant's employment he experienced problems with the teaching staff in the Science Department caused by the resentment as to his appointment.

6   In January 1999 it was necessary for the applicant formally to report the problems he was experiencing to the respondent's Head Teacher, Stella Curd, which resulted in disciplinary action against Howard Bennett in February 1999 and a letter being sent to the teaching staff of the Science Department warning them that they must co-operate with the applicant and assist him in running the Science Department.

7   Importantly, Howard Bennett informed the applicant shortly after the receipt of her written warning that he would make sure that the applicant lived to regret the complaint being made and that he would get him.

8   During the evening of 3 March 1999 the applicant was approached in a public house by Jack Bennett, Howard Bennett's brother. Jack Bennett was acting in an aggressive manner, accusing the applicant of stitching up Howard Bennett. Without cause or provocation, Jack Bennett pushed the applicant off his seat and assaulted him, which required medical attention.

9   On 7 March 1999 the applicant was asked to attend a meeting with Stella Curd during which he was told that he was being suspended following receipt of an anonymous letter in which it stated that the applicant was seen fighting in a public house. Stella Curd refused to provide the applicant with a copy of this letter.

10 The applicant was asked to attend a disciplinary hearing on 12 March 1999. Under the terms of the disciplinary procedure, which forms part of the applicant's contract of employment, it is a requirement that at least one school governor is on the disciplinary panel with a minimum panel of three. Notwithstanding this requirement, the disciplinary panel comprised only of Stella Curd and the respondent's Deputy Head.

11 During the course of the disciplinary hearing the applicant informed the panel that:
    i)   the letter had been sent by Howard Bennett;
    ii) he had not started the fight;
    iii) in all probability he had been set up by Howard Bennett's brother, Jack.

12 At the conclusion of the disciplinary hearing and after only a short adjournment with no further enquiries being made the applicant was dismissed for gross misconduct.

13 The applicant appealed against the decision to dismiss him. At the appeal hearing he was accompanied by a member of the public who had seen the incident on 3 March 1999. The Appeal Panel refused to allow the applicant to call his witness to testify, notwithstanding that under the

disciplinary procedure he is entitled to call any relevant witnesses in support of his appeal. Furthermore and importantly, at the appeal hearing the Appeal Panel was informed about a previous incident at which a member of staff, the Head of Religious Studies (who is white) had assaulted a parent at a Christmas Party but had only received a written warning.

14   In any event, the Appeal Panel failed to discharge its obligation to consider all matters afresh and not simply to review the decision of the disciplinary panel.

15   The Appeal Panel upheld the decision to dismiss.

16   The dismissal was unfair having regard to the equity and substantial merits of the case in that:
   i)   the respondent had failed to comply with the requirements of the disciplinary procedure and, in particular but not exclusively, failed to constitute properly the disciplinary panel, and fettered the obligation imposed on the Appeal Panel to allow the applicant to call relevant witnesses to give evidence;
   ii) the respondent failed to have proper regard to a similar incident when the disciplinary sanction was a written warning;
   iii) the respondent failed to make any further enquiries after the disciplinary panel hearing and, in particular, to make enquiries as to whether Howard Bennett had sent the letter and if so why;
   iv) the fight was engineered and instigated by Jack Bennett;
   v)   the complaint was made by Howard Bennett (who had previously been given a written warning as a consequence of a complaint made by the applicant) and that Jack Bennett was Howard Bennett's brother;
   vi) the assault had occurred outside working hours and away from the respondent's premises;
   vii) the applicant had no previous warnings for misconduct.

17   In all the circumstances, the dismissal of the applicant was unfair.

18   Furthermore, the applicant was treated less favourably on grounds of race in the decision to dismiss him and to reject his appeal against dismissal rather than subjecting him to a disciplinary sanction short of dismissal. The applicant will rely on the previous incident involving the Head of Religious Studies who was white and also in the comparison between the treatment of him and of Howard Bennett.

19   The applicant seeks a declaration that he has been unfairly dismissed and that he was subjected to unlawful discrimination, compensation and an order for reinstatement.

20   The written reasons for dismissal provided by the respondent following a request for the same were inadequate and/or untrue.

NOTICE OF APPEARANCE

1 The respondent resists the claim of the applicant for unfair dismissal and unlawful discrimination and denies the allegations as alleged or at all.

2 The applicant's employment is governed by a written contract which incorporates the disciplinary code. The disciplinary code treats fighting at work and bringing the school into disrepute as acts of gross misconduct. Acts of gross misconduct may give rise to a summary dismissal.

3 It is accepted that the applicant did report problems he was experiencing at work but these problems were resolved by the intervention of Stella Curd, the Head Teacher, and no further complaint was made in the 11 months thereafter by the applicant. It is denied that the problems associated with this complaint played any part in the dismissal of the applicant. Furthermore, it is not denied by the applicant that the fight occurred.

4 The respondent was informed that the applicant had been involved in a fight in a public house situated immediately outside the school gates. The applicant was initially asked by Stella Curd about this incident and confirmed that it did occur. The respondent thereafter commenced the disciplinary procedure.

5 The disciplinary hearing was held on 12 March 1999. Neither at the time nor shortly afterwards did the applicant complain as to the members of the disciplinary panel.

6 Having considered the representations made by the applicant the panel decided that the only sanction was dismissal without notice.

7 The applicant appealed against this decision. The Appeal Panel considered the appeal. It decided to commute the decision to dismiss without notice to dismissal *with* notice which evidences its independence to the disciplinary panel.

8 In all the circumstances and having regard to the bounds of reasonable responses the applicant's dismissal was fair.

9 In the event that the dismissal is deemed unfair, the respondents will resist an application for reinstatement as the applicant has contributed to his dismissal in such a manner that such an order would not be just.

REQUEST PURSUANT TO RULE 4(3) OF THE RULES OF PROCEDURE (QUESTIONS)

1 Is it accepted that Howard Bennett was acting up as Head of the respondent's Science Department prior to the applicant's appointment in September of 1996?

2   Is it accepted that Howard Bennett applied for the permanent post of Head of the respondent's Science Department in 1996 when the applicant secured his appointment?

3   Is it accepted that all the teaching staff in the respondent's staff in the Science Department commenced employment prior to September 1996?

4   Is it accepted that in or about February 1999 Howard Bennett was issued with a disciplinary warning following a complaint by the applicant?

5   Please provide an explanation as to why Stella Curd did not provide the applicant with a copy of the anonymous letter of 7 March 1999 and thereafter when the request was made in writing.

6   Did Stella Curd seek the advice of any third party in reaching the decision not to provide a copy of the letter of 7 March 1999, and if so, who, and when was the advice given? Please provide details of the advice.

7   Who made the decision formally to discipline the applicant and if the same involved more than one person, when was the decision made, where was it recorded and who was involved in this process?

8   Whose decision was it to go ahead with the disciplinary hearing without a school governor present, and if Stella Curd secured advice in respect of this decision, who did she speak to?

9   Was anyone else consulted in reaching the decision to dismiss the applicant, save for the panel members, and if so, who else?

10   Did the Appeal Panel secure any advice prior to hearing the appeal as to the manner in which they should conduct themselves. If so, who provided them with the advice, when and what was the gist of the advice given?

11   Please confirm that in 1998 the respondent's Head of Religious Studies was in a fight with a parent following which the Head of Religious Studies was issued with a written warning.

12   Please provide details of specific training that the members of the Disciplinary and Appeals Panel secure in equal opportunities, in respect of each member of the Disciplinary and Appeal Panel, give dates of their training, the nature of the training and the duration.

13   In what manner was the incident of 3 March 1999 different to the incident in December 1998 when the respondent's Head of Religious Studies was warned in writing and in particular why was the December 1998 incident less serious?

14   Is it accepted that the dismissal of the applicant following the incident of 3 March 1999 was an act of unlawful discrimination?

15   Who on the Appeal Panel decided to commute the applicant's dismissal from summary to dismissal on notice?

Indirect race or sex discrimination: possibly discriminatory requirements

RACE DISCRIMINATION

Qualifications
- formal qualifications
- qualifications only obtainable in GB
- university degree
- qualifications from certain universities/organisations/Oxbridge
- English language qualifications

Language/expression/culture/confidence
- English language fluency – written/verbal
- communication skills
- writing skills
- essay-based tests and application forms
- psychometric testing
- culturally-biased testing
- articulation/fluency in interview performance
- acquiring new technical skills knowledge, within short time periods/ without special training (difficult in an unfamiliar language/with foreign technology)

Experience/service/paid employment
- previous kinds of work experience
- previous management experience
- already being at a certain grade/holding a certain high level job
- previous (fast) promotions
- previous width/variation of experience
- length of previous experience or service in certain positions/with the employer/in the industry/with past employer
- previous paid employment/paid relevant experience
- previous steady employment/no periods of unemployment
- having attended refresher/training courses (usually unavailable to night staff who tend to be black/women)
- previous acting-up experience
- being on a permanent contract rather than temporary

Dress
- uniform/dress/no turbans
- clean-shaven (eg, affect Sikhs)

Attendance/shifts
- days/hours of work/shifts/flexibility (sabbaths/religious holidays)
- not taking holiday entitlement at one time (visits to family abroad)
- limited unpaid/compassionate leave (need to visit ill family abroad)
- good attendance record (extended holidays/unpaid leave to visit family abroad)
- late travel home (danger of racial attacks)

Keeping it internal/references in and out/being part of the club
- nomination/recommendation by/reference from particular staff/management for recruitment/promotion
- word of mouth recruitment (knowing existing workers)
- favouring children from existing staff
- internal applications only
- customer satisfaction (liability to racist complaints)
- membership of certain organisations, professional bodies or trade unions/certain (culturally specific) leisure activities or interests
- using standing lists of vacancies
- using applications for one job for purpose of filling a different job

SEX DISCRIMINATION
Many of the requirements and conditions set out above would also adversely affect women or married workers. Additional requirements and conditions which would specifically affect women could be:

Attendance/shifts/flexibility/mobility
[Requirements likely to cause difficulty for women – and sometimes for married men – usually due to child-care commitments.]

Hours
- full-time work (refusal to allow job-share or part-time working)
- permitting part-time working, but requiring some hours to be worked each day
- overtime or weekend working
- shift-working, especially rotating shifts varying from day to day or week to week
- requirements to work overtime or varying shifts imposed at very short notice
- specified and inflexible start or finish times (interfering with times of taking or collecting children from school or child-minding)
- all year round working (eg, as opposed to term-time only)
- requirements entailing certain (high) attendance levels/limited absences

Mobility
- long journeys to and from work locations (necessitating earlier departures from and returns to home)
- work trips necessitating staying overnight away from home
- relocation (may be unacceptable *if* woman is not the primary earner in the household)

Note: Flexibility and mobility requirements often do cause women difficulties and should therefore be justified by the employer. However, it would be direct discrimination if an employer wrongly assumed a woman would be less flexible and treated her less favourably for that reason.

Miscellaneous
- age bars (women may be out of the job market during child-bearing age)
- to have acquired a certain level of experience by a certain age
- certain forms of dress or uniform (eg, may indirectly discriminate against Muslim women)
- late finishing hours (possibly dangerous travel home)
- home visits, eg, to patients or tenants unaccompanied (in some circumstances may be dangerous)

Note: Employers should provide a safe system of work for all workers, but should not directly discriminate against women unless allowed by statute (eg, in relation to pregnancy and childbirth).

Situations where discriminatory requirements or conditions may occur
- access to particular jobs – who is shortlisted; who is appointed
- access to promotion – who is eligible; who is shortlisted; who is promoted
- access to acting-up opportunities
- access to training schemes
- earning extra pay – determining the level of basic pay; criteria for rises; performance assessments
- opportunities to earn overtime, additional bonuses and benefits
- grading levels
- entitlement to paid time-off for trade union duties and training[1]
- eligibility for subsidised mortgages, occupational pensions, company cars and other perks
- rules for when and for how long holidays may be taken
- sick pay entitlement
- who gets selected for redundancy
- eligibility to formal disciplinary and grievance procedures

---

Note
1   See *Arbeiterwohlfahrt der Stadt Berlin eV v Botel* 38 EOR 45, ECJ.

Unfair dismissal case study

THE STATEMENT OF CAROL ELSE

1   Since leaving Huyton Catering College in 1975 I have worked in a number of hotels and restaurants as a sous chef. In January 1979 I was working as the head chef of the Kyverdale restaurant.[1]

2   On 14 December 1979 I received a letter from Brian Gerrard of the American Steak House offering me a job as head chef at the Felstead restaurant. This was the company's smallest restaurant. Over the next 12 years I worked at several of the company's other restaurants. Each move was a promotion (more prestigious premises) coupled with an increase in pay. My last move was on 19 December 1991 when I was made the head chef of the Johnson restaurant, the most prestigious and best restaurant in the group.

3   The company, American Steak House, has 150 restaurants throughout the United Kingdom, a substantial number of them are situated in London. The company also has a large head office at 153 Shaftesbury Avenue, London which includes a personnel department headed by Brian Gerrard and employing 25 full-time workers.

4   I never had any time off work for sickness during the 21 years of my employment nor any warnings about my work. I remember Brian Gerrard telling me at my last annual appraisal that he wished all the workers had the same commitment to the company as I did.

5   In April 1999 at the time of the annual appraisal and pay increase I was told that I would get £25,000 a year salary as well as a company car. I had been asking for a company car for some time as I often worked late and had no alternative but to catch a taxi home on those occasions. I was told that it would take about a month to get the car.

6   On 20 September 1999 I had an audit meeting. At this meeting I asked Brian Gerrard about my company car. He told me to stop going on about

---

Note

1   When taking a statement for the purpose of an unfair dismissal claim it is important to establish the previous work record (if it is good) and the qualifications that the worker has acquired. If the person has worked for a long time for one employer this should be emphasised at the tribunal hearing, particularly in cases of conduct/capability dismissals. Workers should tell the tribunal if they are well qualified, have had considerable experience in the industry, have worked for well-known employers, and held important positions in the past.

it as I was becoming 'too expensive for the company'. The company had a reputation of being tight with money especially where workers were concerned. I decided that I was not going to let them get away with this and continued to pester Brian Gerrard every time I saw him about my car.

7   On 9 January 2000 I was asked to attend a meeting with Brian Gerrard. I thought the meeting was about a new trainee programme which the company was implementing. It had been arranged for a number of weeks, as Ms Hillman the managing director of the company was also attending and it had been in her diary for at least eight weeks.

8   At the meeting I was told that I was being dismissed on the ground of redundancy because of the economic climate. I was devastated. I had no prior warning that I might be losing my job. I still do not understand why they should dismiss their longest serving worker.

9   I tried to enter into a discussion about my dismissal, seeking an explanation for this decision. They kept saying that I had been made redundant and that I should not take it personally. I was given a letter by Brian Gerrard which contained a brief statement that my dismissal was on the ground of redundancy, my P45 form, and my final pay slip. I was told that I was not required to work out my notice and that I would be paid 12 weeks' pay in lieu of notice, and £2,000 as an ex gratia payment. I asked about my holiday pay, I was told that as I had never been given a written contract, I was not entitled to any accrued holiday pay on dismissal. I was told that holidays were always at the discretion of management and as I had been paid £2,000 I would not get any holiday pay. I had four weeks owing to me.

10   I asked whether there were any other jobs for me in the company but Brian Gerrard said that there was nothing suitable. By the end of the meeting I was very angry. As I left, I said the letter was not good enough and that I wanted the real reasons for my dismissal in writing to be sent to my home address.

11   I was so shocked by my dismissal that I went to see my GP that same evening. It was the first time that I had seen my GP for nearly 10 years. She prescribed me tablets to take for my nerves and for shock. It was the first time that I had been sacked in all my working life.

12   I remember telephoning Ms Hillman on 10 January 2000 asking for a meeting but she told me there was no point as the decision would stand. She did say that she would give me a very good reference as soon as I asked for one.

13   About two weeks after my dismissal I saw Brian Gerrard's secretary in Berwick Street market. She told me that my dismissal had not been a complete surprise to her as she remembered writing to the finance company cancelling the application for my company car. This she thought was in the first week of May. She felt so strongly about the way

that I had been treated that she told me that she would be prepared to go to court with me.

14   Since my dismissal I have been trying without success to secure other employment. I saw a full-page advert in the Hotel and Catering magazine for five different jobs at the American Steak House, and I could have done any of them. It was then that I realised that I was not wanted by the company. You can imagine how I felt. This was in the February 2000 edition. I have also signed-on at a number of specialist agencies.[2]

Signed_____   5 February 2000.[3]

LETTER OF DISMISSAL

American Steak House Ltd
153 SHAFTESBURY AVENUE, LONDON W1

Ms Carol Else
12 Wesley Place
Hackney
London E8

9 January 2000

Dear Carol,

Further to our meeting today with myself and Ms Hillman the managing director, I very much regret that I have to confirm that your position as head chef is now redundant.

You have been given 12 weeks' pay in lieu of your notice entitlement and in the circumstances you are not required to attend work during this period.

I will endeavour to find you suitable alternative employment within the company. Should any position or vacancy arise we will notify you.

May I take this opportunity to thank you for the considerable service you have given to this company.

Yours faithfully

Brian Gerrard
Personnel manager

Notes

2 It is important that the worker can demonstrate that s/he has attempted to mitigate his/her losses. Prior to the hearing it will be necessary to obtain letters from specialist job agencies or the Department of Employment stating when the worker first signed on, what type of jobs s/he was prepared to do, what vacancies are available in the industry, and whether any jobs were offered.

3 It is important to get the worker to sign the statement and date it. A copy should then be given to the worker. If at the hearing s/he cannot remember something contained in the statement, the tribunal may allow the worker to be reminded as to what s/he had said in the statement or the statement could be offered as evidence. The tribunal will attach more importance to evidence given by the worker without reference to this statement, so this ploy should be used only as a last resort.

INITIAL LETTER TO THE EMPLOYER
London Employment Project
12 MALVERN ROAD, LONDON E8 3LT

Brian Gerrard, Personnel Manager
The American Steak House Ltd
153 Shaftesbury Avenue, London W1   12 January 2000

Dear Sir,

Re: Carol Else

I act on behalf of the above named in respect of all matters pertaining to her employment at the American Steak House Ltd, and the termination thereof.

In order that I can advise my client further in respect of her several claims against the company, please supply the following:

1   My client's main terms and conditions of employment or her contract of employment. In particular will you supply me with the following particulars:
    a) My client's contractual right to holiday pay, with sufficient particulars to calculate her entitlement to accrued holiday pay on the termination of her employment. Your attention is drawn to section 1(4)(d) of the Employment Rights Act 1996.
    b) My client's disciplinary and grievance procedure.[4]
2   All other documents which purport to vary my client's contract of employment.
3   Details of the company's redundancy procedure including the selection criteria.
4   The written reasons for my client's dismissal. As you are no doubt aware, if the reasons given in purported compliance of this request are inadequate or untrue, the company will have failed to discharge its legal obligation. The reasons were requested by my client on 9 January 2000. Your attention is drawn to section 92 of the Employment Rights Act 1996.[5]

Notes

4   The employer is obliged by virtue of ERA 1996 s3 to have supplied the worker with a statement containing these details. However, rather than asking for the statement itself, ask specifically for each of the statutory terms and conditions which are needed for the case. If there is a dispute about holiday entitlement ask for these particulars. Always ask for a copy of the employer's disciplinary and grievance procedure.
5   Even if the employer has supplied the written reasons the adviser is entitled to ask for them pursuant to ERA 1996 s92 and it will be these reasons which the tribunal will consider. If they are different to the previous statement, both can be referred to. To apply pressure on the employer, add the statement concerning the adequate and true reasons. If the reasons were requested orally confirm this in the letter to avoid dispute later.

5   All monies which are owed to my client including her holiday pay and her redundancy payment.

My client will be seeking an order for reinstatement or re-engagement as her primary remedy before the industrial tribunal. To this end please supply me with all vacancies within the company, the terms and conditions attributable to each job and the salary, so that my client can consider applying for the vacancy.[6]

Please supply the above information within the next fourteen days.

Yours faithfully

Jacquie Sparky
The London Employment Project

Note

6   If the worker wants the job back it is important that this is made known to the employer at the earliest opportunity. It will also assist in obtaining an additional award from the tribunal (see para 14.4 and 14.30 above) if the employer was put on notice at an early stage.

Application to an Employment Tribunal

For office use

Received at ET

- If you fax this form you do not need to send one in the post.
- This form has to be photocopied. Please use CAPITALS and black ink (if possible).
- Where there are tick boxes, please tick the one that applies.

Case number	
Code	
Initials	

1 Please give the type of complaint you want the tribunal to decide (for example, unfair dismissal, equal pay). A full list is available from the tribunal office. If you have more than one complaint list them all.[7]

Unfair dismissal

2 Please give your details

Mr ☐ Mrs ☐ Miss ☐ Ms ☐ Other ☐ _____

First names Carol

Surname Else

Date of birth 19/08/48

Address 12 Wesley Place
London

Postcode E8

Phone number

Daytime phone number

Please give an address to which we should send documents if different from above

Postcode

3 If a representative is acting for you please give details[8]
(all correspondence will be sent to your representative)

Name Jacquie Sparky

Address
The London Employment project
12 Malvern Road
London
Postcode E8 3LT

Phone 020 8437 4455 | Fax

Reference

4 Please give the dates of your employment

From 14/01/80 to 09/01/2000

5 Please give the name and address of the employer, other organisation or person against whom this complaint is being brought

Name The American Steak House LTD

Address
Shaftesbury Avenue
London

Postcode W1

Phone number

Please give the place where you worked or applied to work if different from above

Address

Postcode

6 Please say what job you did for the employer (or what job you applied for). If this does not apply, please say what your connection was with the employer

Chef

IT1(E/W)

Notes

7 All claims being made must be stated on the ET1 form and in the details of the complaint at para 11.

8 If a representative is put on the application all correspondence will be sent to the representative including notice of the hearing date.

7 Please give the number of normal basic hours worked each week Hours per week 65	9 If your complaint is not about dismissal, please give the date when the matter you are complaining about took place

8 Please give your earning details

Basic wage or salary

£ 25,000 :   per Year

Average take home pay

£   :   per

Other bonuses or benefits [9]

£ Company car, Meals,Travel   per

10 Unfair dismissal applicants only

Please indicate what you are seeking at this stage, if you win your case

☑ Reinstatement: to carry on working in your old job as before (an order for reinstatement normally includes an award of compensation for loss of earnings).

☐ Re-engagement: to start another job or new contract with your old employer (an order for re-engagement normally includes an award of compensation for loss of earnings).

☐ Compensation only: to get an award of money

11 Please give details of your complaint

If there is not enough space for your answer, please continue on a separate sheet and attach it to this form.

Please see attached sheet

12 Please sign and date this form, then send it to the address on the back page of this booklet.

Signed   *Carol Else*   Date   28/01/00

T1(E/W)

Note

9 All benefits and bonuses should be stated and if it is not possible to put a value to them either be generous in the assessment or leave the figure blank.

Details of complaint

1 The respondent is a public company operating 150 restaurants through-out the United Kingdom. A substantial number of these restaurants are situated in or around London. In addition to the administrative and personnel functions performed by each of the managers, the respondent has a large personnel department situated at head office employing some 25 full-time employees.[10]

2 The applicant commenced employment on 14 January 1980 with the respondent as a chef at its Felstead restaurant. Thereafter, the applicant was promoted on several occasions and at the time of her dismissal she was employed as the head chef of the respondent's Johnson restaurant which is the most prestigious in the group.[11]

3 At no time during the currency of the applicant's employment did she receive any written or verbal warnings as to her conduct or capability.[12]

4 On 9 January 2000 the applicant was first informed that she was being dismissed on the ground of redundancy at a meeting convened by the respondent's managing director Ms Hillman, and the personnel man-ager Brian Gerrard. At no time prior to this meeting had the applicant been consulted as to her impending dismissal nor had she been informed as to the nature or purpose of this meeting. The applicant was told at this meeting that she was not to return to work.[13]

5 At the conclusion of this meeting the applicant was handed a letter dated 9 January 2000, a copy of which is hereto attached.

6 The applicant's dismissal was unfair in that:[14]
   a) The dismissal of the applicant was not attributable wholly or mainly to a redundancy situation. The duties which the applicant performed

---

Notes

10 If the employer is a large company then it is imperative that this is stated on the application as the tribunal must consider, in determining the fairness of the dismissal, the size and administrative resources of the employer's undertaking (ERA 1996 s98(4)).

11 If the worker has been promoted or commended during his/her employment state this.

12 If there have been no warnings during the worker's employment state this.

13 In determining the fairness of a redundancy dismissal the tribunal has to be satisfied that the employer properly consulted with the worker prior to dismissal unless it was utterly pointless to do so (see paras 7.68–7.72 above and *Polkey v AE Dayton Services* [1987] IRLR 503, HL).

14 Depending on the facts, set out each of the considerations which the tribunal has to address in determining the fairness of the dismissal. The tribunal's capacity to get the law wrong should never be under-estimated!
   (a) ERA 1996 s139; and see para 7.76 above.
   (b) See n13; and see paras 7.68–7.72 above.
   (c) See paras 7.73–7.74 above;
   (d) See paras 7.75–7.77 above.

pursuant to her employment contract had neither diminished nor ceased.

b) The respondent failed to consult with the applicant prior to the meeting on 9 January in respect of her impending dismissal notwithstanding both statutory and common law obligations to do so.

c) The respondent unfairly selected the applicant for dismissal in contravention of what is currently regarded as a fair selection criterion. The applicant was the longest serving employee.

d) Having regard to the nature of the respondent's undertaking, and its size and administrative resources, the respondent failed adequately to seek or to offer the applicant alternative employment.

7   At the conclusion of the meeting on 9 January 2000 the applicant sought the written reasons for her dismissal. To date the respondent has unreasonably refused to comply with this request. The applicant seeks a declaration as to the reasons for dismissal and compensation.[15]

8   The respondent unlawfully and without authority deducted four weeks' holiday pay from the applicant's final wage. The applicant seeks a declaration that this sum has been unlawfully deducted and an order for repayment of this sum.[16]

9   The applicant seeks an order for reinstatement and/or compensation.

Signed_____   Dated 28 January 2000.

Notes

15 The claim for the failure to supply the written reasons must be set out in the details of the complaint.

16 ERA 1996 Pt II.

THE EMPLOYMENT TRIBUNALS
NOTICE OF APPEARANCE BY RESPONDENT

In the application of:

Case Number:
(please quote in all correspondence)

---

* This form has to be photocopied, if possible please use Black Ink and Capital letters
* If there is not enough space for your answer, please continue on a separate sheet and attach it to this form

1. Full name and address of the Respondent:	3. Do you intend to resist the application? (Tick appropriate box)

1. Full name and address of the Respondent:

The American Steak House LTD
153 Shaftesbury Avenue
London

3. Do you intend to resist the application? (Tick appropriate box)

YES ☑   NO ☐

4. Was the applicant dismissed? (Tick appropriate box)

YES ☑   NO ☐

Please give
reason below

Reason for dismissal:

5. Are the dates of employment given by the applicant correct? (Tick appropriate box)

YES ☑   NO ☐
please give correct dates below

Post Code: W1

Began on:

Telephone number:

Ended on:

2. If you require documents and notices to be sent to a representative or any other address in the United Kingdom please give details:

David Hart
Ince, Webb & Co
Knighton House
13 Edwards Street
London

6. Are the details given by the applicant about wages/salary, take home or other bonuses correct? (Tick appropriate box)

YES ☑   NO ☐
Please give correct details below

Basic Wages/Salary	£	Per
Average Take Home Pay	£	Per
Other Bonuses/Benefits	£	Per

PLEASE TURN OVER

for office use only
Date of receipt   Initials

Post Code: EC2H 1PE

Reference: DH

Telephone number: 020 7232 7201

Form IT3 E&W - 1/95

The notice of appearance

1   In January 2000 the kitchen at the Johnson restaurant was reorganised and decisions regarding menu planning, costing, standards, gross profits and budgets were, in future, to be dealt with by Ms Hughes, the executive director, who was based at the Rusty restaurant.

2   In the early autumn of 2000 it was also decided that the kitchen of the Johnson restaurant would be used as a development for senior chefs de partie and junior sous chefs at the Rusty restaurant (the largest of the respondent's restaurants) to develop their management skills. These persons were to assume responsibility for running the kitchen but would report directly to Ms Hughes.

3   As soon as the decision was made, a meeting was arranged between the applicant, Brian Gerrard the personnel manager and Lucy Hillman the managing director of the respondent company. This took place on 9 January 2000. The applicant was told of the reorganisation of the kitchen and how in future it would be used as a development for senior chefs in the respondent company. This meant that there was no need for a head chef at the Johnson restaurant and in consequence thereof the position had been made redundant following the reorganisation of the kitchen. Brian Gerrard told the applicant that every effort would be made to find her alternative employment.

4   There has been no suitable alternative employment available since this date.

REQUEST FOR FURTHER PARTICULARS AND DISCOVERY
London Employment Project
12 MALVERN ROAD, LONDON E8 3LT

David Hart
Ince, Webb & Co, Solicitors
Knighton House, 13 Edwards Street
London EC2H 1PE   12 March 2000

  Re: Carol Else v American Steak House Ltd
  Case Number 24234/93/LS/A

Please will you forward to this office within the next 14 days[17] the following further particulars of the notice of appearance:

OF 'In the early autumn of 1999 it was also decided that the kitchen of the Johnson restaurant would be used as a development for senior chefs de partie and junior sous chefs at the Rusty restaurant . . .'

Note
17   State a time limit with which to comply.

PLEASE STATE

1 The precise date in the early summer when it was decided that the Johnson restaurant would be used for this alleged development, who made the decision, and who else was present at the time.[18]

OF 'The position had become redundant following the reorganisation of the kitchen'.

PLEASE STATE

1 The names of all other members of staff who were dismissed on the ground of redundancy as a consequence of this reorganisation.[19]

OF 'Every effort was made to find her alternative employment within the company'.

PLEASE STATE

1 The efforts made to secure the applicant alternative employment, who was responsible for this exercise, and the manner and extent of the enquiries made.[20]

OF 'There has been no suitable alternative employment available since this date'.

PLEASE STATE

1 Each and every vacancy within the company, the position and salary attributable to the position.[21]

2 Each and every vacancy which had been considered unsuitable for the applicant for the period 1 September 1999 until and including 2 April 2000.

Please will you also supply me, within 14 days, with the following documents:

1 A list of all chefs employed by the company on 1 September 1999, 1 January 2000 and 1 April 2000, their location and the date on which they commenced employment.[22]

Notes

18 It is important to try to ascertain the precise date when the decision was reached to dismiss the worker. From this date the employer would be expected to consult with the worker.

19 This information is necessary to ascertain whether the worker was the only person dismissed and, if not, the other types of workers who were dismissed.

20 The failure to find alternative employment can make the dismissal unfair. The tribunal will have to consider the efforts made, in relation to the size and administrative resources of the employer's undertaking. This comparison cannot be made without this information.

21 With this information it will be necessary to consider all the vacancies and to list those which the worker could have been offered (within his/her capability). If none of these jobs was offered it will be necessary to ascertain at the hearing the reason why they had not been offered to the worker.

22 Needed to ascertain whether the selection of the worker was unfair. The most important criterion is the length of service provided that it is not indirectly discriminatory in that workplace.

2   A list of all job vacancies for kitchen staff within the company from 1 September 1999 until 1 April 2000, the job title, place of employment and the salary.[23]

3   All notes, minutes or memoranda of all meetings at which the reorganisation of the kitchen of the Johnson restaurant was discussed.[24]

4   Copies of all documents which purport to evidence the applicant's contract of employment.[25]

5   All other documents on which you intend to rely at the hearing.[26]

If you are unable to supply the above within the next 14 days, please contact this office in order that a further extension of time can be agreed.[27]

Yours faithfully,

Ms Jacquie Sparky
The London Employment Project

cc Regional Office of the Employment Tribunal[28]

REQUEST FOR ORDER FOR FURTHER PARTICULARS AND DISCOVERY

London Employment Project
12 MALVERN ROAD, LONDON E8 3LT

The Assistant Secretary of the Tribunals
London South Tribunal   12 April 2000

Dear Sir/Madam,

Re: Employment Tribunal Application 24234/93/LS/A
    Carol Else v American Steak House Ltd

On 12 March 2000 I requested from the respondent's solicitors further particulars of the notice of appearance and discovery of certain documents. A copy of this request is attached.

Notwithstanding the time limit given, there has been no reply nor a request for an extension of time. Please will you exercise your discretion and make an

---

Notes

23   Needed for the purpose of determining the question of alternative employment.
24   Needed to ascertain when the decision to dismiss was made, who made it and how it was proposed to deal with those workers being dismissed
25   Standard request to prevent any damaging documents being presented on the day of the hearing.
26   Ibid.
27   This paragraph should be included so that the tribunal cannot say that it was not reasonable to expect the employer to comply with the request within the time limit given.
28   Always copy this letter to the tribunal.

order for those matters sought in my letter of 12 March 2000. It is essential for my client's case to have this information, to establish that she has been unfairly dismissed.

Yours faithfully,

Jacquie Sparky
The London Employment Project

REQUEST FOR WITNESS ORDER

London Employment Project
12 MALVERN ROAD, LONDON E8 3LT

The Assistant Secretary of the Tribunals
London South Tribunal   18 April 2000

Dear Sir/Madam,

Re: Industrial Tribunal Application 24234/93/LS/A
    Carol Else v American Steak House Ltd

I apply to the tribunal for a witness order for the following person to attend the hearing listed for 14 June 2000.

Margaret Spillar
23 Miller Court
London EC3

Margaret Spillar is employed by the respondent as a secretary to the personnel manager. She can give evidence in respect of the respondent's decision to dismiss the applicant.

Margaret Spillar is not prepared to attend voluntarily as she is still in the employ of the respondent.[29]

Yours faithfully,

Jacquie Sparky
The London Employment Project

Note

29 In obtaining a witness order it is necessary to give the witnesses' full names and addresses (for the purpose of effecting service), a brief statement of their evidence, which must be material, and to state that they are not prepared to attend voluntarily.

FURTHER PARTICULARS OF DEFENCE
Ince, Webb & Co.
KNIGHTON HOUSE, 13 EDWARDS STREET, LONDON EC2H 1PC

Jacquie Sparky
The London Employment Project
12 Malvern Road, London E8 3LT   15 May 2000

Dear Madam,

Re: Case Number 24234/90/LS/A

In reply to the employment tribunal order of 2 May 2000 for further and better particulars of the notice of appearance:

OF 'In the early autumn of 1999 it was also decided that the kitchen of the Johnson restaurant would be used for the development for senior chefs de partie and junior sous chefs at the Rusty restaurant . . . '

PLEASE STATE

1 The precise date in the early summer when it was decided that the Johnson restaurant would be used for this alleged development, who made the decision, and who else was present at the time.

REPLY

The decision was made at a meeting on 10 September 1999 attended by Brian Gerrard and Lucy Hillman. It was a decision reached as part of a reorganisation of the company which was felt to be in the best future interest of all concerned.

OF 'The position had become redundant following the reorganisation of the kitchen'.

PLEASE STATE

1 The names of all other members of staff who were dismissed on the grounds of redundancy as a consequence of this reorganisation.

REPLY

No other person was dismissed.

OF 'Every effort was made to secure the applicant alternative employment within the company'.

PLEASE STATE

1 The efforts made to secure the applicant alternative employment, who was responsible for this exercise, and the manner and extent of the enquiries made.

REPLY

After 9 January 2000 Brian Gerrard personally dealt with this matter. He decided to offer the applicant any future vacancy at head chef level in the larger restaurant. There was no point offering her any other position as she would not have accepted such an offer.

OF 'There has been no suitable alternative employment available since this date'.

PLEASE STATE

1 Each and every vacancy within the company, the position and salary attributable to the position.

REPLY

The respondent is a large organisation and the turnover of staff in the industry is high. There were many vacancies for other positions within the company, but they were not suitable. The respondent did not take these positions into consideration as they were not relevant.

Yours faithfully,

David Hart

TERMS OF SETTLEMENT

The respondent undertakes:

to pay the applicant on or before 2 July 2000 the sum of £7,500 in full and final settlement of all claims that she has arising out of her employment and the termination thereof, save for any claim for personal injury;[30] and

to supply the following reference and only this reference, if requested for the same, and not to depart from it unless with the express permission of the applicant. If the reference is requested in writing, to supply the same on headed notepaper, dated and duly signed.[31]

'Carol Else has been employed by American Steak House Ltd since January 1980 until her dismissal on the ground of redundancy on 9 January 2000. She was promoted on several occasions and at the time of her dismissal was employed as the senior head chef. Throughout her employment we found her to be honest, hard working and enthusiastic. She had a pleasant personality and was liked by the other members of staff, as well as by management. We have no hesitation in recommending her for future employment in a similar capacity.'[32]

The applicant undertakes to withdraw her application to the employment tribunal on receipt of the above sum, and in the meanwhile the case is adjourned generally.[33]

Notes

30 Always put in a date for compliance, and always insist that claims for personal injury are excluded with unfair dismissal claims. ACAS will encourage this exception.

31 If a reference forms part of the agreement, which it should (see para 16.85 above), this undertaking must be secured from the employer.

32 Set out in full the reference.

33 If the worker undertakes to withdraw the application on receipt of the sum, if there is non-payment the worker can return to the tribunal or sue for the agreed sum through the courts. If the worker returns to the tribunal s/he should apply for costs on the grounds of unreasonable conduct (ET Regs Sch 1 r12).

Glossary

Admissible evidence
Evidence to the ET may be in documents or oral. Some forms of evidence will not be allowed by the ET and are termed inadmissible. The ET operates very lax rules of evidence. Most forms of evidence will be admissible although some may not be given much weight, eg, hearsay, written unsworn statements from absent witnesses, incomplete or unclear tape recordings.

Applicant
The formal term for the worker in ET proceedings.

Breach of contract
Breaking or not complying with one of the agreed terms of a contract (of employment). A **fundamental** or **repudiatory breach** of contract is an extremely serious breach going to the heart of the employment relationship. If done by the employer, it may entitle a worker to resign and claim **constructive dismissal**. If done by the worker, it may entitle the employer to dismiss without notice.

Burden of proof
This refers to which party (employer or worker) has the responsibility of proving matters, such as whether a dismissal took place or whether unlawful discrimination happened. The party with the burden of proof cannot simply make an allegation and ask the other party to disprove it.

Civil courts
Strictly-speaking, civil courts are those dealing with civil law, eg, the County Court, High Court, Court of Appeal and House of Lords as opposed to criminal law, eg, the Magistrates' Court and Crown Court. Technically, employment tribunals are civil rather than criminal courts, but the term is sometimes used to distinguish the County Court or High Court with their more formal processes, heavier costs risks and (sometimes) legal aid, from employment tribunals.

Complainant
Another legal term for the worker, used in the questionnaire procedure under the SDA 1975, RRA 1976 or DDA 1995.

Conciliation officer
A person from ACAS automatically appointed on most cases to liaise between the parties off the record in an attempt to encourage a settlement (see para 16.80).

Compromise agreement
A settlement agreement through legal or other authorised representatives meeting specified requirements so as to be binding on the **applicant**.

Consolidation
Where separate cases with one or more of the same parties are put together for the purposes of preparation and a joint hearing. Strictly speaking the term **consolidation** is not used in the ET system and the phrase used is that the cases be 'considered together'.

Constructive dismissal
This is where a worker resigns due to the employer's fundamental or repudiatory breach of the employment contract. See para 6.41.

Contract workers
This is often used to refer to workers employed on fixed-term contracts who may or may not have unfair dismissal rights, according to whether they meet the eligibility criteria (see para 6.21). It is also a precise term with a slightly different meaning under the discrimination legislation (see para 9.14).

COT 3
The standard form on which an ACAS **conciliation officer** records an agreement negotiated through him/her.

Directions; hearing for directions
Directions are orders and guidance given by the ET before any hearing concerning preparation of the case. A **hearing for directions** is where such matters are discussed between a duty chair and the parties and usually covers matters such as discovery, particulars and hearing dates. A hearing for directions is also known as an **interlocutory** hearing.

Discovery
The process of one party disclosing relevant documents to the other.

DL56
The standard form on which a **questionnaire** under the DDA 1995 is usually written.

Domestic law
This term is usually used to distinguish the national law of an EU member state from European law, ie, law laid down by European legislation and case-law which applies to all member states.

EAT
Employment Appeal Tribunal, the first level of appeal from an **ET** Decision.

Employee
Different categories of **worker** are eligible to claim different employment rights. Certain rights can only be claimed by employees. For definition of employee under the ERA 1996, see s229. The definition under discrimination law is wider, see DDA 1995 s68, RRA 1976 s78, SDA 1975 s82.

ET
Employment Tribunal, formerly known as Industrial Tribunal (IT). Most employment cases are heard in ETs.

ET1, ET3
The ET1 (formerly 'IT1') is the standard form on which the **applicant's originating application** is usually written. The ET3 (formerly 'IT3') is the standard form on which the employer's **notice of appearance** is usually written. These documents are often referred to by the names of the forms rather than their full names.

Ex parte
This is when a procedural step is taken by one party in the ET without notifying the other party. Requests for **interlocutory** orders are usually made **ex parte** and not **on notice**.

Evidence-in-chief
The evidence given in an ET hearing by a witness before s/he is cross-examined. The evidence is usually given to his/her own representative, who will be conducting an examination-in-chief.

Fact – questions of fact; fact findings
If something is a **question of fact** for the ET, it means that the issue is decided on the facts of the particular case as opposed to on the law alone. A **fact finding** is the ET's decision on where the truth lies between two conflicting pieces of evidence.

Final submissions
The closing speech in an ET hearing. The **final submissions** are sometimes put in writing. They may also be known as **closing submissions**.

Fundamental breach
See Breach above.

Held
Where something is **held by** a court or tribunal, this is its decision.

Indirect discrimination
This has a specific legal meaning under the RRA 1976 and SDA 1975 (see paras 9.51–9.81).

Interlocutory
This refers to all procedural matters between lodging the claim and the hearing. An interlocutory hearing deals with such matters.

Interrogatories
A formal process whereby one party can ask material questions of another in the preparation of the case. This is also known as the question and answer procedure (see para 16.33).

IT1, IT3
See **ET1, ET3**.

Jurisdiction
The ET may adjudicate only on certain claims brought by certain workers. These are matters 'within its jurisdiction'. The ET has no discretion to decide claims outside its jurisdiction, eg, where a worker has insufficient qualifying service.

Lay members
Otherwise known as **wing members**, these are the representatives from each side of industry who sit on most ET hearings.

Liability; hearing on liability
The issue as to whether or not the worker wins his/her case, ie, whether the employer is found 'liable' for unfair dismissal, discrimination, etc, as distinct from the issue as to what compensation or remedies the worker should receive.

Lodging documents
This usually refers to lodging the ET1 or lodging trial bundles at the ET. It simply means delivering the relevant document to the ET by whatever means.

Merits; merits hearing
This is the same as the hearing on **liability** (see above).

Mitigate; mitigation
Mitigation refers to reasonable steps which should have been taken or were taken by a worker to find fresh employment so as to mitigate (ie, reduce) the loss of earnings resulting from his/her dismissal.

Motion, of its own
An **ET** has power to make **interlocutory** orders and take other steps on its own initiative, ie, of its own motion, as well as at the request of either party.

Notice of appearance
The employer's reply or defence, usually written on an ET3 form.

Obiter
Where a higher court makes a statement of legal principle or interpretation, on which the decision in that particular case does not depend. It is therefore not a binding **precedent** but is of persuasive authority.

On notice
Where a party takes a procedural step in the ET having informed the other party, as opposed to ex parte.

Originating application
The worker's document which starts the ET proceedings, usually written on an ET1.

Pleadings; to plead
Pleadings are the documents which set out each party's case, ie, the ET1, ET3 and any further and better particulars. **To plead** something is to put it into any of these documents.

Pre-hearing review
A hearing before the ET without any verbal or written evidence, where the ET decides, on the basis of the **pleadings** and what the parties' representatives say, whether the claim or defence (as the case may be) has reasonable prospects of success. If not, it requires a deposit of up to £150 as a condition of proceeding further.

Precedent
The courts decide cases by applying and interpreting the law to given facts. There is a hierarchy of courts and tribunals for employment law purposes, ie, House of Lords, Court of Appeal, High Court, EAT, ET. Each level of court/ tribunal is compelled to follow legal principles and interpretations set by higher level courts unless a case can be 'distinguished' on its facts. Where no higher level decision exists, the courts (except the ET) follow the interpretation of other courts of the same level. **Precedent** may also be referred to as 'authority'.

Preliminary hearing
A full hearing with evidence before the ET on a preliminary issue which can be separated from the main claim. It is usually on a matter of **jurisdiction**, eg, whether a worker has sufficient continuous service to claim unfair dismissal.

Presenting the ET1
An ET1 is presented at the ET when it is received at the relevant regional ET.

Proof
A proof is a statement taken by an adviser from his/her own client or witness purely for his/her private purposes in the preparation of a case. If a barrister is used at the hearing, the proof is given to the barrister as a way of letting him/her know what the witness will say. It is not seen by the other side. (This should not be confused with a **witness statement**.)

Question and answer procedure
See **Interrogatories** above.

Questionnaire
A special procedure available under the RRA 1976 , SDA 1975 and DDA 1995 (see para 17.3).

Quantum
Financial compensation.

Remedies; remedies hearing
Remedies are the compensation in money and other forms which a worker receives if s/he wins. A **remedies hearing** is sometimes dealt with separately from the hearing on liability.

Repudiatory breach
See **Breach**.

Respondent
This is the legal term for the employer in ET proceedings.

Review
An **ET** can review a Decision it has made on a number of specific grounds under Sch 1 r11 of the ET (Constitution and Rules of Procedure) Regulations 1993. This is different from appealing to the **EAT** and has a shorter time-limit (see paras 16.74–16.75 above).

RR65
The standard form on which a **questionnaire** under the RRA 1976 is usually written.

SD74
The standard form on which a **questionnaire** under the SDA 1975 is usually written.

Serving proceedings
Delivering/sending documents to the other party.

Skeleton argument
A written outline of a representative's final speech at the ET hearing, which s/he will hand to the ET panel and expand verbally.

Submissions, closing or final submissions
An ET at a hearing (and often immediately before the closing speeches) may invite a representative to make **submissions** on a particular point. This usually means the representative is required to make comments or arguments on law or evidence.

Summary dismissal
This occurs when a worker's conduct is sufficiently grave as to justify immediate termination of the employment contract without notice. The worker is not entitled to either notice or pay in lieu of notice when summarily dismissed.

TUPE
This abbreviation is commonly used by trade unions to refer to the Transfer of Undertakings (Protection of Employment) Regulations 1981.

Wing members
Otherwise known as **lay members**, these are the representatives from each side of industry who sit on most ET hearings.

Witness order
An ET can issue a witness order to compel an unwilling witness to attend the hearing.

Witness statement
A statement taken from each witness including the **applicant**, which it is intended to disclose to the other side in advance of the hearing or at the hearing itself. With the ET's permission, the witness statement may replace most or all of the witness's **evidence-in-chief**. Note that the witness must still attend the hearing unless the other side agrees that s/he need not do so (see paras 16.53–16.58).

Worker
Different employment rights have different eligibility requirements: some are available only to employees and others to 'workers' on a wider basis. These terms can themselves have different definitions according to the employment right concerned. See ERA 1996 s230 for definitions relevant to rights under that Act. Note that the word 'worker' used generally in this

book is in its non-legal sense and does not differentiate between employees and workers unless indicated.

Vicarious liability

Where an employer is responsible for the unlawful acts of his/her employees, regardless of whether s/he knew or approved of those acts. In the employment field, it is mainly relevant to discrimination law (see para 9.17).

Redundancy payments table

READY RECKONER FOR CALCULATING THE NUMBER OF WEEKS' PAY DUE

Age (years) \ Service (years)	2	3	4	5	6	7	8	9	10	11	12	13	14	15	16	17	18	19	20
20	1	1	1	1	—														
21	1	1½	1½	1½	1½	—													
22	1	1½	2	2	2	2	—												
23	1½	2	2½	3	3	3	3	—											
24	2	2½	3	3½	4	4	4	4	—										
25	2	3	3½	4	4½	5	5	5	5	—									
26	2	3	4	4½	5	5½	6	6	6	6	—								
27	2	3	4	5	5½	6	6½	7	7	7	7	—							
28	2	3	4	5	6	6½	7	7½	8	8	8	8	—						
29	2	3	4	5	6	7	7½	8	8½	9	9	9	9	—					
30	2	3	4	5	6	7	8	8½	9	9½	10	10	10	10	—				
31	2	3	4	5	6	7	8	9	9½	10	10½	11	11	11	11	—			
32	2	3	4	5	6	7	8	9	10	10½	11	11½	12	12	12	12	—		
33	2	3	4	5	6	7	8	9	10	11	11½	12	12½	13	13	13	13	—	
34	2	3	4	5	6	7	8	9	10	11	12	12½	13	13½	14	14	14	14	—
35	2	3	4	5	6	7	8	9	10	11	12	13	13½	14	14½	15	15	15	15
36	2	3	4	5	6	7	8	9	10	11	12	13	14	14½	15	15½	16	16	16
37	2	3	4	5	6	7	8	9	10	11	12	13	14	15	15½	16	16½	17	17
38	2	3	4	5	6	7	8	9	10	11	12	13	14	15	16	16½	17	17½	18
39	2	3	4	5	6	7	8	9	10	11	12	13	14	15	16	17	17½	18	18½
40	2	3	4	5	6	7	8	9	10	11	12	13	14	15	16	17	18	18½	19
41	2	3	4	5	6	7	8	9	10	11	12	13	14	15	16	17	18	19	19½
42	2½	3½	4½	5½	6½	7½	8½	9½	10½	11½	12½	13½	14½	15½	16½	17½	18½	19½	20½
43	3	4	5	6	7	8	9	10	11	12	13	14	15	16	17	18	19	20	21
44	3	4½	5½	6½	7½	8½	9½	10½	11½	12½	13½	14½	15½	16½	17½	18½	19½	20½	21½
45	3	4½	6	7	8	9	10	11	12	13	14	15	16	17	18	19	20	21	22
46	3	4½	6	7½	8½	9½	10½	11½	12½	13½	14½	15½	16½	17½	18½	19½	20½	21½	22½
47	3	4½	6	7½	9	10	11	12	13	14	15	16	17	18	19	20	21	22	23
48	3	4½	6	7½	9	10½	11½	12½	13½	14½	15½	16½	17½	18½	19½	20½	21½	22½	23½
49	3	4½	6	7½	9	10½	12	13	14	15	16	17	18	19	20	21	22	23	24
50	3	4½	6	7½	9	10½	12	13½	14½	15½	16½	17½	18½	19½	20½	21½	22½	23½	24½
51	3	4½	6	7½	9	10½	12	13½	15	16	17	18	19	20	21	22	23	24	25
52	3	4½	6	7½	9	10½	12	13½	15	16½	17½	18½	19½	20½	21½	22½	23½	24½	25½
53	3	4½	6	7½	9	10½	12	13½	15	16½	18	19	20	21	22	23	24	25	26
54	3	4½	6	7½	9	10½	12	13½	15	16½	18	19½	20½	21½	22½	23½	24½	25½	26½

Service (years)	2	3	4	5	6	7	8	9	10	11	12	13	14	15	16	17	18	19	20
55	3	4½	6	7½	9	10½	12	13½	15	16½	18	19½	21	22	23	24	25	26	27
56	3	4½	6	7½	9	10½	12	13½	15	16½	18	19½	21	22½	23½	24½	25½	26½	27½
57	3	4½	6	7½	9	10½	12	13½	15	16½	18	19½	21	22½	24	25	26	27	28
58	3	4½	6	7½	9	10½	12	13½	15	16½	18	19½	21	22½	24	25½	26½	27½	28½
59	3	4½	6	7½	9	10½	12	13½	15	16½	18	19½	21	22½	24	25½	27	28	29
60	3	4½	6	7½	9	10½	12	13½	15	16½	18	19½	21	22½	24	25½	27	28½	29½
61	3	4½	6	7½	9	10½	12	13½	15	16½	18	19½	21	22½	24	25½	27	28½	30
62	3	4½	6	7½	9	10½	12	13½	15	16½	18	19½	21	22½	24	25½	27	28½	30
63	3	4½	6	7½	9	10½	12	13½	15	16½	18	19½	21	22½	24	25½	27	28½	30
64	3	4½	6	7½	9	10½	12	13½	15	16½	18	19½	21	22½	24	25½	27	28½	30

Notes

1 A maximum of 20 years' employment is counted.

2 Any service below the age of 18 is ignored. [However, if using this Schedule for a basic award, you should consider service below the age of 18.]

3 In the final year before retirement the redundancy payment is reduced by 1/12th for each completed month.

Index